Handbook of Austrian Literature

Introduced and edited by Frederick Ungar

Frederick Ungar Publishing Co.
New York

Copyright © 1973 by Frederick Ungar Publishing Co., Inc.
Printed in the United States of America
Library of Congress Catalog Card Number: 71-125969
Designed by Anita Duncan
ISBN: 0-8044-2929-4

Handbook of Austrian Literature

*In memory of three Austrian writers
whose books I was privileged to publish
forty years ago in Vienna:*

Heimito von Doderer

Otto Stoessl

Ernst Waldinger

The majority of the entries have been translated from Hermann Kunisch's *Handbuch der deutschen Gegenwartsliteratur*, published by Nymphenburger Verlagshandlung, Munich. A triangle next to the name of the contributor indicates that the article has been specially prepared for this American edition. The entry on Peter Altenberg, contributed by Franz H. Mautner, was previously published in the *Columbia Dictionary of Modern European Literature*, Columbia University Press, New York.

Contents

Introduction	xiii
Ilse Aichinger	
Walther Huder	3
Peter Altenberg	
Franz H. Mautner	5
Hans Carl Artmann	
Ivar Ivask	7
Raoul Auernheimer	
Donald G. Daviau	10
Ingeborg Bachmann	
Charlotte Nennecke	14
Hermann Bahr	
Donald G. Daviau	18
Richard Beer-Hofmann	
Gerhart Baumann	23
Thomas Bernhard	
Wilfried Schwedler	26
Richard Billinger	
Lutz Weltmann	28
Franz Blei	
Karl Strobl	31
Imma von Bodmershof	
Otto Heuschele	34
Hermann Broch	
Walter Weiss	36
Max Brod	
Lutz Weltmann	41
Ferdinand Bruckner	
Clemens Heselhaus	45
Martin Buber	
Hans Kohn	48
Christine Busta	
Wolfram Mauser	55
Elias Canetti	
Joachim Schickel	57

Paul Celan
Victor Lange 59
Franz Theodor Csokor
Lutz Weltmann 62
Theodor Däubler
Eckart Peterich 65
Heimito von Doderer
Herbert Eisenreich 70
Marie von Ebner-Eschenbach
Horst Jarka 75
Albert Ehrenstein
Günther Erken 80
Herbert Eisenreich
Karl August Horst 83
Sigmund Freud
Ulrich Sonnemann 85
Erich Fried
Wieland Schmied 91
Egon Friedell
Frank Trommler 93
Gertrud Fussenegger
Gertrude C. Schwebell 95
Franz Grillparzer
Heinz Politzer 97
Albert Paris Gütersloh
Herbert Eisenreich 105
Enrica von Handel-Mazzetti
Wilhelm Grenzmann 108
Peter Handke
Nicholas Hern 111
Fritz von Herzmanovsky-Orlando
Herbert Eisenreich 115
Fritz Hochwälder
Irene Ruttmann 117
Hugo von Hofmannsthal
Hermann Kunisch 119
Ödön von Horváth
Horst Jarka 132
Franz Kafka
Jacob Steiner 138
Rudolf Kassner
Eudo C. Mason 146

Contents

Theodor Kramer	
Wieland Schmied	151
Karl Kraus	
Frederick Ungar	153
Alfred Kubin	
Wolfgang Schneditz	159
Christine Lavant	
Inge Meidinger-Geise	162
Josef Leitgeb	
Eugen Thurnher	164
Nikolaus Lenau	
Donald G. Daviau	166
Alexander Lernet-Holenia	
Frank Trommler	171
Jakov Lind	
Martin Gregor-Dellin	174
Georg Lukács	
Günter Albrecht Zehm	175
Max Mell	
Clemens Heselhaus	179
Gustav Meyrink	
K. H. Kramberg	182
Erika Mitterer	
Annemarie Groß-Denker	185
Robert Musil	
Gerhart Baumann	187
Franz Nabl	
Ernst Alker	192
Johann Nestroy	
Max Knight and Joseph Fabry	194
Robert Neumann	
K. H. Kramberg	198
Alfred Polgar	
Nino Erné	201
Ferdinand Raimund	
Horst Jarka	204
Rainer Maria Rilke	
Hermann Kunisch	209
Joseph Roth	
Gerhart Baumann	223
Ferdinand von Saar	
Donald G. Daviau	226

George Emmanuel Saiko
Robert Mühlher 230
Richard von Schaukal
Charlotte Nennecke 232
Arthur Schnitzler
Gerhart Baumann 235
Karl Schönherr
Walter Weiss 241
Adalbert Stifter
J. P. Stern 244
Otto Stoessl
Frederick Ungar 248
Friedrich Torberg
Herbert Eisenreich 252
Georg Trakl
Hans Szklenar 254
Franz Tumler
Eugen Thurnher 259
Johannes Urzidil
Karl August Horst 262
Ernst Waldinger
Frederick Ungar 264
Hans Weigel
Herbert Eisenreich 266
Josef Weinheber
K. H. Kramberg 268
Ernst Weiß
Dieter Lattmann 270
Franz Werfel
Anneliese Kuchinke-Bach 273
Martina Wied
Wolfram Mauser 279
Anton Wildgans
Lutz Weltmann 281
Ludwig Wittgenstein
Joachim Schickel 283
Herbert Zand
Alfred Doppler 286
Stefan Zweig
K. H. Kramberg 288

Index 291

Introduction

Is there an Austrian literature? Is it not true that the works of Austrian writers have always been regarded as part of German literature? To the first question the answer is yes, there *is* an Austrian literature. To the second, a more detailed reply is required. If Austrian writing were to be considered just part of German literature, then the term "English literature" would be entirely appropriate for both English and American literatures, not to mention the indigenous writing of Canada, Australia, New Zealand, and South Africa. None of those countries, and certainly not the United States, would submit to having their literature subsumed in such a way. Nor would Austria.

A clear recognition of the individual identity of Austrian literature is obscured by the fact that its language is the same as that of German literature. But are they really the same? When examined closely, they turn out to be no more alike than the British and American idioms. The German of Austria and of Germany could not well be identical in light of the entirely different histories of these countries. Furthermore, Austria was an empire whose many races influenced and enriched its language.

The Austrian writer Otto Basil puts it very well:

> Language is the mirror of a nation. The *lingua Austriaca* represents the essence of the Austrian character. Even today we hear the Latin-Romance heritage vibrate in it, the golden bells of Rome, and we feel the Celtic luster in its veins. This language, formed by Bavarian and Alemanic dialects, with its ingredients from the Czech and Slovak and the German spoken in Prague, from the Hungarian, the Croatian, the Yiddish, even from the Turkish, with its residual echoes of the French military vernacular left behind by Napoleon's armies, with its reminiscences of the idioms of romanized Celts and South Slavs, makes up a resonant mosaic that, with historical passage of time, has melted into a homogeneous accord.

Austrian literature is thus the literature of a common national destiny and a common language area, born out of its military and political history, its ethnic composition, and the supranational structure of its national consciousness. It is not surprising that this supranational structure, Austria's noblest claim, lacked the strength to counteract the centrifugal forces that tore the empire apart, or the vigor to overcome the rebellious nationalism in the many races that constituted the Hapsburg empire and in its dominant German population as well. Looking at today's world, it would hardly be fair to blame those then in power for lacking the practical wisdom and dispassionate humanism that alone could have prevented Austria's collapse—and probably, too, the subsequent holocaust of World War II and a postwar world teetering on the brink of atomic disaster.

The Austrian empire represented at least an attempt, although an inadequate one, to form a multinational state. It is no accident that it was an Austrian, Count R. N. Coudenhove-Calergi, who fathered the idea of Pan-Europe just at the time the League of Nations foundered. It was Hans Weigel, a contemporary writer and acknowledged expert on Austria, who said that

> Austria, which likes to call herself a bridge, is in truth something more, and something, moreover, essentially different, namely a synthesis of worlds, a test case of integration, of supranationality, a country in which one can be counted as German-speaking without being German; in which one may be called Novotny (Czech), Esterhazy (Magyar), or Nicolussi (Italian) and yet consider German his mother tongue; Austria is preserving Prague, Görz (Gorizia), and Laibach (Ljubljana), Budapest and Czernowitz (Cernăuti) through the present into the future. It represents a hibernation of the races, a pocket edition of the empire, a blueprint for a United Europe.

Up to the 1830s Austria had produced no writers of great accomplishment. But with Goethe's death in 1832, when the great age of German literature came to an end, there emerged, as if out of nowhere, three great Austrian writers—Grillparzer, Raimund, and Nestroy, who were to carry on the heritage of the German classical and romantic writers. It was these three who laid the foundation of Austrian literature and reflected in their writing the essence of the Austrian character.

Hugo von Hofmannsthal, in a much-quoted essay "The Prussian and the Austrian," contrasted the characteristic differences of the two types. Only a few of his points are paraphrased here:

The Prussian's outlook changes with little consideration for positions taken in the past. He lacks historical sense, favors unlimited authority, and acts according to orders. He is strong in the realm of the abstract. He is more efficient, has much self-confidence, and pushes toward crises. He is self-righteous, arrogant, schoolmasterly. Incomparable in the exact performance of tasks, he is ambitious. He has little ability to put himself in another's position.

Introduction

The Austrian's outlook is traditional. He has historical sense and strikes out for unlimited individualism. He acts according to what he thinks right. He has little inclination for the abstract, is more humane, and indulges in self-irony. He avoids crises. He is vain, witty, and pleasure-seeking. He is apt to put himself in another person's position to the point of unprincipledness. He has a remarkable ability to extricate himself from difficulties and to take care of himself with resourcefulness.

Hofmannsthal obviously believed that "German" and "Austrian" were not the same.

A second flowering of Austrian literature, its real golden age, developed after the turn of the century. In its first three decades by far the greater part of what traditionally has been called the peaks of German literature is actually Austrian literature: Hugo von Hofmannsthal, Arthur Schnitzler, Rainer Maria Rilke, Franz Kafka, Karl Kraus, Hermann Broch, Robert Musil.

The end of World War I, which brought with it the dismemberment of the Austro-Hungarian monarchy, did not end the golden age of Austrian literature. The different nationalities formed new states, while their German-speaking minorities maintained their bonds with Vienna, still the literary and intellectual center for the components of the former empire. The real end of the old Austria, and a temporary suspension of Austrian literature, came in 1938 with the Nazi invasion and Austria's incorporation into the German Reich.

Reduced in size to a small country since 1918, Austria, as a result of World War II, lost also many of its former cultural ties with the countries that once were parts of Austria and now follow the life style of communist states. Austria's literature lives on, but its glory lies largely in the past.

To quote the well-known Austrian writer Friedrich Torberg: "The continuity within Austrian literature has been broken, but not necessarily its tradition. Austria's writers still walk the same crooked little streets, past the same baroque palaces and out to the same woods and vineyards, as did Hofmannsthal and Schnitzler and Musil. Something of all that remains alive."

The genius *loci* and *linguae*, then, justifies the hope that a new generation of Austrian writers will preserve, in our own time and beyond, the tradition of *humanitas*, established by the three great playwrights of the nineteenth century and by the writers who followed them.

Austrian literature has been a reality for a long time. Recognition of that fact has been slow in developing in Western literary criticism.

This handbook is the first in the English language whose subject is Austrian literature. It will acquaint the English-speaking reader with a number of major writers he may not know. This is by no means a complete roster. Many more writers would have been included had space permitted. All writers represented were born in the territory of the Austro-Hungarian monarchy and wrote, or still write, in German. The first essay on Austrian literature to be published within the covers of an American book is the comprehensive article written by Ivar Ivask, editor of *Books Abroad,* for *The Encyclopedia of World Literature in the Twentieth Century.**

It is a deep satisfaction to me that I can publish this book for an American audience and so repay a debt to Austrian writers who have enriched my life, both during my youth in Austria and my later life in my new homeland.

F. U.

* Published by Frederick Ungar Publishing Co., 1967–71.

Handbook of Austrian Literature

Ilse Aichinger

Born 1 November 1921 in Vienna. Ilse Aichinger spent her childhood in Linz and completed her *Gymnasium* education in Vienna in 1939. Following the Anschluß, she and her family were persecuted, and she was required to do compulsory service during World War II. She gave up her medical studies (begun after 1945) in the fifth semester in order to complete her first novel. In 1949 in Vienna, and later in Frankfurt, she worked in the editorial department of the publishing house of S. Fischer. In Ulm she collaborated with Inge Scholl in establishing the Institute of Creative Writing. Married to the writer Günter Eich since 1953 and mother of two children, she now lives in Lenggries (Upper Bavaria).

Ilse Aichinger is a master of "unveiled language." Her works are a verbal synthesis of the antitheses of human existence. In them she brings together the possible and the actual, the past and the present, the particular and the universal of existence, merging them into an unobtrusive unity in a rendering that seems as real as it is dreamlike, as uncomplicated as it is many-faceted. In emulation of Franz Kafka, she has succeeded in developing the modern narrative form, the parable, to convey truth. In doing so, she forgoes the use of the stylistic devices of surrealism, absurd phantasmagoria, and ironic distance. In the noncontradictory, calm, but relentless mirror of her narratives, the image of man and his world can no longer lie. The material she makes use of may seem modest, but it is marked by the pivotal points of human existence. In the novel *Die größere Hoffnung* (1948), a wrenching of reality takes place before the horrified eyes of a persecuted Jewish girl: home and homeland are becoming a prison, adults are becoming phantoms, and childhood is becoming the end of life. The apocalypse of the Hitler era is not just about to break forth; it has already arrived and is present. But "the greater hope" lies in the future, though a shell blast ends the lives of those who hope.

Sartre's idea of man being constantly bound to the human condition, which is that of the individual "condemned to be free," finds narrative expression in the story *Der Gefesselte* (1953). *Spiegelgeschichte* (1954) turns around the notion of "running ahead into one's own death": the events of a dead girl's life are traced back from bier to birth. It is precisely the situations at the fringe of human existence that turn out to be the springboard into the actuality of existence.

Ilse Aichinger's works—her stories, verse, dialogues, and radio plays—considered as a whole, are patterns of perception. They achieve their resolution through a special narrative technique of representation: narrated reality is reduced to situations and incidents that contain direct existential truths. In her collection of stories *Eliza, Eliza* (1965) she therefore turns toward a "concrete prose" that achieves, without any symbolic paraphrase, transcendental significance in the word, which is simultaneously an actual sign and an abstraction.

Works: *Die größere Hoffnung* (1948; Eng. tr., Herod's Children, 1963); *Rede unter dem Galgen* (1952; published in Germany as *Der Gefesselte*, 1953; Eng. tr., Bound Man, and Other Stories, 1955); *Knöpfe* (radio play, 1953; drama, 1957; Buttons); *Spiegelgeschichte* (1954; Mirror Story); *Zu keiner Stunde* (1957; At No Hour); *Besuch im Pfarrhaus* (1961; includes *Paßübergang, Weiße Chrysanthemen, Nicht vor Mailand*; Visit to the Parsonage: Going through the Mountain Pass, White Chrysanthemums, and Not before Milan); *Wo ich wohne* (1963; Where I Live); *Eliza, Eliza* (1965); *Auckland* (1969); *Nachricht vom Tag* (1970; News of the Day).

English translations in collections: Selected Short Stories and Dialogues (1968).

Bibliography: Allridge, J. C., *Ilse Aichinger*, 1969. Lübren, R., "Die Sprache der Bilder," *Neue Rundschau* 76 (1965):626–36. On *Bound Man*, in *Saturday Review*, 16 January 1956. On *Herod's Children*, in *Book Week*, 17 November 1963, p. 6. *New York Times*, 24 November 1963.

Walther Huder

Peter Altenberg

Peter Altenberg (pseudonym of Richard Engländer), Austrian writer of prose sketches, was born in Vienna 8 March 1859 and died there 8 January 1919. Widely known as a bizarre character frequenting literary cafés, he was also revered as the friend of frank and free souls in the lower walks of life. In his published works and in his famous table talk alike he was a restless apostle of beauty and health and a brilliant philosophical humorist who adored nature and kindness and nonchalantly unmasked the despicable "bourgeois."

Having, in his own words, fervently loved ladies both noble and very ignoble, loitered in the woods, been a law student and a medical student, but never having actually studied either law or medicine, Altenberg published at the age of thirty-seven his first book, *Wie ich es sehe* (1896). "As I see it"—with the stress on *see*—was to be the approach also in his other writings, the *it* always being "life itself" (Vita ipsa, 1918), filled with most "real" fairy tales (*Märchen des Lebens*, 1908) and pictures, beautiful and revealing (*Bilderbögen des kleinen Lebens*, 1909). Altenberg wanted to give "extracts of life, dehydrated and canned in two or three pages." Whether these extracts be descriptive or narrative, monologue or dialogue, sublime or abusive, his bohemian existence is their background, explicit or implied. His impressions are submerged in the effort to disclose the values he cared for and to win his readers over to his enthusiastic beliefs—that physiological perfection is the basis of moral, intellectual, aesthetic perfection; that mental genius in men has its counterpart in aesthetic perfection in women; that radical "faithfulness to one's self," accompanied by unselfishness, is the highest good. These convictions pervade the witty and melancholic, shocking and delicate aphorisms, idyls, prose poems and manifestoes of Altenberg's remaining books: *Was der Tag mir zuträgt* (1901), *Pródromos* (1906), *Neues Altes* (1911), *Semmering 1912* (1913), *Fechsung* (1915), *Nachfechsung* (1916), *Mein Lebensabend* (1919), *Der Nachlaß* (1925). He attacks all that seems hypocritical in a vapid civilization. He praises, with equal enthusiasm, nobleness of mind and of body, finding these in the socially humblest creature as well as in a famous actress. Animals, children, adolescent girls—creatures nearer to nature than the boring world of man—are the preferred objects of his admiration.

Altenberg has a supreme talent for conveying impressions and implications with a minimum of visible effort in concentrated prose or in a revealing dialogue of a few lines. Outstanding is his gift for making silent things resonant and for muffling the loud ones. His last books are full of bitterness and misanthropy. Alone in his sickroom, he turned his power of observation on himself, reflecting upon his passing life, describing the intermittent approach of death—until a few days before the end.

Works: *Wie ich es sehe* (1896; As I See It); *Ashantee* (1897); *Was der Tag mir zuträgt* (1901; What the Day Brings); *Prodromos* (1906); *Die Auswahl aus meinen Büchern* (1908; My Selections from My Books); *Märchen des Lebens* (1908; Fairy Tales of Life); *Bilderbögen des kleinen Lebens* (1909; Picture-sheets of the Small Life); *Neues Altes* (1911; New Old Things); *Semmering 1912* (1913); *Fechsung* (1915; Harvest); *Nachfechsung* (1916: Second Crop); *Vita ipsa* (1918); *Mein Lebensabend* (1919; Evening of My Life); *Das Altenbergbuch* (ed. E. Friedell, 1921; The Book about Altenberg); *Der Nachlaß* (ed. A. Polgar, 1925; Posthumous Works); *Nachlese* (ed. M. Mauthner, 1929–30; Gleanings); *Peter Altenberg: Auswahl aus seinen Büchern* (ed. K. Kraus, 1932; Peter Altenberg: Selections from His Books); *Briefe* (ed. F. Glück, 1947 Letters); *Auswahlausgaben* (ed. G. Martin, 1960; ed. W. Kraus, 1961; ed. E. Randak, 1961; Selected Editions); *Das Glück der verlorenen Stunden* (1961; Happiness of Lost Hours).

English translations in collections: *Alexander King Presents Peter Altenberg's Evocations of Love* (1960).

Bibliography: Friedell, E., *Ecce Poeta*, 1912. Hofmannsthal, Hugo von, *Gesammelte Werke*, Prosa I, pp. 313–22, 1950. Malmberg, H., *Widerhall des Herzens—Ein Peter-Altenberg-Buch*, 1961. Mann, Thomas, *Altes und Neues*, pp. 697–701, 1953. Martin, G., *Peter Altenberg—Reporter der Seele*, 1960. Polgar, Alfred, *Der Nachlaß von Peter Altenberg*, pp. 149–54, 1925. Rosenwald, Henry M., *Jahrhundertwende*, pp. 47–48, 1968.

Franz H. Mautner

Hans Carl Artmann

Born 12 June 1921 in Vienna. Artmann's father was a shoemaker in Breitensee, an outskirting area of Vienna where Artmann grew up. A well-read, amazing polyglot, his formal education did not go beyond elementary school. During the period 1950–60, he was one of the founders and became one of the most successful members of the so-called Vienna Group of avant-garde writers, who experimented with everything from black-humor verse in Viennese dialect to concrete poetry and Happenings inspired by dadaism and surrealism (see *Die Wiener Gruppe: Achleitner, Artmann, Bayer, Rühm, Wiener*, edited by Gerhard Rühm, 1967).

Artmann's role as the leading spirit of the Vienna Group has been compared to that of Ezra Pound in his day. Of established writers, Doderer encouraged the Vienna Group (see his introduction to Artmann's *hosn rosn baa*; written with Friedrich Achleitner and Gerhard Rühm, 1959), just as the painter-writer Albert Paris Gütersloh was the mentor of the Vienna School of Phantastic Realism, a group equally indebted to surrealism and, in many ways, a close parallel to the Vienna Group during the same fruitful postwar years.

Artmann gained public acclaim in 1958 when his macabre-surrealistic dialect poems appeared under the title *med ana schwoazzn dintn*, one of the few mid-20th-century Austrian collections of verse to become a bestseller. Yet this popularity was due to a misunderstanding on the part of the public, which appreciated the dialect more than the ends to which Artmann used it.

Artmann left Vienna in 1960 and subsequently lived in Berlin, Malmö, and Graz. Recently, however, he has been traveling extensively and frequently stays in Brittany. His translations include a selection from the religious poetry of the Celts (*der schlüssel des heiligen patrick*, 1959), a novel by Francisco de Quevedo (*Der abenteuerliche Buscón*, 1963), Carl von Linné's travel diaries (*Lappländische Reise*, 1964), versions of Edward Lear's nonsense poetry, and François Villon's ballads, which Artmann rendered in the Viennese dialect (*Baladn*, 1968).

Artmann, with the other members of the Vienna Group, gave dialect poetry a new lease on life. This achievement points to his original inspiration—Vienna, in particular one of the outskirts, and its dialect, by means of which he created a union of nature lyricism and the macabre. Yet, in his other poetry and in his prose and plays, he has gone far beyond this initial stage. *Ein lilienweißer brief aus lincolnshire* (1969) is the first collection of all his nondialect poetry from 1945 to 1966. His early writing shows that he was influenced by Rainer Maria Rilke, Georg Trakl, and Frederico García Lorca. But he soon found his own voice and style.

Artmann is an Alexandrian poet who incorporates out-of-the-way bits of erudition and information in his poetry with surprising effect. This poetry is nourished by a fairy-talelike wonder and an ironical-satirical abandon with which he roams the realms of world literature. Like James Joyce, he seems to be at home in many ages and milieus. He is a verbal juggler and a multilingual punster always balancing on that fine edge between genuine humor and less convincing intellectual gambols. Again and again he returns to his favorite age, the baroque (see such cycles as *Vergänglichkeit und Auferstehung der Schäfferei* or *persische quatrainen*), which has so decisively shaped Austrian literature to this very day.

Artmann's first prose volume, *von denen husaren und anderen seiltänzern* (1959), is a parody of baroque adventures. *Grünverschlossene Botschaft: 90 Träume* (1967), *fleiß und industrie* (1967), and *die anfangsbuchstaben der flagge* (1969) range from phantastic prose poems to parodies of once-popular novels and sample sentences from foreign-language readers. Artmann's most sustained prose work is the quasi-autobiographical *das suchen nach dem gestrigen tag, oder schnee auf einen heißen brotwecken* (1964), obviously inspired by Linné's diaries. Using the technique of diary entries, Artmann comments on travels, far-ranging reading, memories of Vienna, and ideas for future works already in progress. A melancholy humor pervades the book.

In *die fahrt zur insel nantucket* (1969), which reveals the hand of the poet as much as that of the prose writer, Artmann collected all his theatrical works written between 1952 and 1966. The influences are of an extraordinary variety: commedia dell'arte, the Viennese popular comedy, Grand Guignol, Sherlock Holmes, Abott-and-Costello movies, Samuel Beckett, Eugène Ionesco, Gertrude Stein, and others. But even in works that show none of these apparent influences, Artmann's imagination is fertile: in *die liebe fee pocahontas oder kasperl als schildwache* he takes the Viennese Kasperle (similar to the Punch and Judy show) to the American Civil War; in *Erlaubent, Schas, sehr heiß bitte* he evokes a ghostly Hitler in a Viennese café in the year 1995. The punning dialogue between the characters tau and lau in *nebel und blatt* (1955) is actually a long poem. *Kleinere taschenkunststücke,* despite its mixing of illusion and reality, is not as Pirandellian as might be expected. Instead, it lies more in the main tradition of Austrian theater from Franz Grillparzer to Arthur Schnitzler. The most impressive of these theater pieces remains *Kein Pfeffer für Czermak* (1954). In this full-length play that modernizes and demonizes the Ferdinand Raimund-Johann Nestroy kind of popular Viennese theater, a sadistic grocer dies agonizingly from apoplexy after having reveled in his perverse power over poor customers and his ward.

The legend that has grown up around Artmann during his lifetime—like that around Rilke before him—is not dispelled but rather deepened by the *festschrift* edited in his honor by G. Giesinger and Peter O. Chotjewitz and entitled *Der Landgraf zu Camprodon* (1966).

Works: *med ana schwoazzn dintn* (1958; In Black Ink); *von denen husaren und anderen seiltänzern* (1959; About Those Hussars and Other Tightrope Dancers); *hosn rosn baa* (with F. Achleitner and G. Rühm, 1959; Pants, Roses, and Bone); *das suchen nach dem gestrigen tag, oder schnee auf einen heißen brotwecken* (1964; The Search for Yesterday, or Snow on a Hot Loaf of Bread); *fleiß und industrie* (1967; Diligence and Industry); *Grünverschlossene Botschaft: 90 Träume* (1967; Green-sealed Message: 90 Dreams); *Herzlose Reime für herzlose Heime* (with H. Graham, 1968; Heartless Poems for Heartless Homes); *die anfangsbuchstaben der flagge* (1969; The Initial Letters of the Flag); *ein lilienweißer brief aus lincolnshire* (1969; A Lily-white Letter from Lincolnshire); *die fahrt zur insel nantucket* (1969; The Voyage to Nantucket); *The Best of Hans Carl Artmann* (1970, in German); *Das im Walde verlorene Totem: Prosadichtungen 1949–1953* (1970; The Totem Lost in the Forest); *Die Jagd nach Doktor Unspeakable* (1971; The Hunt for Doctor Unspeakable); *How much, Schatzi?* (1971, in German); *Der Aeronautische Sindbart* (1972; The Aeronaut Sindbart).

Bibliography: Alldridge, J. C., "H. C. Artmann and the English Nonsense Tradition," in *Affinities: Essays in German and English Literature,* edited by R. W. Last, pp. 168–83, 1971. Chotjewitz, Peter O., in *Literatur und Kritik,* 1966, pp. 26 ff. Ivask, Ivar, on *ein lilienweißer brief aus lincolnshire,* in *Books Abroad,* 1970, p. 307.

Ivar Ivask[▲]

Raoul Auernheimer

Raoul Auernheimer was born on 15 April 1876 in Vienna, and he grew up in a stable, middle-class environment. Because of his mixed heritage—his father was a German Protestant from the Nuremberg region, and his mother, who was Jewish, came from Hungary—Auernheimer regarded himself as a genuine *Wiener Kind* (son of Vienna). Almost all of his writings are inextricably interwoven with his native city, which he truly loved. He received his law degree from the University of Vienna and was destined for a career in law. The renaissance of the arts in Vienna, however, stimulated his literary talent, and early success determined him to earn his living as a writer. Under the influence and on the model of his eminent distant cousin, Zionist Theodor Herzl, a feature writer for the *Neue Freie Presse*, the most influential newspaper in Vienna at that time, Auernheimer became a journalist. He wrote feuilletons and drama reviews (he was the Burgtheater critic) for this prestigious newspaper from 1906 to 1933. He continued to write for the *Basler Nationalzeitung* until 1948.

Immediately following the Anschluß in 1938, Auernheimer was imprisoned for approximately six months in Dachau. He was released through the intervention of the American attaché in Berlin, Prentice Gilbert, who had translated two of Auernheimer's plays into English. Auernheimer lived briefly in New York before settling in Oakland, California, and became an American citizen in 1944. The effects of a heart condition caused his death on 7 January 1948.

Auernheimer represents a type of writer that flourished at the turn of the century, namely, a talented writer who was predominantly a journalist and critic but who also wrote a considerable number of belletristic works. Many of the outstanding journalists of that period, such as Herzl, Hermann Bahr, and Felix Salten, fit this same pattern—unless a writer was independently wealthy, he had little other choice, for very few authors found it possible to live on the proceeds of their literary works alone. It is a measure of Auernheimer's stature both as an individual and as a writer that he was accepted into the group known as Young Vienna, which included the outstanding Austrian literary figures Hugo von Hofmannsthal, Arthur Schnitzler, and Richard Beer-Hofmann. Like these men, Auernheimer was dedicated to the preservation of the humanistic tradition.

As a journalist, Auernheimer took his responsibilities toward the public seriously. He considered the feuilleton to be a "people's university" that served to educate and broaden the public view. His theater reviews helped overcome critical resistance to literary innovation in Vienna, and it is a tribute to his objectivity and discernment that many of his ideas and judgments have now found general acceptance. A number of his essays were later published in book form: *Das ältere Wien: Bilder und Schatten* (1920), *Die Wienerin im Spiegel der Jahrhunderte* (1928), and *Wien: Bild und Schicksal* (1938).

Auernheimer achieved considerable popularity with his psychological novellas and his light comedies, the dramatic form that was his specialty, as attested by the numerous new editions of his works published during his lifetime and the frequency with which his dramas were performed both in Austria and Germany and in translation in other countries as well. Auernheimer's narrative works show the influence of Schnitzler, and he freely admitted his indebtedness to the latter, whom he esteemed most highly of all of his contemporaries.

Auernheimer's narrative approach shows little development throughout his career. For the most part his novellas and stories, collected in more than a dozen volumes, contain seemingly endless variations on the basic theme of playing with love. Their chief appeal lies in the quality of the style and the imaginativeness of the situations, which are sustained by complicated twists of plot. Despite the apparent lightness of his approach, Auernheimer was an unusually perceptive observer of Viennese behavior, and his writings, including *Rosen, die wir nicht erreichen* (1901), *Der gußeiserne Herrgott* (1911), and *Das wahre Gesicht* (1916), form an honest but sympathetic chronicle of Viennese society after 1900. Several of his individual short stories—*Der Leichenbestatter von Ebenbrunn* (1911), *Laurenz Hallers Praterfahrt* (1913), *Der Geheimniskrämer* (1919), and *Evarist und Leander* (1931)—are particularly distinguished and represent the pinnacle of his narrative achievement. His later novels *Das Kapital* (1923) and *Die linke und die rechte Hand* (1927), in which he attempted to reflect the changed conditions of post-World War I Vienna, found little response. A more successful novel, *Gottlieb Weniger dient der Gerechtigkeit* (1934), takes place in the Austrian milieu of the 1830s, during the period of Metternich's influence, the historical period in which Auernheimer felt most at home.

Since the comedy of manners is Auernheimer's forte, it is not surprising that drama was the genre most suitable to his talents. In subject matter and technique there is little difference between the dramas and the novellas, as is suggested by the title *Lustspielnovellen*

(1922), a designation that Auernheimer applied to all of his shorter prose writings. Like the narrative works, his light comedies treat the theme of love and seduction. They are all characterized by witty, sophisticated (for that era) dialogue, and spiced by antithesis, gentle irony, and satire, whether they have a contemporary setting—*Die große Leidenschaft* (1905), *Das Paar nach der Mode* (1913), and *Gewitter auf dem Rigi* (1932)—or an historical background—*Der gute König* (1908), *Die verbündeten Mächte* (1915), and *Casanova in Wien* (1924).

Auernheimer's internment in 1938 not only put an end to the world as he knew it, but it also virtually finished his career as a writer. Although his first book written in America, *Metternich, Staatsmann und Kavalier* (1947; first published in English, *Prince Metternich, Statesman and Lover*, in 1940), received favorable reviews, he was unable to duplicate this initial success. His literary estate contains many unpublished essays, aphorisms, movie scripts, dramas, and biographies. His autobiography, *Das Wirtshaus zur verlorenen Zeit*, a biography entitled *Grillparzer, der Dichter Österreichs*, a psychological portrait of the Austrian national poet, were published posthumously in Vienna in 1948.

Auernheimer is of particular interest to the cultural and literary historian, for his life and writings epitomize the strengths and weaknesses of Viennese culture at the turn of the century. Born into an age of relative security and blessed with early and easy success, Auernheimer, like many of his contemporaries, led a fundamentally aesthetic existence with almost total avoidance of political interest and responsibility. Only when confronted by the harshness of political reality in 1938 and forced out of the mainstream of society did Auernheimer finally recognize this fundamental deficiency of his generation. Nevertheless, he merits recognition as a typical representative of his generation both in Austria and in exile. Above all, he deserves remembrance as an idealistic human being, who in his writings and through the example of his life, left a legacy of dedication to eternal humanistic values.

Works: *Talent* (1900); *Rosen, die wir nicht erreichen* (1901; Unattainable Roses); *Koketterie* (1902; Coquetry); *Die Lügenbrücke* (1902; The Bridge of Lies); *Renée* (1902); *In festen Händen* (1903; In Firm Hands); *Die Verliebten* (1903; People in Love); *Lebemänner* (1903; Men about Town); *Karriere* (1904; Career); *Die Dame mit der Maske* (1905; The Lady with the Mask); *Die große Leidenschaft* (1905; The Grand Passion); *Die ängstliche Dodo* (1907; The Fearful Dodo); *Der gute König*

(1908; The Good King); *Die glücklichste Zeit* (1909; The Happiest Time); *Die man nicht heiratet* (1909; Those One Does not Marry); *Gesellschaft* (1910; Society); *Renée und die Männer* (1910; Renée and the Men); *Der gußeiserne Hergott* (1911; The Cast Iron God); *Der Unverschämte* (1912; The Insolent Man); *Das dumme Glück* (1912; Dumb Luck); *Das Paar nach der Mode* (1913; The Fashionable Couple); *Laurenz Hallers Praterfahrt* (1913; Laurenz Haller's Ride through the Park); *Die verbündeten Mächte* (1915; The Allied Powers); *Das wahre Gesicht* (1916; The True Face); *Herzen in Schwebe* (1916; Hearts in Abeyance); *Frau Magda im Schnee* (1919; Mrs. Magda Snowbound); *Der Geheimniskrämer* (1919; The Secretmonger); *Maskenball* (1920; Masked Ball); *Das ältere Wien* (1920; Older Vienna); *Lustpielnovellen* (1922; Comic Novellas); *Das Kapital* (1923; The Capital); *Casanova in Wien* (1924; Casanova in Vienna); *Die linke und die rechte Hand* (1927; The Left and the Right Hand); *Die Wienerin im Spiegel der Jahrhunderte* (1928; The Viennese Woman in the Mirror of Centuries); *Die Feuerglocke* (1929; The Firebell); *Gewitter auf dem Rigi* (1931; Thunder Storm on the Rigi); *Evarist und Leander* (1931); *Der gefährliche Augenblick* (1932; The Dangerous Moment); *Geist und Gemeinschaft* (1932; Spirit and Community); *Gottlieb Weniger dient der Gerechtigkeit* (1934; Gottlieb Weninger Serves Justice); *Wien—Bild und Schicksal* (1938; Vienna—Portrait and Destiny); *Prince Metternich, Statesman and Lover* (1940; German edition, *Metternich, Staatsmann und Kavalier*, 1947); *Franz Grillparzer, der Dichter Österreichs* (1948; Franz Grillparzer, The Poet of Austria); *Das Wirtshaus zur verlorenen Zeit* (1948; The Inn at the Sign of Lost Time).

Bibliography: Daviau, Donald G., "Raoul Auernheimer—In Memoriam," *Modern Austrian Literature* 3 (Winter 1970):7–21. Daviau, Donald G., and Johns, Jorun B., *The Correspondence of Arthur Schnitzler and Raoul Auernheimer*, 1972. Johnson, Hal, "New American Citizen," *Berkeley Daily Gazette*, 28 December 1944, p. 4. Kleiber, O., "Raoul Auernheimer," *Basler Nationalzeitung*, 12 January 1948, p. 1. Rollett, Edwin, "Abschied von Auernheimer," *Wiener Zeitung*, 10 January 1948, p. 2.

Donald G. Daviau[▲]

Ingeborg Bachmann

Born 25 June 1926 in Klagenfurt. Grew up in Carinthia. Studied philosophy in Innsbruck, Graz, and Vienna. Received her Ph.D. in 1950 with the dissertation "Kritische Aufnahme der Existentialphilosophie Martin Heideggers." From 1953 to 1957 Ingeborg Bachman lived in Italy, primarily in Rome. In 1955 she went to America for further study. Later she lived intermittently in Munich, Rome, and Zurich. From 1959 to 1960 she was the first lecturer in the new Chair for Poetry at Frankfurt, and in 1964 she was awarded the Büchner Prize. She presently lives in Berlin.

From the beginning Ingeborg Bachmann's poems commanded attention. In imploring tones they proclaimed the end of time. *Herbstmanöver der Zeit* sounded the awakening: the release of man from all existing, now worthless ties. The poems were a command, in the hour of "the afterbirth of horror," to voice a final *no* to comfortable self-adjustment, a final *no* to escape behind the mask into traditional, crumbly beauty and jerry-built pseudoorder. The summons sounded: "Do not look back. Tie your shoe. Chase the dogs back. Throw the fish into the sea. Harder days are coming." The often extravagant pictorial and verbal evocations of her language were received with fascination but also with startled confusion. Here were visions—begotten in delirium and lucid wakefulness—transformed into expansive, glowing pictures or reduced to terse magic formulas full of warning and promise: "See to it that you stay awake!" "Redeem the promises." "Pour yourself out and come back knowing. . . ."

The very titles of her first two volumes of poetry—*Die gestundete Zeit* (1953) and *Anrufung des großen Bären* (1956)—are warning signals of the approaching end. The poems in these collections define the situation: "Borrowed time, now recalled, grows visible on the horizon"; the "creature of cloudlike fur, . . . with tired flanks, and the sharp, half-bared teeth" stands threateningly in the sky. Positioned under Damocles's sword, man is asked to orient himself anew, to lift himself out of a world in which "all life . . . has wandered away into boxes for toy-building blocks," to step into the "status of the isolated, where wonder takes place." Numerous poem titles are ciphers of farewell and new beginning: "Departure," "Fall Away, Heart,"

"The Great Cargo," "The Game Is Over," "Heap of Fragments," "Songs in Flight," "Land Rush."

Ingeborg Bachmann's poems are testimonials of an unqualified and courageous readiness to accept fate. The solitary path is chosen ("I hold to the course that no one knows anymore"), though fear and horror accompany it ("Oh, if only I had no fear of death"). Unanswerable questions are asked: "But where will we go / when it gets dark and cold / what should we do / and think / in the face of an end / and what will happen / when dead silence / comes? Initiation into love, destruction and loss of love, powerful beauty that can scarcely be "endured"—all are freshly and totally experienced. Hymnically she announces her preparedness for life: "Nothing more beautiful under the sun than to be under the sun . . . my enraptured eyes widen again." Yet: "Like Orpheus I play death on the strings of life . . . like Orpheus I know life on death's side."

A free, heavy, flowing rhythm dominates the form, though in one or two instances we encounter a strict rhyme scheme. The images, taken predominantly from nature but from the world of myth and fairy tale as well, mirror inner conditions and the historical situation. Lines of the most delicate melodies, immediately grasped and in their language as obvious as they are spellbinding, are juxtaposed with wild and impassable lyrical passages. Occasional slips into artificiality and pompousness are outweighed by the presence of a great poetic force pouring forth.

Ingeborg Bachmann's prose works, in which the keynote is noticeably lyrical, also contains extreme experiences of joy and pain and strongest temptations. She almost always concerns herself with attempts to break through the hidden areas of the self, whereby, as she hopes, the world and man might be given a new, more consummate shape. Fully aware of the impossibility of fulfilling this demand, she calls for an unflinching look at "the perfected, the impossible, the unattainable, be it in love, freedom, or in any great dimension" (acceptance speech for the radio play prize of blind war veterans, 1959).

In her radio play *Der gute Gott von Manhattan* (1958), judgement is being passed on the god of lovers, but in reality it is being passed on the boundless and absolute love this god defends. Symbolizing the increasingly exclusive love bond between Jan and Jennifer, the author has them occupy progressively higher rooms in the Atlantic Hotel. Step by step their love (the stages of which are blended into the legal proceedings) removes both of them from the world and its laws in order to bring them closer to "antitime." To the god,

Jan and Jennifer appear worthy of being rocketed to heaven—he sees active in them those "elements of madness," those "scarce elements of luminous and combustible power that disintegrate everything and call the world into question." But Jan forfeits his chance for a modern love-death: in ogling his earlier, insignificant life, though only for a moment, he relapses and therefore becomes unworthy in the eyes of the god

In *Undine geht*, the final, compact prose piece in the volume *Das dreißigste Jahr* (1961), again a man fails, out of weakness, to follow the nymph's call, which is a "cry for the end," for freedom from bonds, for isolation and total freedom. He commits himself to the everyday and thus effects a "renunciation of all truth." Like this story, the others in the volume also deal with the desperate attempt to renounce the "old, infamous order."

Man in his thirtieth year (*cf*. the title story) is man in revolt. He makes another attempt to forcibly bring about a change of direction, a reversal of values: in love, as in *Ein Schritt nach Gomorrha*; in the education of a new man in *Alles*; in the search for absolute truth in *Ein Wildermuth*. Though the rebellions break down and at the end revert to the old order (the radio play *Zikaden*, 1954, also belongs in this thematic group), protest, guilt, and death nevertheless come to be renewing and formative experiences between the act of turning away and the act of turning back.

In her Frankfurt "Lectures in Poetics," Ingeborg Bachmann attempted, among other things, a justification of poetic utterance in our time: "The modifying effect of new works trains us for a new way of perception, a new sense of feeling, a new consciousness." According to her, art gives us "the possibility of discovering where we stand and where we should stand, how our lives are arranged and how they should be arranged." When she asserts that today probably no one believes any longer in the idea "that literature happens outside the historical situation," she is also characterizing her own work.

Ingeborg Bachmann's first artistic collaboration with composer Hans Werner Henze was in 1952, when she wrote the libretto for Tatjana Gsovsky's ballet-pantomime *The Idiot*, for which Henze composed the music. Under the title *Ein Monolog des Fürsten Myschkin*, the libretto was included a year later in the volume *Die gestundete Zeit*. In 1960 she wrote the text for Henze's opera *Der Prinz von Homburg*. But their collaboration has had its greatest success so far with the comic opera *Der junge Lord*, which had its premiere in Berlin in 1965. Ingeborg Bachmann based her libretto on Wilhelm

Hauff's *Der Scheik von Alexandria und seine Sklaven*. She was praised by the critics as an opera librettist of great talent.

Works: *Die gestundete Zeit* (1953; Borrowed Time); *Herrenhaus* (1954; The Manor; radio play based on drama by T. Wolfe); *Zikaden* (1955; Cicadas); *Anrufung des großen Bären* (1956; Evocation of the Great Dipper); *Der gute Gott von Manhattan* (1958; The Good God of Manhattan); *Nachtstücke und Arien* (1958; Nocturnes and Arias); *Musik und Dichtung* (1959; Music and Poetry); *Das dreißigste Jahr* (1961; Eng. tr., The Thirtieth Year, 1964); *Jugend in einer österreichischen Stadt* (1961; Youth in an Austrian Town); *Der Prinz vom Homburg* (libretto, 1963; The Prince of Homburg); *Gedichte, Erzählungen, Hörspiele, Essays* (1964; Poetry, Short Stories, Radio Plays, Essays); *Der junge Lord* (libretto, 1965; The Young Lord); *Ein Ort für Zufälle* (1965; A Place for Coincidences); *Malina* (1971); *Simultan: Neue Erzählungen* (1972; Simultaneous: New Stories).

Bibliography: Härtling, Peter, "Es kommen härtere Tage," in *In Zeiten zuhaus*, pp. 31–37, 1957. Holthusen, Hans Egon, "Kämpfender Sprachgeist," in *Das Schöne und das Wahre*, pp. 246–76, 1958. Lyon, James K., "The Poetry of Ingeborg Bachmann," *German Life and Letters* 17, no. 3 (1964):205–215. Oppens, Kurt, "Gesang und Magie im Zeitalter des Steins: Zur Dichtung Ingeborg Bachmanns und Paul Celans," *Merkur* 17, no. 2 (1963):175–93. Rasch, Wolfdietrich, "Ingeborg Bachmann: 'Mein Vogel,'" *Germanisch-romanische Monatshefte*, Neue Folge 7 (1957): 16–21. Schoolfield, George C., in *Essays on Contemporary German Literature*, edited by Brian Keith-Smith, 1966. Triesch, Manfred, in *Books Abroad*, 1965.

Charlotte Nennecke

Hermann Bahr

Born 19 July 1863, in Linz on the Danube, into a lawyer's family. Began the study of law and classical philology in Vienna but eventually concentrated on economics and political science. Relegated from Vienna in 1883 for unlawful political activity, Hermann Bahr studied briefly in Graz and Czernowitz (now Cernăuţi), and, from 1884 to 1887, in Berlin, where he became closely acquainted with Arno Holz. Following one year of compulsory military training in Austria, Bahr lived for a year in Paris, an important experience that changed his interest from politics to literature. Traveled in France, Spain, and Morocco. Later travels included Russia, Italy, Greece, and England. In 1890 Bahr served as a contributing editor to the journal *Die Freie Bühne*. Returned to Vienna in 1891 to work as a journalist, and from 1894 to 1899 served as joint editor of the liberal newspaper *Die Zeit*. Growing unpopularity in Vienna because of his role as a cultural critic caused Bahr to move to Salzburg in 1912. In 1922 he moved to Munich, where he died on 15 January 1934 after a long paralyzing illness.

Although he was a protean figure of considerable influence and importance in his own generation (he was called the "midwife of modern literature"), Bahr's former European renown has now faded. Because of his prolific writings (more than one hundred volumes of dramas, essays, and narrative prose) and his frequent changes of direction in life (German naturalist, Marxist, atheist, impressionist, Catholic, monarchist), both critics and public alike have had difficulty in understanding Bahr's literary position and contribution. Essentially, Bahr remained an impressionist throughout his life, reacting in his writings to events, personalities, and problems that he felt were important. His central, self-appointed task was to serve as a mediator between the arts and the public and in a broader sense between Austria and the rest of western Europe. His artistic goal was to raise the general cultural level of Austria, while politically he worked to fulfill his vision of a loose-knit federation of European states with a strong, culturally vital Austria as the unifying center.

To achieve these aims, Bahr felt that all of the talented people in Austria must contribute. He therefore frequently "discovered" young writers and artists and occasionally promoted them beyond their intrinsic merits. However, Bahr's praise was not indiscriminate, as is sometimes alleged, and does not reflect any deficiency of critical sensitivity and judgment. Ultimately, he operated within an absolute hierarchical system of values that generously recognized all talent but always on its own level.

As a social critic, Bahr, like most members of his literary generation, was too aesthetically oriented to arrive at any solid understanding of the problems of the Hapsburg monarchy. Although he bitterly attacked the Hapsburgs, the Austrian bureaucratic system, and the Viennese in general in his malicious book *Wien* (1906) and further assailed Austrian political conditions and affairs in *Austriaca* (1911), he, nevertheless, after the republicanization of Austria in 1918, came to an appreciation of the monarchy as a stabilizing force and longed for its return.

In effect Bahr's literary works represent an extension of his journalistic writings and, like the latter, treat topical issues of contemporary but not enduring interest except to the literary and cultural historian. As a result, few of his writings have survived their time. Of his more than two dozen plays, all of which were widely performed at the time, only the comedy *Das Konzert* (1909) is still presented today. Bahr's narrative prose works, which lack solid epic substance, are all out of print. His plan to create a cycle of a dozen novels, analyzing specific aspects of Austrian life under the reign of Emperor Franz Joseph, was never completed.

Concerning Bahr's numerous critical essays, it can probably be safely predicted that of lasting value are his various commentaries on naturalism, impressionism, and expressionism, his *Dialog vom Tragischen* (1904) and *Dialog vom Marsyas* (1905), and the essay *Adalbert Stifter: Eine Entdeckung* (1919), which was influential in reviving popular appreciation of this eminent 19th-century Austrian writer. Bahr's autobiography, entitled *Selbstbildnis* (1923), is perhaps the most important book that he wrote, a fact that is not only a qualitative judgment but one that also reflects the importance of his life to his significance. For his prominence in his own day derived not so much from the intrinsic value of his many works, as from the dynamic forcefulness of his personality. In essence the man ultimately proved more important than his writings. In this connection it is noteworthy that he published a weekly version of his personal diary in the *Neues Wiener Journal* from 1917 to 1929.

In addition to literary and political interests, Bahr also actively supported, among many others, such artists as Gustav Klimt and the adherents of the secessionist movement in Vienna, the architect Joseph Olbrich, the composer Adalbert von Goldschmidt, the director Max Burckhard, and the actress Eleonora Duse, whom he claimed to have discovered. He had a strong interest in the theater, the major artistic forum in Austria, and worked as a director both under Bukovics in Vienna and Max Reinhardt in Berlin. In 1918 he was appointed director of the influential Burgtheater in Vienna but in the chaotic conditions of that transitional period was unable to institute any of his long-planned reforms.

Bahr's importance for Austrian literature lies in his catalytic effect on the arts in Vienna between 1891 and 1905 and in his efforts to overcome the stifling provincialism of Austria by exposing his readers to western European, English, and American influences. Following in the footsteps of Josef Nadler, Bahr also made an important contribution to reawakening in Austria an understanding of its unique baroque tradition, which, as he redefined it, became not only a life style but also a general guide for Austria's future role within the framework of a supranationalistic federation of European states.

Works: *Die neuen Menschen* (1887; The New People); *La Marquese d'Amegui* (1888); *Die große Sünde* (1888; The Great Sin); *Die gute Schule* (1890; The Good School); *Fin de siècle* (1890); *Zur Kritik der Moderne* (2 vols., 1890–91; On Criticism of Modernism); *Die Überwindung des Naturalismus* (1891; The Overcoming of Naturalism); *Die Mutter* (1891; The Mother); *Dora* (1893); *Russische Reise* (1893; Russian Journey); *Aus der Vorstadt* (with C. Karlweis, 1893; From the Outskirts of Town); *Die häusliche Frau* (1893; The Home-Loving Woman); *Neben der Liebe* (1893; Beside Love); *Caph* (1894); *Studien zur Kritik der Moderne* (1894; Studies on Criticism of Modernism); *Josephine* (1895); *Die Nixe* (1896; The Mermaid); *Juana* (1896); *Theater* (1897); *Das Tschaperl* (1898; Sweet Little Blockhead); *Der Star* (1898); *Wenn es euch gefällt* (with C. Karlweis, 1899; If You Like It); *Wiener Theater* (1899; Viennese Theater); *Der Athlet* (1899: The Athlete); *Die schöne Frau* (1899; The Beautiful Woman); *Sezession* (1900; Secession); *Bildung* (1900; Education); *Die Wienerinnen* (1900; Viennese Women); *Der Franzl* (1900; Little Franz); *Der Apostel* (1901; The Apostle); *Der liebe Augustin* (1902; Dear Augustin); *Der Krampus* (1902; The Little Devil of December 6); *Wirkung in die Ferne* (1902; Influence in the Distance); *Premieren* (1902; Opening Nights); *Rezensionen* (1903; Reviews); *Unter sich: Ein Arme-Leut-Stück* (1904; Among Themselves: A Poor-People Play); *Der Meister* (1904; Eng. tr., The Master, 1918); *Dialog vom Tragischen* (1904; Dialogue on the Tragic); *Dialog vom Marsyas* (1905; Dialogue on Marsyas); *Sanna* (1905); *Wien* (1906; Vienna); *Die Andere*

(1906; The Other One); *Der arme Narr* (1906; The Poor Fool); *Joseph Kainz* (1906); *Der Faun* (1906); *Glossen* (1906; Marginal Notes); *Ringelspiel* (1907; Merry-Go-Round); *Grotesken* (1907; Grotesques); *Die gelbe Nachtigall* (1907; The Yellow Nightingale); *Die Rahl* (1908); *Stimmen des Blutes* (1908; The Voices of the Blood); *Das Konzert* (1909; Eng. tr., The Concert, 1910); *Dalmatinische Reise* (1909; Dalmatian Journey); *Drut* (1909); *O Mensch* (1910; O Man); *Das Tänzchen* (1911; The Little Dance); *Die Kinder* (1911; The Children); *Austriaca* (1911); *Das Prinzip* (1912; The Principle); *Inventur* (1912; Inventory); *Erinnerungen an Max Burckhard* (1913; Recollections about Max Burckhard); *Das Phantom* (1913); *Essays* (1913); *Das Hermann-Bahr-Buch* (1913; The Hermann Bahr Book); *Der Querulant* (1914; Eng. tr., The Mongrel, 1924); *Der muntere Seifensieder* (1915; The Cheerful Soap Boiler); *Expressionismus* (1916; Eng. tr., Expressionism, 1925); *Himmelfahrt* (1916; Ascension); *Die Stimme* (1916; The Voice); *Der Augenblick* (1917; The Moment); *Adalbert Stifter: Eine Entdeckung* (1919; Adalbert Stifter: A Discovery); *Die Rotte Korah* (1919; Korah and All His Company); *Ehelei* (1920; Flippant Marriage); *Spielerei* (1920; Childish Dallying); *Der Unmensch* (1920; The Brute); *Burgtheater* (1920); *Summula* (1921); *Liebe der Lebenden* (3 vols., 1921–23; Love of the Living); *Kritik der Gegenwart* (1922; Criticism of the Present); *Selbstbildnis* (1923; Self-Portrait); *Schauspielkunst* (1923; Dramatic Art); *Sendung des Künstlers* (1923; The Artist's Mission); *Altweibersommer* (1924; Indian Summer); *Der Zauberstab: Tagebücher 1924–1926* (1926; The Magic Wand: Diaries 1924–1926); *Der inwendige Garten* (1927; The Internal Garden); *Die Tante* (1928; The Aunt); *Labyrinth der Gegenwart* (1929; The Labyrinth of the Present Time); *Tagebuch* (1929; Diary); *Osterreich in Ewigkeit* (1929; Forever Austria); *Mensch, werde wesentlich* (1934; Thou Man, Become Essential); *Salzburger Landschaft: Briefe und Tagebuchblätter* (1937; Salzburg Landscape: Letters and Diary); *Meister und Meisterbriefe um Hermann Bahr* (ed. J. Gregor, 1947; Masters and Master Letters about Hermann Bahr); *Essays von Hermann Bahr* (ed. H. Kindermann, 1962; Essays by Hermann Bahr); *Kulturprofil der Jahrhundertwende* (ed. H. Kindermann, 1962; Cultural Profile of the Turn of the Century); *Theater der Jahrhundertwende* (ed. H. Kindermann, 1963; Theater of the Turn of the Century); *Zur Überwindung des Naturalismus: Theoretische Schriften 1887–1903* (ed. G. Wunberg, 1968; The Overcoming of Naturalism: Theoretical Papers 1887–1903).

Bibliography: Bahr-Mildenburg, Anna, "Bibliographie deutscher Werke," *Jahrbuch deutsche Bibliophilen* 20 (1934). Buschbeck, Erhard, "Hermann Bahr—heute," *Wort in der Zeit* 4 (1958). Daviau, Donald G., "The Misconception of Hermann Bahr as a 'Verwandlungskünstler,'" *German Life and Letters* 11 (1958); "Dialog vom Marsyas: Hermann Bahr's Affirmation of Life over Art," *Modern Language Quarterly* 20 (1959); "Hermann

Bahr's Nachlaß," *Journal of the International Arthur Schnitzler Research Association* 2 (1963); and "Hermann Bahr's Cultural Relations with America," in *"Österreich und die Angelsächsische Welt*, ed. O. Hietsch, vol. 2, 1968. Kindermann, Heinz, *Hermann Bahr*, 1954. Lehner, Friedrich, "Hermann Bahr," *Monatshefte* 39 (1947). Macken, Mary M., "Hermann Bahr: His Personality and His Works," *Irish Quarterly Review* 15 (1926). Meridies, Wilhelm, *Hermann Bahr als epischer Gestalter und Kritiker der Gegenwart*, 1927.

Donald G. Daviau▲

Richard Beer-Hofmann

Richard Beer-Hofmann was born on 11 July 1886 in Vienna, the son of a lawyer; he died on 26 September 1945 in New York. He was adopted by his uncle Alois Hofmann. Received a degree in law in Vienna. Amateur producer in Berlin and Vienna. In 1938 he fled from Vienna to the United States via Switzerland. He was an active supporter of the Zionist movement. Since 1946 there has been a Beer-Hofmann Society in New York.

In the 1900 Vienna literary circle, which also included Hugo von Hofmannsthal, Leopold Andrian, Arthur Schnitzler, Felix Salten, and Hermann Bahr, Beer-Hofmann was a stimulating influence, thanks to his suggestions, criticism, and his own writings. The young Hofmannsthal admitted to being most deeply indebted to him. After some early conventional endeavors, Beer-Hofmann produced a pioneer work with his novel *Der Tod Georgs* (1900). It is an imaginative permutation of the baroque theme "life is a dream," which Franz Grillparzer had so effectively developed in *Der Traum, ein Leben*.

In his elaborate *Das goldene Pferd* (1955), Beer-Hofmann once more took up the same theme with its characteristic retroflexion. The narrative, full of future implications, makes exemplary use of the achievements of interior monologue; it deploys to the full all the differentiated states of consciousness and emotional levels. By this means, Beer-Hofmann succeeded in condensing the successive into the simultaneous, the temporal into the timeless, and the dream into the waking state.

In *Der Tod Georgs* the death of Georg, the "darling of the Gods," generates concentric circles of reflexes: visions and states of ecstasy, counterpointed by the most detailed objective descriptions, recur and reflect each other, and intertwine in an exquisite and compelling web of associations, which keeps the dream state intact, gives stability to the fleeting moment, and causes instability in the unchangeable. Man makes another's life his own. The present is multiplied by being seen universally with all its reflections, and at the same time the past is ceaselessly evoked. An irresistibly suggestive effect emanates from the expressive power of the language, its fairy-tale splendor and expanding metaphors, its symbolic leitmotifs and severe sobriety, which mercilessly penetrates all the semiconscious and unconscious strata. Beer-Hofmann's contemporaries in Vienna, including Rainer Maria Rilke, have also used language to this effect, but it was left to later narrative writing to make creative use of the multilevel technique.

In *Der Graf von Charolais* (1905), a somewhat capricious adaptation of Philip Massinger's *The Fatal Dowry*, Beer-Hofmann tried out a special structural principle in the drama. Following the Spanish dramatists—who strongly influenced Grillparzer, too—he presented a sequence of autonomous dramatic situations that are not linked by strict functional or causal relationships. Instead, the situations leave room for incidental and episodic interference, indeed, charge it with dramatic tension. Admittedly, the self-sufficient moments' gain of expressive power shows up as a loss of consistency in the whole. The compelling moment on the stage is rarely combined with a consistent plot, and there is always something unsatisfying about chance elevated into law.

In the important draft prologue to his *Ariadne auf Kreta*, Beer-Hofmann proclaimed the principle underlying his dramatic approach. One of the works in which form and idea combine in the purest union is *Jaákobs Traum* (1918), in which he sublimated the sacrifice endured by the chosen, God's "elected whipping boy" whose suffering body God uses forever to convince all nations of His divinity. Here and in the *David* cycle (which remained incomplete) Beer-Hofmann gave compelling expression to the sternness of the Judaic faith, as Rilke was one of the first to note: "while so many Jewish people . . . seem to represent this hard fate only in its catastrophes," Beer-Hofmann gave us an example of its greatness and dignity, "unimpaired in its essentials even in the long and troubled exile."

Beer-Hofmann's few poems are messages of the mind, not atmospheric media of a magic language vibrating to its own sounds. A fine record is the late book of reminiscences, *Paula: Ein Fragment* (1949), in which the personal and the impersonal interpenetrate. Stirring events are brought to life with the detachment of what has irrevocably become a thing of the past, yet with all the bloom of immediacy.

Works: *Novellen* (1893; Novellas); *Der Tod Georgs* (1900; George's Death); *Der Graf von Charolais* (1904; The Count of Charolais); *Gedenkrede auf W. A. Mozart* (1906; Memorial Speech on W. A. Mozart); *Jaákobs Traum* (1918; Eng. tr., Jacob's Dream, 1947); *Schlaflied für Mirjam* (1919; Lullaby for Mirjam); *Der junge David* (1933; Young David); *Das Vorspiel auf dem Theater zu König David* (1936; Prologue on the Stage for King David); *Verse* (1941); *Paula: Ein Fragment* (1949;

Paula: A Fragment); *Das goldene Pferd* (1955; The Golden Horse); *Gesammelte Werke* (Introduction by M. Buber, 1963; Collected Works).

Bibliography: Bithell, Jethro, *Modern German Literature 1880–1950*, pp. 228–29, 1959. Kahler, Erich, in *Neue Rundschau*, 1946, pp. 236–37. Liptzin, Sol, *Richard Beer-Hofmann*, 1936. Schnitzler, O., *Beer-Hofmann*, 1961. Vordtriede, Werner, *Gespräche mit Beer-Hofmann*, 1952.

Gerhart Baumann

Thomas Bernhard

Born 10 February 1931 in Heerlen near Maastricht into a family of Salzburg and Upper Austrian origins. Commercial apprenticeship, four years as courtroom reporter, then librarian at a cultural institute in London. Early travels to nearly all European countries, especially to Yugoslavia. Dramaturgic and stage-direction studies at the Salzburg Mozarteum, concluded in 1957 with a comparative thesis on Bertolt Brecht and Antonin Artaud. Now lives as a writer in Austria. In 1967 received the Great Austrian State Prize for the novel.

Bernhard's first published works are collections of poems, which, like his prose, are imbued with melancholia, dull despair, and existential suffering. The language of these poems often dissolves into surrealist images. His first prose work of any length, the novel *Frost* (1963), depicts a human destiny foundering on the menace of the absolute and on the petty intrigues of other people. This novel already displays Bernhard's unmistakably individual language and choice of themes, which show themselves again in the fragmentary story *Amras* (1964) and in the novel *Verstörung* (1967); they are, like *Frost*, variations on one basic concern.

Bernhard writes with almost fanatical literary obsession, case histories of psychopaths, criminals, suicides, and dying individuals because he wants to show that human existence is in bondage to suffering, that suffering is, indeed, the only reality. Each of his characters lives out his life either in dumb purposelessness, or he gains from his mental disturbance clearsightedness and with it, certainty about the "primordial human tragedy." Bernhard's prose bears the mark of a profoundly serious compassion, not of an annihilating pessimism.

Works: *Die heiligen drei Könige von St. Vitus* (1955; The Three Wise Men of St. Vitus); *Der Schweinehüter* (1956; The Swineherd); *Auf der Erde und in der Hölle* (1957; On Earth and in Hell); *In hora mortis* (1958); *Unter dem Eisen des Mondes* (1958; Under the Iron of the Moon); *Die Rosen der Einöde* (1959; Roses of the Desert); *Psalm* (1960); *Frost* (1963); *Amras* (1964); *Die Jause* (1965; The Afternoon Snack); *Verstörung* (1967; Perturbation); *Prosa* (1967); *Ungemach* (1968; Trouble); *An der Baumgrenze* (1969; At the Timber Line); *Watten* (1969; the Mud Flats);

Thomas Bernhard

Das Kalkwerk (1970; The Lime Works); *Ein Fest für Böris* (1970; Celebration for Boris); *Midland in Stilfs* (1971); *Die Italiener* (1971; The Italians); *Gehen* (1971; To Go); *Der Ignorant und der Wahnsinnige* (1972; The Ignoramus and the Lunatic).

Bibliography: Botond, A., ed., *Über Thomas Bernhard*, 1970. Haberl, Franz P., in *Books Abroad*, 1970, p. 656. Reich-Ranicki, Marcel, *Literatur der kleinen Schritte*, 1967. Stern, Guy, in *Books Abroad*, 1969, p. 341. Zelinsky, Hartmut, "Thomas Bernhards *Amras* und Novalis, mit besonderer Berücksichtigung von dessen Krankheitsphilosophie," *Literatur und Kritik* 1, no. 6 (1966):38–42.

Wilfried Schwedler

Richard Billinger

Born 20 July 1893 in St. Marienkirchen near Schärding, by the Bavarian border. In his autobiographical work *Die Asche des Fegefeuers* (1931), Richard Billinger tells how he was meant to become a priest (his father owned the village general store) but found the education of a "holy boy" not to his liking. He broke off his studies in Innsbruck and tried his luck as a sailor in Kiel. When this did not work out either, he attended classes in philosophy and literature, first in Kiel and soon afterward in Vienna. There, the dancer Grete Wiesenthal discovered Billinger's poetic talents and introduced him to Hugo von Hofmannsthal, who, together with Max Mell, became his patron. Billinger lived for a time in Berlin, Munich, and at Niederpöcking on Lake Starnberg. He died on 7 June 1965 at Linz on the Danube.

The poetic strength of Billinger's dramatic works, a quality that is present to a lesser extent in his lyric poetry, also permeates his novels. In 1934 he published the novel *Das Schutzengelhaus*, which is a loving description of a vacation idyll in his native Inn valley. His novel *Lehen aus Gottes Hand* (1935), set in the milieu of the peasantry, is a naturalistic tale of a fatefully tragic love story. A gloomy and macabre mood permeates the great novel *Das verschenkte Leben* (1937), in which a circus artiste makes a pact with the devil in order to save the life of his seriously ill mother.

In 1924 Billinger's play *Spiel vom Knecht* was produced by an experimental theater in Vienna. It expresses the outlook to be found in all his dramatic works. Rooted in the popular heritage and customs of his native land, it displays a primitive strength that stems from the deep pagan forces that reign beneath the thin crust of Christian civilization. But Billinger's very first volumes of poetry—*Über die Äcker* (1923), *Lob Gottes* (1923), and *Gedichte* (1929), brought together under the title *Sichel am Himmel* (1931)—reveal his weaknesses. Notwithstanding his fervent love of God reposing in the Catholic faith, the elementary power of his emotions, and the originality of his language, which owes much to his native dialect, Billinger came dangerously close to the sort of literature that is addicted to the forces of family origin and ties with the soil.

These same influences inspired the drama *Rauhnacht*, which

was produced by Jürgen Fehling at the Berliner Staatstheater in 1931 and won the Kleist Prize in 1932. On this occasion Werner Kraus played the principal role, an uprooted peasant from the Inn valley who goes to Africa as a missionary and, after his return, is driven by pagan masked rituals to murder. The play was a sensational hit, but a few isolated voices warned of the dangers implicit in Billinger's vital representation of pagan "Germanic" forces.

Billinger's drama *Rosse* (1931; opera by Winfried Zillig) was chosen by Leopold Jessner for his last production before he left the Berliner Staatstheater. This is a play about a farm hand so atavistically attached to his horses that he fights—and loses the battle—against the intrusion of the modern world in the shape of tractors. In Billinger's Sudeten-German play *Der Gigant* (1937; film under the title *Die goldene Stadt*), Prague, the "golden city," causes the ruin of a young peasant woman, "because she did not keep faith with the countryside and the soil on which she was born."

Billinger's plays *Lob des Landes* (1933), *Melusine* (1942), and *Die Fuchsfalle* (1942) degenerate into shallow mannerism. In *Die Hexe von Passau* (1935; opera by Ottmar Gerster) a bishop oppresses the peasants and fights the theater. But the theater wins when a rebel blacksmith's daughter, who travels with an acting company, touches the bishop's heart with her interpretation of the Magdalene role in a passion play. This "victory of the theater"—the theater as mimetic—is symptomatic of Billinger's dramatic writing. It bears the mark of the pantomime, which originated in the stirrings of primitive man and thus became the ancestor both of the realistic and the burlesque play in world literature. When Billinger began to write again after the war, he returned to his old themes, as in *Der Zentaur* (1948), and tried to replace the not always convincing psychological motivations with compellingly dramatized myth.

Works: *Über die Äcker* (1923; Across the Fields); *Lob Gottes* (1923; Praise of the Lord); *Spiel vom Knecht* (1924; The Farmhand); *Das Perchtenspiel* (1928; The Demons' Play); *Gedichte* (1929; Poems); *Die Asche des Fegefeuers* (1931; Ashes of Purgatory); Rosse (1931; Horses); *Rauhnacht* (1931; Evil Ghosts of the Twelve Nights); *Sichel am Himmel* (1931; Sickle in the Sky); *Zwei Spiele* (1932; includes Spiel vom Knecht, and *Reise nach Ursprung* [originally *Das Perchtenspiel*]; Two plays: The Farmhand, and Trip to Ursprung); *Lied vom Glück* (1933; Song of Happiness); *Lob des Landes* (1933; Praise of the Country); *Der Pfeil im Wappen* (1933; The Arrow in the Coat of Arms); *Das Verlöbnis* (1933; The Engagement); *Stille Gäste* (1934; Quiet Guests); *Das Schutzengelhaus* (1934; The House of the Guardian Angel); *Die*

Hexe von Passau (1935; The Witch from Passau); *Lehen aus Gottes Hand* (1935; Fief from God); *Nachtwache* (1935; Night Watch); *Der Gigant* (1937; The Giant); *Das verschenkte Leben* (1937; A Life Given Away); *Triumph des Gottes* (1940; God's Triumph); *Die Windsbraut* (1941; The Whirlwind); *Drei Dramen: Gabriele Dambrone, Melusine, Die Fuchsfalle* (1942; Three Dramas: Gabriele Dambrone, Melusine, The Fox Trap); *Holder Morgen* (1942; Sweet Morning); *Paracelsus* (1943; Paracelsus); *Das Spiel vom Erasmus Grasser* (1943; The Play about Erasmus Grasser); *Zentaur* (1948; Centaur); *Galgenvogel* (1948; Gallows Bird); *Das Haus* (1948; The House); *Palast der Jugend* (1949; Palace of Youth); *Traube in der Kelter* (1951; Grapes in the Wine-Press); *Ein Tag wie alle* (1952; A Day Like All the Others); *Das nackte Leben* (1953; The Bare Life); *Lobgesang* (1953; Song of Praise); *Plumpsack* (1954; Don't Turn About, the Knot's Going Ronud!); *Ein Strauß Rosen* (1954; A Bunch of Roses); *Das Augsburger Jahrtausendspiel* (1955; Augsburg's Millenial Play); *Viktoria* (1955; Victoria; dramatization of K. Hamsun's novel); *Donauballade* (1959; Danube Ballad); *Würfelspiel* (1960; Game of Dice); *Bauernpassion* (1960; Peasants' Passion); *Gesammelte Werke* (12 vols., 1955–60; Collected Works); *Menschen nennen es Schicksal (4 Einakter): Am Nachmittag, Entwurzelte Jugend, Regenszene, Die Schafschur* (1962; People Call it Fate, 4 One-Act Plays: In the Afternoon, Uprooted Youth, Scene in the Rain, Sheep-Shearing).

Bibliography: Gerstinger, H., *Richard Billinger als Dramatiker*, 1947. Grimme, K., "Der Fall Billinger," *Wort in der Zeit* 5 (1959):20–22. Henz, R., Über Richard Billinger," in *Orplid*, vol. 5, 1928. Hering, G., *Der Ruf zur Leidenschaft*, 1959. Lissauer, E., "Richard Billingers Gedichte," *Die Literatur*, 1929.

Lutz Weltmann

Franz Blei

Born 18 January 1871 in Vienna, the son of an immigrant Silesian cobbler who worked his way up to become a building contractor, and a tailor's daughter from Prussian Silesia. Secondary schooling at the Benedictine monastery at Melk, later in Vienna, where he, as early as that, established contact with the socialist labor leaders August Bebel and Viktor Adler. Left the Catholic church in 1887. Studied in Vienna, Paris, Berne, and Zurich, earning a Ph.D. In 1893 married a medical student, Maria Lehmann. Study trips to North America. Returned to Europe in 1900, met Oscar Wilde in Paris. Lived in Munich and Berlin from 1903 to 1914. Served in World War I as a private in the Austrian army and, after a heart attack, was transferred to the army press headquarters (where Hugo von Hofmannsthal and Robert Musil were also assigned).

Between the years 1906 and 1919 Blei edited several literary and bibliophile periodicals. Among other activities he collaborated with Carl Sternheim, Max Scheler, and Albert Paris Gütersloh. Rejoined the Catholic church in 1919, at the same time professing communist ideals. His house at Schwabing became a meeting place of the artistic elite. In 1923 moved to Berlin once more, but, as a passionate opponent of national socialism, retired to Majorca in 1933. Fled to Vienna in 1936, later joined Rudolf Borchardt at Lucca, and subsequently went to southern France, where André Gide supported him. Finally emigrated to North America. Died 10 July 1942 in Westbury, New York.

Blei's writings comprise creative prose and dramatic works, literary criticism and satire, religious and philosophical reform proposals, editorial adaptations and interpretations of past and present cultural currents. But the boundaries between these fields are blurred. The volumes of stories *Die Frivolitäten des Herrn von Disenberg* (1925) and *Erdachte Geschichten* (1911), the novel fragment *Lyswina*, and the comedy *Logik des Herzens* (1961) are among his comparatively few imaginative writings.

Blei was always sparked by the subject, be it the past seen graphically or the present vividly experienced. His characters are timeless, creative portraits—e.g., in *Männer und Masken* (1930), *Glanz und Elend berühmter Frauen* (1927), and *Historische Bildnisse*,

Zeitgenössische Bildnisse (1940), among others. He himself described his series of critical "digressions" as the "mechanics of truths." His style is modeled on the clarity of the French encyclopedists; he approached literary, cultural, political, and economic facts alike with scientific precision.

A somewhat wider group of readers found much to entertain themselves in Blei's *Das große Bestiarium der Literatur* (1920; enlarged edition, 1924), a satire on contemporary writers in zoological terms. There is often a marked erotic touch in his narratives and commentaries, but it never oversteps aesthetic limits. The almost excessive variety of his work is most strikingly reconciled in *Erzählung eines Lebens* (1930), in which poetic invention, description, and meditation are combined.

Works: *Die rechtschaffene Frau* (1893; The Righteous Woman); *Thea* (1895); *Die Sehnsucht* (1900; Longing); *Das Kußmal* (1900; The Kissing Mark); *Prinz Hippolyt* (1903); *Die galante Zeit und ihr Ende* (1904; The Time of Chivalry and Its End); *Von amoureusen Frauen* (1906; On Amorous Women); *Der dunkle Weg* (1906; The Dark Path); *Die Puderquaste* (1908; The Powder Puff); *Scaramuccio auf Naxos* (1909; Scaramouche in Naxos); *Gesammelte Schriften* (5 vols., 1910–13; Collected Works); *Vermischte Schriften* (6 vols., 1911–13; Miscellaneous Writings; I., *Erdachte Geschichten* [Invented Stories]; II., *Gott der Frauen* [The God of Women]; III., *Das Rokoko* [Rococo]; IV., *Das schwere Herz* [The Heavy Heart]; V., *Das dienende Werk* [The Serving Work]; VI., *Der Dichter und das Leben* [The Poet and Life]); *Landfahrer und Abenteurer* (1913; Vagabonds and Adventurers); *Über Wedekind, Sternheim und das Theater* (1914; On Wedekind, Sternheim, and the Theater); *Das Zaubertheater* (1915; The Magic Theater); *Menschliche Betrachtungen zur Politik* (1916; Human Reflections on Politics); *Logik des Herzens* (1916; The Heart's Logic); *Das Lesebuch der Marquise* (1917; The Reading Book of the Marchioness); *Das Evangelium des Apollonius: Phantasien zum Neuen Testament* (1919; The Gospel of Apollonius: Fantasies on the New Testament); *Die Abenteurer* (1920; The Adventurers); *Das große Bestiarium der modernen Literatur* (1920; The Great Bestiary of Modern Literature); *Die verliebte Weisheit der Ninon* (1920; Ninon's Enamoured Wisdom); *Felicien Rops* (1921); *Leben und Traum der Frauen* (1921; Women's Lives and Dreams); *Versprengte Worte Jesu* (1922; Scattered Words of Jesus); *Der Knabe Ganymed* (1923; The Boy Ganymede); *Der Geist des Rokoko* (1923; Rococo Spirit); *Das Kuriositätenkabinett der Literatur* (1924; Curiosity Cabinet of Literature); *Die Frivolitäten des Herrn von Disenberg* (1924; Herr von Disenberg's Frivolities); *Frauen und Männer der Renaissance* (1927; Women and Men of the Renaissance); *Das Erotische* (1927; Erotics); *Frauen und Abenteurer*

(1927; Women and Adventurers); *Glanz und Elend berühmter Frauen* (1927; Splendor and Misery of Famous Women); *Lehrbuch der Liebe* (1928; Manual of Love); *Himmlische und irdische Liebe in Frauenschicksalen* (1928; Heavenly and Earthly Love in Women's Fates); *Formen der Liebe* (1930; Forms of Love); *Männer und Masken* (1930; Men and Masks); *Die Göttliche Garbo* (1930; Divine Garbo); *Erzählung eines Lebens* (1930; Tale of a Life); *Gefährtinnen* (1931; Companions); *Lust der Kreatur* (1931; Creature's Zest); *Talleyrand* (1932); *Zeitgenössische Bildnisse* (1940; Contemporary Portraits); *Schriften in Auswahl* (ed. A. P. Gütersloh, 1960; Selected Writings).

Bibliography: Funk, Phillip, in *Hochland*, 1919, pp. 540–41. Hardekopf, Ferdinand, on *Logik des Herzens*, in *Die Aktion*, nos. 3–4 (22 January 1916). Raabe, Paul, *Kafka-Symposium*, p. 7, 1965. Schönwiese, Ernst, *Franz Blei: Zwischen Orpheus und Don Juan*, 1965. Soergel, Albert, in *Dichtung und Dichter der Zeit*, edited by Curt Hohoff, vol. 2, 1963.

Karl Strobl

Imma von Bodmershof

Born 10 August 1895 in Graz, the daughter of the Prague philosopher Christian Freiherr von Ehrenfels, the founder of the Gestalt theory. At Munich, in the circle of writers, artists, and philosophers then forming around the Bruckmann publishing house, she met and became engaged to the Hölderlin scholar Norbert von Hellingrath, who was killed in the battle of Verdun in 1916. Since 1925 she has been married to Dr. Wilhelm von Bodmershof, and together they manage the farm Rastbach near Gföhl in Lower Austria.

In 1937 Imma von Bodmershof published her first novel, *Der zweite Sommer*, the story of a woman who has inherited a farm but gets into difficulties with its management because, unable to shake off the burden of tradition, she fails to meet the challenge of a different world and time. In this novel, as in her second, *Die Stadt in Flandern* (1939), the intense relatedness of actual processes to deep layers of soul and mind are shown to have a profound emotional and intellectual relevance. Images become symbols.

Imma von Bodmershof's novel *Die Rosse des Urban Roithner* (1950) presents a limited world as a mirror of the world per se. In *Sieben Handvoll Salz* (1958), the rich past of an island swept by the storms of history in the course of millennia is linked with the present to make a novel of rich substance and poetic density.

Imma von Bodmershof's strict linguistic discipline also proved its worth in a volume of stories published in 1953 under the title *Solang es Tag ist*. In 1962 appeared *Haiku*, a voluminous collection in which the verse technique of the Far East is handled with astonishing mastery.

Works: *Der zweite Sommer* (1937; The Second Summer); *Die Stadt in Flandern* (1939; The City in Flanders; new version, *Das verlorene Meer* [1952: The Lost Sea]); *Theres Pirnagl* (1941); *Begegnung im Frühling* (1942; Meeting in Spring); *Die Rosse des Urban Roithner* (1950; Urban Roithner's Horses); *Solang es Tag ist* (1953; As Long as the Day Lasts); *Sieben Handvoll Salz* (1958; Seven Handfuls of Salt); *Haiku* (1962); *Unter acht Winden* (1962; Under Eight Currents of Wind).

Bibliography: Aichinger, Ingrid, "Beides zusammen nur ist das Ganze: Das Werk der österreichischen Dichterin Imma Bodmershof," *Österreich in Geschichte und Literatur* 10 (1966):358–79. Bithell, Jethro, *Modern German Literature 1880–1950*, pp. 515–18, 1959. Fiechtner, Helmut, "Imma Bodmershof," *Wort in der Zeit* 3, no. 6 (1957):1–5.

Otto Heuschele

Hermann Broch

Born 1 November 1886 in Vienna, the son of textile manufacturer. After studying at the Technical Institute in Vienna and the Textile School in Mülhausen (Alsace-Lorraine), Hermann Broch entered his father's firm in 1908. He later managed the business until 1927. As a leading member of the Association of Manufacturers he concerned himself with labor problems. In 1928 he decided to devote himself entirely to intellectual pursuits, and for the next three years he studied mathematics, philosophy, and psychology. During this period he produced his first great novel, *Die Schlafwandler*.

In 1935 Broch made his home in the mountains, first in Mösern near Seefeld in the Tyrol, then in Alt-Aussee (Styrian Alps), where he worked on his *Der Versucher* and wrote essays. Following the Anschluß in 1938, he was arrested and imprisoned in Alt-Aussee to await deportation to a German concentration camp. Under these circumstances he conceived the plan of rewriting his earlier radio play *Die Heimkehr des Vergil* (1936) as a novel, *Der Tod des Vergil*, the work that in 1945 established his world reputation.

Friends abroad secured Broch's release, and he emigrated to the United States, where he lived successively in New York, Princeton, and New Haven. The American Academy of Arts and Letters, the Rockefeller Foundation, and other foundations supported him. During this period, especially after the completion of *Der Tod des Vergil*, Broch shifted his attention more strongly toward scientific scholarship than toward literature. He pursued studies at the Institute for Public Opinion Research in Princeton and worked on his "Massenpsychologie," which he based on a theory of politics and democracy and on his own theory of cognition. He submitted a "Declaration for the Preservation of Human Dignity" to the United Nations, hoping to make his theories immediately politically effective. He became a professor at Yale University in 1950, the same year in which he was nominated for the Nobel Prize. But on 30 May 1951, after years of overburdening himself, he succumbed to a heart attack in New Haven. He was buried in Killingworth, Connecticut. Numerous unfinished manuscripts have been preserved in the Broch Archive in the Goethe Room of the Yale University Library.

Broch did not go successively from manufacturing to writing to scholarship to political thinking. It was precisely in the autonomization of individual compartments of life and their special logic that Broch saw the chief symptom of the disintegration of values that characterizes our age. Broch observed this disturbing process with fascination. He portrayed it, analyzed it, and he also attempted to counter it by what he termed a "unifying platonic attitude." The shift in emphasis in his work resulted from this.

Broch's first published writings, the poem *Mathematisches Mysterium* and two essays, appeared in 1913 in *Der Brenner*, an important journal in the history of ideas. In his novels he was aware, with some reservations, of his indebtedness to James Joyce: *James Joyce und die Gegenwart* (1936). The death problem, omnipresent in his work, binds him to the Austrian writers of the turn of the century (Rainer Maria Rilke, Hugo von Hofmannsthal, Richard Beer-Hofmann, and Georg Trakl). Beginning in the 1930s he sought a way toward the mythic. In his critical essay *The Style of the Mythical Age* (1947; written in English), Broch repeatedly names Joyce (*Ulysses*), Thomas Mann (*Joseph*), and Franz Kafka as models.

Broch's five narrative works are: *Die Schlafwandler* (1931–32); *Die unbekannte Größe* (1933); *Der Versucher* (written, 1936–51; published, 1953), which is a conflation of three versions of the same novel (the unfinished third version was published separately in 1967 under its original title, *Demeter*, and each of the three versions was published in 1969 under the collective title *Bergroman*); *Der Tod des Vergil* (1945); and *Die Schuldlosen: Roman in 11 Erzählungen* (1950). These works revolve around the disintegration of world and values and its consequences. In the trilogy *Die Schlafwandler*, Broch undertakes the paradoxical attempt of giving a total picture of the disintegrating process in three phases (1888, 1903, 1918) and with three characters (von Pasenow, Esch, Huguenau). The conflict between rationality-made-autonomous and irrationality-made-equally-autonomous stands at the center of *Die unbekannte Größe*. In *Der Versucher* Broch portrays in a way that could serve as a laboratory model the outbreak of mass hysteria in an isolated village community somewhere in the Austrian Alps. The existing orders offer no adequate protection.

Der Tod des Vergil originated in a poetic investigation of the theme "literature at the end of a culture," which Broch wrote in 1936 for Radio Vienna. The death agony of a dissolving world, of a world altogether doomed, are mirrored in the interior monologue of the dying poet. The relevance to our own age is obvious.

In *Die Schuldlosen*, especially in its climactic story *Steinerner Gast*, Broch exposes a somnabulistic, irresponsible indifference as the actual guilt of the generation between the wars. The collection's title, like *Die Schlafwandler* and *Die unbekannte Größe*, indicates a relapse into uncontrolled irrationality, which is dialectically tied to the rationality of our age pushed to extremes. The theme of the novels also governs Broch's lectures, essays, and research, as, for example, in *Logik einer zerfallenden Welt* (1930), *Das Böse im Wertsystem der Kunst* (1933), *Geist und Zeitgeist* (1934), *Hofmannsthal und seine Zeit* (1951, 1955), and his "Massenpsychologie."

Against disintegration Broch places the search for the absolute, the ethical-religious postulation. Here, as he saw it, the mystical pathway through the inner depth of the human soul and the rational pathway of deduction of mathematics and epistemology do not preclude one another. In *Der Versucher*, Mother Gisson (anagram for gnosis) is the unflinching opposite of the mass hysteria of the villagers, caused by the tempter Marius Ratti. She lives death and life as one. She does not look toward the end but toward the middle, where the heart is, and the middle beams its light beyond the dark edges of the beginning and the end. Much like the mythical mother is the mythical old man, who is an adaptation of the Stone Guest in the Don Juan myth, in *Steinerner Gast*. With these figures Broch's yearning for a mythic style, which in its archaic simplicity and abstractness could grapple with the chaos of the age, found partial fulfillment.

But literary expression lost its preeminence for Broch in his last years because science (knowledge) as metapolitics and as a herald of the "earthy absolute" seemed to him to be capable of helping man better and more directly. For Broch *l'art pour l'art*, which strives for an end in itself and for autonomous value, is not true art (*Das Weltbild des Romans*, 1933, and *Einige Bemerkungen zum Problem des Kitsches*, 1950–51). The merely beautiful word is evil, doomed to die, and deserving of annihilation. Thus Virgil wants to destroy his *Æneid*, not because it is deficient in art but because it is wanting in human terms. When he later does relinquish it to Augustus, this is not an act of weak submission but the very ethical deed lacking in the work itself. Virgil renounces his urgent wish for the sake of his friend.

The ancillary role that Broch gives to literature does not preclude a strong formal effort. He accomplishes this goal best in the novel and essay. His only drama, *Die Entsühnung* (1933; premiered in 1934 under the title . . . *Denn sie wissen nicht, was sie tun*), and the poems are inferior by comparison. The novels in the trilogy *Die*

Schlafwandler differ stylistically. At the beginning is a social novel of almost Fontane-like mold. Corresponding to the ever more openly emerging anarchy of values, the form progressively disintegrates. In the third novel, portrayal and reflection are directly juxtaposed. In *Der Versucher*, portrayal and contemplation melt together, especially in the splendid nature images. That is made possible through the interpolated narrator, whose memories form a lyrical, unifying filter for the narration.

Paradoxically, in *Der Tod des Vergil*, that great renunciation of literature, Broch came closest to his ideal of a style that would perform both an aesthetic and an ethical function. This style converts the *Nacheinander* (succession) of sequentially arranged, linguistic sentence units into *Miteinander* (simultaneity) and thereby dissolves the very form (in sentence, paragraph, and entire work) of fleeting time striving toward death. The novel achieves ultimately a lyric-platonic unity; it is a single interior monologue by the dying Virgil. In his feverish tremors intensified physical sensations, remembered images, and despairing reflections all fuse at the edge of the inexpressible. The rhythm of Charon's rocking, gliding boat permeates the work from beginning to end and determines sentence structure and word choice. That rhythm is present even in the 1936 radio version, *Die Heimkehr des Vergil*.

Broch's attempt to go beyond language by using the resources of language itself is nevertheless not totally satisfying. The tortuousness of many passages is brought about not by *Die Heimkehr des Vergil*, for it is found in Broch's entire work, sometimes more, sometimes less. Symbolic in this connection is the frantic haste of his last years and the lament shortly before his death about his "cancerously swollen work load." The unresolved tension between a burningly felt, superhuman task and its fulfillment permeates his writing and thinking.

Works: *Die Schlafwandler* (trilogy, 1931–32; Eng. tr., The Sleepwalkers, 1932); *Das Weltbild des Romans* (1933; The Conception of the World as Expressed in Novels); *Die unbekannte Größe* (1933; Eng. tr., The Unknown Quantity, 1935); *Das Böse im Wertsystem der Kunst* (1933; The Evil in the Value System of Art); *Die Entsühnung* (1933; The Atonement; first performance under the title . . . *Denn sie wissen nicht, was sie tun* [1934; For They Know Not What They Do]); *Geist und Zeitgeist* (1934; Mind and Spirit of the Times); *Die Heimkehr des Vergil* (1936; Virgil's Homecoming); *James Joyce und die Gegenwart* (1936; Eng. tr., James Joyce and the Present Age, 1949); *Der Tod des Vergil* (1945; Eng. tr., The Death of Virgil, 1945); *The Style of the Mythical Age* (1947);

Die Schuldlosen (1950; The Guilt-Free); *Hofmannsthal und seine Zeit* (1951; Hofmannsthal and His Time); *Gesammelte Werke* (10 vols., 1952–61; Collected Works); *Der Versucher* (1953; The Tempter; conflation of three version of *Bergroman*); *Hermann Broch der Dichter* (ed. H. Binde, 1964; Hermann Broch the Writer); *Hermann Broch der Denker* (ed. H. Binde, 1966; Hermann Broch the Philosopher); *Demeter* (1967, unfinished third version of *Bergroman*); *Bergroman* (eds. F. Kress and H. A. Maier, 1969; Mountain Novel; three versions); *Zur Universitätsreform* (ed. G. Wienold, 1969; Toward the Reform of the Universities); *Gedanken zur Politik* (ed. D. Hildebrandt, 1970; Thoughts on Politics); *Huguenau, oder Die Sachlichkeit* (1970; Huguenau, or Factuality).

Bibliography: Arendt, Hannah, "The Achievement of Hermann Broch," *Kenyon Review*, no. 11 (1949). Baumann, Walter, in *Modern Language Quarterly*, 1968. Blanchot, M., "Broch," *Nouvelle Revue Française*, no. 3 (1955). Cohn, Dorrit Claire, *"The Sleepwalkers": Elucidations of Hermann Broch's Trilogy*, 1966. Csokor, Franz Theodor, in *German Life and Letters*, 1954–55. Fleischmann, Wolfgang Bernard, in *Wisconsin Studies in Contemporary Literature*, 1967. Kahler, E., *Die Philosophie von Hermann Broch*, 1962. Waldinger, Ernst, in *Books Abroad*, 1961. Weigand, Hermann J., "Broch's *Death of Virgil*: Program Notes," *Publications of the Modern Language Association of America*, no. 62 (1947); and "Hermann Broch's *Die Schuldlosen*: An Approach," *Publications of the Modern Language Association of America*, no. 68 (1953). Ziolkowski, Theodore, *Hermann Broch*, 1964

Walter Weiss

Max Brod

Max Brod, born 27 May 1884, was, like Rainer Maria Rilke, Franz Kafka, and Franz Werfel, a child of Prague. His efforts in bringing the work of his friend Kafka, a year his senior, to the attention of the public are well known. But he also discovered Werfel, who was six years younger than he, and, as long ago as 1910, introduced Werfel to the public by a reading of his poems in Berlin. In Prague Brod studied law, earned a law degree, and became successively an official of the finance ministry, of the post office, and of the courts. Was a member of the Czechoslovak Council of Ministers in Prague, and later was theater and music critic of the *Prager Tagblatt*. In 1939 Brod, a confirmed Zionist who cherished an "affection" for Germany, preferably from a distance, went to Israel, where he became consultant to the Habimah Theater at Tel Aviv. He died 20 December 1968 in Tel Aviv.

Disinclined to any nationalist fanaticism, Brod believed that the reverse of Franz Grillparzer's phrase "From humanity through nationality to bestiality" had to be taught and lived. There is no break between what he published before and after his emigration. He completed a trilogy of novels about the Renaissance entitled *Ein Kampf um Wahrheit*, the first of which, *Tycho Brahes Weg zu Gott* (1916), made him famous. The second part, *Rëubeni, Fürst der Juden* (1925), earned him the Czechoslovak State Prize in 1925. In spite of the fact that he did not use Hebrew, the language of his adopted country, for even the concluding volume, *Galilei in Gefangenschaft* (1948), he was awarded Israel's Bialik Prize in 1948.

In the best novels, Brod combines philosophy and narrative skill. *Der Meister* (1952), an antinihilist novel, attempts to reconcile the Christian and the Jewish concepts of Jesus. It is characteristic of Brod's religious convictions that he believed God needs the active help of man in order to be an effectual force on earth. Similarly, Brod's *Armer Cicero* (1955), despite his philosopher's vanity, rises above the confusion of pagan Rome. In *Mira* (1958), "a novel about Hofmannsthal," as in his novel on Kafka, *Das Zauberreich der Liebe* (1928), he manages to evoke the nature of a writer while avoiding anything in the form of a *roman à clef*.

To Brod we owe the preservation and publication of Kafka's posthumous novels *Der Prozeß*, *Das Schloß*, and *Amerika* (1925–27), and the later collected editions (1935 to 1937 and others). Brod's three studies *Franz Kafkas Glauben und Lehre—Kafka und Tolstoi* (1948), *Franz Kafka als wegweisende Gestalt* (1951), and *Verzweiflung und Erlösung im Werk Franz Kafkas* (1959) are devoted to introducing Kafka and to an interpretation of his works that has not remained undisputed. Part of Brod's writing about Kafka appeared again in 1966 in the omnibus book *Über Franz Kafka*.

In addition, Brod also wrote polished, entertaining novels such as *Die Frau, nach der man sich sehnt* (1927), which was made into a film starring Marlene Dietrich. Its sequel, *Die Frau, die nicht enttäuscht* (1934), is more important as a document of the crisis into which Brod was plunged in 1933 as a result of his expulsion from the world of German language and culture.

In his later life in Israel, Brod recalled his formative years in Prague: *Beinahe ein Vorzugsschüler, oder Pièce touchée* (1952), *Der Sommer, den man zurückwünscht* (1952), *Rebellische Herzen* (1957; published under the original title *Prager Tagblatt: Roman einer Redaktion*, 1968), *Jugend im Nebel* (1959), *Die Rosenkoralle* (1961), and *Der Prager Kreis* (1966). But his actual autobiography he reserved for the volume *Streitbares Leben* (1960).

One of his few dramas, the biblical play *Schaul* (1944), his only work in Hebrew, was written for the Habimah Theater. Among his earlier plays were *Lord Byron kommt aus der Mode* (1929) and, in 1928, *Schweijk*, a dramatic adaptation of Hašek's novel *The Good Soldier Schweik*. Loyalty to Kafka as well as his own dramatic ambitions prompted his dramatization of Kafka's *Das Schloß* in 1953.

No less important than his fiction are Brod's writings on religion and philosophy, *Heidentum, Christentum, Judentum* (1921) and *Diesseits und Jenseits* (1947)—the latter includes the two volumes *Von der Krisis der Seelen und vom Weltbilde der neuen Naturwissenschaften* (1946) and *Von der Unsterblichkeit der Seele, der Gerechtigkeit Gottes und einer neuen Politik* (1947). In these books the fundamental idea is the distinction between "noble" misfortune—misfortune that we should accept as God's dispensation—and "ignoble" misfortune—misfortune that we should resist as evil caused by man. A substantial part of *Heidentum, Christentum, Judentum* was reissued in 1949 under the title *Das Diesseitswunder*.

Brod was a born intermediary, not least in music (see his monographs on Leoš Janáček, Carl Nielsen, Gustav Mahler, Adolf Schreiber). *Israels Musik* (1951) is a short survey devoted to Israel's musical life. A biography of Karel Sabina, the librettist of Smetana's *The Bartered Bride*, written with the enthusiasm of the discoverer, appeared in 1962. His biography *Heinrich Heine* (1934) was republished in 1949.

Works: *Tod den Toten!* (1906; Death to the Dead!); *Experimente* (1907; Experiments); *Der Weg des Verliebten* (1907; The Road of the Man in Love); *Schloß Nornepygge* (1908; Castle Nornepygge); *Ein tschechisches Dienstmädchen* (1909; A Czech Maid); *Die Erziehung zur Hetäre* (1909; The Education of a Courtesan); *Jüdinnen* (1911; Jewesses); *Arnold Beer* (1912); *Der Bräutigam* (1912; The Bridegroom); *Abschied von der Jugend* (1912; Farewell to Youth); *Weiberwirtschaft* (1913; Petticoat Management); *Über die Schönheit häßlicher Bilder* (1913; On the Beauty of Ugly Pictures); *Die Höhe des Gefühls* (1913; The Height of Feeling); *Die erste Stunde nach dem Tode* (1916; The First Hour after Death); *Tycho Brahes Weg zu Gott* (1916; Eng. tr., The Redemption of Tycho Brahe, 1928; part I of the trilogy *Ein Kampf um Wahrheit* [A Fight for Truth]); *Das gelobte Land* (1917; The Promised Land); *Die Retterin* (1917; The Rescuer); *Eine Königin Esther* (1918; A Queen Esther); *Das große Wagnis* (1919; The Great Venture); *Ausgewählte Romane und Novellen* (6 vols., 1919; Selected Novels and Novellas); *Die Fälscher* (1920; The Forgers); *Sozialismus im Zionismus* (1920; Socialism in Zionism); *Im Kampf um das Judentum* (1920; Fighting for Jewry); *Heidentum, Christentum, Judentum* (2 vols., 1921; Paganism, Christianity, Judaism); *Adolf Schreiber* (1921); *Das Buch der Liebe* (1921; The Book of Love); *Franzi, oder Eine Liebe zweiten Ranges* (1922; Franzi, or A Second-Class Love); *Klarissas halbes Herz* (1923; Klarissa's Half-Heart); *Leben mit einer Göttin* (1923; Life with a Goddess); *Sternenhimmel* (1924; Starry Sky); *Prozeß Bunterbart* (1924; Trial of Bunterbart); *Rëubeni, Fürst der Juden* (1925; Eng. tr., Reubeni, Prince of the Jews, 1928; part II of the trilogy *Ein Kampf um Wahrheit*); *Leoš Janáček* (1925); *Zionismus als Weltanschauung* (1925; Zionism as Weltanschauung); *Die Frau, nach der man sich sehnt* (1927; The Woman One Longs For); *Das Zauberreich der Liebe* (1928; Eng. tr., Three Loves, 1929); *Lord Byron* (1929); *Lord Byron kommt aus der Mode* (1929; Lord Byron Is Going out of Fashion); *Liebe im Film* (1930; Love on the Screen); *Stefan Rott, oder Das Jahr der Entscheidung* (1931; Stefan Rott, or The Year of Decision); *Die Frau, die nicht enttäuscht* (1934; The Woman Who Does Not Disappoint); *Heinrich Heine* (1934; Eng. tr., The Artist in Revolt, 1956); *Novellen aus Böhmen* (1936; Novellas from Bohemia); *Rassentheorie und Judentum* (1936; Race Theory and Jewry); *Annerl* (1937; Little Anne); *Die Berauschten* (1937; The Intoxicated); *Franz Kafka* (1937; Eng. tr., Franz Kafka, 1947); *Schaul* (1944); *Diesseits und Jenseits* (2 vols., 1947; The Here and Hereafter); *Franz Kafkas Glauben und Lehre* (1948; Franz Kafka's Belief and Teachings); *Galilei in Gefangenschaft* (1948; Galileo in Prison; part III of the trilogy *Ein Kampf um Wahrheit*); *Das Diesseitswunder* (1949; Miracle in This Life); *Neue Gedichte* (1949; New Poems); *Unambo; Roman aus dem jüdisch-arabischen Krieg* (1949; Eng. tr., Unambo: A Novel of the War in Israel, 1952); *Franz Kafka als-wegweisende Gestalt* (1951; Franz Kafka as a Pathmarking Figure); *Musik Israels* (1951; Eng. tr., Israel's Music, 1951); *Der Meister* (1952; Eng. tr., The Master, 1952); *Beinahe ein Vorzugsschüler, oder Pièce touchée* (1952; Almost an Honor Student, or Pièce touchée); *Der Sommer, den man zurückwünscht* (1952; The Summer You Want Back); *Das Schloß* (1953; The Castle; a dramatization of Kafka's novel); *Ein Abenteuer Napoleons* (1954; An Adventure of Napoleon); *Armer Cicero* (1955; Poor Cicero); *Rebellische Herzen* (1957; Rebellious Hearts; republished under the original title *Prager Tagblatt: Roman einer Redaktion* [1968; Prager Tagblatt: Novel of an Editorial Desk]); *Amerika* (1957; dramatization of Kafka's novel); *Mira* (1958); *Verzweiflung und Erlösung im Werk Franz Kafkas* (1959; Desperation and Salvation in Franz Kafka's Work); *Jugend im Nebel* (1959; Youth in a Fog); *Streitbares Leben* (1960; Valiant Life); *Gustav Mahler* (1961); *Die Rosenkoralle* (1961; Pink Coral); *Die verbotene Frau* (1962; Forbidden Woman); *Die verkaufte Braut* (1962; The Bartered Bride); *Durchbruch ins Wunder* (1962; Breakthrough to the Miracle); *Johannes Reuchlin und sein Kampf* (1965; Johannes Reuchlin and His Fight); *Gesang einer Giftschlange, Wirrnis und Auflichtung* (1966; Song of a Viper, Confusion and Elucidation); *Der Prager Kreis* (1966; The Literary Circle in Prague); *Das Unzerstörbare* (1968; The Indestructable); *Von der Unsterblichkeit der Seele* (1969; On the Immortality of the Soul).

Bibliography: On *Reubeni*, in *New York Herald Tribune*, 8 November 1928. On *Three Loves*, in *New York Herald Tribune*, 21 July 1929. On *The Biography of Franz Kafka*, in *Time*, 28 April 1947. Fitzgerald, Edward J., in *Saturday Review*, 8 March 1952. Rosenfeld, Sidney, in *Books Abroad*, 1970. Sullivan, Richard, in *New York Times Book Review*, 11 November 1951. Weltmann, Lutz, in *German Life and Letters*, 1950–51. Zohn, Harry, in *Books Abroad*, 1969. Zweig, Stefan, introduction to *The Redemption of Tycho Brahe*, 1928.

Lutz Weltmann

Ferdinand Bruckner

Ferdinand Bruckner (pseudonym of Theodor Tagger) was born on 26 August 1891 in Vienna. He studied various subjects in Vienna and Paris and then settled in Berlin and tried to establish himself as a writer. After his first attempts at writing poems and stories he became, by way of practical work in the theater (in 1923 he founded the Renaissance Theater and directed it until 1927), a productive playwright. But despite interesting subjects and effective theatrical treatment, he never succeeded in making a breakthrough, as Bertolt Brecht or Carl Zuckmayer did. In 1933 he emigrated to Paris and in 1936 to New York. His plays were performed a number of times outside Germany, but this still did not make him a dramatist of European stature. When he returned to Berlin after World War II, he again failed to achieve any considerable success and, indeed, did not even arouse as much interest as in earlier years. He died on 5 December 1958 in Berlin.

Bruckner's many plays waver between extreme modernism and a return to the classical tradition. His early analyses of the age, such as *Krankheit der Jugend* (1926 and 1928), *Die Verbrecher* (1928), and *Die Kreatur* (1930), show how the bounds of morality or society are broken by unnatural or impulsive crime. This analysis of society is demonstrated by means of a group of students, of people living together or belonging together. In theatrical terms, the group diagnosis leads to the modern multiple setting (in *Die Verbrecher* the stage consists of three floors, on which separate rooms are illuminated one by one and become the scene of action). This "drama of the side by side" is paralleled in the paratactic structure of the primitive dialogue: the abnormal becomes commonplace and the ordinary becomes criminal.

The diagnostic acuteness and the disturbing vehemence of these plays are especially notable characteristics of Bruckner's political drama *Die Rassen* (1933), in which a group of students, as a result of terrorism and demoralization, falls victim to the organized criminality of the Nazi party. (On anti-Semitism the Nazi plot was: "We must create a new concept—that of the *publicly prosecuted.* That is, in brief, the Jew.") In place of the immoral hero, Bruckner rediscovered in this play the moral hero—in the person of the persecuted victim. This hero is even more clearly seen in the later resistance plays, *Denn seine Zeit ist kurz* (1943–45; on the Norwegian church struggle) and *Die Befreiten* (1943–45; on the Italian resistance after the liberation).

In addition to his topical plays, Bruckner wrote a series of historical dramas. He had his biggest success with *Elisabeth von England* (1930; later filmed; also televised, 1961). The character studies of Elizabeth and her lover, Essex, are extremely subtle, and the simultaneous scenes at the courts of London and Madrid are effectively constructed. In an artistically convincing way, inherent human elements and impulses are shown to be the decisive influences that shape history. Less striking are the later comedies about Napoleon and Madame de Staël: *Napoleon der Erste* (1936–37) and *Heroische Komödie* (1942–46). In these plays the artistic montage of scenes is reduced to a simple sequence of pictures, which is also particularly true in *Simon Bolivar* (1942). It is an indication that the moral had become more important for Bruckner than the form.

Bruckner's return to the ethical character of the theater after his period of emigration parallels on the whole his return to the "theater of greatness." *Pyrrhus und Andromache* (1951–52), a tragedy in verse, is based on themes from classical antiquity and French classical drama (Euripides and Racine). Tragic fate is demonstrated by means of a group from the realm of myth (Pyrrhus of Epirus, Andromache, Hermione, Orestes). Tragedy is "the daily struggle for a better life," even if the one is futile and the other a mere illusion. This effort to recover the idea of tragedy is reflected in the three versions of *Timon* (1932, 1948, and 1956).

Works: *Die Vollendung eines Herzens* (1917; Perfection of a Heart); *Der Herr in den Nebeln* (1917; The Gentleman in the Fog); *Psalmen Davids* (1918; Psalms of David); *Der zerstörte Tasso* (1919; The Ruined Tasso); *Peters Traum* (1920; Peter's Dream); *Die Komödie vom Untergang der Welt* (1920; The Comedy of the Extinction of the World); *Auf der Straße* (1920; In the Street); *Kapitän Christoph* (1921; Captain Christoph); *Krankheit der Jugend* (1926; Sickness of Youth); *Die Verbrecher* (1928; The Criminals); *Tedeum* (1929; Te Deum); *Die Kreatur* (1930; The Creature); *Elisabeth von England* (1930; Elizabeth of England); *Timon* (1932; revised versions, 1948, 1956); *Die Marquise von O.* (1933; The Marchioness von O.); *Die Rassen* (1933; The Races); *Mussia* (1935); *Napoleon der Erste* (1936–37; Napoleon the First); *Negerlieder* (1945; Negro Songs); *Simon Bolivar* (1942); *Heroische Komödie* (1942–46; Heroic Comedy); *Dramen unserer Zeit* (1945; includes *Denn seine*

Ferdinand Bruckner 47

Zeit ist kurz, and *Die Befreiten;* Dramas of Our Time: For His Time Is Short, and The Liberated); *Jugend zweier Kriege* (1947; Youth of Two Wars; includes *Krankheit der Jugend, Die Verbrecher,* and *Die Rassen*); *Die Namenlosen von Lexington* (1947; The Nameless of Lexington); *Fährten* (1949; Trails; republished as *Spreu im Wind* [1952; Chaff in the Wind]); *Pyrrhus und Andromache* (1951–52; Pyrrhus and Andromache); *Früchte des Nichts* (1952; Fruits of Nothingness); *Die Buhlschwestern* (1954; The Paramours); *Clarissa* (1956); *Der Tod einer Puppe* (1956; A Doll's Death); *Schauspiele nach historischen Stoffen* (1956; Plays on Historical Topics); *Der Kampf mit dem Engel* (1957; Wrestling with the Angel); *Das irdene Wägelchen* (1957; The Little Earthen Carriage); *Vom Schmerz und von der Vernunft* (1961; On Pain and Reason); *Die Himmel wechseln* (1961; The Skies Change).

Bibliography: Bankloh, Friedhelm, "Ein Forscher der Wirklichkeit: Der Dramatiker Ferdinand Bruckner," *Wort in der Zeit* 2 (August 1956): 1–7. Csokor, Franz Theodor, "Größe und Nichtigkeit des Menschen: Zum Hinscheiden des Dichters Ferdinand Bruckner," *Wort in der Zeit* 5, no. 1 (1959):3–6. Harper, Anthony J., "Ferdinand Bruckner's Treatment of the 'Timon' Theme," *German Life and Letters* 17, no. 3 (1964):259–69. Mann, Otto, "Exkurs über Ferdinand Bruckner," *Deutsche Literatur im 20. Jahrhundert* [34], vol. 1, pp. 162–78, 1961. Schreyvogl, Friedrich, "Ferdinand Bruckner," *Eckart Jahrbuch* 30 (1961):95–97. Schwiefert, Fritz, "Ferdinand Bruckner," *Maske und Kothurn* 4 (1958):358–70.

Clemens Heselhaus

Martin Buber

Religious and social philosopher, born 8 February 1878, Vienna; died 13 June 1965, Jerusalem, Israel. As a result of his parents' divorce, Martin Buber went at the age of three to his grandfather, Salomon Buber, a man of great wealth and profound Hebrew scholarship. There, in Lwow (then the capital of the Austrian province Galicia; today Lviv, in the Ukraine), Buber studied in a Polish *Gymnasium* and received a thorough education in Hebrew and Judaism. He spent the summers near Sadagora and Czortkow, seats of famous dynasties of Hasidic leaders, and thus established a first contact with Hasidism, whose interpreter he later became.

In 1896 Buber entered the University of Vienna and there, as well as in Leipzig, Zurich, and Berlin, he studied philosophy and the history of art. Of his teachers, Wilhelm Dilthey and Georg Simmel impressed him most. The years 1898–1900 became in many ways decisive for his development. He started reading the German mystics of the Renaissance and Reformation periods; married a Bavarian costudent at the University of Zurich, Paula Winkler, who later published several novels of great originality under the pen name of Georg Munk; and became an active worker in the Zionist movement, founded in 1897 by Theodor Herzl at the first Zionist Congress in Basel. Buber took part in the third Congress in Basel in 1899. He insisted there on the importance of Jewish cultural life. Later he settled in Berlin-Zehlendorf.

At the fifth Zionist Congress (1901) Buber broke with Herzl. He was, together with Chaim Weizmann, a leading member of the *kulturell-demokratische* opposition to Herzl's political Zionism, and, on behalf of this group, he delivered a long report on the importance of a Jewish cultural renaissance of art and literature. The rejection of his proposals by the Congress led to his withdrawal from active participation. He devoted the following years to a close study of Hasidism. The result was several books, which translated the Hasidic legends and sayings into the language of the "new style," the *Jugendstil* of the early 20th century. In 1906 appeared his *Die Geschichten des Rabbi Nachman* (Nachman ben Simcha of Brazlaw [1771–1810]), and in 1908 his *Die Legende des Baal Schem* (Israel ben Eliezer Baal

Schemtow [1700–1760], founder of the Hasidic movement and Nachman's great-grandfather). Later on, Buber's interpretations of Hasidism became less poetic. They were collected in his *Die chassidischen Bücher* (1927) and in *Die Erzählungen der Chassidim* (1950). In his early books Buber saw the Hasidic movement as part of the "subterranean," mystical tradition of Judaism, opposed to the "official" rabbinic rationalistic main current. During that period, which lasted until World War I, Buber published also editions of mystical writers of other religions, the most important being *Ekstatische Konfessionen* (1909).

Buber's interpretation of Hasidism and of mysticism, his affirmation of life and life-enhancing values, was strongly influenced by Nietzsche. Buber emphasized man's responsibility, his creative response to God's challenge. His mysticism was characterized by his *Weltfrömmigkeit* and *Weltfreudigkeit*; he interpreted Jewish history as the ever-present encounter of God and His people, of God's call ("Hear, O Israel") and Israel's willing acceptance or obstinate refusal of the difficult yoke of God's demands. At the same time the chief responsibility was not on the people but on the individual personality. In his first "Rede über das Judentum" Buber defined the Jewish problem not as a social, political, or economic one, but as an individual, personal one of an authentic existence: "The true Jewish problem is an inwardly individual one, the attitude of each individual Jew to his inherited substance [*Wesensbesonderheit*]."

This "Rede über das Judentum" opened a new period of Buber's Zionist activity. It was delivered in January 1909 before the Jewish student association, Bar Kochba, of Prague. The important *Drei Reden über das Judentum* (1911) and the more comprehensive *Reden über das Judentum* (1923) elaborated Buber's new definition of Zionism. It was on the one hand influenced by the then prevailing German neoromanticism, which emphasized the fundamental importance of "blood" (biological descent) and the God-willed connection of a people with "its" soil; and on the other, by the universalistic ethics of the Hebrew prophets. Buber never succeeded in fully accepting one of these two contradictory tendencies. This ambivalence increased his influence on Central European Jewish youth in the years between 1910 and 1930, two decades of great spiritual unrest and changes in the intellectual climate of a disintegrating society. The Jew, Buber said in his *Reden*, feels "in the immortality [of the chain] of generations the community of the blood, and he feels it as . . . the duration of his individual self. He discovers the blood as the deeply rooted and nourishing power in the individual; he discovers that the deepest layers of our existence are determined by the blood, that our thought and our will are colored by it in their innermost substance."

At the same time, to a large part under the influence of his friend Gustav Landauer (1870–1919), an idealistic, anti-Marxist anarchist whose posthumous works Buber edited, Buber praised the communal living and spirit of the workers' settlements (*Kevutsof*) in Palestine as the voluntary and nonviolent realization of socialism. World War I intensified in Buber, as in Landauer (and in the two Hebrew writers who were Buber's older contemporaries, Achad Haam [Asher Ginzberg, 1856–1927] and A. D. Gordon [1856–1922], both Russian Hebrew writers), his opposition to war and violence. In this sense Buber spoke at the twelfth Zionist Congress in Karlsbad (Karlove Vary, Czechoslovakia) in 1921 against a Jewish state in Palestine, for brotherly cooperation with the Arabs, who then formed the large majority of the country's population, and for a binational state that would safeguard the rights of both peoples on the basis of equality, irrespective of their numbers. This failure to influence the Congress and the Zionist movement brought about a second period of withdrawal from active participation in the movement. From 1916 to 1923 Buber published an important monthly, *Der Jude*. After his withdrawal he replaced it in 1926 with a more general theological and philosophical quarterly, *Die Kreatur*, in which a Catholic German and a Protestant German were his coeditors.

In 1916 Buber moved from Berlin to Heppenheim (near Frankfurt), where he lived until 1938, when Hitlerism forced his emigration to Palestine. In that period he taught Jewish theology and ethics at the University of Frankfurt on the Main, and later social philosophy at the Hebrew University of Jerusalem. Buber's years in Heppenheim were characterized by two decisive events. The first was the abandonment of mysticism in his book *Ich und Du* (1922). In this new interpretation of man's relationship to God there is no longer a question of their union (*unio mystica*). God is real, but man is real too; likewise the world. God and man can meet. In this encounter man enters into a true and demanding reality. This encounter always happens in a concrete situation; it is not part of theology, but of existence. God speaks to man; man realizes himself in his response. But an I-Thou relationship can also exist between human beings. Man lives a real life if he responds to his "Thou." There is no "I" except in the relationship to a "Thou." But the I-Thou is not the only relationship between human beings. There is also the I-it (*Ich-Er, Sie, Es*) relationship, in which the "it" is no longer a true partner, but an object in daily experience. The I-it is also the world of science, of politics and economics.

The second decisive event in the Heppenheim period was Buber's encounter with the Bible, which now took the place of his encounter with Hasidism twenty-five years before. As a result of this encounter Buber, with his friend Franz Rosenzweig (1889–1929), started a new translation of the Old Testament into a German that would faithfully render the meaning of the Hebrew text. The first volume appeared in 1925, the last one, following a revision of the former volumes, in 1962. Connected with his renewed study of the Bible, Buber published *Königtum Gottes* (1932; 3rd ed., 1956), a study in the origins of messianism, and *Der Glaube der Propheten* (1950). In agreement with his general philosophy Buber saw in the Bible a voice speaking to the reader; as in all true life, in the Bible, too, is a life of dialogue; a life of confrontation of I and Thou. This "Thou" is everyone who hears the "Thou" and responds to it. In that way man participates in God's work.

True education is also a form of the life of dialogue. Hence Buber's growing interest in education, and in adult education. With the threat of Hitlerism growing, and later in Palestine and in Israel, Buber devoted more and more of his time to "teaching." He was in depth and clarity an incomparable teacher. *Rede über das Erzieherische* (1926), *Dialogisches Leben: Gesammelte philosophische und pädagogische Schriften* (1947), and *Reden über Erziehung* (1953) contain his main contributions in the field that grew ever more important to him.

Buber's life in Jerusalem brought him into direct contact with the "Arab problem." Once more, and in a much more difficult situation, he demanded, together with a very small group of Palestinian Jews (among them the Chancellor of the Hebrew University, Dr. Judah L. Magnus), due consideration of the rights of the Arab Palestinians. Together they proposed, in 1946, a program of "Palestine a Binational State." Their opinion did not prevail. Even after the new State of Israel had been created in a war against the Arabs, Buber continued to plead for the civil and political rights of what had become an Arab minority in a Jewish state. As a unique gesture in the history of Israel, Arab students of the Hebrew University laid a wreath at the bier when Buber was lying in state after his death.

During the last years of his life Buber's influence, which remained very small in Israel, spread in the English-speaking world and was reestablished in Germany. He received the Goethe Prize from the City of Hamburg in 1953, and the Peace Prize of the German Book Trade in 1955. In each instance, a reason stated for awarding the prize was Buber's achievement as a writer of prose fiction in German. Solidly rooted in the stylistic traditions of romantic narrative prose,

Buber imposes formal elements of the 19th-century German *Novelle* upon the traditions of Hasidic storytelling. The highly evocative, "magical" effect of this fusion upon readers of Buber's prose has been frequently noted. He visited the United States for the first time in 1951–52, when he lectured mainly at the Jewish Theological Seminary in New York and at the College of Jewish Studies in Los Angeles. During his following visits, in 1957 and 1958, he conducted seminars at Columbia University and at Princeton University. By then he was regarded among non-Jews as the representative Jewish thinker of the time. Many of his books were translated into English. One of the most important of them, with which he resumed and concluded his revelation of the Hasidic world, was his only novel, called *Gog und Magog* (1949). It describes the crises and tensions in the Hasidic world during the Napoleonic war against Russia. One school believed that this great struggle inaugurated the coming of the messianic times, while another, the Hasidic school, rejected this belief as heretical, because the coming of the Messiah does not depend on battlefields but on the inner life of man. Buber manifestly sided with this second interpretation.

Buber's philosophic thought remained centered on the individual, but not in the same way as Kierkegaard or Heidegger, with whom Buber was frequently compared as an "existentialist" thinker. For Buber man is never man by himself, but man-with-man: "The fundamental fact of existence is not man, but man-with-man." (*Das Problem des Menschen*, 1948, p. 165). Salvation cannot be found in individualism, which glorifies man's loneliness, nor in collectivism, which shifts responsibility from the individual to the group. Beyond subjectivism and objectivism, on the narrow ridge where "I" and "Thou" meet, is the realm of the dialogue (*"das Reich des Zwischen"*). Buber's philosophy had become in 1923 a philosophy of dialogue, of the authentic and immediate relationship of man to man, and so it remained throughout the rest of his life. In an open dialogue, not in the "unmasking" of the "adversary," Buber saw the hope, the *"Hoffnung für diese Stunde,"* the hope for our time and for all times.

Works: *Lesser Ury* (1903); *Die Geschichte des Rabbi Nachman* (1906; Eng. tr., Tales of Rabbi Nachman, 1956); *Die Legende des Baal Schem* (1908; Eng. tr., Legend of the Baal Schem, 1955); *Ekstatische Konfessionen* (1909; Ecstatic Confessions); *Drei Reden über das Judentum* (1911; Three Speeches on Judaism); *Daniel* (1913; Eng. tr., 1964); *Vom Geist des Judentums* (1916; About the Spirit of Judaism); *Die jüdische Bewegung* (2 vols., 1916–20; The Jewish Movement); *Völker, Staaten* und Zion (1917; Peoples, Nations, and Zion); *Die Rede, die Lehre und das Lied* (1917; The Sermon, the Lesson, and the Song); *Ereignisse und Begegnungen* (1917; Events and Confrontations); *Mein Weg zum Chassidismus* (1918; My Way to Hasidism); *Der heilige Weg* (1919; Eng. tr., The Holy Way, 1967); *Worte an die Zeit* (2 vols., 1919; Words Addressed to Our Times); *Cheruth* (1919; Eng. tr., Herut, on Youth and Religion, 1967); *Der große Maggid* (1921; The Great Maggid); *Ich und Du* (1922; Eng. tr., I and Thou, 1937); *Reden über das Judentum* (1923; Speeches about Judaism); *Das verborgene Licht* (1924; The Hidden Light); *Die Schrift* (translation, with Franz Rosenzweig; 15 vols., 1925–38; The Old Testament); *Reden über das Erzieherische* (1926; Discourses on Pedagogics); *Die chassidischen Bücher* (1927; The Hasidic Books); *Hundert chassidische Geschichten* (1930; One Hundred Hasidic Stories); *Zwiesprache* (1930; Eng. tr., Between Man and Man, 1947); *Königtum Gottes* (1932; Eng. tr., Kingship of God, 1967); *Kampf um Israel* (1933; Fight for Israel); *Erzählungen von Engeln, Geistern und Dämonen* (1934; Eng. tr., Tales of Angels, Spirits, and Demons, 1958); *Deutung des Chassidismus* (1935; Eng. tr., Hasidism and Modern Man, 1958); *Die Stunde und die Erkenntnis* (1936; The Hour and Recognition); *Zion als Ziel und Aufgabe* (1936; Zion, a Goal and a Mission); *Die Frage an den Einzelnen* (1936; Eng. tr., The Silent Question, 1967); *Die Schrift und ihre Verdeutschung* (with Franz Rosenzweig, 1936; The Scripture and Its Rendering in German); *Worte an die Jugend* (1938; Words to Youth); *Chassidismus* (1945; Eng. tr., Hasidism, 1948); *Dialogisches Leben* (1947; Eng. tr., Dialogues on Realization, 1964); *Moses* (1948; Eng. tr., 1958); *Das Problem des Menschen* (1948; Eng. tr., Knowledge of Man, 1965); *Der Weg des Menschen nach der chassidischen Lehre* (1948; Am. tr., The Way of Man, 1950; Brit. tr., Way of Man according to the Teachings of Hasidism, 1963); *Gog und Magog* (1949; Eng. tr., For the Sake of Heaven, 1945); *Der Glaube der Propheten* (1950; Eng. tr., The Prophetic Faith, 1949); *Zwei Glaubensweisen* (1950; Eng. tr., Two Types of Faith, 1951); *Die Erzählungen der Chassidim* (1950; Eng. tr., Tales of the Hasidim, 2 vols., 1947); *Israel und Palästina* (1950; Eng. tr., Israel and Palestine, 1952); *Pfade in Utopia* (1950; Eng. tr., Paths in Utopia, 1950; republished as *Der utopische Sozialismus* [1967; Eng. tr., The Utopian Socialism, 1967]); *Urdistanz und Beziehung* (1951; Original Distance and Correlation); *Zwischen Gesellschaft und Staat* (1952; Between Society and State); *Die chassidische Botschaft* (1952; The Hasidic Message); *An der Wende* (1952; Eng. tr., At the Turning, 1952); *Bilder von Gut und Böse* (1952; Am. tr., Good and Evil, 1961; Brit. tr., Images of Good and Evil, 1953); *Deutung einiger Psalmen* (1952; Interpretation of Some Psalms); *Bücher und Menschen* (1952; Books and Men); *Recht und Unrecht* (1952; Eng. tr., Right and Wrong, 1953); *Gottesfinsternis* (1953; Eng. tr., Eclipse of God, 1952); *Reden über Erziehung* (1953; Discourse on Pedagogics); *Einsichten* (1953; Insights); *Hinweise* (1953; Eng. tr., Pointing the Way,

1957); *Die Schriften über das dialogische Prinzip* (1954; Eng. tr., The History of the Dialogical Principle, 1965); *Sehertum* (1955; Prophetry); *Der Mensch und sein Gebild* (1955; Eng. tr., The Knowledge of Man, 1965); *Stationen des Glaubens* (1956; Eng. tr., To Hallow this Life, 1958); *Schuld und Schuldgefühle* (1958; Guilt and Feelings of Guilt); *Die Juden in der UdSSR* (with Goldmann, 1961; The Jews in the USSR); *Begegnungen* (1961; Encounters); *Werke* (3 vols., 1962–64; Works); *Schriften zur Philosophie* (1962; Writings on Philosophy); *Der Jude und sein Judentum* (1963; Eng. tr., Judaism and the Jews, 1967); *Elija: Ein Mysterienspiel* (1963; Elijah: A Miracle Play); *Schriften zum Chassidismus* (1963; Writings on Hasidism); *Pegishot* (1965); *Nachlese* (1965; Gleanings); *Die fünf Bücher der Weisung* (with Franz Rosenzweig, 1968; The Pentateuch).

English translations in collections: Israel and the World: Essays in a Time of Crisis (1948); Writings (1956); On the Bible: Eighteen Studies (Am. tr., in Collection of Different Works, 1968); Biblical Humanism (Brit. tr., in Collection of Different Works, 1968).

Bibliography: Balthasar, Hans Urs von, *Martin Buber and Christianity*, 1961. Berkovits, E., *A Jewish Critique of the Philosophy of Martin Buber*, 1962. Cohen, A. A., *Martin Buber*, 1957. Diamond, M. L., *Martin Buber, Jewish Existentialist*, 1960. Friedman, M. S., *Martin Buber: The Life of Dialogue*, 1955. Pfuetze, P. E., *Self, Society, Existence, Human Nature and Dialogue in the Thought of Herbert Mead and Martin Buber*, 1961. Waldinger, Ernst, in *Books Abroad*, 1961.

Hans Kohn[▲]

Christine Busta

Christine Busta (pseudonym of Christine Dimt), born 23 April 1915 in Vienna, grew up in very modest circumstances and without a father. Despite poverty she completed secondary school in 1933. In 1936, owing to a serious illness, she had to give up her university studies of German and English languages and literatures. She then worked as an assistant teacher and in 1940 married the musician Maximilian Dimt (missing in Russia since 1944). In the postwar years, she was an interpreter and hotel employee. Since 1950 she has been librarian in the Vienna municipal libraries.

In spite of early poetical attempts, Christine Busta found her way to the public comparatively late, by means of contributions to periodicals and anthologies. Her lyrical work grew out of poverty, sorrow, disappointment, and solitude. Her poetic message is closely connected with her personal fate.

In form *Der Regenbaum* (1951), her first book, is still in the Austrian lyrical tradition. Nevertheless, the poems are powerfully original, even if there is no attempt at experiment. The language is beautiful, sonorous, and rich in symbols. Her themes circle round the mystery of life, which is made up as much of guilt, solitude, and ceaseless change as of trustful love for God and all creatures. Her undogmatic Christianity is inspired by strong compassion: "I am not here to hate my neighbor, but to love him."

The volume of poetry *Lampe und Delphin* was published in 1955. In a menacing and hopeless world, the lamp and the dolphin appear as symbols of the guiding, healing, and redeeming forces of life. With the volume *Die Scheune der Vögel* (1958), the poet went further along the laborious road of spiritualization, as in *Heimgang ins fremdgewordene Innen*. "My basic theme," she says, "is the transformation of fear, terror, and guilt into joy, love, and redemption." With the increasingly individual tone goes a progressive emancipation from the fetters of traditional form and a leaning toward the free verse of modern writing. Vividness, graphic detail, and the mark of a strong personality are also evident in her *Bethlehemitische Legende* (1956) and her poems for children, *Die Sternenmühle* (1959).

Works: *Jahr um Jahr* (1950; Year after Year); *Der Regenbaum* (1951; The Rain Tree); *Lampe und Delphin* (1955; Lamp and Dolphin); *Bethlehemitische Legende* (1956; Bethlehemitic Legend); *Die Scheune der Vögel* (1958; The Bird Barn); *Die Sternenmühle* (1959; The Star Mill); *Das andere Schaf* (1959; The Other Sheep); *Steyrer Krippenspiel* (1960; Styrian Nativity Play); *Unterwegs zu älteren Feuern* (1965; On the Way to Older Fires); *Unveröffentlichte Gedichte* (1965; Unpublished Poems).

Bibliography: Fleischmann, Wolfgang Bernard, "New Look at Austrian Literature," *America*, 17 September 1960, pp. 644–47. Fritsch, Gerhard, "Christine Busta," *Wort in der Zeit* 5, no. 2 (1959):3–6. Horst, Karl August, *Kritischer Führer durch die deutsche Literatur der Gegenwart*, p. 251, 1962. Waldinger, Ernst, in *Books Abroad*, 1961.

Wolfram Mauser

Elias Canetti

Born 25 July 1905 in Ruse, Bulgaria. As a result of family circumstances Elias Canetti grew up in England, Austria, Switzerland, and Germany. He was brought up a polyglot: as a child he spoke the 15th-century Spanish of his Sephardic parents; at six he learned English, at eight German. From 1924 to 1929 he studied natural sciences in Vienna, and after earning his Ph.D., he lived there as a writer.

Fascinated by Karl Kraus's readings of his own works, Canetti developed into an art his own talent for recitation. From the example set by Hermann Broch, with whom he was on friendly terms, he was able to understand the writer as a "dog of his time," as a man of universal insight, as an adversary of death. But a longer-lasting influence on him than individuals were the phenomena of masses and power, by which he was confronted for the first time in Vienna. The impressions made on him by certain outer experiences, such as political demonstrations, and certain inner experiences, such as reading Suetonius's biographies of the Caesars, led him to devote his life to the study and representation of these phenomena.

The political events of 1938 forced Canetti to emigrate, via Paris, to England, where he has been living since. In his novel *Die Blendung* he made a tremendous effort to pursue his aims in both an artistic and a philosophic direction. This novel is the story of the futile self-assertion and inevitable self-destruction of the isolated individual; it is a natural history of evil, a view of the deluded and dark side of mankind, which since the beginning of fascism had become a normal, respectably established thing. It is history imagined in advance, and therefore it aroused no response in Germany at its first and second publication (1935 and 1948). But with its third edition in 1963, it was at last understood.

Not until 1960, in *Masse und Macht*, did Canetti provide the anthropological substantiation for *Die Blendung*. As massively as *Die Blendung* it illustrates how, outside the conventional disciplines (in this case, sociology or cultural anthropology), fresh thinking is possible; how, from the phenomena masses and power themselves, it is possible to develop adequate concepts for representing and interpreting them. *Masse und Macht*, drawing on rich material about primitive instead of civilized behavior, an archaic typology of the contemporary world, gives an implicit reason for reading *Die Blendung*. Both books are written in the same suggestive style, often of a crystalline beauty, and are always of a concise clarity that opens up new possibilities for both fictions and essays.

In his dramas Canetti employs a technique that he calls the "acoustic mask," wherein each of his characters is vividly outlined solely by his unique style of speech. But he brings to the stage the same problems that preoccupy him elsewhere. In his *Komödie der Eitelkeit* (finished, 1934; published, 1950), a ban on all mirrors brings about a mass psychosis. *Die Befristeten* (first performance, 1956) is a didactic play about the amount of time allotted to each character to spend until death, many aspects of which are also discussed in *Masse und Macht*. The stage has yet to show how effective in practice this theoretician is in his theatrical guise.

Works: *Hochzeit* (1932; The Marriage); *Die Blendung* (1935; Am. tr., The Tower of Babel, 1947; Brit. tr., Auto da fé, 1946); *Die Affenoper* (1950; The Monkey Opera); *Komödie der Eitelkeit* (1950; Comedy of Vanity); *Fritz Wotruba* (1953); *Die Befristeten* (1956; Eng. tr., The Numbered, 1964); *Masse und Macht* (1960; Eng. tr., Crowds and Power, 1963); *Welt im Kopf* (1962; The World in My Head); *Dramen* (1964; Dramas); *Aufzeichnungen 1942–1948* (1965; Notes 1942–48); *Die Stimmen von Marrakesch* (1968; The Voices of Marrakesh); *Der andere Prozeß: Kafkas Briefe an Felice* (1969; The Other Trial: Kafka's Letters to Felice); *Die gespaltene Zukunft* (1973; The Split Future).

Bibliography: Angerer, Elisabeth, in *Books Abroad*, 1965. Fremantle, Anne, in *Commonweal*, no. 45 (4 April 1947), p. 620. Sisk, John P., in *Commonweal*, no. 77 (15 February 1963), p. 544. Weisstein, Ulrich, in *Books Abroad*, 1970. On *Crowds and Power*, in *Times Literary Supplement*, 2 November 1962, p. 839.

Joachim Schickel

Paul Celan

Paul Celan (pseudonym of Paul Antschel) was born on 23 November 1920, in Cernăuti (in Bucovina, northern Rumania), the son of German-speaking parents. After the outbreak of World War II he had to discontinue his medical studies, begun at Tours in 1938. He then took up the study of Romance languages in Cernăuti. After the occupation of Bucovina—since 1940 a part of the Soviet Union—by German and Rumanian troops, he was sent to a labor camp in Rumania. In 1943 he returned to Cernăuti and resumed his studies.

In 1945 Celan left the Soviet Union and worked as a translator and publisher's reader in Bucharest. In 1947 he published his first poems in the Rumanian anthology *Agora*, which also contained texts in German. During the same year he emigrated to Vienna, then in 1948 to Paris, where he studied German and linguistics and became a French citizen. In 1950 he received his *licence-ès-lettres* (B. A.), and after that he worked as a writer and translator in addition to holding a teaching post at the École Normale Supérieure of the University of Paris. In 1958 he was awarded the Literary Prize of the Free Hanseatic City of Bremen and in 1960 the Georg Büchner Prize. In April 1970 Celan took his own life—he was forty-nine years old.

Celan's literary work grew out of the fullness of his varied linguistic and cultural heritage. The memories of his Hasidic and biblically oriented youth, the impetus of expressionist literature (Trakl, Lasker-Schüler), the encounter with modern French poetry, especially surrealism (he had personal ties in Paris with Yvan Goll), and the Eastern *Weltanschauung* (he did translations of Russian writers): all are integrated into the experiential sphere of his poems, a sphere of intellectual validation where reality is being sought and created.

Celan's poems are images and gestures—a perceiving thought process. Though the poet relates all appearances to an inner self, the sphere of the self created by him always remains in contact with things from the visible world—like flowers, tears, stones—which condense into codes of existential assertion. Each of the varying forms of these poems is a new attempt to show ways "where language becomes resonant, ways of a voice toward a perceiving you, as creatures on the same earth, adumbrations for a way of life, a sending-oneself-ahead toward oneself in search of oneself. . . ."

In the first volume, *Der Sand aus den Urnen* (1948; later included as Part I of *Mohn und Gedächtnis*), his affinity to his models is still apparent, but in the volumes that follow, Celan achieved an increasingly conscious relationship to the word and thus distance, independence.

By an artistic interweaving of sensuous mental images, by the linking together of apparently disparate images and paradoxical attributes, but above all by a language as disciplined as it is magically associative, Celan attempts in *Mohn und Gedächtnis* (1952)—which contains the *Todesfuge*—to transcend the logical forms of experience. Reminding and entreating, out of the *Ineinander* (into-one-another) of multiply mirrored or reverberating voices, Celan, in *Von Schwelle zu Schwelle* (1955), shapes the poetic form of a modern state of consciousness.

The Jean Paul-like metaphor in the title of the next volume, *Sprachgitter* (1959), already points out the boundaries as well as the outermost objectifying possibilities of a relationship-to-reality made absolute in language, of an actualized language—as Celan formulated it in his acceptance speech for the Büchner Prize (published as *Der Meridian*, 1961)—"set free under the sign of a radical individualization, mindful at the same time of the verbal limits and unlocking possibilities posed by that language itself." When Celan calls to mind the "strong inclination to become silent," which seems to be the distinct characteristic of modern poetry, the paradoxical task of literature nevertheless remains "a going-beyond the human, a transferring of self into a realm, alien, uncanny, yet inclined toward the human."

The title of the poetry volume *Die Niemandsrose* (1963) is the cipher to such a transcendence, in spite of knowing the shapelessness of that realm. In its meaninglessly beautiful flowering out of nothing, form without content is conceived as mystery. But that Celan's ultimate concern, in this volume too, is with the relationship between world and spirit is shown by the incantation of many names that, more clearly than in his previous work, reveal a recognition of the consciousness born out of the Jewish tradition: to designate the world and so create it. At the limit of the unutterable, the poems still preserve fragments of a represented world; but the way into the language landscape, drawn through constellations, leads through the visible world into a reality that eludes the shaping word. *Atemwende* (1967) is the attempt to give expression to such a way of thinking that is detached from the image concepts of language.

Works: *Der Sand aus den Urnen* (1948; Sand from the Urns); *Mohn und Gedächtnis* (1952; Poppy and Memory); *Von Schwelle zu Schwelle* (1955; From Threshold to Threshold); *Sprachgitter* (1959; Language Lattice); *Gedichte* (1959; Poems); *Der Meridian* (1961; The Meridian); *Die Niemandsrose* (1963; No Man's Rose); *Atemkristall* (1965; Breath-Crystal); *Atemwende* (1967; Turn of Breath); *Todtnauberg* (1968); *Ausgewählte Gedichte* (1968; Selected Poems); *Fadensonnen* (1968; Filaments of Suns); *Ausgewählte Gedichte* (ed. K. Reichert, 1970); *Schneepart: Letzte Gedichte* (1971; Share of Snow: Last Poems).

English translations in collections: Selections in *Twentieth-Century German Verse* (ed. P. Bridgewater, 1963); *Contemporary German Poetry* (ed. G. Schwebell, 1964); *Selected Poems* (1972).

Bibliography: Duroche, L. L., in *Modern Language Notes*, 1967, p. 476. Exner, Richard, in *Books Abroad*, 1968, p. 253. Horst, Karl August, *Kritischer Führer durch die deutsche Literaur der Gegenwart*, 1962. Lyon, James K., "The Poetry of Paul Celan: An Approach," *Germanic Review* 39 (1964):50–67. Middleton, J. C., in *German Life and Letters*, 1959–60, pp. 60–61. Prawer, Siegbert, in *Essays on Contemporary German Literature*, edited by Brian Keith-Smith, 1966.

Victor Lange

Franz Theodor Csokor

Born 6 September 1885 in Vienna; died 5 January 1969, there. Studied history of art in Vienna, fought in World War I, traveled in Russia, Poland, Italy, and France. Csokor served as a dramatic consultant in Leningrad. Later in Vienna he worked in the same capacity and also did some directing at the Raimund Theater (1923–27) and was employed by the Deutsches Volkstheater. After emigrating in 1938, Csokor lived successively in Poland, Rumania, and Yugoslavia. He returned to Vienna in 1946, and from 1947 until his death was president of the Austrian P.E.N. Club.

Csokor's first writings belong to expressionism. In conception and execution they are tied to his time. They are also characterized by the fact that their content has more meaning than is apparent on the surface. The early plays *Der große Kampf* (1915)—which describes the struggle of the individual against the multitude—and *Die rote Straße* (1918) are dominated by a revolutionary approach. For all that—their topicality notwithstanding—they owe much to the Austrian mystery plays and the traditional Viennese "magic play" (*Zauberstück*). The tragedy *Dritter November 1918* (1936) is the first play of his *Europäische Trilogie*. Although Csokor's sure dramatic sense allowed him to see both sides of a problem and to give convincing arguments to each partner in the dialogue, his sympathies were on the side of the conservatives in 1923, when he wrote the first version of the play. At heart he was a royalist Catholic who felt that the collapse of the Hapsburg monarchy was a loss for Europe. Three years before Hanns Johst's *Schlageter*—a play, a literary result of Johst's pro-Nazi sentiments, much performed in the 1930s—Csokor treated a similar theme in his drama about the Ruhr Valley, *Besetztes Gebiet* (1930). But this play was so free from chauvinism that in 1952 it was easily made the second part of the *Europäische Trilogie*, which closed with a drama on the Yugoslav partisans, *Der verlorene Sohn* (1947).

This dramatic sequence dealing with the period 1914–45 was followed by another trilogy, *Olymp und Golgatha* (1954), which treats of the world upheaval between the time of the murder of Caesar and the crucifixion of Jesus. Csokor drew a parallel between this epoch and the period from 1914 to 1945, both so restless and both generating so much that was new, in the epilogue to *Pilatus* (1949), one of the plays of the *Olymp und Golgatha* trilogy. The other two are *Cäsars Witwe* (1953)—Calpurnia and young Augustus caught in the struggle for "this" world—and *Kalypso* (1942)—"Christian" sentiments in paganism. *Kalypso* was written in 1941 under the impact of Csokor's first encounter with the Mediterranean, the last stop on his flight from Hitler.

Csokor is at his most impressive in two prose works. The first of these is the record of his odyssey in Poland and the Balkans, which was published in 1955 under the title *Auf fremden Straßen*. It had previously appeared in two separate parts, *Als Zivilist im polnischen Krieg* (1940) and *Als Zivilist im Balkankrieg* (1947). His other outstanding prose work is the Anabaptist novel *Der Schlüssel zum Abgrund* (1955), which first appeared in 1932 under the title *Ein Reich gegen die Welt* and again in 1933, as a drama, under the title *Das Reich der Schwärmer*. Csokor gave epic breadth to the novel by bringing in contemporaneous events outside the action's causal nexus.

Csokor was much interested in Georg Büchner. Both Csokor's stage experience and his political concerns were very useful to him when, in 1928, he adapted Büchner's drama fragment *Woyzeck* with sensitive faithfulness to Büchner's style. The last scene harks back to the first: again the captain is being shaved, but the patient batman Woyzeck is now replaced by his comrade, Andres, whose fingers are itching to cut the captain's throat. Csokor also wrote a play about Büchner, *Gesellschaft der Menschenrechte* (1929), in which he projected onto the character of Büchner his own conflict between his desire to produce poetic writing and his desire to protest. Csokor was a man who could not remain silent: on the occasion of the 1933 P.E.N. Club Congress in Yugoslavia, he publicly raised his voice against the Nazi book burnings, with the result that his own works were forbidden in Germany.

Works: *Die Gewalten* (1912; The Powers); *Der große Kampf* (1915; The Great Struggle); *Der Dolch und die Wunde* (1918; The Dagger and the Wound); *Die rote Straße* (1918; The Red Street); *Die Sünde wider den Geist* (1918; The Sin against the Spirit); *Die Stunde des Absterbens* (1919; The Hour of Death); *Der Baum der Erkenntnis* (1919; The Tree of Knowledge); *Schuß ins Geschäft* (1924; The Shot into the Store); *Der Fall Otto Eisler* (1925; The Otto Eisler Case); *Das Geschenk* (1925; The Present); *Ewiger Aufbruch* (1926; Eternal Start); *Ballade von der Stadt* (1928; Ballad about the City); *Gesellschaft der Menschenrechte* (1929; Society for Human Rights); *Besetztes Gebiet* (1930; Occupied Zone; part

II of the *Europäische Trilogie*); *Gewesene Menschen* (1932; The Hasbeens); *Die Weibermühle* (1932; The Women Mill); *Der tausendjährige Traum* (1933; The Millennial Dream); *Das Thüringer Spiel von den zehn Jungfrauen* (1933; The Thuringian Play about the Ten Virgins); *3.November 1918* (1936; part I of the *Europäische Trilogie*); *Über die Schwelle* (1937; Over the Threshold); *Jadwiga* (1939); *Gottes General* (1939; The Lord's General); *Satans Arche* (1940; Satan's Ark); *Als Zivilist im polnischen Krieg* (1940; Am. tr., A Civilian in the Polish War, 1941); *Wenn sie zurückkommen* (1941; When They Return); *Kalypso* (1942; Calypso; part of the trilogy *Olymp und Golgatha*); *Medea Postbellica* (1946); *Schwarzes Schiff* (1946; Black Ship); *Der verlorene Sohn* (1947; The Prodigal Son; part III of the *Europäische Trilogie*); *Als Zivilist im Balkankrieg* (1947; A Civilian in the Balkan War); *Pilatus* (1949; Pilate; part of the trilogy *Olymp und Golgatha*); *Immer ist Anfang* (1952; All the Time Is a Beginning); *Europäische Trilogie* (1952; European Trilogy); *Cäsars Witwe* (1953; Caesar's Widow; part of the trilogy *Olymp und Golgatha*); *Olymp und Golgatha* (1954; Olympus and Golgotha); *Der Schlüssel zum Abgrund* (1955; The Key to the Abyss; first published as *Ein Reich gegen die Welt*, 1932; published as drama *Das Reich der Schwärmer*, 1933); *Auf fremden Straßen* (1955; On Foreign Roads; includes *Als Zivilist im polnischen Krieg*, and *Als Zivilist im Balkankrieg*); *Hebt den Stein ab* (1957; Lift up the Stone); *Der zweite Hahnenschrei* (1959; The Second Crowing of the Cock); *Treibholz* (1959; Driftwood); *Du bist gemeint* (1959; You Are Meant); *Vom Schmerz und von der Vernunft* (1960; On Pain and on Reason); *Das Zeichen an der Wand* (1962; The Sign on the Wall); *Zeuge einer Zeit: Briefe aus dem Exil 1933–1950* (1964; Witness of an Epoch: Letters from Exile, 1933–1950); *Die Kaiser zwischen den Zeiten* (with C. Hauser, 1964; The Emperors between the Times); *Ein paar Schaufeln Erde* (1965; A Few Shovels of Dust); *Du silberne Dame du* (with L. Rüthner, 1966; You Silvery Lady, You).

Bibliography: Battaglia, Otto Forst de, "Franz Theodor Csokor," *Frankfurter Hefte*, 1953. Bithell, Jethro, in *German Life and Letters*, 1954–55, pp. 38–40. Parker, L. J., "Two Drama Trilogies of Franz Theodor Csokor," *The South Central Bulletin* 21 (1961):37–43. Werner, Alfred, in *German Life and Letters*, 1948–49, p. 211.

Lutz Weltmann

Theodor Däubler

Born 17 August 1876 at Trieste, then part of Austria; died 13 June 1934 at St. Blasien in the Black Forest. He always felt that fate had given his life a special meaning by allowing him to be born to German parents on the shores of the Mediterranean. It made him, he said, "the most Mediterranean of German poets." When, at the age of eleven, he first saw neighboring Venice with astonished and delighted eyes, he declared it the capital of his dream realm, which, besides Italy, soon came to encompass the Hellenic parts of the old Venetian empire. But Italy remained the country, destined to be the center of his life and work: "It was at the foot of Vesuvius that I began writing *Das Nordlicht* in the German tongue." This was in 1898, when Däubler was twenty-two years old.

Das Nordlicht, one of the longest poems in world literature, came into being and unfolded over a period of twelve years spent wandering through Italy, France, and Germany—years that were as lacking in material rewards as they were rich in spiritual ones. Däubler completed *Das Nordlicht* only in 1910, after he had found friendly help and inner peace in the circle around the sculptor Paul Peterich at Florence. Soon afterward it was published in a subscription edition, thanks to the good offices of Däubler's friend Möller van den Bruck. To the end of his life Däubler complained bitterly, and sometimes heartrendingly, that virtually no one had read the whole of *Das Nordlicht*, let alone understood it. His later, far less voluminous works did give him access to a somewhat wider circle of readers.

After 1910, two more poetic works "erupted" (to use an expression from Däubler) in Italy; namely, *Hesperien* (1915) and *Hymne an Italien* (1916). Again on the shores of the Mediterranean, in the then newly discovered Tuscan seaside resort Forte dei Marmi, he wrote, for the first time, poetry in prose—autobiographical fragments published in 1914 under the title *Wir wollen nicht verweilen*. Forced by World War I to leave Italy, he went to live both in Berlin and Dresden.

In 1916 Däubler published *Der neue Standpunkt*, the first important book in German on the revolution in the arts at that time. Another book of poems, *Der sternhelle Weg* (1915), was followed in

1916 by a selection entitled *Das Sternenkind*, which was published as one of the short volumes of the "Inselbücherei" and was the only one of his works to reach a relatively wide public. A second, enlarged edition of *Das Nordlicht* that Däubler had begun in 1919 at Geneva was completed in 1921 on the island of Ithaca, where he was staying as the guest of Greek friends. He continued living in Greece until 1926, mostly in Athens, and from this base he traveled to Istanbul, Asia Minor, Palestine, and Egypt.

Däubler's six years in Greece proved to be the second of his major creative periods. Together with friends he rented a small house at Kalamaki, the ancient Halimus, on the Attic coast, and living there in very modest comfort during the years 1922–23, he wrote more poems, collected in the two volumes *Päan und Dithyrambos* (1924) and *Attische Sonette* (1924). But Däubler's main preoccupation of those years was working on what he called "my Greece book," in which he meant to "venture on a new debate with antiquity." This he did not accomplish, nor did he ever complete the book, though fairly lengthy fragments of it were published. Two of the fragments, *Der heilige Berg Athos* and *Sparta*, appeared in 1923 in book form, and the long essay *Delos* (about Apollo as the patron divinity of the Western world) was printed in 1925 in *Deutsche Rundschau*. Numerous other pieces on Greek and Hellenic themes, some of them important and exquisite, others on a smaller scale and in a lighter, journalistic vein—ones that could hardly have been written for inclusion in the planned book—were published posthumously by Max Sidow in a volume entitled *Griechenland*. But this volume did not appear until 1946, after the fall of the Nazi regime, which had no use for Däubler's works and had prevented earlier publication.

During his years in Greece, Däubler also began working on a third version of *Das Nordlicht*. This is the so-called Athens edition, which he completed in 1930 during a journey to France. It has never been published, and the manuscript is now in the Goethe and Schiller Archive at Weimar.

In 1932 Däubler was found to be suffering from severe tuberculosis. In August 1933 he was taken to a sanatorium at St. Blasien in the Black Forest, where his condition rapidly deteriorated. It did not help that he was deeply affected by the political catastrophe that had overtaken Germany—one which he had indeed predicted years before. He breathed his last on the evening of 13 June 1934, "firm in the evangelical Christian faith," as he said in his will, written during the last days of his life.

Däubler led a restless, sometimes adventurous life, a life always difficult and often harsh, but brimful of the highest spiritual joys, which he owed above all to his alert perception and also to his enthusiasm and warm vitality. These qualities gripped his friends and continued to quicken them well after his death. Däubler was romantic in the highest degree and at the same time passionately devoted to classic art; he was a troubadour of Mediterranean beauty and the Greek gods, yet a pioneer of the most daring modernity. As such he did not fit in any way into the intellectual and artistic trends of the Germany of his time, and he found himself isolated and lonely.

Däubler is counted among the expressionists but with little justification. He praised and championed expressionism in the visual arts, but as a poet he went an entirely different direction: the ways of the classical as well as the romantic. In matters of language, he was above all a disciple of Rimbaud, of whose poem *Le Bateau Ivre* he did an excellent translation. The content of his poetry hardly ever owes anything to his own time. He had a most lively mind, and, to the extent that he took his subject matter from literary sources—which he drew on far less than on landscapes, myth, and the visual arts—he took it from the Greeks, the *Divine Comedy*, the second part of *Faust*, Byron, and Victor Hugo. By language he was a German poet, but at the same time a European, and this more than almost anybody else. Even in his language he trespassed beyond the national frontiers, for the dominant sound elements in the music of his language are Romance, especially Italian, cadences. For this reason, even those among his German contemporaries who admired him often felt him to be alien. This impression is obvious even in what his close friend Barlach wrote about him. Italians and Greeks, on the other hand, who did not know a word of German, always felt Däubler to be one of themselves.

The last line of *Das Nordlicht* reads: "The spirit reconciles and drowns the sounds of the world." Basing his ideas on this line, Carl Schmitt interpreted the poem in the sense that for Däubler the aurora borealis was the earthly witness and guarantor of mankind's salvation by the spirit. This is not an idea but an image. The northern lights, so Schmitt writes in an interpretation prefacing the Geneva edition, are "autobiographical in a symbolical sense." Däubler intensified this poetic autobiography into a cosmological myth rooted partly in the myths of pre-Christian peoples and in Christianity and partly in his own childhood, to which, with his characteristic absolute innocence—perhaps the most powerful of his creative forces—he always returned whenever he was in the throes of one of his poetic "eruptions."

Däubler's art of poetry is above all an art of rhyming. Before rhyme lost all meaning for many poets, or indeed became, as with some of the more recent critics, the subject of a stupid (because veristic and reactionary) condemnation, Däubler once more reveled in rhyme, as hardly any great poet has done since Goethe. He found his rhymes with the troubadour's unfailing certainty, sought out and enjoyed rare ones, but did not scorn the hackneyed ones either. He could never have enough rhymes, sometimes repeating a rhyme eight or even ten times, and he mastered both the loose and the strict rhyme forms such as the sonnet, of which he was fond, the terza rima, and the ottava rima. Unrhymed verse is rare in Däubler, and even when used, it always has a strong melody. He liked internal rhymes; even more he liked alliteration. The underlying note of Däubler's verse is rounded, ceremonious or at least festive, and its tone color always unmistakably that of the Romance languages. The stormy flow of his language is often interrupted by little metric breaks, discords, jokes, indeed naughtiness, by playful turns and drollery; some satyr element in his nature comes to full life, but is ultimately always sublimated.

Das Nordlicht is the work of Däubler's youth and at the same time his main work. As such it contains all the essential elements of form, kinds of imagery, and themes of his poetry, above all the whole range of Mediterranean motifs, taken from both landscape and myth. In this respect, the so-called *Symphonie*—namely, the *Hesperien* series of hymns, written in 1914 at Florence, and the *Hymne an Italien*, written about the same time—are in every way akin to *Das Nordlicht*, while the poems in *Der sternhelle Weg* (written between 1908 and 1915) include some shorter, songlike poems on non-Mediterranean subjects. This is perhaps why they have become relatively more popular. When Däubler gave a reading, the public always wanted to hear such poems as *Die Fichte, Die Buchen, Katzen, Schwäbische Madonna, Schnee,* or *Mittag.*

The poems of Däubler's years in Greece, however, are again wholly Mediterranean creations, except that the Hesperian motifs are replaced by Hellenic ones. Dominant among them are the myths that, in accordance with Däubler's most powerful impression of Greece, penetrate the landscape and hence all the scenic metaphors, leading to new, always astonishing, and sometimes baroque elaborations of imagery. Both *Attische Sonette* and the sequence *Päan und Dithyrambos,* subtitled *Phantasmagorie,* show Däubler at the age of almost fifty following the same poetic paths that the young man took when he intoned the first songs of *Das Nordlicht* at the foot of Vesuvius; the sole difference is that these paths in the meantime led him from

Italy to Greece. When staying at Askra on Helicon, Däubler once said: "Hesiod is taught by the Muses, the sweet springs; I by the bitter ones, the Nereids. What I have written is the melody of the Mediterranean." It lingers on in Däubler's poems as in sea shells.

Works: *Das Nordlicht* (3 vols., 1910; rev. ed., 2 vols., 1921; Aurora Borealis); *Ode und Gesänge* (1913; Ode and Hymns); *Wir wollen nicht verweilen* (1914; We Do Not Want to Linger); *Hesperien* (1915; Hesperia); *Der sternhelle Weg* (1915; The Starlit Way); *Hymne an Italien* (1916; Hymn to Italy); *Mit silberner Sichel* (1916; With a Silver Sickle); *Der neue Standpunkt* (1916; The New Point of View); *Das Sternenkind* (1916; The Star Child); *Lucidarum in arte musicae* (1917); *Im Kampf um die moderne Kunst* (1919; Struggle for Modern Art); *Die Treppe zum Nordlicht* (1920; Stairs to the Northern Light); *Perlen von Venedig* (1921; Pearls of Venice); *Der heilige Berg Athos* (1923; The Holy Mountain of Athos); *Sparta* (1923); *Päan und Dithyrambos* (1924; Paean and Dithyramb); *Attische Sonette* (1924; Attic Sonnets); *Der Schatz der Insel* (1925; The Treasure of the Isle); *Bestrickungen* (1927; Enthrallments); *L'Africana* (1928); *Der Fischzug* (1930; The Catch); *Der Marmorbruch* (1930; The Marble Quarry); *Die Göttin mit der Fackel* (1931; The Goddess with the Torch); *Can Grande della Scala* (1932); *Heimgang der Stämme* (1942; Homecoming of the Tribes); *Hades* (1943); *Gleichgewicht im Kosmos* (1943; Balance in the Universe); *Griechenland* (1946; Greece); *Dichtungen und Schriften* (ed. F. Kemp, 1956; Poems and Prose).

Bibliography: Bithell, Jethro, *Modern German Literature 1880–1950*, pp. 248–50, 1959. Fontana, Oskar Maurus, in *Wort und Wahrheit*, 1957. Helwig, W., "Das letzte Bekenntnis," *Akzente* 11 (1964):280–87. Müller, Joachim, *Die Akte Däubler*, 1967. Ulbricht, H., *Theodor Däubler: Eine Einführung in sein Werk und eine Auswahl*, 1951.

Eckart Peterich

Heimito von Doderer

Born 5 September 1896 at Weidlingau, near Vienna, into a family with roots not only in Austria but also in Germany, France, and Hungary (distantly related to Lenau). His father made a name building mountain railways. From 1916 to 1920, Doderer was a prisoner of war in Siberia, the decisive experience of his youth, which awakened the writer in him. After his return he studied history in Vienna and received his Ph.D. in 1925. His first book, a volume of poems entitled *Gassen und Landschaft*, appeared in 1923. He had to interrupt his writing when he was called up for military service in World War II, and served in the army from 1940 to 1945. Returning to his home in Vienna after the war, he not only took up his literary work again but also his historical studies, and in 1950 he became a member of the select Institute for Historical Research. After an early marriage that soon ended in divorce, Doderer married again in 1952. His second wife was a relative of the Bavarian writer Ludwig Thoma. Thereafter he lived alternately in Vienna and at Landshut until his death in Vienna on 23 December 1966.

Doderer's early publications enjoyed no lasting success, perhaps because they were few and appeared at irregular intervals and also because he had little contact with the more influential writers of the interwar period. Even at that time, however, and until the end of his life, he was an admiring, but not uncritical friend of the slightly older writer and painter Albert Paris Gütersloh: their fundamental artistic principles were almost identical, even in their wording. It was during this period of isolation that Doderer, in 1931, began working on *Die Dämonen*, a novel in the Dostoyevski manner. The first of the three parts was ready by 1937 but was held back by the author and publisher in view of the political situation in Germany. Instead, there appeared in 1938 the psychological crime novel, *Ein Mord, den jeder begeht*. Though somewhat labored in composition, this novel is masterly in parts, especially as regards the incomparable description of a man's youth (to some extent, no doubt, Doderer's own). Soon afterward, in 1940, he published the baroque novel *Ein Umweg*.

Doderer was fifty-five, however, before his novel *Die Strudlhofstiege* (1951) achieved a breakthrough with the critics and the public. Thereafter, he consolidated his position as a narrative writer by a few smaller, though in part highly important works and, at long last, after twenty-five years of work, by the great novel *Die Dämonen* (1956). In 1958 he was awarded the Great Austrian State Prize. There followed a surprise for his readers with the novel *Die Merowinger, oder Die totale Familie* (1962), a bizarre, humorous, and supremely authoritative analysis of contemporary society. In 1963 Doderer published *Die Wasserfälle von Slunj*, the first part of his planned but uncompleted tetralogy, *Roman No. 7*. The tetralogy was conceived in the grand manner and was to describe what "happened despite history" during the period between 1880 and 1960. In addition to fourteen narrative works (and a few essays), Doderer published poems that bear witness less to a lyrical than to an epigrammatical talent.

Doderer's true qualities became apparent only in the works of the second half of his life, beginning with *Ein Mord, den jeder begeht* and *Ein Umweg*. The very title of the latter (a detour) suggests the characteristic feature of Doderer's life and writing. He was really concerned with only one theme, that of humanization by way of detours, and this theme steadily grew with him, and he with it. The bitter lesson that life taught him, that "we never manage to achieve what we really mean to," became an artistic principle. Help in life (help for one's own as well as for the reader's life) can be achieved only by the detour of art:

> For already we had made the discovery of paramount importance for this our life, which was a discovery in the mechanics of the mind no less than of external events—that is, the indirect path, the method of adapting thought to life, as diametrically opposed to the universal and ever-renewed attempts to adapt life to thought, all these attempts being doomed to end up in doctrinairism, reforming mania, and eventually the totalitarian state. . . . Already we have discovered how much more important it is to see what is than to state what should be; for, first of all, the latter is possible, generally speaking, only by absolutization, and secondly it leads to the refusal of apperception (of what actually is)—that is, to that devastating form of modern stupidity that as of now simply rules out any agreement even on the simplest things—by means of what we call our convictions. (1953)

This is an eminently political attitude, but Doderer exemplifies it not by events that are reported (disregarding the blood-stained 15 July 1927 in *Die Dämonen*), but in individuals. He does so because there is always a correspondence, or at least a correlation, between what goes on inside people and what goes on outside them, and because what subsequently becomes known as history must first have happened in human hearts. From *Ein Mord, den jeder begeht* onward, no single book of Doderer's appeared in which the characters fail to be involved in such a "second reality" and either perish in it or else, at the end of a salutary detour, arrive at goals of which they have hardly dared to dream.

As for the object of his work, Doderer ranks supreme for the most precise description of Vienna during the first third of this century, ranging from the nobility's town houses to assignation hotels, from the boardroom of a bank to the café in the outskirts, from the tennis court to the sewage system—and all that from personal experience. He depicts not merely one class or group or clique, but society as a whole. In *Ein Umweg* and in *Das letzte Abenteuer* (1953), Doderer delved further back into the past, in the one case to the end of the Thirty Years' War and in the other to a period when there were still not only knights but also dragons. *Die Merowinger, oder Die totale Familie,* on the other hand, constitutes a crowning synthesis in this respect: the early Middle Ages and the present are merged precisely because it is not the subject matter that counts, but form as "the entelechy of all content."

As regards technique, Doderer belongs to the tradition of naturalism (though without affinity to its views). It is self-evident for him that a novel should have a plot, and this, too, rests on his awareness of the correspondence between what happens inside and outside an individual. A person's external fate—such as being run over and losing a leg, or coming into an inheritance, or having to serve in the war—is no accident, nor is it anything that can be discarded or ignored at one's discretion or inwardly opposed. On the contrary, to be "sound of fate," man must inwardly agree to his external fate; he must incorporate it, as it were.

Just as there is no solely external or solely internal life, so Doderer admits of no novel that is either solely external or solely internal; hence his critical dissociation on the one hand from mere eyewitness reporting, from the novel about current events, from "journalism in book form," and on the other hand from such writers as James Joyce and Robert Musil. In contrast to Musil, Doderer is a precise architect who literally plans his novels on the drawing board (and, thanks to the principles so laid down, can subsequently let himself go on spinning his tale). The reader, to be sure, is unaware of the calculation hidden in colorful description and a multiplicity of strands of action, which, seemingly impossible to disentangle, are suddenly woven into an artful pattern. What has been said about many an

Austrian writer, is, therefore, really true of Doderer; namely, that in him the baroque still lives on.

In a critical appreciation of Doderer's works the topmost rank will no doubt be accorded to the group made up of *Die erleuchteten Fenster, oder Die Menschwerdung des Amtsrates Julius Zihal* (1950), *Die Strudlhofstiege*, and *Die Dämonen*. Together, these amount to the first really universal picture of Vienna, illuminated by the signs of the times—and this applies to more than just the brilliant description in *Die Dämonen* of the fire that destroyed the Palace of Justice in 1927. *Die Dämonen* is the greatest novel of the three, written in a dry, epigrammatic style in comparison with the exuberance of *Die Strudlhofstiege*, while *Der Menschwerdung des Amstrates Julius Zihal* is a sort of witty and humorous private footnote of the author's to the greater whole.

After the twenty-five hundred pages of *Die Dämonen*, Doderer demonstrated, in *Die Posaunen von Jericho* (1958), how to make do with the minute space of a mere sixty pages by a wholly successful combination of descriptive lingering over the subject and the unresting advance of the action. In the story *Das letzte Abenteuer* he set down his confession as a humane being.

In *Die Merowinger, oder Die totale Familie* Doderer is shown at the height of his mastery of language. Through the often grisly humor of the book he expresses, without laboring the point, the essence of his philosophy—adapting thought to life rather than life to thought. In *Die Wasserfälle von Slunj* this philosophy is presented in a mixture of simplicity and mastery comparable only with Stifter.

Like Jean Paul, Doderer is a writer who arouses either glowing admiration or cold rejection, but when everything is said for and against his work, there is no denying the author's immense psychological gifts, even though he himself rated psychology merely as one among several ancillary sciences. The novelist, Doderer once said, is essentially not a psychologist but a "fatologist." It is only thereby that his art, in clear contrast to the 19th-century psychological novel, reaches the highest level of which it is capable and becomes "the science of life."

Works: *Gassen und Landschaft* (1923; Little Streets and Open Country); *Die Bresche: Ein Vorgang in 24 Stunden* (1924; The Breach: Proceedings in 24 Hours); *Der Fall Gütersloh: Ein Schicksal und seine Deutung* (1930; The Gütersloh Case: Its Destiny and Its Interpretation); *Das Geheimnis des Reichs: Ein Roman aus dem russischen Bürgerkrieg* (1930; The Secret of the Realm: A Novel of the Russian Civil War); *Ein Mord,* *den jeder begeht* (1938; Eng. tr., Everyman a Murderer, 1964); *Ein Umweg* (1940; A Detour); *Die erleuchteten Fenster, oder Die Menschwerdung des Amtstrates Julius Zihal* (1950; Light in the Windows, or the Humanization of Magistrate Julius Zihal); *Die Strudlhofstiege* (1951; Teh Strudlhof Stairway); *Das letzte Abenteuer* (1953; The Last Adventure); *Die Dämonen* (1956; Eng. tr., The Demons, 1961); *Ein Weg im Dunkeln* (1957; A Way in the Dark); *Die Posaunen von Jericho* (1958; The Trumpets of Jericho); *Grundlagen und Funktionen des Romans* (1959; The Underlying Principles and Functions of the Novel); *Die Peinigung der Lederbeutelchen* (1959; The Torment of Little Leather Purses); *Der Konservative* (1959; The Conservative); *Wege und Umwege* (1960; Ways and Detours); *Die Merowinger, oder Die totale Familie* (1962; The Merowingians, or the Total Family); *Die Wasserfälle of Slunj* (1963; Eng. tr., Waterfalls of Slunj, 1966; part I of the uncompleted tetralogy *Roman No. 7* [Novel No. 7]); *Tangenten* (1964; Tangents); *Unter schwarzen Sternen* (1966; Under Black Stars); *Meine neunzehn Lebensläufe und neun andere Geschichten* (1966; My Nineteen Lives, and Nine Other Stories); *Der Grenzwald* (1967; The Border Forest; part II of the uncompleted tetralogy *Roman No. 7*); *Frühe Prose* (1968; Early Prose); *Repertorium* (1969; Repertory).

Bibliography: Blauhut, R., *Österreichische Novellistik des 20. Jahrhunderts*, pp. 236–44, 1966. Csokor, Franz Theodor, in *German Life and Letters*, 1954–55. Eisenreich, H., *Reaktionen*, pp. 166–214, 1964. Hamburger, M., *From Prophecy to Exorcism*, pp. 131–39, 1965. Hatfield, H., "Vitality and Tradition," *Monatshefte* 47 (January 1955):19–25. Horst, Karl August, in *Books Abroad*, 1963. Ivask, Ivar, "Heimito von Doderer's *Die Dämonen*," *Books Abroad* 31 (Fall 1957):363–65; also "Poet of the Vibrant Equilibrium," *Books Abroad* 40 (Fall 1966):415–18; and in *Wisconsin Studies in Contemporary Literature*, 1967. Jones, D. L., "Proust and Doderer: Themes and Techniques," *Books Abroad* 37 (Winter 1963):12–15. Morton, F., "For a Literary Epic the Place Is Vienna," *New York Times*, 24 September 1961. Politzer, H., "Realismus und Realität in Heimito von Doderers *Posaunen von Jericho*," *Germanic Review* 38 (January 1963): 37–51. Schoolfield, George C., in *German Quarterly*, 1953. Waidson, H. M, "Heimito von Doderer's *Demons*," *German Life and Letters* 11 (April 1958):214–24. Winter, H. von, "Heimito von Doderer," *Wort in der Zeit* 1 (July 1955):3–6.

Herbert Eisenreich

Marie von Ebner-Eschenbach

Marie Freifrau von Ebner-Eschenbach was born on 13 September 1830, at Zdislawitz Castle near Kremsier (now Kroměříž), in Moravia; she died on 12 March 1916, at Zdislawitz Castle. One of the most significant prose writers of the era of Franz Joseph I (her life span, 1830–1916, was the same as the emperor's). Her family background was typically Austrian in that it was greatly diversified: her father, Count Dubsky, descended from the Catholic Czech aristocracy, her mother from a Protestant German family; her upbringing was multilingual (Czech, French, and German). At eighteen she married her cousin, Moritz Freiherr von Ebner-Eschenbach, a high-ranking officer, fifteen years her senior. In 1910 Marie von Ebner-Eschenbach was awarded an honorary doctorate from the University of Vienna, the first woman to receive this honor. She died during the war that was to put an end to the world to which she had given form in her work.

Marie von Ebner-Eschenbach's talents matured slowly. Performances at the Burgtheater (of Friedrich Schiller's works) fired her idealism, and like Ferdinand von Saar and Conrad Ferdinand Meyer, she entertained vain hopes of becoming a great dramatist. Instead, she found her voice as a prose writer. Recognition came slowly; she was fifty when, with the publication of *Lotti, die Uhrmacherin* in the magazine *Die deutsche Rundschau* in 1881, she gained her first public acclaim. She greatly admired Gottfried Keller but learned most from Ivan Turgenev. She followed the works of the young generation with detached interest.

The best introduction to Marie von Ebner-Eschenbach's personality as a writer are her childhood memories—*Meine Kinderjahre* (1906), vivid sketches of her early life at Zdislawitz Castle, which demonstrate her skill in characterization and her sense of humor—and her aphorisms, which are the purest expression of her didactic intent, her deep moral sense, her tolerance, and her insight into human nature and into her own time.

The title *Dorf- und Schloßgeschichten* (1883; Tales of Village and Manor) suggests the social range and tensions in most of Marie von Ebner-Eschenbach's work. The emphasis in this collection is on the typical Austrian upper classes—the high-ranking civil servants and officers, the aristocrats in their Vienna drawing rooms and on their country estates—and on the peasants. The middle class is represented in some of her finest works: for example, *Wieder die Alte* (1886) and *Der Vorzugsschüler* (1898). The setting is Vienna and non-German-speaking parts of the monarchy, especially Moravia. (With works such as *Mašlans Frau* in 1897, she originated the stories of Moravian village life that were to be continued by Jakob Julius David and, with psychoanalytic emphasis, by Oskar Jellinek.) Marie von Ebner-Eschenbach's regionalism was never a limitation.

In her work, most of which was written after 1870, we find various modifications of 19th-century realism. *Das Gemeindekind* (1887), a novel in which she attempts to disprove the power of heredity and environment, is typical of much of her work and of what Saar nostalgically called the literature of "Real-Idealismus." Yet in the same work the treatment of human misery and baseness is as stark as any naturalist's. Her realism is primarily concerned with states of mind—"Not what we experience but how we experience determines our lives."

Apart from *Das Schädliche* (1894), which deals with the nature of evil, Marie von Ebner-Eschenbach's work does not treat metaphysical questions. (*Glaubenslos?*, which deals with a religious theme, is one of her weakest works.) Marie von Ebner-Eschenbach's purpose in writing was "to describe human beings above all, real people." She created this very human world with the acute observation and psychological insight gained in a socially rich life, with tolerance and understanding, and, significantly, with humor. Her humor could be gentle and whimsical (*e.g., Die Kapitalistinnen*, 1889), goodnaturedly satirical (*Die Freiherren von Gemperlein*, 1878), or ironical (*Komtesse Muschi*, 1884). That her tolerance was not permissiveness is evident from the bitter sarcasm with which she castigated prejudice and hypocrisy. Her loving description of what is often a quite ordinary life lived by ordinary people and her compassion for every living creature point to the root of her realism: humility and reverence for life ("The closer I approach old age, the deeper my veneration becomes for what is"). Some of her best-known stories, such as *Krambambuli* (1886) and *Die Spitzin* (1901), deal with the suffering of animals.

Basic human relationships were the chief concern of Marie von Ebner-Eschenbach, and love and marriage play an important role in her work. Though not always immune to the weaknesses of "family fiction"—sentimentality, melodrama, "idyllic" sweetness—she avoids simple solutions ("The simplest person is still a most complex being").

The happiness her characters attain is not easily won; often only after long years of frustration and lost illusions (*Lotti, die Uhrmacherin*; *Rittmeister Brand*, 1896). Some works trace the slow, painful course from pride to humility: in *Der Kreisphysikus* (1886) an embittered Jewish doctor is transformed into a true Samaritan during the Galician revolt of 1846, and a radical Christian agitator for drastic social change resigns himself to helping people in his immediate small circle. Similarly, in *Glaubenslos?* (1893) a priest who has suffered self-torturing doubts and speculations renounces a career as church dignitary for the life of a village priest. In *Oversberg* (1891) resignation reaches almost saintly self-sacrifice. Works like these bring to mind the inner radiance of Adalbert Stifter's *Kalkstein*, and they also remind us of Franz Grillparzer's *Der arme Spielmann*.

The many examples of failure to attain happiness, of bitter estrangement between people (the tyrannical, even sadistic, father and husband is a recurring figure), and of isolation show Marie von Ebner-Eschenbach's deep concern with loneliness. Not always is resignation blessed through meaningful sacrifice, as it is in *Wieder die Alte*. In *Das tägliche Leben* (1910), one of her most bitter comments on family life, years of suffering behind a façade of contentment end in a catastrophe, and in *Der Vorzugsschüler* a boy is driven to suicide by an overambitious father.

Marie von Ebner-Eschenbach's sense of justice and her compassion made her a keen social critic. She never, however, favored radical solutions. Nor did she attack the existing order but rather individuals who betray their responsibilities. She ridiculed aristocrats for their "untrained brains" and exposed what E. M. Forster was to term "the undeveloped hearts" of the ruling classes, their inability to treat their inferiors as human beings. Her indignation at man's cruelty to man found its most bitterly ironic expression in *Er läßt die Hand küssen* (1886), in which brutality and idyllic sentimentality are juxtaposed. In stories such as *Der Muff* (1888) and *Bettelbriefe* (1891), she revealed the problematical nature of charity: "Many a person thinks he has a good heart when in reality he only has weak nerves."

Marie von Ebner-Eschenbach's social criticism was not restricted to the nobility and the clergy when they sacrificed a human being to convention and dogma. In *Das Gemeindekind* the brutality of the poor to the poor and the hardness of small-property owners toward the have-nots were drawn with unrelenting realism; she knew the country folk too well to idealize them. She was profoundly concerned with all inhuman barriers that people of any class set up between each other. Her warnings and unsentimental pleas for a sane humanism and social responsibility still have validity for our time: "We are in deadly fear that the love of neighbor might spread too far, and we erect barriers against it—the nationalities."—"We live in an especially instructive age. Never before has man been warned more distinctly: Don't be selfish—if for no nobler reason than that of self-preservation. . . . All (but the utterly blind) will find that because of their neighbor's empty plate they cannot enjoy their meal—the good ones out of a sense of justice, the cowards out of fear."

Beneath the apparently fixed world in Marie von Ebner-Eschenbach's work, we sense the undercurrents of a time in transition, a social order that is outliving itself. Her criticism shows how questionable institutions and conventional concepts (of marriage, of family life) had become to her. Her stories about artists (all are stories about failure), for example, *Ein Spätgeborener* (1875) and *Verschollen* (1897), not only suggest an uncertainty about her own work but also an awareness of the tiredness of a whole culture. Though she watched the final decline of the aristocracy, her own class, with regret, her wise open-mindedness made it possible for her to accept, even to welcome, change: "I believe that all of us, consciously or unconsciously, are at work compiling the alphabet of a new language of the morality of the future. In that language much of what is now called a noble sacrifice will be called a crime."

Marie von Ebner-Eschenbach's work escapes easy labeling. Much has been made of her compassion, her all-embracing motherliness. But to see her only as a writer with a heart is to overlook the most precious gifts that characterize her best work: a warm rationality; a sober detachment evident in a lucid, unadorned style; a refreshing matter-of-factness; and irony.

Wide and varied as the social and psychological spectrum of Marie von Ebner-Eschenbach's work is, the large epic scope was not at her command. Her longest works are among her less successful; usually those that go beyond single, linear plots are marred by stereotyped secondary characters and situations: *Unsühnbar* is an example of this, or the final scene in *Božena* (1876), which is sheer melodrama.

Like Saar and Arthur Schnitzler, Marie von Ebner-Eschenbach was a master of the short narrative form. Her apprenticeship as a dramatist bore fruit in her novellas, particularly in the dialogue, formally perhaps the most outstanding feature of her work. Though not an innovator in the genre of the novella, she was a master of variation of structure and technique to the point of being overingenious. Her work shows a striking preference for antithetical situations, parallelisms and reversals in plot, and constellation of characters. She never intrudes as a writer; she shows great skill in the use of the frame story (for example, in *Oversberg*) and of techniques that indirectly reveal states of mind: there are stories comprised of diary entries, of letters, (one even of postcards). Her stories often culminate in surprise endings that reveal her values with special poignancy: *Die Poesie des Unbewußten* (1881), *Erste Trennung* (1915), *Uneröffnet zu verbrennen* (1901). That Marie von Ebner-Eschenbach was one of the early masters in the short-story genre, and thus went beyond the traditional 19th-century forms of fiction, has not yet been fully recognized.

Works: *Erzählungen* (1875; Tales); *Božena* (1876); *Aphorismen* (1880; Eng. tr., Aphorisms, 1883); *Neue Erzählungen* (1881; New Tales; includes *Lotti, die Uhrmacherin* [Lotti, the Watchmaker]); *Dorf- und Schloßgeschichten* (1883; Tales of Village and Manor); *Zwei Komtessen* (1885; Eng. tr., The Two Countesses, 1893); *Neue Dorf- und Schloßgeschichten* (1886); *Krambambuli* (1886; Eng. tr., 1915); *Der Kreisphysikus* (1886; Eng. tr., The District Doctor, 1915); *Das Gemeindekind* (1887; Eng. tr., The Child of the Parish, 1893); *Miterlebtes* (1889; Experiences); *Unsühnbar* (1890; Eng. tr., Beyond Atonement, 1892); *Drei Novellen* (1892; Three Novellas); *Parabeln, Märchen und Gedichte* (1892; Parables, Fairy Tales, and Poems); *Glaubenslos?* (1893; Without a Creed?); *Gesammelte Werke* (10 vols., 1893–1911; Collected Works); *Das Schädliche. Die Totenwacht* 1894; Harmfulness. Death Watch); *Rittmeister Brand* (1896; Eng. tr., A Man of the World, 1912); *Alte Schule* 1897; Old School); *Aus Spätherbsttagen* (2 vols., 1901; From Late Autumn Days); *Agave* (1903); *Die arme Kleine* (1903; The Poor Little One); *Meine Kinderjahre* (1906; My Childhood Years); *Altweibersommer* (1909; Indian Summer); *Genrebilder* (1910; Genre Pictures); *Stille Welt* (1915; Silent World); *Meine Erinnerungen an Grillparzer* (1916; My Memories of Grillparzer); *Sämtliche Werke* (12 vols., 1928; Complete Works); *Weisheit des Herzens* (ed. H. Rieder, 1947; Wisdom of the Heart).

Bibliography: Bettelheim, Anton, *Marie Freifrau von Ebner-Eschenbach,* 1925. Bietak, W., "Marie von Ebner-Eschenbach," *Österreich in Geschichte und Literatur* 10 (1966). Hofmiller, Josef, "Marie von Ebner-Eschenbach," in *Letzte Versuche,* 1934. Martini, Fritz, *Deutsche Literatur im bürgerlichen Realismus,* pp. 481–98, 1964. Mühlberger, Josef, "Marie von Ebner-Eschenbach," in *Die großen Deutschen,* vol. 5, 1957. Sauer, August, *Marie Freifrau von Ebner-Eschenbach,* 1923.

Horst Jarka[▲]

Albert Ehrenstein

Born 23 December 1886 in Vienna, the son of a Hungarian couple. From the outset Albert Ehrenstein's life was one of poverty and loneliness. He grew up in the lower-middle-class narrowness of Ottakring, on the outskirts of Vienna. Many of his later stories reflect his unhappy youth. He studied history and philosophy, earning a doctorate in 1910.

Karl Kraus discovered Ehrenstein's gift as a writer and published his first melancholy poems and bizarre prose sketches in *Die Fackel*. In November 1911 Ehrenstein's first book, the tragicomic story *Tubutsch*, was published. *Tubutsch* created a sensation among the literary avant-garde and to this day has remained his best-known work. Oskar Kokoschka, who illustrated the book, brought its author into contact with Berlin and Herwarth Walden's review *Der Sturm*, to which Ehrenstein was soon to become a fairly frequent contributor.

Ehrenstein moved to Berlin and thereafter published creative and critical writings in nearly all the major democratic daily papers and, above all, in journals of the young, revolutionary generation of writers. He often became involved in feuds, in which pun-strewn pamphlets were his weapons. During World War I he lived temporarily in Switzerland. As a pacifist, he joined the circle around *Die Aktion* and *Die weißen Blätter* and made himself the spokesman of ardent accusation in the name of the "murdered brothers." His bitterness at the emergence of "Barbaropa" (barbarian Europe) and inner restlessness drove Ehrenstein into a life of fitful wandering in the 1920s. His travels took him to Africa and the Middle East and, allegedly, even as far as China, among other places. In 1932 he emigrated to Switzerland, and in 1941 to New York, where he died in poverty on 8 April 1950, after a long illness. He had published nothing after 1933.

What Ehrenstein shows himself most keenly aware of in his work is the transitoriness and senselessness of life, to the point of considering even death meaningless. A despairing, perpetual reoccurence of everything marks the monotony of life. The dominant moods are lament and cynical gaiety. His often parodistic form derives from a perplexed feeling of having outlived everything, such as is expressed by one of his characters—that is, to have been born with so penetrating a knowledge of things that the future has long become part of the past, that it has been lived through already. "I am weary of life and death"—such is the title of one of his poems. Erotic disappointment, which recurs so often as the theme of his works that it assumes a traumatic quality, increases his loathing of life. Human relationships are fragile and of no help, and God has forgotten men in their misery and loneliness.

Ehrenstein shows people at the mercy of the tritest of everyday conditions. In an illusionless close-up, things reveal how ugly and incoherent they are; they begin to grow grotesquely and ominously and threaten to monopolize the entire field of vision. Animals are compassionately seen as symbols: two flies that have fallen into the inkwell, the suicide of a tomcat (*Selbstmord eines Katers*, 1912), or a slaughtered rabbit oppress the soul more heavily than the so-called great destinies. This narrow world is confronted with an imaginary realm of myth and fairy tale. Poetic imagination soars into infinite dimensions of space and time. It encompasses the sun and the stars in a paradoxical "discreation" myth of birth and decline and conjures up the gods of Greece and the Orient in dreamlike or parodistic parables.

Ehrenstein achieved perfection in few of his poems, but many of them contain lines of strong, original imagery. Neologisms and bold word combinations, which lend expressiveness to his language, sometimes seem to derive from a mania for the most unexpected linguistic homologies and satirical punning. Friedrich Hölderlin's influence is unmistakable in the broad rhythms of Ehrenstein's hymns. Among his prose pieces, only *Zaubermärchen* (1919) makes any pretense at some sort of narrative continuity. In the largely autobiographical notes and sketches, *Bericht aus einem Tollhaus* (1919), every event floats on an undercurrent of sad or bizarrely humorous reflection. As a prose writer Ehrenstein may well have been influenced by Franz Kafka and by Rainer Maria Rilke's *Malte Laurids Brigge*.

What Ehrenstein writes is immediate confession, closely connected with the expressionist movement as regards means of expression. The two-thirds of his work written before 1917 is the more important part. On the whole his creative talent waned with the expressionist decade. By 1919 and 1920 he began collecting his output and revising it, but the many alterations do not indicate any process of maturing. During the 1920s, Ehrenstein occupied himself mainly with editorial work and with adaptations of Chinese poetry and novels.

Works: *Tubutsch* (1911); *Der Selbstmord eines Katers* (1912; Suicide of a Tomcat); *Die weiße Zeit* (1914; The White Time); *Der Mensch schreit* (1916; Man Screams); *Nicht da, nicht dort* (1916; Neither Here, nor There); *Die rote Zeit* (1917; The Red Time); *Eros* (1918); *Bericht aus einem Tollhaus* (1919; Report from a Madhouse); *Den ermordeten Brüdern* (1919; To Our Murdered Brothers); *Zaubermärchen* (1919; Magic Fairy Tales); *Die Gedichte* (1920; The Poems); *K. Kraus* (1920); *Die Nacht wird* (1920; The Night Is Coming); *Die Heimkehr des Falken* (1921; The Return of the Falcon); *Dem ewigen Olymp* (1921; To the Eternal Olympus); *Wien* (1921; Vienna); *Briefe an Gott* (1922; Letters to God); *Herbst* (1923; Autumn); *Menschen und Affen* (1926; Men and Apes); *Ritter des Todes* (1926; Knights of Death); *Räuber und Soldaten* (1927; Eng. tr., Robbers and Soldiers, 1929); *Mörder aus Gerechtigkeit* (1931; Murderer for Justice); *Mein Lied* (1931; My Song); *Gedichte und Prosa* (ed. K. Otten, 1961; Poems and Prose); *Ausgewählte Aufsätze* (ed. M. Y. Ben-gavriêl, 1961; Selected Essays); *Stimme über Barbaropa* (ed. J. Jahn, 1967; Voice about Barbaropa).

Bibliography: Ayscough, Florence, in *Saturday Review*, 17 August 1929. Ben-gavriêl, M. Y., ed., preface to *Albert Ehrenstein: Ausgewählte Aufsätze*, 1961. Otten, K., ed., preface to *Gedichte und Prosa*, 1961. Sokel, Walter H., *The Writer in Extremis*, 1958. On *Robbers and Soldiers*, in *New York Herald Tribune*, 9 June 1929, p. 18.

Günther Erken

Herbert Eisenreich

Born 7 February 1925 in Linz on the Danube, he grew up in Upper Austria and in Vienna. Called into the German army at the age of eighteen, Eisenreich was wounded and taken prisoner. After his release, he completed his secondary schooling in 1946. Studied German literature and language in Vienna for a short time, made a living with various jobs of no particular interest, and began to have his writings published. Established fairly close contacts with a group of Austrian writers and artists (Albert Paris Gütersloh, Heimito von Doderer, Wotruba, Qualtinger). Lived as a professional writer in Hamburg (1952–54), then in Stuttgart until 1956, and again in Vienna until 1958. He now lives in Sandl, in Upper Austria.

Eisenreich's first novel, *Auch in ihrer Sünde* (1953), established his reputation in literary circles as a writer with an original narrative style. The basic element of this style in novel writing is the "story," which, according to Eisenreich's definition, in his own handling "is distinguished from other narrative methods by the almost total absence of any object with recognizable natural features." The novel's characters share no common reality, and this is expressed in the labyrinthine fable that never allows the reader to deviate even a little from the carefully traced line of individual destinies. Connected with this principle is the relativization of the friend/foe relationship, the exchange of identities, the loss of personality—and all this in the concave mirror of total dissolution. *Auch in ihrer Sünde* is the negative projection of a conservative who measures distortion by means of a system that would do justice to human dignity.

The underlying mood of the short stories in *Böse schöne Welt* (1957) is one of bitterness in the face of ineluctable decay, mixed with the passionate but resigned wishful thought that "perhaps love will succeed in making the world as round as it should be." Looked at closely, so much that is destructive in the world today, that is vulgar, ephemeral, and futile, is revealed as the result of a break with a system—one it is the mission of modern man to reshape.

Wovon wir leben und woran wir sterben (radio play, 1955; in book form, 1964) exposes the emptiness of marital intimacy, and, with its dry disillusionment, is reminiscent of Alberto Moravia and the novels, largely in dialogue, of the English writer Henry Green.

Works: *Einladung, deutlich zu leben* (1951; Invitation to Live Distinctly); *Sebastian, oder Die kleine Chance und das große Risiko des Märtyrers* (1953; Sebastian, or The Small Chance and the Great Risk of the Martyr); *Auch in ihrer Sünde* (1953; Even in Their Sin); *Die Ketzer, oder Mehrere Arten, der Wahrheit behilflich zu sein* (1954; The Heretics, or Several Ways to Help the Truth); *Böse schöne Welt* (1957; Evil, Beautiful World); *Carnuntum* (1960); *Eheliches Spiel* (1960; Marital Play); *Große Welt auf kleinen Schienen* (1963; Big World on Narrow Rails); *Wovon wir leben und woran wir sterben* (1964; What We Live On and What We Die From); *Der Urgroßvater* (1964; The Great-Grandfather); *Reaktionen* (1964; Reactions); *Sozusagen Liebesgeschichten* (1965; Love Stories, So to Speak); *Ich im Auto* (1965; I in the Car); *Die Freunde meiner Frau* (1966; My Wife's Friends); *Das kleine Stifterbuch* (1967; The Little Stifter Book); *Ich im Auto* (1969; I in the Car).

Bibliography: Friedl, Hermann, "Herbert Eisenreich, oder Schreiben, um leben zu lernen," *Wort in der Zeit* 7, no. 8 (1961):6–12. Horst, Karl August, *Kritischer Führer durch die deutsche Literatur der Gegenwart*, pp. 205–206, 1962. Ivask, Ivar, in *Books Abroad*, 1968, p. 122. Schmidt-Dengler, Wendelin, "A Commentary on Herbert Eisenreich," *Dimension* 1 (1968):480–90.

Karl August Horst

Sigmund Freud

Sigmund Freud, the founder of psychoanalysis, was born on 6 May 1856 in Freiberg (now Příbor) in Moravia, the son of a textile merchant. In 1860 Freud's family moved to Vienna, where in 1873 Freud began the study of medicine. From 1876 to 1882 he worked at the Vienna Institute of Physiology and then took up his work in the General Hospital. In 1886 Freud was appointed lecturer in neuropathology, and following this he studied for a while under Charcot at the Salpêtrière hospital in Paris. In 1889 he studied hypnosis with Bernheim and Liebault. In 1898 he began writing *Die Traumdeutung* (1900). In 1909, together with Carl Gustav Jung, he gave a series of lectures at Clark University in Worcester, Massachusetts. In 1938 he emigrated to London where, on 23 September 1939, he died of a chronic illness.

Freud's place in the history of ideas and literature cannot be properly appreciated by considering only his immediate influence as a psychologist—his significance, say, for the later Thomas Mann or T. S. Eliot, and even more markedly for minor writers during the decades after World War I, from whom, it is true, Freud remained aloof. It is becoming increasingly clear that essential elements in the contemporary view of man and of consciousness can only be understood as a consequence of the unprecedented disillusionment of man about himself that Freud brought about. It becomes clear, too, that not only did the history of ideas in the late 19th and 20th centuries find in this pessimistic doctor one of its decisive pioneers and revolutionaries, but that it did so, not in spite of, but because of the claim of his theory to be science and nothing more.

The importance of Freud's thinking for civilization and for man's understanding of himself is attributable to his methodical approach. In it the last consequence of Cartesian dualism, we find the scarcely fathomable contradiction of the objectivization of personality realized. Subjectivity, which is the implicit condition of knowledge, is dissolved. This puts man's own existence scientifically at his disposal, or anyway will do so. This impasse is most evident in the epistemological extension that, in fact if not in intent, Freud gave in his later years to his theory of projection, which originally was restricted to clinical phenomena.

In principle this theory leaves no room for any "objective" criterion of knowledge that is not dependent on the unconscious. Thereby the theory cut the ground from under its own feet, a fate anticipated in Hegel's famous mockery of "psychological necessity." It must be emphasized, however, that this does not in any way diminish Freud's significance as a theoretician, as an interpreter of the automatic psychic processes and, beyond that, of the sexuality of early childhood, its genesis, and the influence of its traumata on the formation of neuroses in adult life. On the contrary, it greatly enhances Freud's significance, for it is only thanks to his work that the fundamental set of problems in question, which is essentially one for the anthropological sciences as a whole, has generally become recognized as such. As a result, of course, we are not only forced to distinguish more sharply between Freud the discoverer and Freud the theoretician, but we are also in duty bound to think through more radically than hitherto the problem of psychological objectivity.

This fundamental problem concerns the fate of psychoanalysis in the history of science rather than the revolutionary impulse of its original conception. The latter remains most intimately bound up with the emancipation of the human psyche as a pure natural being. It is only by considering the disrupted situation of the prevailing theory into which Freud's work burst that we can measure the historical importance of this emancipation, in its particular blend, so typical of Freud's period, of progressive and chthonic-vitalistic strains of thought.

On the one hand the psyche was considered as "object," as a purely physiological complex of functions, and thus as a field of physical investigation of the organic, to which it was causally reduced. On the other hand it was considered as "subject," as the quintessence of a theologically or metaphysically autonomous *a priori* freedom. Freud's achievement was that he defended the psyche, in its immediacy of self-knowledge, against the claims of natural science, and that he did so by subordinating it to scientific law—i.e., the determinist principle. Thus he sacrificed that very claim to freedom that was inherent in the concept of the psyche, that was in fact its essential tradition. In so doing, he caused the psyche for the first time to be understood as being also "nature." For this reason the psyche must necessarily be more than it knows itself to be.

Thus consciousness shrinks to a precarious surface reflex, to the purely controlling ego diplomatically mediating between the psyche and the "reality principle," while everything spontaneous, everything that truly stems from the psyche, is ruled by the obscure, purely "objective" operation of forces (which can, however, be rationally illuminated by psychoanalysis): that is, by the unconscious, blind id of the instincts and by the super-ego, which, equally unconscious, checks them. What is doubtful about this doctrine—*i.e.*, its too narrow conception of the conscious—derives from the uncritical concept of reality, the prejudiced character of the "reality principle."

It may be said of psychoanalysis as a whole that its epistemological approach could not remain limited to the purely clinical. Once the principle of "total psychic" determinism was established in such boundless form as was virtually forced upon Freud by the uncritical (because unphenomenological) concept of reality, that principle was bound to lead to the relativization of civilization and of the intellectual life as a whole—which Freud undertook in *Totem und Tabu* (1922), *Die Zukunft einer Illusion* (1927), and *Das Unbehagen in der Kultur* (1930). As Marx looked at man in his poverty, Freud looked at him in his weakness. This meant that while Freud himself was subjectively a fanatic for truth (which is what creates the paradox), the question he asked when faced by the claim of a different subjectivity that logic should always prevail was basically never, "Is that true?" but always "Why does he say that?" The break in the logic that nourished his psychologism, with its claim to the whole truth about man, was concealed, probably even from himself, by the exceptionally high degree of systematization in all his thinking. This was not something, as it were, acquired or forced upon his thought, but something inherent in it, even to the literary elements of his style, and it produced the famous lucidity of his diction, to which it lent a semblance of logic. Its condition was the tacit, probably "unconsciously" predetermined selection of only such empirical data as ever got into Freud's theoretical focus at all, because they fitted it and served his deductions, in fact or appearance.

As things are, it may be stated *theoretically* that it is not merely impossible so far to verify experimentally the fundamental hypotheses of psychoanalysis but that it is in principle impossible to do so at all. *Historically*, the corollary is that the decisive step beyond Freud came from phenomenology, in particular from the work of Ludwig Binswanger. Phenomenology admittedly owes much to Freud, but it provides a corrective to his theory, above all through an understanding of the epistemological problem that Freud's theory unintentionally bequeathed to the human consciousness. Phenomenology has critically examined the basic ideas of psychoanalysis, both as psychological doctrine and as therapeutic method—e.g., transference, resistance, rationalization, sublimation, repression—from the point of view of their ability to stand up to the test of anthropological phenomenology. The aim of such an examination is, theoretically, to construct a system of existential analytical rules that will serve as a critical regulative or psychoanalytical objectivism. In practice, the aim is to discover a methodical access to the healing of psychoses and of those neuroses which, as Freud himself admitted, are not accessible to psychoanalytic treatment. This failure, for ominously consequential reasons, resulted from the initial preoccupation of psychoanalysis with the special structure of the hysterical personality.

While the depth psychology that Freud created is developing into an anthropology freer from logical contradictions, it is becoming easier to distinguish the one-sidedness and limitations, as well as the human greatness, of Freud's subjectivity from the vast system of thought he developed, the influence of which, chiefly on the society and civilization of the United States, is far greater than can as yet be assessed. To understand this subjectivity, it is important first of all to take into account the determining influence of an underlying stream in German intellectual history of the 19th-century, from Schopenhauer's metaphysics of the will to Eduard von Hartmann's philosophy of the unconscious and Nietzsche's passionate desire to bring his unconscious drives into the open and to liberate himself from them. Secondly, there was the impulse of protest against the Viennese *fin-de-siècle* society of the 1890s that sprang from the quasi-puritanical spirit of Freud's Jewish family. Thirdly, there was the special masculinity of his character, which both marked and limited his understanding of the human in general. Finally, and this is a highly personal opinion, there was his extreme lack of musical sensibility, which at an early stage set all too narrow limits to his range of experience in culture and in personal life. But the liberating sincerity and power of his personality were more deeply felt precisely by those who absorbed his influence with greater critical detachment—as for instance by Franz Kafka and Jean Paul Sartre in literature and by Max Ernst in the plastic arts—than it was absorbed by some of those mentioned earlier. As one of mankind's great teachers, one of its enlighteners and emancipators, of the stamp and tradition of Jean-Jacques Rousseau, he will be remembered for what he himself understood his achievement to be and once tersely summed up to Ludwig Binswanger in these words: "Mankind knew well it had a mind. I had to show that it also had instincts."

Works: *Neue Vorlesungen über die Krankheit des Nervensystems, insbesondere der Hysterie* (1886; New Lectures on Diseases of the Nervous System, Especially Hysteria); *Die Suggestion und ihre Heilwirkung* (1888; Suggestion and Its Curative Effect); *Zur Auffassung der Aphasien*

Sigmund Freud

(1891; On the Understanding of Aphasias); *Neue Studien über Hypnotismus, Suggestion und Psychotherapie* (1892; New Studies on Hypnotism, Suggestion and Psychotherapy); *Poliklinische Vorträge* (1892; Policlinical Lectures); *Zur Kenntnis der cerebralen Diplegien des Kindesalters* (1893; Toward Knowledge of Cerebral Diplegias of Infancy); *Die infantile Cerebrallähmung* (1897; Infantile Cerebral Paralysis); *Die Traumdeutung* (1900; Am. tr., Dream Psychology, 1921; Brit. tr., The Interpretation of Dreams, 1913); *Über den Traum* (1901; Eng. tr., On Dreams, 1914); *Zur Psychopathologie des Alltagslebens* (1901; Eng. tr., Psychopathology of Everyday Life, 1914); *Drei Abhandlungen über Sexualtheorie* (1905; Eng. tr., Three Contributions on Theory of Sex, 1910); *Der Witz und seine Beziehung zum Unbewußten* (1905; Eng. tr., Wit and Its Relations to the Unconscious, 1916); *Bruchstücke einer Hysterie* (1906; Fragments of a Hysteria); *Sammlung kleiner Schriften zur Nervenlehre aus den Jahren 1893–1906* (5 vols., 1906/22; Collection of Short Writings on Neurology, from the Years 1893–1906); *Der Wahn und die Träume* (1907; Eng. tr., Delusion and Dreams, 1917); *Eine Kindheitserinnerung des Leonardo da Vinci* (1910; Eng. tr., Leonardo da Vinci: A Psychological Study of an Infantile Reminiscence, 1916); *Über Psychoanalyse* (1910; Eng. tr., A General Introduction to Psychoanalysis, 1927); *Zur Geschichte der psychoanalytischen Bewegung* (1914; On the History of the Psychoanalytical Movement); *Zeitgemäßes über Krieg und Frieden* (1915; Eng. tr., Reflections on War and Peace, 1918); *Vorlesungen zur Einführung in die Psychoanalyse* (3 vols., 1916–17; Eng. tr., An Introduction to Psychoanalysis, 1920); *Zur Psychoanalyse der Kriegsneurosen* (1919; On Psychoanalysis of War Neuroses); *Jenseits des Lustprinzips* (1921; Eng. tr., Beyond the Pleasure Principle, 1922); *Massenpsychologie und Ich-Analyse* (1921; Eng. tr., Group Psychology and the Analysis of the Ego., 1922); *Totem und Tabu* (1922; Eng. tr., Totem and Tabu, 1928); *Neue Folge der Vorlesungen zur Einführung in die Psychoanalyse* (1922; Eng. tr., New Introductory Lectures on Psychoanalysis, 1933); *Das Ich und das Es* (1923; Eng. tr., The Ego and the Id, 1927); *Eine Teufelsneurose im siebzehnten Jahrhundert* (1923: A Devil's Neurosis in the Seventeenth Century); *Zur Technik der Psychoanalyse und zur Metapsychologie* (1924; On the Technique of Psychoanalysis and on Metapsychology); *Psychoanalytische Studien an Werken der Dichtung und Kunst* (1924; Psychoanalytical Studies on Works of Literature and Art); *Neue Arbeiten zur ärztlichen Psychoanalyse* (1924; New Writings on Medical Psychoanalysis); *Beiträge zur Psychologie des Liebeslebens* (1924; Contributions to the Psychology of Sex Life); *Zur Einführung des Narzißmus* (1924; Introduction to the Problem of Narcism); *Gesammelte Schriften* (12 vols., 1924–34; Eng. tr., Collected Papers of S. F., 10 vols., 1924ff.); S. F.: *Autobiographie* (1925; Eng. tr., Autobiographical Study, 1935); *Die Frage der Laienanalyse* (1926; Eng. tr., The Problem of Lay-Analysis, 1927); *Hemmung, Symptom, Angst* (1926; Am. tr., The Problem of Anxiety, 1936; Brit. tr., Inhibitions, Symptoms, Anxiety, 1936); *Die*

Zukunft einer Illusion (1927; Eng. tr., The Future of an Illusion, 1927); *Dostojewski und die Vatertötung* (1928; Dostoyevski and Patricide); *Das Unbehagen in der Kultur* (1930; Eng. tr., Civilization and Its Discontent, 1930); *Kleine Schriften zur Sexualtheorie und zur Traumlehre* (1931; Short Papers on Sex Theories and on the Teachings on Dreams); *Theoretische Schriften 1911–1925* (1931; Theoretical Papers); *Schriften zur Neurosenlehre und zur psychoanalytischen Technik 1913–1926* (1931; Papers on Neurology and on Psychoanalytical Technique); *Vier psychoanalytische Krankengeschichten* (1932; Four Psychoanalytical Case Histories); *Briefwechsel mit Albert Einstein: Warum Krieg?* (1933; Correspondence with Albert Einstein: Why War?); *Selbstdarstellung* (1936; Eng. tr., An Autobiographical Study, 1963); *Der Mann Moses und die monotheistische Religion* (1939; Eng. tr., Moses and Monotheism, 1939); *Schriften aus dem Nachlaß 1892–1938* (1941; Posthumous Papers); *Aus den Anfängen der Psychoanalyse: Briefe an Wilhem Fließ, Abhandlungen und Notizen, 1887–1902* (1950; From the Beginnings of Psychoanalysis: Letters to Wilhelm Fließ, Treatises and Notes); *Gesammelte Werke* (18 vols., 1952–68; Collected Works); *Briefe 1873–1939* (eds. E. and L. Freud, 1960; Eng. tr., Letters 1873–1939, 1960); *Briefwechsel mit Oskar Pfister 1909–1939* (1963; Correspondence with Oskar Pfister); *Briefwechsel mit Karl Abraham 1907–1926* (1965); *Briefwechsel mit Lou Andreas-Salomé* (1966); *Briefwechsel mit Arnold Zweig* (1968); *Brautbriefe* (1968; Letters to His Fiancée); *Briefwechsel mit Sandor Ferenczi* (in preparation).

English translations in collections: Selected Papers on Hysteria and Other Psychoneuroses (1909); Dream Psychology: Psychology for Beginners (1921); Introductory Lectures on Psychoanalysis (1922); Modern Sexual Morality and Modern Nervousness (1931); A General Selection from the Works of Sigmund Freud (1937); The Basic Writings of Sigmund Freud (1938); Civilization, War and Death (1939); The Living Thoughts of Sigmund Freud (1941); An Outline of Psychoanalysis (1949); The Case of Dora and Other Papers (1952); Major Works of Sigmund Freud (1952); The Standard Edition of the Complete Psychoanalytical Works of Sigmund Freud (1953–66); Character and Culture (1963).

Bibliography—on literature and Freud: Fraiberg, L., *Psychoanalysis and American Literary Criticism*, 1960. Hoffmann, F. J., *Freudianism and the Literary Mind*, 2nd edition, 1957. Holland, N., "Freud on Shakespeare," *Publications of the Modern Language Association* 75 (1960):163–73; and *Psychoanalysis and Shakespeare*, 1966. Phillips, W., ed., *Art and Psychoanalysis*, 1957. Trilling, Lionel, "Freud and Literature," in *The Liberal Imagination*, pp. 34–57, 1950; and *Freud and the Crisis of Our Culture*, 1955.

Ulrich Sonnemann

Erich Fried

Born 6 May 1921 in Vienna. Erich Fried emigrated in August 1938 to London, where he has been living since, employed successively as an unskilled laborer, dairy chemist, librarian, and worker in a glass factory. His first publications appeared in 1940, and since 1946 he has been entirely concerned with literary work. In 1950 he became an editor of the review *Blick in die Welt*. From 1952 until 1968, when he left for political reasons, he worked on a permanent basis for the German service of the BBC.

Fried has translated into German poetic dramas of Dylan Thomas, works by T. S. Eliot, Graham Greene, Laurie Lee, and J. M. Synge, and some Shakespeare plays. But he is as well known for his original writings—poems, cycles of poems, prose, radio plays, and essays—as he is for his translations. In an epilogue to his 1958 volume *Gedichte*, Fried protested against the reproach of "writing English poems in the German language" and of being influenced by Dylan Thomas. In effect certain common conceptions and admirations—for example, Gerard Manley Hopkins, James Joyce, Wilfred Owen, e. e. cummings —did attract Fried to the Welsh poet.

Fried's poetry is his most essential work. The poems are dominated by three elements: (1) his predilection for the world of magic, the archaic, and the fairy tale, for the vocabulary of old nursery rhymes, myths, proverbs, and children's counting songs; (2) his pleasure in wordplay, in verbal repetitions, alliterations, and word transformations, with experiments not so much with language and syntax as with the individual word, which he strips to its roots and enriches with new meanings; and (3) his passionately active commitment to contemporary affairs, to the unsolved problems and unhealed wounds of the present, a commitment that makes him feel at home quite as much in political as in love poems. In his best poems topical relevance is combined with inventive language and magic depth into compact, indissoluble unity. By taking the world of fairy tales and its language literally, Fried often achieves astonishing and profound relevance to the present.

Fried's novel *Ein Soldat und ein Mädchen* (1960) can best be described as a mosaic of divergent prose parts put together from a report, from notes, symbols, dreams, and commentaries. The novel deals with the encounter of a Jewish American soldier with a German girl who was a warden in a concentration camp and sentenced to death after the war. Fried tries to find in this encounter a solution to the problem of unforgivable guilt.

Works: *Deutschland* (1944; Germany); *Österreich* (1945; Austria); *Genügung* (1947; Moderateness); *Gedichte* (1958; Poems); *Izanagi und Izanami* (1960); *Ein Soldat und ein Mädchen* (1960; A Soldier and a Girl); *Die Expedition* (1962; The Expedition); *Reich der Steine* (1963; Realm of Stone); *Überlegungen* (1964; Reflexions); *Warngedichte* (1964; Warning Poems); *Kinder und Narren* (1965; Children and Fools); *und Vietnam und* (1966; and Vietnam and); *Anfechtungen* (1967; Temptations); *Befreiung von der Flucht* (1968; Freedom from Flight); *Zeitfragen* (1968; Modern Problems); *Unter Nebenfeinden* (1970; Among Close Enemies); *Shakespeare Übersetzungen* (1973; Translations of Shakespeare).

English translations in collections: *Last Honors* (1968); *On Pain of Seeing* (1969).

Bibliography: Adolf, Helen, on *und Vietnam und*, in *Books Abroad*, 1967, pp. 320–21. Glenn, Jerry, in *Books Abroad*, 1969, p. 414. Hagspiel, Robert, on *Kinder und Narren*, in *Books Abroad*, 1966, pp. 438–39. Opitz, Kurt, on *Die Beine der größeren Lügen*, in *Books Abroad*, 1970, p. 480. Reich-Ranicki, Marcel, *Literatur der kleinen Schritte*, 1967.

Wieland Schmied

Egon Friedell

Born 21 February 1878 in Vienna, the son of a well-to-do businessman. Man of letters, actor, historian, and Viennese "original." In 1904 Egon Friedell, having first withdrawn a dissertation on Hebbel and one on Lichtenberg, earned his Ph. D. at Heidelberg with the dissertation *Novalis als Philosoph*. Became author and manager of the cabaret "Die Fledermaus" and of an avant-garde theater in Vienna. From 1919 to 1922 he was a theater critic, and from 1922 to 1927, an actor of bit parts in Max Reinhardt's theater ensemble. At that time he began detailed preliminary work for his history of civilization. On 16 March 1938, shortly after Hitler's march into Vienna, Friedell, in the belief that he would be arrested because of his Jewish origin, jumped to his death from the fourth floor of his house.

These biographical details give some idea of the sort of man who could conceive so daring a venture as *Kulturgeschichte der Neuzeit* (3 vols., 1927–31). It was this work that quickly won fame for Friedell well beyond Vienna. In it, he invokes Oswald Spengler, who asserted that "nature should be dealt with in scientific treatises, history in poetry"; nevertheless, Friedell goes his own way in the style and approach. He tells "today's legend of the modern age" in a free rendering, well aware of how provisional his standpoint must be, but unhindered by the straitjacket of any rigorous system. The only way of getting hold of history, in his view, is creative reenactment. This process helps the writer to clarify for himself his own position. Friedell begins his interpretation of events between the end of the Middle Ages and World War I by singling out a significant detail, often an anecdote. He does not mind exaggerations, and he gives prominence to the great personalities in whom the representative currents of an age converge. Thanks largely to his vivid, graphic language, Friedell succeeds in making the multiplicity of political, cultural, and economic facts come to life in one organic unity.

The 17th and 18th centuries are Friedell's best; the 19th begins to burst at the seams. He was highly critical of his own work, but this does not prevent some doubts about his methods forcing themselves upon the mind of the reader vis-à-vis the two companion volumes that Friedell had very nearly finished when he died; *Kulturgeschichte des Altertums* (Vol. 1, *Agypten und Vorderasien*, 1936; Vol. 2, *Kulturgeschichte Griechenlands*, posthumously, 1949).

During the years when Friedell was active at the cabaret, he wrote, together with Alfred Polgar, a number of successful skits and farces: *Goethe in Examen, Die Musteroperette, Sherlock Holmes, Der Petroleumkönig, Soldatenleben im Frieden*. His play *Die Judastragödie* (1920) did well at the Burgtheater.

Friedell also has some sparkling aphorisms and essays to his credit, but his claim to originality rests on being the poet-historian of the *Kulturgeschichte der Neuzeit*. Admittedly, the specialists said hard things about it, often not without justification. Though Friedell's judgments were well documented, he often shifted the emphasis and made labored comparisons. But it is precisely because he approached history as an outsider that he managed to bring it to life, with intelligence and wit, presenting it from a bird's-eye view. As a "human" history, it remains an adventure full of imagination. In the meantime this light-hearted man of many facets has himself become part of history.

Works: *Novalis als Philosoph* (1904; Novalis as Philosopher); *Der Petroleumkönig* (with A. Polgar, 1908; The Petroleum King); *Soldatenleben im Frieden* (with A. Polgar, 1910; Soldier's Life in Peacetime); *Ecce Poeta* (1912); *Von Dante zu D'Annunzio* (1915; From Dante to D'Annunzio); *Die Judastragödie* (1920; The Tragedy of Judas); *Das Jesusproblem* (1921; The Question of Jesus); *Steinbruch* (1922; Quarry); *Altenberg-Buch* (1922; The Book of Altenberg); *Kulturgeschichte der Neuzeit* (3 vols., 1927–31; Eng. tr., A Cultural History of the Modern Age, 3 vols. 1930–32); *Kulturgeschichte des Altertums* (2 vols.; Cultural History of Antiquity; I., *Ägypten und Vorderasien* [1936; Egypt and the Near East]; II., *Kulturgeschichte Griechenlands* [1949; Cultural History of Greece]); *Die Reise mit der Zeitmaschine* (1946; The Journey with the Time Machine); *Friedell-Brevier* (ed. W. Schneider, 1947; Friedell-Breviary); *Das Altertum war nicht antik* (ed. W. Schneider, 1950; Antiquity Was Not Antique); *Kleine Porträtgalerie* (1953; Little Portrait Gallery); *Aphorismen zur Geschichte* (ed. W. Schneider, 1955; Aphorisms on History); *Briefe* (ed. W. Schneider, 1959; Letters); *Ist die Erde bewohnt?* (ed. W. Schneider, 1961; Is the Earth Inhabited?).

Bibliography: On volume 1 of *A Cultural History of the Modern Age*, in *New York Times*, 9 February 1930, p. 1; on volume II, in *New York Times*, 13 September 1931, p. 1; on volume III, in *New York Times*, 2 October 1932, p. 1. On *A Cultural History of the Modern Age*, in *Yale Review* 21 (1932):416. Biographical and critical material may be found in W. Schneider's introductions to selections from Friedell's works (*see* Works, above) and in Zuckmayer, Carl, *Als wär's ein Stück von mir*, 1966.

Frank Trommler

Gertrud Fussenegger

Gertrud Fussenegger (pseudonym of Gertrud Dietz), novelist, poet, and dramatist, was born 8 May 1912, in Plzeň, Czechoslovakia. Gertrud Fussenegger grew up in Bohemia and in the Tyrol; she studied history, philosophy, and art history in Munich and Innsbruck. She has lived in Munich, and in Hall (in the Tyrol) since 1944. She is married to the sculptor Aloys Dorn.

Gertrud Fussenegger's realistic social and historical novels are of a traditional mold. They have depth and are rich in characters and symbols. She treats of the basic problems that beset man—guilt and suffering—and his often vain attempts to overcome these afflictions. Her stories cover a wide span of time. Her first novel, *Geschlecht im Advent* (1937), is set in the 9th century in the time of the Carolingians. In *Mohrenlegende* (1937, 1957) she depicts the fate of a Negro child in the Tyrol. And *Zeit des Raben, Zeit der Taube* (1960) is a biographical novel about Madame Curie and Léon Bloy. While some of her stories have a bohemian background of a nightmarish quality, reminiscent of Franz Werfel and Franz Kafka, she displays a preference for delineating the interplay of rural and urban cultures, and also the clashes of the German and the Slavic worlds (*Die Brüder von Lasawa*, 1948). Gertrud Fussenegger also writes poetry, radio plays (*Die Reise nach Amalfi*, 1963), and she translates from Danish. She was awarded the Stifter Prize in 1951, and the Drama Prize of the Oldenburg State Theater in 1956.

Works: *Geschlecht im Advent* (1937; The Rise of a Noble Family); *Mohrenlegende* (1937, 1957; Moor's Legend); *Eines Menschen Sohn* (1939; A Man's Son); *Der Brautraub* (1939; The Rape of the Bride); *Die Leute auf Falbeson* (1940; The People on Falbeson); *Eggebrecht* (1943); *Böhmische Verzauberungen* (1944; Bohemian Enchantments); *Die Brüder von Lasawa* (1948; The Brothers of Lasawa); *... wie gleichst du dem Wasser* (1949; ... How Like the Water You Are); *Falkenberg* (1949); *Das Haus der dunklen Krüge* (1951; The House of the Dark Jugs); *Die Legende von den drei heiligen Frauen* (1952; The Legend of the Three Holy Women); *In deine Hand gegeben* (1954; Into Your Hand); *Iris und Muschelmund* (1955); *Das verschüttete Antlitz* (1957; The Buried Face); *Victorin* (1957); *Südtirol* (1959; South Tyrol); *See-Oberitalien* (1959; Lake-Northern Italy); *Zeit des Raben, Zeit der Taube* (1960;

Time of the Raven, Time of the Dove); *Der Tabakgarten* (1961; The Tobacco Garden); *Die Nachtwache am Weiher* (1963; The Nightwatch at the Pond); *Die Reise nach Amalfi* (1963; The Trip to Amalfi); *Die Pulvermühle* (1968; The Powder Mill); *Bibelgeschichten* (1972; Bible Stories).

Bibliography: Hohoff, C., "Zeit des Raben, Zeit der Taube," *Rheinische Post*, 15 October 1960. Schmidt, A., *Dichtung und Dichter Österreichs im 19. und 20. Jahrhundert*, 1964 ff.

Gertrude C. Schwebell▲

Franz Grillparzer

Born 15 January 1791, in the very center of Vienna. Franz Grillparzer's father, Wenzel Grillparzer, was a lawyer who had acquired a modest fortune without living long enough to enjoy it; he died when he was forty-nine years old and Franz was eighteen. In his autobiography, *Selbstbiographie* (published in editions of Grillparzer's collected works), Grillparzer, the oldest of four sons, recalls that his father considered him his favorite, "although he never gave me a sign of his favors." Franz's mother, Anna Franziska née Sonnleithner, a woman to whom music meant much, was irritable and sickly. Grillparzer wrote that after the death of his father, "she saw in me both son and husband. . . . From our living together I could deduce that my nature was not opposed to a marital relationship, although I was never able to establish one." In 1819 she committed suicide.

Grillparzer had such a deep attachment to his mother that none of his heroes was permitted to have a mother during the dramatic action of the play. His whole life was determined by this fixation. He had many affairs but, when he was forty years old, he wrote in his diaries: "The evening dawns." He did, however, have a long relationship with his "eternal fiancée," Katharina Fröhlich, whom he met in the winter of 1820/21. Six years later he confided to his diary his "capriciously observed decision not to enjoy her sexually." When he was fifty-six years old he moved in with her and her sisters. Though he proposed to her in the year before his death, he died a bachelor, on 21 January 1872.

Grillparzer spent all his life in Vienna. Through the years he traveled to Italy (in 1819), to Germany (in 1826 and in 1847), to France and England (in 1836), and to Turkey and Greece (in 1843). A professional civil servant, he entered government service in 1813 and left it as a *Hofrat* (an honorary title for one holding a high civil-service position), in 1856. In 1861 Emperor Franz Josef I appointed him to the upper chamber of the parliament, which he attended without ever giving a speech.

After the success of the tragedy *Sappho* (in 1818), Grillparzer became the official poet of the Court's Theater. In 1859 he received an honorary doctorate from the universities of Vienna and Leipzig, and in 1864 he was made an honorary citizen of Vienna.

Despite the recognition he received, he decided in 1838 to stop writing dramas, ostensibly because of the débacle of his comedy *Weh' dem, der lügt!* Thereafter he spent his life in ever-increasing alienation and bitterness. This early withdrawal was due to a loss of vitality rather than to a lack of response and respect on the part of his fellow citizens. Easily wounded, he suffered most from the wounds he inflicted on himself.

Grillparzer lived during the great epoch of Viennese music. He knew Franz Schubert, who was a visitor to the salon of the Fröhlich sisters. *Melusina* (1823), a libretto he originally wrote for Ludwig van Beethoven, was set to music by Conradin Kreutzer. Grillparzer wrote the funeral orations for both Schubert and Beethoven.

During Grillparzer's life he witnessed the siege Napoleon laid to Vienna in 1806, the "Dancing Congress" held there in 1814 and 1815, and the revolution of 1848, for which he had longed and about which he ranted after it had happened. He suffered from the censorship imposed on both the literature and politics of the prerevolutionary years, and from his fear of the rule of the masses during the later decades of his life. He witnessed the industrialization of Austria, the ascent to power of the *grande bourgeoisie*, and the first signs of the disintegration of the Hapsburg empire. He was a faithful though surly loyalist, a more than skeptical Roman Catholic, a reluctant traditionalist, and a cautious "original." Deeply steeped in the lore of myth, legend, and history, he was influenced to an equally deep extent by the psychological insights the medical school of Vienna had been developing since the days of Gerhard von Swieten, the personal physician of Empress Maria Theresia. He was born in the year in which Mozart's *The Magic Flute* was first performed; when he died, Sigmund Freud was a sixteen-year-old student.

Myth and psychology underlie most of Grillparzer's works. The drama that established his fame, *Die Ahnfrau* (first performance, 1817), was both hailed and attacked. It was parodied as a tragedy of fate in the Gothic fashion. Yet in spite of its romantic trappings, this play about a noble brigand who harbored an unconscious love for his sister and who killed his father, unaware that he was his father, is an Oedipal tragedy as well as a *drame à thèse* on the theme of heredity. To a certain extent it anticipated Ibsen's *Ghosts*.

Sappho (1818) carried Grillparzer's fame beyond the boundaries of the German tongue. Reading it in 1821, Lord Byron exclaimed: "Grillparzer—a devil of a name, to be sure, for posterity; but they *must* learn to pronounce it." A tragedy of the artist, in the wake of Goethe's *Torquato Tasso* (1790), *Sappho* presents us with the psychological portrait of an aging woman—her drives, fears, and eventual self-destruction. It defines the abandoment of the artist to art as fatal, and the artist as a congenitally suicidal character.

The trilogy *Das goldene Vließ* (1821; *Der Gastfreund, Die Argonauten,* and *Medea*) is the purest example of Grillparzer's skill in illuminating a mythical episode psychologically. Medea, the barbarian, is uprooted from her native land by Jason, the Greek. When Jason decides to desert her to marry another woman, Medea kills their children. Within the boundaries of the myth a tragedy of confused emotions enfolds. There are as many male traits in Medea's character as there are female characteristics in Jason's psychological makeup. For the first time on the European stage, marriage is seen as a complementary neurosis: through the weaknesses of one partner and the failures of the other, an insoluble bond is forged, thereby producing a discord that is as lasting as it is devastating. The classical theme—treated by Euripides, Seneca, and Corneille—is thoroughly modernized by Grillparzer's use of psychology. Anticipating August Strindberg's and even Eugene O'Neill's acerbic presentations of marriage problems, the "eternal bachelor" Grillparzer concentrated on the nightmarish sides of married life. He succeeded, however, in preserving fully Medea's tragic stature.

The third and last of Grillparzer's Greek dramas, *Des Meeres und der Liebe Wellen* (1831), harks back to another archetypal model, the myth of Hero and Leander. Lyrically the most accomplished of Grillparzer's works for the stage, it combines the graces of hellenistic art and Viennese Biedermeier. The fourth act presents Hero, fatigued, on the morning after a night of love with Leander. By failing to keep the tower light burning that is supposed to guide Leander, who is swimming to shore, she causes his death. Thus the catastrophe is precipitated by Hero's physical tiredness, an idea that was as realistic as it was surprising at the time when the play was produced. The playwright himself was taken aback at the novelty of this fourth act when he saw it performed. He called it "ineffective" and added, "The task was immense. If I had succeeded in finding a solution, the gain for dramatic poetry would have been great. But I failed." Only a neoromantic like Hofmannsthal ranked this play on a par with, and even preferred it to, Shakespeare's *Romeo and Juliet.*

Grillparzer's historical and semihistorical plays are similarly characterized by their tendency to present characters in mythological and psychological terms. In *König Ottokars Glück und Ende* (1825) Grillparzer elevated Rudolf I, the founder of the Hapsburg dynasty, to the level of a secular saint, modest though monumental. Rudolf's antagonist, the Bohemian king Ottokar, is contrasted to him by means of complex, psychological detail. Ottokar's fall is the decline of an aging man; his tragedy begins in his marital bed and ends on the battlefield. Yet his death, like Hero's, releases speeches of grandeur. There is tragic irony in the fact that he fails to meet Rudolf when he has attained a human stature comparable to Rudolf's imperial stance. This is Grillparzer at his most patriotic. The emergence of the house of Hapsburg after the battle on the Marchfeld in Act V is a telling testimony to Grillparzer's loyalty. Moreover, the eulogy delivered in Act III by the scribe Ottokar von Horneck (whose chronicle the author had used as a source of his play) has survived to the present day as a favorite paean of Austria.

Ein treuer Diener seines Herrn (1829) was also conceived to pay homage to the dynasty. If Rudolf I was meant to conjure up the wishful dream of the good emperor, Bancban, an aging man like King Ottokar, acts out, sometimes grotesquely, the myth of the true servant. The almost sanctimonious message of the play is interrupted by asides replete with insights into the psychopathology of love, perversion, and ambition. Emperor Franz I, who privately admired the play, tried to suppress it by offering to buy the manuscript "for his own use."

On the surface, *Der Traum ein Leben* (1834) is a fantasy play of the kind being written by Ferdinand Raimund and the early Johann Nestroy and performed at that time on the popular stage of Vienna. Complicated stage effects like falling bridges and dream sequences behind gauzy curtains were expected and readily understood by the audiences. In Grillparzer's dream play even the serpent from *The Magic Flute* makes an appearance. Basically, however, Grillparzer was interested in the phenomenon of dreams, their censorships and revelations. By way of a dream he bares the unconscious of the hero, Rustan. Day residuals emerge as nightmares; suppressed fears and aggressions are released in dreams; the restless soul of the dreamer is allowed to act out the desires hidden in its obscure recesses. Because of its seemingly happy ending—Rustan's awakening from his nightmare—this play has often been called escapist. Actually, however, Grillparzer is offering here a diagnosis of an age, in which few aspirations could be fulfilled because of the social and political conditions of Austria before the 1848 revolution.

Popular elements are also prevalent in Grillparzer's one and only comedy, *Weh' dem, der lügt!* (1838). It not only introduces a picaresque hero, the young cook Leon, but also boasts a veritable buffoon in the person of the half-mute, Galomir. Galomir's stammerings provide the clue to the inner structure of the play. Basically it is a parable on the possibility of human communications; Galomir represents the state of inarticulateness, Leon the artistic dimension of human speech, and Bishop Gregor the metaphysical dimension. Language seems to have been pushed to its limits in this loosely knit fantasy: nothing short of divine interference can redeem the confusion created by the word as it oscillates between truth and lie. Since Grillparzer did not believe in miracles, one cannot help noticing a certain resignation, a wise, smiling despair, in the last work he entrusted to the stage. (The first act of his fragment *Esther* was performed, however, under the auspices of a charitable organization, in 1840.)

After Grillparzer's death, Katharina Fröhlich, his sole heir, permitted the performance of three more tragedies from Grillparzer's estate. Considering them unfinished and imperfect, he originally directed that they be destroyed but thought better of it when he felt his death approaching.

Of them, *Libussa* (completed about 1847) is the most difficult to realize on the stage. It combines the myth of the founding of Prague with another demonstration of the psychological antagonism between the sexes. Primislaus, the plowman, falls in love with the Bohemian princess Libussa, yet, is too proud to confess his feelings. Upon her father's death, Libussa tries to govern her country but is doing it badly. When Primislaus reappears, she marries him, hoping he will solve the country's problems. A fairy tale with melodramatic and mildly comical passages tossed in for good measure, the play unexpectedly rises to the level of high tragedy in the last act. Primislaus has by now taken over the reins of Bohemia. As the mythical ancestor of the Bohemian house of the Premislids, he founds Prague. But Libussa, who turns against Primislaus because he has become a conqueror, commits suicide. As death approaches, her farewell speeches rise to the level of political prophecy. Presenting an organic vision of history, as opposed to Hegel's dialectical one, the play reaches its peak with the proclamation of humility as the governing principle of mankind. Pointing to the Slavs as the future rulers of a "tired" world, Libussa prophesies a Kingdom of God in Bohemia, which will adopt the phrase "Man is good" as its national motto.

Die Jüdin von Toledo (completed in 1851) again deals with what Grillparzer's contemporary and antagonist Friedrich Hebbel called "the trial pending between the sexes." Rahel, the Jew, is seduction incarnate, a true descendant of the biblical Eve. Beyond good and evil, she sweeps across the stage as an elemental force, playful and passionate, calculating and sensitive; she is a fairy queen, a witch, and, above all, a personification of lust. She seduces young King Alphons, the noblest and weakest of Grillparzer's lovers. Married to the English queen Eleonore, who is a puritan before the emergence of historical Puritanism, the king easily falls prey to the game of attraction, fulfillment, jealousy, and ennui. Eleonore orders Rahel killed; and the spectator is offered the rehabilitation of Alphons, his awakening, his relapse into his fantasy world, and his eventual return to reality. Sadness pervades this drama, which is a play about the mysteries of sexual passion. Extreme eroticism in the love scenes is countered by the sober grandeur that distinguishes the political action. Rahel's sister, Esther, is about to pronounce judgment on the misdeeds of the Christians. But on finding her father digging up the gold he has made by Rahel's short-lived luck, she exclaims: "We all stand in the row of sinners." *Die Jüdin von Toledo* is Grillparzer's most balanced and objective drama.

Grillparzer's heir on the Austrian stage, Hugo von Hofmannsthal, has hailed his predecessor's *Ein Bruderzwist in Habsburg* (probably completed after 1848) as "the most significant historico-political tragedy of the Germans." The late-sixteenth-century dispute between Catholics and Protestants, the domestic disunion within the *casa d'Austria*, and the outbreak of the Thirty Years' War are shown as the results of the interplay of obsolete authority and of the evil ambition to change the world by violent means. The title of the play ("A quarrel between brothers") to the contrary notwithstanding, the true counterpart of Rudolf II is not one of his kin, but Bishop Klesel, a baker's son. In speeches that remain monologues, even though they are addressed to others, Rudolf formulates his testament to a Europe torn and tattered by fraternal strife. Discontent with his own existence, averse to *any* action, he only serves to brake the universal destruction he deems imminent and inevitable. In this play Grillparzer anatomizes the subsequent decline of Austria. Yet the figure of Rudolf, the "quiet emperor," dominates the five acts of the play. In fact this dominance is most strongly conveyed in the fifth act, which takes place after his death. Rudolf is an antihero, paradoxically great in his nonactions and immortal through his frailty.

Of Grillparzer's poetic *oeuvre*, it is most often the epigrams and satires that are remembered. Yet he was a lyrical poet whose brittle and occasionally ardent verse is redeemed when the lyricism breaks through the all-too-polished form. Himself a musician *manqué*, he filled his poetry as well as his dramas with the music of speech, thought, and feeling. Yet he knew also the destructiveness of music. In a famous poem, he called Paganini, the violin virtuoso of his day, a "murderer of his own soul" and "suicide." Sappho sacrifices herself for the greatness of her song. As a prelude to his death, Rudolf II hears a melody inaudible to the others. Music was both the most creative and destructive ingredient of Grillparzer's genius.

Grillparzer wrote two novellas. *Das Kloster bei Sendomir* (1828) presents another of his daimonic females, Elga, in a thoroughly inappropriate romantic garb. *Der arme Spielmann* (published in 1847) is, on the other hand, one of the few perfect prose narratives in the German language. The artist as a social misfit and outcast, as a lover frustrated by his overwhelming tenderness, as a saintly fool and grotesque martyr—this theme, not unusual in nineteenth- and early twentieth-century literature, is treated with an irony and a human delicacy not often encountered in European letters. Franz Kafka admired this piece of prose and, grudgingly, paid it tribute.

Grillparzer did try to give the society of his day what he thought was its due: the Austrian version of a tradition that originated in Goethe's humanity and Schiller's idealism of liberty. Yet he enriched this tradition with his baroque heritage and a contrary streak that was a harbinger of our own sensitivities. "I have sprung from different times," he said, "and hope to see different ones." He was a poet between eras and cultures, and as such the founding father of modern Austrian literature.

Works: *Blanka von Kastilien* (1809; Blanca of Castilia); *Die Ahnfrau* (1817; first performance, 1817; The Ancestress); *Sappho* (1819; first performance, 1818; Eng. tr., 1953); *Das goldene Vließ* (triolgy, 1822; first performance, 1821; Eng. tr., The Golden Fleece [I., The Guest-Friend, 1942; II., The Argonauts, 1942; III. Medea, 1941]); *König Ottokars Glück und Ende* (1825; first performance, 1825; King Ottokar's Happiness and End); *Das Kloster bei Sendomir* (1828; The Cloister at Sendomir); *Ein treuer Diener seines Herrn* (1830; first performance, 1829; A Faithful Servant of His Master); *Melusina* (libretto, 1833); *Des Meeres und der Liebe Wellen* (1840; first performance, 1831; The Waves of the Ocean and of Love); *Der Traum ein Leben* (1840; first performance, 1834; The Dream Is a Life); *Weh dem, der lügt!* (1840; first performance, 1838; Woe unto Him Who Lies!); *Der arme Spielmann* (1847; Eng. tr., The Poor Fiddler, 1967); *Selbstbiographie* (1853; Autobiography); *Esther* (first performance, 1868; Eng. tr., 1953); *Ein Bruderzwist in Habsburg* (1872; first performance, 1872; Eng. tr., Family Strife in Hapsburg, 1940); *Gedichte* (1872; Poems); *Libussa* (1872; first performance, 1874); *Die Jüdin von Toledo* (1873; first performance, 1872; Eng. tr., The Jewess of Toledo, 1953).

Bibliography: Baumann, G., *Franz Grillparzer: Dichtung und österreichische Geistesverfassung*, 2nd edition, 1966. Burkhard, A., *Franz Grillparzer in England and America: An Annotated Bibliography*, 1961. Klarman, A. D., "Grillparzer und die Moderne," *Die neue Rundschau* 67 (1956):137–52. Nadler, J., *Franz Grillparzer*, 2nd edition, 1952. Reich, E., *Grillparzers dramatisches Werk*, 1938. Stern, J. P., "Beyond the Common Indication: Grillparzer," in *Reinterpretations*, pp. 42–77, 1964. Straubinger, O. Paul, "Grillparzer: Bibliographie 1937–1952," in *Jahrbuch der Grillparzer-Gesellschaft*, series 3, vol. 1, pp. 33–80, 1953. Yates, D., *Franz Grillparzer: A Critical Biography*, 1946.

Heinz Politzer[▲]

Albert Paris Gütersloh

Albert Paris Gütersloh (pseudonym of Albert Conrad Kiehtreiber) was born on 5 February 1887 in Vienna. The course of his life has led him to almost every field of culture, and so of art. After attending the humanistic monastery schools at Melk and Bozen (now Bolzano), he studied dramatic art simultaneously with painting (under Klimt). He worked until 1921 (with interruptions) in Berlin, Vienna, and Munich, among other places, as actor, producer, and stage designer. In 1909 he wrote his first novel, *Die tanzende Törin* (1910; new version, 1913), one of the founding works of expressionism. Then came an essay on Schiele, contributions to the periodical *Die Aktion*, and reporting from Paris for Budapest newspapers.

In 1913 Gütersloh married the dancer Emma Berger, who died three years later in giving birth to a daughter. Gütersloh volunteered for military service during World War I; after a serious illness he went, upon Robert Musil's recommendation, into the war press office. There he met Franz Blei, with whom he published the periodical *Die Rettung* after the war. In 1921 he married a second time. Four volumes of his prose were published in quick succession. In 1923 he was awarded the Fontane Prize.

From 1923 on, however, it was the painter who stepped into the foreground; for years Gütersloh worked on his painting while living in the south of France. And from Paris he received the Grand Prix for a tapestry design. In 1929 he became a professor at the Vienna School of Industrial Arts. At this time he published only minor writings—stories, essays, and reviews—in Viennese and Prague journals. He ostentatiously bid farewell to belles-lettres and in 1935 began the "historical novel of the present," *Sonne und Mond* (1962). As a painter he received the distinction of a second Grand Prix, but as a writer he seemed to be almost forgotten. With the Anschluß in 1938 he was forbidden, as being a "degenerate artist," to exercise his profession and was compelled to work as a laborer and then as a clerk in a munitions factory.

In 1945 Gütersloh became a professor at the Academy of Fine Arts in Vienna (of which he was rector from 1953 to 1955). At that time Gütersloh the writer reappeared with two collections of stories, a volume of poems, and the novel *Eine sagenhafte Figur* (1946), which he had previously written in France. Like the painter who had earlier received two Grand Prix, he was now honored by Austria's most distinguished prizes. But it was *Sonne und Mond* that really brought the fifty-seven-year-old author back to the notice of the literary world in German-speaking countries.

Gütersloh's inner life is as circuitous and multifarious as that of the outer man. It is true that one is justified in considering his work to date, taken in its entirety, as a brilliantly successful attempt to carry the sensualization of thought, the incarnation of the mind ("profundity is outward"), beyond the limits hitherto existing in German. But this was accomplished in a number of different attempts, not in one continuous effort, and from a number of different directions, not from a standpoint adopted once and for all. Expressionism was only a transitional phase. When the Fontane Prize heralded his coming literary fame, Gütersloh turned from literature to theology. His publications since 1946, in particular, can hardly be grouped within the usual conceptions of a personal style or adherence to a school. In his tales and stories especially, he provides (and in this he is comparable to Picasso) a kind of outline, with examples, of literary history. Thus, the Kleist-style anecdote and the naiveté of Johann Hebel reappear in an entirely new fashion, along with the sobriety of Stendhal and the Protean manner of Laurence Sterne. Any subject matter suits him: a child murder in the country or a love letter gone astray, the assassination of the Austrian prime minister Count Stürgkh in 1916 or something completely fictitious. In *Sonne und Mond* Gütersloh provides a *summa* of everything he has learned to see, to say, and to interpret.

With ostentatious naiveté, Gütersloh confesses to being an artist. He knows all about the literary industry game, but he refuses to play it. Instead, he adheres to those straightforward principles, which, from Homer through Cervantes to William Faulkner, have guaranteed the continuum of the storyteller's art:

> A man who is skilled in words ought not to relinquish any situation to silence. This would be too easy, it would not do in the sight of God. And to whomever he loves but does not consider able to understand him, he ought not to speak as though to a child or an obtuse pupil. For that is not the point—though it is the point for us; but then, what do we know of what we really ought to know? The point is not to be understood by this particular individual here and at this very moment, but to say what can be said only now or never, by us and by no one else.

Logically there is, then, no time or need to note the existence of a crisis or to ride a new wave; we need only put our trust in this:

Albert Paris Gütersloh

"What constitutes a novel is what the one who happens to be writing it decides."

In actual fact the criteria that have been derived, for instance, from the work of Heimito von Doderer, should not be applied to the novels of Gütersloh, and vice versa. The forms of epic verse are still at work concealed in Doderer's epic narrative style, but "Gütersloh's sentences are static." Gütersloh's works are governed by "the view of the world through a fly's eye, with its four hundred facets. Narrative drive comes to a standstill in the face of the clarity of a world that is more being than happening" (Doderer). The fact that something does happen in the narration is, just after Musil's failure in the matter, an intellectual event of inexhaustible significance. Gütersloh himself points the way when he justifies his use of the royal "we":

> Thus, our storyteller certainly goes on foot like an ordinary man, but, like the disciples going to Emmaus, three at a time. In fact the storyteller consists of three men: one who experiences the formless; one who forms what is experienced; and one who interprets the formed experience. And these three are so thoroughly distinct that what is sequence in time appears as juxtaposition in thought.

Works: *Die tanzende Törin* (1910; new version, 1913; The Dancing Fool); *Egon Schiele* (1911); *Die Vision vom Alten und vom Neuen* (1921; The Vision of the Old and the New); *Der Lügner unter Bürgern* (1922; The Liar among the Burghers); *Innozenz, oder Sinn und Fluch der Unschuld* (1922; Innozenz, or the Meaning and Curse of Innocence); *Die Rede über Blei* (1922; The Speech on Blei); *Kain und Abel* (1924; Cain and Abel); *Bekenntnisse eines modernen Malers* (1926; Confessions of a Modern Painter); *Der Maler Alexander Gartenberg* (1928; The Painter Alexander Gartenberg); *Eine sagenhafte Figur* (1946; A Legendary Figure); *Die Fabeln vom Eros* (1947; The Fables of Eros); *Musik zu einem Lebenslauf* (1957; Music Accompanying a Life); *Sonne und Mond* (1962; Sun and Moon); *Laßt uns den Menschen machen* (1962; Let Us Create Man); *Gewaltig staunt der Mensch* (1963; Man Is Awesomely Amazed); *Zur Situation der modernen Kunst* (1963; On the State of Affairs of Modern Art); *Der innere Erdteil* (1966; The Inner Continent); *Die Fabel von der Freundschaft: Ein sokratischer Roman* (1969; The Fable of a Friendship: A Socratic Novel).

Bibliography: Basil, O., Eisenreich, Herbert, and Ivask, Ivar, *Das große Erbe*, 1962. Blei, Franz, *Schriften in Auswahl, Nachwort von Albert Paris Gütersloh*, pp. 288–94, 1960; and *Albert Paris Gütersloh: Autor und Werk*, 1962. Doderer, Heimito von, *Der Fall Gütersloh: Ein Schicksal und seine Deutung*, 1930: Ivask, Ivar, "Sonne und Mond," Books Abroad 37 (Summer 1963):304–305.

Herbert Eisenreich

Enrica von Handel-Mazzetti

Enrica Freiin von Handel-Mazzetti was born on 10 January 1871 in Vienna. The scion of a widely ramified aristocratic family, she is representative of the nobility of the Austro-Hungarian monarchy.

Enrica von Handel-Mazzetti's life, little disturbed by external events, was spent in the familiar surroundings of her native home. At fifteen she went to school at the Institut der Englischen Fräulein in Saint Pölten. Her natural inclination toward conventual seclusion and piety was accentuated by the school's influence. After leaving the Institut, she studied German and French, as well as ancient and modern literature, in Vienna. After a period at Steyr (1905–1911) she moved to Linz on the Danube. Entirely devoted to her work, she remained there until her death on 8 April 1955.

Enrica von Handel-Mazzetti began her literary career when she was only nineteen by contributing short stories to newspapers, in particular to the *Wiener Zeitung*. She found her own style and gained public recognition with her first full-length novel, *Meinrad Helmpergers denkwürdiges Jahr* (first published in a review, 1897; published separately, 1900). Still weak and blurred though the diction of this book is, she built up, on the basis of chronicles, a gripping structure of conflicts. *Jesse und Maria* (1906) was published in *Hochland* and was considered by its editor, Carl Muth, a hopeful sign of a new narrative art inspired by Catholicism. It deals with the problem of a conflict of conscience during the Counter Reformation. A variation on the theme appears in the novel *Die arme Margaret* (1910). Of all her books, *Stephana Schwertner* (1912–14) is the most colorful and the richest in characters and presents a picture of the Counter Reformation on a broad canvas.

Enrica von Handel-Mazzetti's second theme is that of the "bride of Christ." Following the early tale *Die Braut des Lammes*, the theme is taken up again in the *Rita* novels—*Brüderlein und Schwesterlein* (begun, 1898; completed and published, 1913), *Ritas Briefe* (1915–21), and *Ritas Vermächtnis* (1922). Enrica von Handel-Mazzetti's patriotic feeling is best displayed in the novel *Der deutsche Held* (1920). The archduke Charles is probably the most successful character she ever created. In the trilogy *Das Rosenwunder* (1924–26), she displays her mastery of the narrative even in a small compass.

At the end of her career she produced another trilogy, *Frau Maria* (1929–31), the story of the canoness Maria von Bronnen.

Enrica von Handel-Mazzetti's narrative art is in the Austrian baroque tradition. Its dominant characteristic is a virtuoso command of antithesis as a stylistic device. She creates an animated set of contrasting characters who have to live out together the tensions of life and the dangerous conflicts of the age. Antithesis also dominates the construction of her novels. Apparent reconciliations alternate with conflicts all the more acute; suffering under torture is juxtaposed with the Virgin Mary and the most tender mysticism; the pomp of a great pageant, with the mental anguish of a poor woman.

The tendency to antithetical treatment led Enrica von Handel-Mazzetti to the scene of religious controversy between Catholics and Protestants. The tragic event of schism was for her the cause of grave conflicts of conscience, of struggles, crime and guilt. Her fundamentally religious outlook, which imposes the duty of decision on all her characters, is, in the human sphere, directed toward the resolution of opposites. For her, all contradictions are reconciled by love.

Works: *Nicht umsonst* (1892; Not for Nothing); *Pegasus im Joch* (1895; Pegasus under the Yoke); *Meinrad Helmpergers denkwürdiges Jahr* (1900; Meinrad Helmperger's Memorable Year); *Der Verräter* (1902; The Traitor); *Skizzen aus Österreich* (1903; Sketches from Austria); *Erzählungen* (2 vols., 1903; Stories); *Novellen* (1906; Novellas); *Jesse und Maria* (2 vols., 1906; Eng. tr., 1931); *Deutsches Recht und andere Gedichte* (1908; German Law, and Other Poems); *Acht geistliche Lieder* (1908; Eight Religious Songs); *Historische Novellen* (1909; Historical Novellas); *Die arme Margaret* (1910; Poor Margaret); *Imperatori* (1911); *Geistige Werdejahre* (2 vols., 1911–13; Years of Intellectual Development); *Stephana Schwertner* (3 vols., 1912–14); *Napoleon II. und andere Dichtungen* (1912; Napoleon II, and Other Poems); *Weihnachts- und Krippenspiele* (1912; Christmas and Nativity Plays); *Brüderlein und Schwesterlein* (1913; Little Brother and Sister); *Ritas Briefe* (1915–21; Rita's Letters); *Ilko Sumtniak* (1917); *Der deutsche Held* (1920; The German Hero); *Ritas Vermächtnis* (1922; Rita's Legacy); *Das Rosenwunder* (trilogy, 1924–26; The Miracle of the Roses); *Johann Christian Günther* (1928); *Frau Maria* (3 vols., 1929–31; Lady Maria); *Christiane Kotzebue* (1934); *Die Waxenbergerin* (1934; The Waxenberg Woman); *Das heilige Licht* (1938; The Holy Light); *Graf Reichard* (1939; Count Reichard); *Renate von Natzmer* (1951); *Ein groß Ding ist die Liebe—Magna res est caritas* (ed. K. Vancsa, 1958; A Great Thing Is Love—Magna res est caritas).

Bibliography: Berger, F., and Vancsa, K., eds., *Enrica von Handel-Mazzetti: Festschrift zur 75. Jahrfeier*, 1946. Bourgeois, Joseph E., "Ecclesiastical Characters in the Novels of Enrica von Handel-Mazzetti," dissertation (University of Cincinnati), 1956; and "Enrica von Handel-Mazzetti's Tribute to Schiller," *Monatshefte* 51 (1959):313–14. Hemmen, A., "The Concept of Religious Tolerance in the Novels of Enrica von Handel-Mazzetti," dissertation (University of Michigan), 1945. Siebertz, P., et al., *Enrica von Handel-Mazzettis Persönlichkeit, Werk und Bedeutung*, 1930. Vancsa, K., ed., introduction to *Ein groß Ding ist die Liebe*, 1958.

Wilhelm Grenzmann

Peter Handke

Born 6 December 1942 in Griffen (in the province of Carinthia), Austria, the son of a bank employee. Peter Handke's schooling in Griffen and Klagenfurt, led to law studies at Graz University (1961–65), during which time his work first appeared in little magazines. In 1966 the publication of his first novel, the premiere of his first play, and his antiestablishment outburst at the Gruppe 47 conference in Princeton, New Jersey, combined to precipitate him into the public eye. In 1967 he was awarded the Gerhart Hauptmann Prize, and in 1968 his first full-length play was nominated "Play of the Year." After stays in Düsseldorf, Berlin, and Paris, he moved in 1972 to Frankfurt, headquarters of Verlag der Autoren, a thriving authors' agency set up on cooperative lines in 1969 by Handke and ten other playwrights. He is married but lives apart from his wife. They have one child.

Although he has essayed most forms of writing, it is as a playwright that Handke has achieved most impact. His first play, *Publikumsbeschimpfung* (published and performed, 1966), is deliberately antitheatrical: four actors repeatedly tell the audience that what they are watching is not a play but simply a stage with four people on it telling the audience that what they are watching is not a play. This hour-long piece ends with the actors alternately insulting the audience and complimenting them on their "performance," a strategy that often provokes extreme audience reaction. There followed three less extravagant plays—*Selbstbezichtigung* (published and performed, 1966), *Weissagung* (published and performed, 1966), and *Hilferufe* (performed, 1967)—which nonetheless have in common with *Publikumsbeschimpfung* an absence of plot, character, and dramatic construction. Handke calls these plays *Sprechstücke* (speech plays), possibly an analogy with Brecht's *Lehrstücke* (didactic plays). The purpose of the *Sprechstücke* is not to "revolutionize, but to make aware."

This is also the aim of *Kaspar* (published and performed, 1968), Handke's first full-length play, in which he moved away from the *Sprechstücke* with the creation of a dramatic character (albeit an abstract one). Basing his play on the story of the real-life Kaspar Hauser, who had been shut up by himself in a small room since birth and first came into contact with the rest of the world at the age of sixteen, Handke created a nonspecific parable to "make the audience aware" of how accepted modes of expression are imposed on an individual, stifling and circumscribing his originality. Kaspar, a clumsy, clownish innocent, is indoctrinated by disembodied voices into becoming an orderly, articulate, integrated member of society. Then, surrounded by carbon copies of himself, Kaspar gradually lapses into incoherence as he realizes the arbitrariness of his new personality. Mastery of language should have enabled him to think for himself, to *be* himself. But language contains predetermined values; learning the language means accepting those values; and accepting the values means being unable to think thoughts free from the values implicit in the language in which they are framed. Kaspar's strength lies in the force with which this Wittgensteinian impasse is presented in theatrical terms.

The educative process that is at the center of *Kaspar* (as well as of the earlier *Selbstbezichtigung*) is seen in another light in *Das Mündel will Vormund sein* (performed, 1969), a sixty-minute scenario in which two half-masked men (reminiscent, as is Kaspar, both of Beckett's clowns and of the comics of the silent screen) perform rituals of domination and subservience in and around a picture-book farmhouse. Not a word is spoken throughout: a surprising volte-face by the author of the *Sprechstücke*, but a logical progression from the mistrust of language evidenced in *Kaspar*. "Domination," says Handke, "is best practiced in silence." The result is an oddly compelling piece of theater, that has been seen as an allegory of management and labor but has equal force as an abstract rendering of the common factors in all relationships between dominant and subservient human beings.

After *Quodlibet* (performed, 1970), a disappointingly unsuccessful word game, Handke explored an idea suggested by a 19th-century ballad about a horseman who rides unsuspectingly across the thinly frozen Lake Constance and dies of fright when told of the danger he was in. *Der Ritt über den Bodensee* (published and performed, 1971) assembles a weird collection of characters in an indeterminate period setting. They exist on the thin ice between wakefulness and sleep, reality and imagination, sanity and madness. Their conversations are allusive, inconsistent, full of half-completed anecdotes; their actions are likewise disjointed, as if compiled at random from stock theatrical business. Using the conventions of commercial theater as his metaphor, Handke is questioning the assumption that those who conform to set patterns of speech and behavior are sane, and that those who do not are insane. He is indicating the depths beneath the thin veneer of language and conformity—depths which, like the horseman, one becomes aware of at his peril.

If as a playwright Handke has not entirely shaken off the *enfant terrible* image with which he began his career, he is winning himself a considerable reputation as a novelist. His first two novels, *Die Hornissen* (1966) and *Der Hausierer* (1967), use familiar genres but at the same time call into question their validity, in much the same way as the *Sprechstücke* used and abused the conventions of the theater. But with his third novel, *Die Angst des Tormanns beim Elfmeter* (1970), Handke makes the same leap forward as he had done with *Kaspar* in the theater, and, while maintaining much of the formalistic self-consciousness of the earlier novels, he introduces a story strong enough to support the concrete style. The concentration on the nature of the fear felt by a murderer as he awaits inevitable discovery by the police steers the book lightly in the direction of Kafka, just as his first novels call to mind those of Frisch and Raymond Chandler.

Handke's most recent novel, *Der kurze Brief zum langen Abschied* (1972), the story of a picaresquely haphazard trip across the U.S.A., is interspersed with quotations from books, plays, and films, recountings of dreams and memories, and descriptions of random details of American life. Although the stylistic objectivity and absence of psychological insight remain, in other respects this semifactual, semifantastic "report" on modern American seen through European eyes is a refreshing departure for Handke the novelist.

Handke's other writing—his prose pieces, essays, and short stories (many collected in *Begrüßung des Aufsichtsrats*, 1967), his poems in *Die Innenwelt der Außenwelt der Innenwelt* (1969), his radio plays (collected in *Wind und Meer*, 1970), and his television screenplay, *Chronik der laufenden Ereignisse* (1971)—shows many of the concerns and stylistic devices of his larger scale works. Yet despite experimentation with many different media, Handke's work retains its own identity and overall similarity of aim. His purpose is to make his readers/listeners/spectators aware, by demonstration, that the connection between words and things is fundamentally arbitrary, and that language is not the helpful, comforting, order-instilling phenomenon it is taken to be, but a limited and limiting tyrant. That Handke succeeds in using language to expose language in this way is his greatest achievement.

Works: *Die Hornissen* (1966; The Hornets); *Publikumsbeschimpfung und andere Sprechstücke* (1966; first performances, 1966; Offending the Audience and Other Speech Plays; also includes *Selbstbezichtigung*

[Self-Accusation] and *Weissagung* [Prophecy]); *Der Hausierer* (1967; The Peddler); *Begrüßung des Aufsichtsrats* (1967; Welcoming the Board of Directors); *Hilferufe* (first performance, 1967; Eng. tr., Calling for Help, in *Drama Review*, January 1971); *Kaspar* (1968; first performance, 1968); *Das Mündel will Vormund sein* (first performance, 1969; Eng. tr., My Foot My Tutor, in *Drama Review*, January 1971); *Die Innenwelt der Außenwelt der Innenwelt* (1969; The Inner World of the Outer World of the Inner World); *Deutsche Gedichte* (1969; German Poems); *Peter Handke: Prosa Gedichte Theaterstücke Hörspiel Aufsätze* (1969; Peter Handke: Prose, Poems, Theater Pieces, Radio Plays, Essays); *Quodlibet* (first performance, 1970); *Wind und Meer* (1970; Wind and Sea); *Die Angst des Tormanns beim Elfmeter* (1970; Eng. tr., The Goalie's Anxiety at the Penalty Kick, 1972); *Der Ritt über den Bodensee* (1971; first performance, 1971; Eng. tr., The Ride across Lake Constance, in *Contemporary German Drama*, 1972); *Chronik der laufenden Ereignisse* (1971; Chronicle of Current Events); *Der kurze Brief zum langen Abschied* (1972; The Short Letter for the Long Farewell); *Ich bewohne einen Elfenbeinturm* (1972; I Live in an Ivory Tower); *Wunschloses Unglück* (1972; Wishless Misfortune).

English translations in collections: *Kaspar, and Other Plays* (1969; includes *Offending the Audience* and *Self-Accusation*).

Bibliography: Arnold, Heinz Ludwig, ed., "Peter Handke," *Text und Kritik*, no. 24 (1969). Heißenbüttel, Helmut, "Peter Handke and His Writings," *Universitas* (Wayne State) 12, no. 3 (1970):243–51. Hern, Nicholas, *Peter Handke*, 1972. Scharang, Michael, ed., *Über Peter Handke*, 1972. Rischbieter, Henning, *Peter Handke*, 1972.

Nicholas Hern▲

Fritz von Herzmanovsky-Orlando

Born 30 April 1877 in Vienna; died 27 May 1954 at Merano in northern Italy, where he had been living since 1917. His name discloses his background as the scion of German-Austrian, Moravian, and Italian (-Byzantine) families. As such he shared in the constituent elements of the Austrian nature—the German, the Slav, and the Mediterranean. Originally an architect, he was forced by a lung disease to give up his profession, and, like his friend Alfred Kubin, he then devoted all his time to his artistic ambitions as a painter and writer. "He was an amateur in the finest and literal sense of the word—one who loved the arts not only by inclination but also by imagination" (Friedrich Torberg).

During his lifetime only one of Herzmanovsky-Orlando's books was published, the scurrilous tale *Der Gaulschreck im Rosennetz* (1928). He became widely known after his death, when a few of his plays, difficult as they were to produce, were performed as well as broadcast in Munich and Vienna. From 1957 to 1963 his collected works were published, which involved the editor (Torberg) in fighting his way through a gigantic accumulation of notes, sketches, drafts, plans, fragments, variants, etc., and in laboriously sifting the plentiful chaff from the wheat. Clearly, Herzmanovsky-Orlando had been interested only in the brainstorms as they occurred to him, and hardly ever in their literary and economic exploitation.

These ideas seem like the bizarre inventions of an eccentric, but on closer inspection it becomes apparent that they have some humoristically veiled similarity with known reality. Anyone who studies Herzmanovsky-Orlando's work in depth will perceive it to be a sometimes staggeringly accurate description of the world, a sort of officially detached stock-taking of it, albeit of a precisely circumscribed section and in a precisely determined perspective. Herzmanovsky-Orlando acted like a magnet on highly strung, eccentric personalities; he had a gift for discovering oddities like that of a dowser for water.

To that extent, and particularly in the light of the discrepancy between sober language and a subject matter run wild, it is correct to say that Herzmanovsky-Orlando was "a Kafka deflected into the scurrilous"; but while Kafka struggled with his God, Herzmanovsky-

Orlando practiced the art of making an accommodation with his gods. He was not a biblical poet, but one attuned to the spirit of antiquity, with a nature like that of Pan, so to speak. His subject matter, to be sure, is more genuine old Austrian than that of any other writer, and he went into the most meticulous details of cultural history, which contributes an essential element to his comic writing. Everything—antique and modern, Olympus and jazz, mothers' rights and railways, prostitution and irredentism, Cythera and Bohemia—was turned by his pen into Biedermeier, though often far less respectable than the first half of the German word suggests. Generally speaking, Herzmanovsky-Orlando had the knack of making his readers laugh about just those things that are ordinarily far from laughable. In short, he was a singular person of extraordinary status quite unclassifiable, whose "Tarockania" is the necessary, satyric reverse of Musil's "Kakania."

Works: *Der Gaulschreck im Rosennetz* (1928; Scare-nag in the Rose Net); *Gesammelte Werke* (ed. F. Torberg, 4 vols., 1957–63; Collected Works).

Bibliography: Akselrad, R.-M., "Fritz von Herzmanovsky-Orlando," *Books Abroad* 38 (1964):376–80. Eisenreich, Herbert, "Der Illusionist und seine Wirklichkeiten," *Merkur* 18 (1964):494–96. Torberg, Friedrich, "Die Österreichische Spirale," *Wort in der Zeit* 10, no. 4 (1964):1–6.

Herbert Eisenreich

Fritz Hochwälder

Born 28 May 1911 in Vienna, the son of an artisan. Fritz Hochwälder is himself a skilled upholsterer. His parents were Jewish and perished in Poland. But in 1938 Hochwälder escaped to Switzerland, where he formed a friendship with Georg Kaiser. He now lives in Zurich, though still of Austrian nationality.

Hochwälder's first dramatic attempt, *Jehr* (1932), is a tragedy on the theme of incest. This was followed in 1936 by a comedy, *Liebe in Florenz*, based on a short story by Cervantes. Hochwälder achieved a world hit with his play *Das heilige Experiment* (written, 1941; published, 1947), in which he chose the example of the Jesuit welfare state in Paraguay and its forcible dissolution by the king of Spain in 1767 to treat of "eternal problems of mankind, the questions of social justice and the realm of God on earth."

The most notable among Hochwälder's fifteen plays so far are: the comedy *Hôtel du Commerce* (1945), based on Maupassant's story *Boule de suif*; *Der öffentliche Ankläger* (1954), a "devil's comedy" of the criminal type, in which, in a free adaptation of history, Fouquier-Tinville, public prosecutor during the French revolution, unwittingly conducts his own secret trial; *Donadieu* (1953), a drama, suggested by Conrad Ferdinand Meyer's ballad *Die Füße im Feuer*, that treats of the cruel inner conflict of a Huguenot nobleman who spares his wife's murderer in order to save from destruction those who share his faith. In *Die Herberge* (1956), a "dramatic legend," a theft leads to the discovery and expiation of hidden guilt.

Hochwälder's plays belong to the tradition of the Viennese popular stage. His aim is "unliterary, unpretentious, popular theater." He mostly takes historical situations and presents them in a colorful, concentrated, and theatrically effective way as a means of dealing with timeless conflicts.

Works: *Jehr* (1932); *Liebe in Florenz* (1936; Love in Florence); *Esther* (1940); *Hôtel du Commerce* (1945); *Die verschleierte Frau* (1946; The Veiled Woman); *Meier Helmbrecht* (1947); *Das heilige Experiment* (1947; Eng. tr., The Strong Are Lonely, 1943); *Der Flüchtling* (1948; The Fugitive); *Der Unschuldige* (1949; The Innocent); *Vier Paragraphen*

(1951; Four Paragraphs); *Virginia* (1951); *Donadieu* (1953); *Der öffentliche Ankläger* (1954; Eng. tr., The Public Prosecutor, 1958); *Die Herberge* (1956; The Inn); *Donnerstag* (1959; Thursday); *Über mein Theater* (1959; On My Theater); *Dramen* (2 vols., 1959–64; Dramas); *1003* (1964); *Der Himbeerpflücker* (1965; The Raspberry Picker); *Der Befehl* (1967; The Order); *Dramen* (1968).

Bibliography: Fontana, Oskar Maurus, "Fritz Hochwälder zum 50. Geburtstag," *Wort in der Zeit* 7, no. 5 (1961):10–14. Hochwälder, Fritz, "Über mein Theater," *German Life and Letters* 12 (1959):102–14. Loram, Ian C., "Fritz Hochwälder," *Monatshefte* 57 (1965):8–16. Theobald, Erika, in *American-German Review*, August-September 1966. Wellwarth, George E., "Fritz Hochwälder: The Drama within the Self," *Quarterly Journal of Speech* 49 (1963): 274–81.

Irene Ruttmann

Hugo von Hofmannsthal

Born 1 February 1874, in Vienna; died 15 July 1929, in Rodaun. Hofmannsthal left no actual autobiographical writings. His *Buch der Freunde* (1922) and the posthumous notebooks and diaries (now included in *Aufzeichnungen*, 1959) consist of aphorisms, memories, excerpts from his reading, poetic ideas, first attempts at putting into words his adumbrations and interpretations of the problems of life and their poetic representation. But these have only a slight connection with his actual life. *Ad me ipsum* (1930; enlarged editions, 1942 and 1954; republished in *Aufzeichnungen*) was begun in 1916 but remained a fragment. In it Hofmannsthal makes allusion to the aim and significance of his works in a series of notes that are difficult to classify, often overlap, and are often more in the nature of key words. The framework for this self-exegesis consists of "pre-existence" (freedom from fate) and the path into "existence" through "integration with life," which can be accomplished either via introversion (the mystical way) or via sacrifice and social action. In one of his later works, *Die Frau ohne Schatten* (1919), Hofmannsthal himself considered that "all subjects are unified and integrated." These unsystematic notes are supplemented by his letters. The correspondence with Richard Strauss is especially important for an understanding of Hofmannsthal's work.

Hofmannsthal was the son of the Viennese banker Hugo Hofmann von Hofmannsthal. With its varied origins (Austrian, Jewish, Lombard), the family was representative of the bourgeois and aristocratic culture of the old Austria. After his schooling in Vienna, Hofmannsthal first studied law (1892) and then, after 1895, Romance languages and literatures. In 1898 he obtained his Ph.D. with a dissertation on linguistic usage among the poets of the *Pleiade*. His first publications appeared in 1890, while he was still at school, under the pseudonym Loris. At the same time he came to know the Viennese writers Arthur Schnitzler, Richard Beer-Hofmann, and Hermann Bahr, as well as Stefan George (in whose *Blätter für die Kunst* some of his writing was published, 1892–1904); he broke off relations with George in 1892, and in 1893 he separated from the inner *Blätter* circle. In 1893 he struck up a friendship with the poet and later politician Leopold von Andrian.

Hofmannsthal's period of hesitation between an artistic and an academic career ended in 1901 when he gave up his plan of trying to qualify for a position as lecturer on the basis of a thesis on Victor Hugo (which has survived). In the same year he married Gertrud Schlesinger and settled at Rodaun near Vienna, where he lived until his death. Life at Rodaun was interrupted by summer and fall visits to Alt-Aussee in the Salzkammergut, by military service, and by a political mission during World War I in more or less close connection with which he undertook studies on Austrian culture, on Prince Eugen and Maria Theresia. He edited the Österreichische Bibliothek (26 volumes, 1915–17) for the Insel Verlag, the first volume of which he prepared and introduced—a selection from Franz Grillparzer entitled *Grillparzers politisches Vermächtnis* (1915). He traveled frequently in Italy (Venice), Switzerland, Germany (Berlin, Weimar, Dresden, Munich), France (Paris), England, and Greece, meeting people and taking part in discussions, often in connection with productions of operas for which he had written librettos or of his plays.

In his middle and later years Hofmannsthal enlarged the circle of his personal and intellectual contacts to include Rudolf Alexander Schröder, Rudolf Borchardt, Rudolf Kassner, Otto Brahm, Harry Graf Kessler, Rainer Maria Rilke, Eberhard von Bodenhausen, Carl Jacob Burckhardt, Anton Wildgans, Hans Carossa, and others. He took an active part in Max Reinhardt's Salzburg Festivals. Hofmannsthal's theoretical efforts on behalf of the overall concept of this festival (a European art based on the popular theatrical tradition of Austria) attempt a more profound justification of the venture. From the time of the Mozart centenary celebration in 1891, Salzburg, which Hofmannsthal had often visited, meant much to him as the expression of an intellectual and artistic tradition. In 1906 he began his collaboration with Richard Strauss, the composer of the music for his librettos, from *Elektra* (drama, 1904; opera libretto, 1909) to *Arabella* (1933). It was a collaboration that lasted until Hofmannsthal's death, and while not devoid of tension, it was a fertile one for him.

Even as a young man, Hofmannsthal displayed an intellectual originality, which subsequently gained in depth and richness and which can be traced in his notes and letters about his encounters, occupations, and plans. He played his part in the literary, artistic, and political aspirations of his time—an era he reflected with sensitivity. And he made his own the great tradition of the West since the Greeks, which he defended seriously and with dignity as an inalienable birthright. To this tradition he added the legendary world of *The Thousand and One Nights* for an element of imagery.

In all this Hofmannsthal was one of the last universal representatives of a European consciousness centered upon the old Austria in its intellectual role. The collapse of the Austro-Hungarian empire destroyed the very foundations on which he had passionately and high-spiritedly based his whole existence as a poet. More than once he attempted to define the connections of his role as a poet with his time and with the timeless forces: first, early in his career, in 1906 in the lecture *Der Dichter und diese Zeit* and finally, against all hopes and beliefs, in the great Munich speech of 1927, *Das Schrifttum als geistiger Raum der Nation*. Concurrently, in various versions of *Der Turm* (1902; later versions, 1923, 1925, 1927) he was concerned with the nobility and impotence of the true ruler in the face of violence. Between the speech and the drama there is a hidden connection.

Hofmannsthal's grapplings with contemporary events and with the foundations of Western culture found expression in a body of prose work that was large in extent, distinguished in its connoisseurship, and perfect in style. Besides his essays on poetry, his preoccupations were his reform of comedy and opera, and the poet's role as exemplified in essays on Greece, Shakespeare, Beethoven, Goethe, and Grillparzer. His work as an editor ("Neue deutsche Beiträge," 1922–27) and the great anthologies *Deutsche Erzähler* (1912), *Deutsches Lesebuch* (2 parts, 1922/23), *Deutsche Epigramme* (1923), and *Wert und Ehre deutscher Sprache* (1927) are the fruits of superior knowledge and mature judgment. Other anthologies were planned but not carried out: German poetry of the 17th century, letters, testimonies to the encounter of the German mind and antiquity.

Hofmannsthal's creative work comprises poems, which belong almost exclusively to the early period, stories that range from the early intimations of "preexistence" (*Märchen der 672. Nacht*, 1905) to *Andreas, oder die Vereinigten* (1932) and *Die Frau ohne Schatten*, and, as the most richly represented category, plays in various forms from the "lyrical dramas," through the comedies and opera librettos, to the "mythology opera." Behind all his work lies a subtle experience of life and development ("pre-existence" and life), of the Austrian cultural heritage, and of theatrical tradition ranging through Greece, the Middle Ages, the Austrian folk theater, and above all the baroque "theater of the world." Hofmannsthal's conception of the theater was based especially on the Middle Ages and on the baroque in its Austrian and Catholic form as contrasted with the northern and Protestant form (exemplified, in his view, by Friedrich Hebbel and Henrik Ibsen), though, of course, denominational contrasts, in the narrower sense, are not in question. He defined this difference in its most acute form as that between "expression" and "communication."

Hofmannsthal's work as a whole developed through three stages.

The transitions between these are in reality more manifold and fluid than appears in the following classification, which aims at making distinctions. Even in the first phase, for instance, it is possible to find evidence that Hofmannsthal was already surpassing the "subtle, refracted, impressionist," that he was feeling a "need for living actuality," and knew of the impoverishment that comes from the "beautiful life," such as is rejected and surpassed in *Der Tor und der Tod* (1893).

The three stages of Hofmannsthal's work, which are nevertheless distinguishable as a basic pattern, are connected by a problem that is recognizable throughout from the early poems and the first dramatic effort, *Gestern* (1891), to the late works. Hofmannsthal himself discussed the problem in detail in a letter to Richard Strauss in which he defended his *Ariadne auf Naxos* (1912) libretto against the composer's criticisms and explained it—a letter that, revised as *Der Ariadne-Brief* (written, 1911; published, 1912), is now included in his prose works. The problem may be summed up in the antinomic companions—constancy and change—that recur throughout his work in many variants: *e.g.*, yesterday/today; remembrance/forgetting; loyalty/disloyalty; persistence/change; eternity/time; being/becoming; dream/reality.

The antinomy grows all the stronger the more speech becomes the vehicle of this problem. In *Der Ariadne-Brief*, Hofmannsthal admits: "I will never cease to be astonished my whole life long at the eternal mystery of this contradiction." In short, he says: "Change is the life of life, the true mystery of creative nature; persistence is petrification and death. To live, a man must get beyond himself, must transform himself. He must forget. Yet all man's dignity is bound up with persistence, with not forgetting, with loyalty. This is one of the unfathomably profound contradictions upon which life is based, like the Delphic temple upon its bottomless chasm."

This fundamental problem is connected with the relationship of "pre-existence" and existence, as set forth in *Ad me ipsum*, by its closer definition of the manner of "integration with life," *i.e.*, the attempts to exist. Existence as contrasted with "pre-existence" is necessary to fulfilled being. But life is realized through a difficult process that necessitates a choice between the two forms, change and constancy. This problem of life was for Hofmannsthal fascinatingly embodied in the figure of Casanova, the man who changes and hence is full of life, the faithless man who thereby injures man's dignity. The most diverse refractions of this figure appear in Hofmannsthal's work, from Andrea in *Gestern*, through the adventurer Florindo and the Marschallin, to the sister of Arabella, the Dyer's wife, and the

Egyptian Helena. The antitype, sometimes developing from an originally Casanova-like figure such as the Marschallin and Helena, appears in Silvia, Cristina, Ariadne, the Empress, the Dyer, and Sigismund. From this viewpoint the whole of Hofmannsthal's work is encompassed in a single great idea; this idea confers dignity on the work and gives it human validity that transcends its era. Parallel with the concentration and spiritualization of the basic theme, we find a compression of the language in which the theme is expressed, from the flowing, dark lyricism of the early poems to the restrained objectivity of the comedies and the simplicity and intense warmth of his mythology operas and the story of *Die Frau ohne Schatten*.

Monologues: The Fool

Hofmannsthal's preoccupation in the first stage of his work may be summarized in the name of one of the early dramatic characters, that of the Fool in the lyrical drama *Der Tor und der Tod*. The Fool is the individual who persists in the state of "pre-existence," of freedom from fate, who, from fear of "integration with life," fails to take the step into conscious, fateful being. He is the man who lacks the courage to make contact, who avoids commitments and loyalties, and who takes refuge in the noncommitment of aesthetic pleasure. At the moment of death he realizes that instead of living he has lost himself in "artifice," has lived life "like a book," and has thus missed the possibilities of real contact with his mother, his beloved, and his friend. That is why he is a Fool—one for whom knowledge comes only in the hour of death. The prototype for many other characters in Hofmannsthal's early work, he is perhaps their most moving and most profound representative.

This early stage of Hofmannsthal's work comprises the poems and the *Kleine Dramen*, which is essentially what appeared in 1907 in the three volumes *Die gesammelten Gedichte*, *Kleine Dramen I*, and *Kleine Dramen II*, and in 1911 (in a different selection) in one volume, *Die Gedichte und kleinen Dramen*. The essential poems, in which the state that precedes individual fate is presented in dark, evocative symbols, strange and difficult to interpret, are *Lebenslied*, *Weltgeheimnis*, *Ballade des äußeren Lebens*, and *Erlebnis*. Among the dramas the following may be grouped with *Der Tor und der Tod*: the unfinished version of *Das Bergwerk zu Falun*, *Der Kaiser und die Hexe* (1900), *Die Frau im Fenster* (1897), *Der weiße Fächer* (1897), and *Das kleine Welttheater* (1903). To these may also be added the fragment *Der Tod des Tizian* (1892) and the "Characters" in the poems. The most convincing presentation of the connection between the problem of sinful persistence in "pre-existence" and that of change and constancy is given in *Der Tor und der Tod* and in *Das Märchen der 672. Nacht.*

The distinguishing mark of this first phase of Hofmannsthal's writing is the rich, flowing, musical language, the magical ability to discuss precociously the greatest mysteries, the intermingling of alertness and veiled symbolism. It was the exquisite language of this early work that established Hofmannsthal's reputation and for long prevented a just appreciation of his later work. In itself it was of great perfection, but it was not everything that he was destined to achieve. The verbal magic of the poems and dramas is a result of the precise expression of Hofmannsthal's inner state and of that of his characters; the language is monologuelike, self-centered, and a sensitive circling without reference to any addressed and listening human counterpart; it corresponds to the "pre-existential" form of being, remote from life. Even the dramas are not real plays. They have no dialogue involving interlocutors in the real sense. Each character speaks for himself and alongside the other, not with the other. This form is most clearly reflected in *Der Tor und der Tod* and *Das kleine Welttheater*. In them the characters appear one after the other, but not in interplay with or against each other; the fundamental problem of change and constancy is presented and is reflectively discussed as a condition. Thus, there is no essential difference between the "Characters" of the poems and those of the dramas. They all speak the same language—nervous, vibrant, and veiled. None of the characters is outlined by means of his language; each is enveloped in it as by a robe. Characteristically, there is no hiatus between these poetic works and Hofmannsthal's reviews of contemporary publications. Everywhere there is the same vivid recording of every nuance in the exposition of intellectual and spiritual circumstances.

Society: Change and Constancy

In the second stage of his works Hofmannsthal was primarily concerned with the representation of "integration with life" in society, that is, the emergence from "pre-existence," the world of the Fool. Essentially this second period is that of the comedies, a new form of artistic expression for Hofmannsthal that was reached only after many hesitations and false starts. To begin with, Hofmannsthal undertook experiments to find a form of language corresponding to this new form of life, life in society. The earliest experiment is represented by the three dramas of 1899, *Die Hochzeit der Sobeide, Der Abenteurer und die Sängerin,* and *Das Bergwerk zu Falun.* At first Hofmannsthal himself published only the first act of *Das Bergwerk zu Falun,* as a "Prologue," probably feeling that despite the incomparable beauty of language, the whole did not meet his expectations. (Acts 2, 4, and 5 were each published separately between 1902 and 1911, and the whole work was published for the first time in 1933.) A second experiment, the Greek dramas, is more a preliminary exercise in the diction—made necessary by the representation of societal life—than a completely new diction.

Going beyond his early formative experience of Greece, which was later more profoundly expressed in the books *Griechenland* (1922) and *Augenblicke in Griechenland* (1924), and the safety provided by the dramatic structure of Greek tragedy, Hofmannsthal now attempted dramatic representation transcending the monologue form. The attempt was only partially successful. The experimental and assimilative character of these plays (to which may be added, as far as its experimental character goes, *Das gerettete Venedig,* 1904–1905, "adapted from an old tragedy by Thomas Otway") is also evidenced by the fact that they developed out of free translations, which at first followed more closely the Greek originals—*Alkestis,* after Euripides (written, 1893/94; published, 1911) and *König Ödipus* (written, 1906; published, 1907—into adaptations and independent creations—*Elektra,* "freely adapted from Sophocles" (written, 1903; published, 1904) and *Ödipus und die Sphinx* (written, 1905; published, 1906). The form was still verse, approximating the early dramas in cadence.

It was not until the comedies, beginning in 1907, that Hofmannsthal really succeeded in creating a dramatic form appropriate to the mutual interplay of characters. These comedies constitute the heart of his dramatic work; they are not a sideline, still less, as contemporaries often felt, a failure or retrogression. It is true that after his experiments Hofmannsthal still had to struggle to master the new dramatic form, as is clear from the genesis of the early plays *Silvia im Stern* (1907) and *Cristinas Heimreise* (1910). Here, as always when he needed to make sure of his own procedures, he advanced by way of translation (*Die Heirat wider Willen,* 1910, and *Die Lästigen,* 1916, were based on plays by Molière) and adaptation (*e.g., Ariadne auf Naxos,* 1912; new version, 1916), just as later in the historical works (*Das kleine Welttheater* and *Der Turm*) he grappled with the spirit and form of Calderón.

The outcome of this effort was a convincing and independent series of comedies and opera librettos extending to the late form of "mythology opera" in *Die ägyptische Helena*: namely, *Silvia im Stern* (new attempts as late as 1921–23); *Cristinas Heimreise*; *Der Rosenkavalier* (1911); *Der Schwierige* (written, 1918; published, 1920, 1921); *Der Unbestechliche* (written, 1922; published, 1923); *Die ägyptische Helena* (1927). These comedies form a world of their own originating in a renewal of language. In fact, the opera librettos, in particular *Der Rosenkavalier,* can stand on their own as comedies, performed without music, and indeed many scenes are all the better without the music. To call such works *Lustpiele* (farces) does not describe them correctly; it would be better to call them *Komödien* (comedies), on which Hofmannsthal had his own theories as to form and style. By comedy he understood a particular way of interpreting the world with reference to society, for which reason he went so far as to maintain that in times of crises it was the only possible dramatic form. In any event it may be said that in comedy (which here includes *Ariadne auf Naxos* and *Die ägyptische Helena*) Hofmannsthal found the dramatic form in which he could most clearly express his own particular vision.

The new dramatic form was preceded by a language crisis. This resulted from the language of the monologue pieces, which left nothing unsaid, a language for which there was nothing it could not say. Hofmannsthal described this crisis in the *Brief des Lord Chandos an Francis Bacon* (1902), the confessional character of which cannot be denied. In the letter Chandos explains why he will write no more. His silence is a "sickness of the mind"; "an unbridged abyss" separates him from his earlier work. The "unity" of existence is smashed. He cannot grasp it in words, for things will not go into words any more. The new form, as he envisioned it, would no longer organize the subject matter, but penetrate it and replace it. This language of expression—to use a later concept of Hofmannsthal's—he is not able to discover; all he can do in "good moments" is to establish unity with things through "thinking with the heart." This occurs with "a material that is more immediate, liquid, and fiery than words." This singular text, which in an accomplished style reshapes and extends an ancient tradition, deserves thorough exposition. Here it is only possible to mention two ideas that stand out above all: words can do nothing; love of language does not save one from betrayal of language. Secondly, there is, beyond words, a mysterious entranced life that sets one apart from ordinary life. This "awkward strangeness" explains the originality both of the characters in the comedies (*e.g.,* in *Der*

Schwierige) and of Sigismund in *Der Turm*, whose creation was made possible only on the foundation of the comedies.

Hofmannsthal did not remain silent like Chandos. He was too much an artist to be able to live without creating. But the succeeding comedies constituted a new path, as is seen from its effects on the language. Distrust of language persists after this crisis. Hofmannsthal's comedies are built on the knowledge of all that is provisional and perilous in language. This means in the first place that the question of speech, of not being able to speak, of silence, of understanding and not understanding, becomes the subject and theme of the comedies. More important, however, is the fact that dramatic action no longer takes the form of juxtaposition of characters, but of their symbiosis in the realm of speech and silence. Hans Karl Buhl, the "difficult man," is difficult because he suffers from language. Now the characters are presented in their speech or silence; their way of speaking characterizes them; each speaks his own language. Language is the form in which they exist. The problem of "integration with life," of symbiosis, is set forth in the new diction. The societal realizes itself in speech, and for that reason the "constellations" of the characters are primarily a relation of language. The spiritual of speech is what is realized in the comedies. Its highest expression is "celebration," exemplified in the theme of marriage, as with Silvia, Cristina, the Rose Bearer, Ariadne, the Difficult Man, Helena. This prose language becomes reserved, allusive, tender, and reticent. Between the speakers lies the field of the mind in which the problem is "disposed of," precisely as Hofmannsthal laid down in his *Grillparzer-Rede* (1922): "Only in the created form is the problem disposed of."

History: Freedom and Guilt

At the last stage, which to some extent overlaps in time with the second stage, the societal is transposed into the historical. The same process of social symbiosis takes on an historical quality. Deep down these two ways lie close together. Hofmannsthal's deepest concern was perhaps with the comedies. This may be the explanation of why the great "historical" works *Jedermann* (1911), *Die Frau ohne Schatten* (written, 1911–19), *Das Salzburger große Welttheater* (written, 1921/22; published, 1922), and *Der Turm* (new versions written, 1920–26) were followed by the two operas of the comedies period, *Die ägyptische Helena* (written, 1923/24) and *Arabella* (written, 1927–29).

In the comedies the characters gain their freedom by existing with and alongside others. Ariadne, the Difficult Man, and Helena carry the problem of integration into the unique encounter. The question of guilt is solved either with witty melancholy, as in *Der Rosenkavalier*, by putting it all onto God ("he couldn't have done it differently"), or through love. It becomes a problem only in the historical sphere, where social integration acquires, in a more crucial sense, the character of responsibility and moral decision.

Here, too, Hofmannsthal began with the adaptation of foreign stimuli. Medieval and baroque conceptions of man's behavior toward one another and before God were used to pose the fundamental question of the meaning of man's mission in the world—as, for example, in *Jedermann* and in *Das Salzburger große Welttheater*, which, in contrast to the early *Das kleine Welttheater*, is a play about conscious, responsible life that must be accounted for under moral law.

The kind of universal responsibility associated with Christian ideology does not mean revolution by "changing roles," but the creation of a new "world estate." Although he took over atmospheric coloring from *The Thousand and One Nights* and from Calderón, Hofmannsthal used his own means to pursue the discussion in *Die Frau ohne Schatten* and *Der Turm*. *Die Frau ohne Schatten* handles the problem of symbiosis in human relations. They lead to a necessity —the child. By self-surrender to this necessity, man finds himself. In *Der Turm* the question of freedom is treated in an essentially historical sense. The man who voluntarily surrenders, who goes back into the tower, who remains behind the "wall," is, by this self-conquest, by this renunciation of power, the true survivor. The man who overcomes violence in himself wins the victory of mind: "All is vanity save the speech of mind to mind." The problem of speech and silence from *Der Schwierige* here recurs in fateful form. Inability to speak is here accepted freely and ensures survival in destruction. Sigismund goes back into his silence as into a dungeon where nothing further reaches him, and he averts the impending destruction. This is the utmost freedom in his own mind, no longer in bondage to causality.

The language of these late works is, like that of the late comedies, "expression" rather than "communication"; a language in which the characters appear as what they are; a diction that aims at nothing more than to make present. In the "fairy story" *Die Frau ohne Schatten* this is done through the symbol, the net of relationships that imparts significance; in the dramas, through the dialogue, which is unpsychological, unargumentative, "undirected." In his conception of language, Hofmannsthal, as he said, was on the side of Shakespeare and Goethe against Ibsen and Hebbel. The absence of any intent to convince, as a human attitude and in speech, is the real advance of the comedies period (gracefully personified in the character of the clown Furlani), and Hofmannsthal carried it over into the dramas. It is this that Sigismund, along with the Difficult Man, most convincingly represents. They are brothers but in different spheres, one in the sphere of society and the other in that of history. In these works Hofmannsthal realized his greatest potentialities and found his true form, a form that was playful in the comedies and fateful in the historical dramas.

Works: *Gestern* (1891; Yesterday); *Der Tod des Tizian* (1892; Eng. tr., The Death of Titian, 1913); *Der Tor und der Tod* (1893; Eng. tr., Death and the Fool, 1913); *Poesie und Leben* (1896; Poetry and Life); *Der weiße Fächer* (1897; Eng. tr., The White Fan, 1909); *Die Frau im Fenster* (1897; Eng. tr., Madonna Dianora, 1916); *Die Hochzeit der Sobeide* (1899; Eng. tr., The Marriage of Sobeide, 1899); *Der Abenteurer und die Sängerin* (1899; Eng. tr., The Adventurer and the Singer, 1917); *Theater in Versen* (1899; Theater in Verses; includes *Die Frau im Fenster*, *Die Hochzeit der Sobeide*, and *Der Abenteurer und die Sängerin*); *Der Kaiser und die Hexe* (1900; The Emperor and the Witch); *Erlebnis des Marschalls von Bassompierre* (1900; Eng. tr., An Episode in the Life of the Marshal de Bassompierre, 1952); *Studie über die Entwicklung des Dichters Victor Hugo* (1901; Study of Victor Hugo's Development); *Der Brief des Lord Chandos an Francis Bacon* (1902; Eng. tr., The Letter of Lord Chandos, 1952); *Der Turm* (1902; later versions, 1923, 1925, 1927; Eng. tr., The Tower, 1927); *Der Schüler* (1903; The Pupil); *Ausgewählte Gedichte* (1903; Selected Poems); *Das kleine Welttheater* (1903; Eng. tr., The Little Theater of the World, 1945); *Elektra* (drama, 1903; Eng. tr., Electra, 1908); *Unterhaltung über literarische Gegenstände* (1904; Conversation on Literary Subjects); *Das gerettete Venedig* (1904–05; Eng. tr., Venice Preserved, 1915); *Das Märchen der 672. Nacht* (1905; The Fairy Tale of the 672nd Night); *Der Dichter und diese Zeit* (1906; The Poet and Our Time); *Ödipus und die Sphinx* (1906; Oedipus and the Sphinx); *Kleine Dramen* (2 vol., 1906–1907; Little Dramas); *Die prosaischen Schriften* (3 vols., 1907–1917; The Prose Writings); *Silvia im Stern* (1907; Silvia in the Star); *König Ödipus* (1907; King Oedipus); *Die gesammelten Gedichte* (1907; Collected Poems); *Vorspiele* (1908; Introductory Pieces); *Reitergeschichte* (1908; Horseman Story); *Elektra* (libretto, 1909; Eng. tr., Electra, 1966); *Cristinas Heimreise* (1910; Eng. tr., Christina's Journey Home, 1917); *Lucidor* (1910); *Der Rosenkavalier* (1911; Eng. tr., The Rose Bearer, 1912); *Alkestis* (1911; Alcestis); *Die Gedichte und kleinen Dramen* (1911; The Poems and the Little Dramas); *Jedermann* (1911; Eng. tr., The Play of Everyman, 1917); *Ariadne auf Naxos* (1912; Eng. tr., Ariadne on Naxos, 1913); *Der Ariadne-Brief* (1912; The

Ariadne Letter); *Eine Joseph Legende* (1914; Eng. tr., A Legend of Joseph, 1914); *Kantate* (1914; Cantata); *Die Frau ohne Schatten* (libretto, 1916; The Woman without a Shadow); *Der Bürger als Edelmann* (1918; The Commoner as a Gentleman); *Die Frau ohne Schatten* (story, 1919); *Der Schwierge* (1920; The Difficult One); *Reden und Aufsätze* (1921; Speeches and Essays); *Die Salzburger Festspiele* (1921, The Salzburg Festivals); *Buch der Freunde* (1922; The Book of Friends); *Das Salzburger große Welttheater* (1922; Eng. tr., The Salzburg Great Theater of the World, 1968); *Grillparzer-Rede* (1922; Speech on Grillparzer); *Griechenland* (1922; Greece); *Florindo* (1923); *Der Unbestechliche* (1923; The Incorruptible); *Augenblicke in Griechenland* (1924; Moments in Greece); *Die Ruinen von Athen* (1924; The Ruins of Athens); *Gesammelte Werke* (6 vols., 1924; Collected Works); *Briefwechsel Richard Strauss-Hugo von Hofmannsthal* (1926; Eng. tr., Correspondence between Richard Strauss and Hugo von Hofmannsthal, 1927); *Früheste Prosastücke* (1926; Earliest Works); *Das Schrifttum als geistiger Raum der Nation* (1927; Literature as the Nation's Spiritual Realm); *Die ägyptische Helena* (1927; Eng. tr., Helen in Egypt, 1928); *Das Spiel von der Menge* (1927; The Play of the Crowd); *Loris* (1930); *Ad me ipsum* (1930); *Berührung der Sphären* (1931; Contact of the Spheres); *Andreas, oder Die Vereinigten* (1932; Eng. tr., Andreas, 1936); *Das Bergwerk zu Falun* (1933; The Mine at Falun); *Arabella* (1933; Eng. tr., 1955); *Nachlese der Gedichte* (1934; Later Selection of Poems); *Gesammelte Werke* (3 vols., 1934; Collected Works); *Dramatische Entwürfe aus dem Nachlaß* (1935; Dramatic Drafts from Posthumous Papers); *Briefe 1890–1909* (2 vols., 1935–37; Letters 1890–1909); *Briefwechsel Hugo von Hofmannsthal–Wildgans* (1935; Correspondence Hugo von Hofmannsthal–Wildgans); *Briefwechsel Hugo von Hofmannsthal–Stefan George* (1938); *Gedichte und Lyrische Dramen* (1946; Eng. tr., Poems and Verse Plays, 1961); *Gesammelte Werke in Einzelausgaben* (ed. E. Steiner, 15 vols., 1951–63; Collected Works in Single Editions); *Danae, oder Die Vernunftheirat* (1952; Danaë, or The Marriage of Convenience); *Briefe der Freundschaft: Hugo von Hofmannsthal–Eberhard von Bodenhausen* (1953; Letters of Friendship: Hugo von Hofmannsthal–Eberhard von Bodenhausen); *Briefwechsel Hugo von Hofmannsthal–Rudolf Borchardt* (1954); *Briefwechsel Hugo von Hofmannsthal–Carl Burckhardt* (1956); *Briefwechsel Hugo von Hofmannsthal–Josef Redlich* (1956); *Ausgewählte Werke* (2 vol., 1957; Selected Works); *Aufzeichnungen* (1959; Notes); *Briefwechsel Hugo von Hofmannsthal–Arthur Schnitzler* (1964); *Briefwechsel Hugo von Hofmannsthal–Helene von Nostiz* (1965); *Briefwechsel Hugo von Hofmannsthal–Edgar Karl von Bebenberg* (1966); *Briefe an Marie Herzfeld* (1967; Letters to Marie Herzfeld); *Briefwechsel Hugo von Hofmannsthal–L. von Andrian* (1968); *Briefwechsel 1898–1929 mit H. Graf Kessler* (1968); *Ein Briefwechsel—Hugo von Hofmannsthal und Willy Haas* (1968).

English translations in collections: *The Lyrical Poems of Hugo von*

Hofmannsthal (1918); *Selected Writings: Prose* (1952; Introduction by H. Broch); *Selected Writings, Poems and Verse Plays* (1961; Introduction by T. S. Eliot and Michael Hamburger); *A Working Friendship: Correspondence between Richard Strauss and Hugo von Hofmannsthal* (1961); *Selected Plays and Libretti* (1963); *Three Plays* (1966).

Bibliography: Alewyn R., *Über Hugo von Hofmannsthal*, 1958. Borchardt, R., *Rede über Hofmannsthal*, 1905. Broch, H., "Hofmannsthal und seine Zeit," in *Essays*, 1955. Butler, E. M., "Alcestis in Modern Dress," *Journal of the Warburg Institute*, 1937. David, C., "Le dernier homme de lettres," *Critique* 11 (1955). Fahrner, R., *Dichterische Visionen menschlicher Urbilder in Hofmannsthals Werk*, 1956. Hamburger, Michael, *Hugo von Hofmannsthal*, 1964. Heuschele, Otto, *Hugo von Hofmannsthal*, 2nd edition, 1965. Jacoby, K., *Hugo von Hofmannsthal Bibliographie*, 1936. Kommerell, M., *Hugo von Hofmannsthal*, 1930. Krüger, K. J., *Hugo von Hofmannsthal und R. Strauss*, 1935. Naef, K. J., *Hugo von Hofmannsthals Wesen und Werk*, 1938. Pulver, E., *Hofmannsthals Schriften zur Literatur*, 1956. Rey, William H., "Tragik und Verklärung des Geistes in Hofmannsthals 'Turm,'" *Euphorion* 47, no. 2 (1953).

Hermann Kunisch

Ödön von Horváth

Born 9 December 1901 in Fiume. Horváth described his family background as being a "typical Old-Austro-Hungarian mixture: Hungarian, Croatian, German, and Czech." Because the father was a diplomat, the family moved frequently (Belgrade, Budapest, Munich, Bratislava, Vienna, Budapest). Horváth wrote all his works in German. In 1924, after a few terms at the University of Munich, Horváth moved to Berlin, where, in the early 1930s, he enjoyed a few years of success as a dramatist (Kleist Prize, 1931, at Carl Zuckmayer's recommendation). With the advent of Hitler his anti-Nazi convictions made further productions impossible. In 1933 he went to live in Austria. In March 1938, the Anschluß forced him to go into exile. During a brief stay in Paris he was killed on 1 June 1938 in an unusual accident—a falling branch hit him as he was walking along the street.

Horváth grew up at a time when the values of the late 19th century were disintegrating. "All my childhood memories I forgot during the war. My life began with the declaration of war." Of his generation he said: "We were calloused, felt neither pity nor respect. We had neither any sense for museums nor for the immortality of the soul—and when the grown-ups collapsed, we remained intact. In us nothing had collapsed because we had only been watching." In Horváth, the traditional cosmopolitanism of Austrian writers took on a matter-of-fact aloofness: "I do not have a home country and, of course, I do not suffer from this homelessness but rather enjoy it since it frees me of an unnecessary sentimentality." Horváth's critical detachment and his intuitive psychological insights enabled him to become one of the most perceptive analysts of society in the interwar period, a time of economic, political, and spiritual insecurity. A master of irony and satire in the tradition of Johann Nestroy and Karl Kraus, Horváth recognized the pseudovalues, escape mechanisms, and aggressive tendencies in a society ready to embrace fascism.

Horváth combined ironic distance with a profound moral sense, a light touch with social consciousness. A problem that incurred his criticism at the very beginning of his playwriting career, and that recurs in many of his later works, is that of the social inequality between men and women, of sex and exploitation. *Zur schönen Aussicht* (written, 1927) is a farce, rich in verbal humor and biting satire, about the change in attitude of men toward a poor woman who suddenly comes into money. *Rund um den Kongreß* (written, 1929) exposes the hypocrisy surrounding prostitution, the absurdity of moral indignation in an amoral commercial society, the cold abstractness of conferences when they are nothing but organized "shows" pretending human concern.

The dangerous susceptibility of the common man to political ideologies is the central theme of *Sladek, der schwarze Reichswehrmann* (written, 1928). Of this play Horváth wrote: "Sladek is the representative of the generation that, born in 1902, experienced the 'great time,' war and inflation, the typical unrooted individual . . . who becomes the prototype of the fellow traveler. Without being a murderer, he commits murder. . . . Since I see the main problems of humanity from a social point of view, my intention in writing *Sladek* was to show the social forces that create this type of person."

Die Bergbahn (written 1927) was based on actual events occurring during the building of a cable car up the Zugspitze. It is a workers' drama in the vein of Gerhart Hauptmann's *Die Weber*. A sudden change in the weather brings to open conflict the tensions between labor, capital, and the engineer, who is the ambitious irresponsible intellectual belonging to neither class. The workers' lives are to be risked so that a lucrative tourist attraction will be ready on schedule. *Die Bergbahn* was the first of Horváth's plays to be performed (1929). Although not a success on the stage, it made the Berlin theater world aware of his talent.

It was in this play that Horváth first grappled with the technique of the *Volksstück*, a genre that he significantly modified and in which he was to create his most characteristic and most important plays. To Horváth, a *Volksstück* was a play that dealt with the problems of ordinary, simple people in a way they would understand. Horváth, being aware of the changes in the social structure of his time, redefined *Volk* as "established or would-be bourgeoisie." He felt that, in the 20th century, the conventional *Volksstück* could only perpetuate illusions, that it could no longer reflect the actual life of the common man in modern industrial society. "With full knowledge I am now destroying the old *Volksstück*, its form as well as the ethics behind it —and I am trying to find the new form of the *Volksstück*." Actually, the *Volksstück* before Horváth had not been only sentimental and idyllic. Horváth's perspective can be linked to the social criticism in Nestroy, Ludwig Anzengruber, Ludwig Thoma, and Marieluise Fleißer.

Horváth's most original contribution to 20th-century German-language drama was the ironic and grotesque twists he gave to the form and content of the *Volksstück*: the ironic contrasts he achieved with popular melodies and songs, the dialogue in which he aimed at a "synthesis of realism and irony," the idiom that he had his characters speak. Horváth realized that people in an urban, kitsch-and-propaganda-ridden mass society no longer spoke a homogeneous dialect. Instead they spoke what he called *Bildungsjargon*, a conglomerate of dialect remnants, pseudoerudite clichés, and other grotesque incongruities of style that reflect their loss of identity, their intellectual and spiritual impoverishment, their inability to communicate. Horváth had an extremely sensitive ear for nuances of language that are simultaneously comic and terrifying and that reveal the conflicts between the conscious and the subconscious. "To unmask consciousness" was the foremost goal of the moralist Horváth. By laying bare the sterile, socially conditioned modes of thought and feeling with which we disguise our aggressions and egotistic desires, he hoped to increase the self-awareness of his audience. Horváth's most successful plays were his diagnostic *Volksstücke* in which he attacked "stupidity and deceit" and in which he pleaded for "reason and sincerity": *Italienische Nacht* (written, 1930), *Geschichten aus dem Wiener Wald* (written, 1931), *Kasimir und Karoline* (written, 1932), and *Glaube Liebe Hoffnung* (written, 1932). The last three have been aptly called banal tragedies of Everyman in our time.

The plays Horváth wrote after 1932 are ample evidence of his versatility. *Die Unbekannte aus der Seine* (written, 1933) combines exposure of petty-bourgeois mentality with the macabre and the supernatural. In *Hin und Her* (written, 1934), Horváth gave the conflict between the individual and society, that is, its inhuman bureaucratic machinery, a farcical turn. (In *Glaube Liebe Hoffnung* the same conflict is in tragic terms.) *Himmelwärts* (written, 1934) is a fairy-tale-like play, which, though rich in verbal comedy, is not unlike the conventional *Volksstück* Horváth had rejected. In *Ein Dorf ohne Männer* (written, 1937) Horváth, incorporating elements of the novel of that name by Kálmán Mikszáth, created a charming romance about marital loyalty and wise government. In terms of the political situation of those years and Horváth's intense awareness of it, these plays indicate his withdrawal into a resigned, gentle humanism. In 1935, Horváth wrote: "In a restless time like ours when nobody knows what will be tomorrow, it may be grotesque to set up a program for writing plays. Nevertheless, I dare to do just that, although I don't know what I will eat tomorrow. . . . So I have set myself the task, free from confusion, to write the comedy of man ... keeping in mind that, taken as a whole, human life is always a tragedy; only in the individual case is it a comedy."

In two of his late plays, Horváth succeeded in giving present-day relevance to traditional literary heroes: in *Figaro läßt sich scheiden* (written, 1937), elements of the Beaumarchais-Mozart story are fused with the problems of emigration and the humanization of revolution in a most original manner, though Horváth's Figaro—a rebel who first turns bourgeois, then political opportunist, and ends up as an apostle of tolerance—is not one of Horváth's most carefully delineated characters. In *Don Juan kommt aus dem Krieg* (written, 1937) Horváth returned to the atmosphere of disintegration after World War I, now emphasizing the moral problem of guilt that in his later works takes on a particular prominence.

In *Der jüngste Tag* (written, 1937), the only one of Horváth's plays ever to be performed at the prestigious Burgtheater in Vienna (1969), human irresponsibility is clearly seen from a Christian point of view—as the result of man's innate fallibility. Horváth's last play, *Pompeji: Komödie eines Erdbebens* (written, 1937), which calls to mind the expressionistic theme of regeneration, deals with the overthrow of the pagan, inhuman order and the dawning of the new era of Christian love and forgiveness. In the light of the political reality at the time, Horváth's hope for a spiritual rebirth through the individual's conscience seems naive for one who knew the mentality of his contemporaries so well. That it was a hope born of despair is clear from his last novel, *Ein Kind unserer Zeit*.

In spite of the wealth of ideas, the theatrical effectiveness, the technical experiments (*e.g.*, the masks in *Pompeji*), the plays Horváth wrote after 1932 have not survived well on the stage. The repertory of German-language theaters since the early 1960s shows that Horváth's importance as a dramatist rests on the modern *Volksstücke* he wrote at the beginning of the 1930s. They have been a vital stimulus to the theater of our time. Productions by some of the most imaginative directors (Schenk, Kehlmann, Palitzsch, Hollmann, and others) have shown that Horváth's insights into the consciousness of people in a mass society have lost nothing of their relevance today. The influence of his style of playwriting, especially his dialogue, can be seen in the work of such young dramatists as Martin Sperr and Franz Xaver Kroetz, among others.

Horváth's significance as a playwright has tended to overshadow his achievements as a writer of fiction. His early *Sportmärchen* (written, 1924–26) are grotesquely humorous parables. In 1930 he published *Der ewige Spießer*, a satirical novel full of verbal humor and sociological insights. In the late 1930s, when the German stages were closed to him and when even in Austria he received little encouragement, he turned to writing novels again. *Jugend ohne Gott* (1938)—an immediate worldwide success after its publication in Holland—deals with the moral conflict of a teacher in a fascist country, where children are brainwashed in school and prepared for war in premilitary camps. He overcomes his apathy and cowardice and, though forced to leave the country, leaves behind him an example of integrity and decency. Such faith in at least the possibility of moral regeneration is abandoned in Horváth's last novel, *Ein Kind unserer Zeit* (1938). The central character, who brings Sladek to mind, finds refuge from isolation and unemployment in the army. He awakens to the horror of war but cannot escape the vicious circle of misery and violence. He commits a murder and freezes to death in a snowstorm—Horváth's symbol for a time of inhuman coldness. Memories of the aftermath of World War I and prophecies of the war to come merge in this, Horváth's final evocation of the wasteland that his generation was born into and from which it was unable to escape. Like *Jugend ohne Gott*, *Ein Kind unserer Zeit* is a first-person, confessional, journal-like narrative that effectively draws the reader into the consciousness Horváth is unmasking. In the persuasive lyrical tone of these two novels, a quality in Horváth's work becomes especially prominent: the desperate melancholy that so often accompanied even his most bitter criticism.

Works: *Das Buch der Tänze* (1922; The Book of Dances); *Die Bergbahn* (first performance, 1929; The Cable Car; originally entitled *Revolte auf Côte 3018* [first performance, 1927; Revolt at Benchmark 3018]); *Sladek, der schwarze Reichswehrmann* (first performance, 1929; Sladek, the Man of the Black Army); *Der ewige Spießer* (1930; The Eternal Bourgeois); *Italienische Nacht* (first performance, 1931; Italian Night); *Geschichten aus dem Wiener Wald* (first performance, 1931; Tales from the Vienna Woods); *Kasimir und Karoline* (first performance, 1932); *Hin und Her* (first performance, 1934; Back and Forth); *Mit dem Kopf durch die Wand* (first performance, 1935; Beating One's Head Against the Wall); *Glaube Liebe Hoffnung* (first performance, 1936; Faith Hope Charity); *Himmelwärts* (first performance, 1937; Heavenward); *Don Juan kommt aus dem Krieg* (first performance, 1937; Don Juan Comes Back from the war); *Figaro läßt sich scheiden* (first performance, 1937; Figaro Gets a Divorce); *Der jüngste Tag* (first performance, 1937; The Day of Judgment); *Ein Dorf ohne Männer* (first performance, 1937; A Village without Men); *Jugend ohne Gott* (1938; Eng. tr., Youth without God, in

The Age of the Fish, 1939); *Ein Kind unserer Zeit* (1938; Eng. tr., A Child of Our Time, in *The Age of the Fish*, 1939); *Die Unbekannte aus der Seine* (first performance, 1949; The Unknown Girl from the Seine); *Zeitalter der Fische* (1953; The Age of the Fish; includes *Jugend ohne Gott* and *Ein Kind unserer Zeit*; 1968 edition also includes *Der ewige Spießer*, and a story); *Pompeji* (first performance, 1959); *Unvollendet* . . . (ed. F. T. Csokor, 1961; Unfinished); *Stücke* (ed. T. Krischke, 1961; Plays); *Dramen* (eds. D. Huhn and H. Schneider, 1969); *Sportmärchen* (1969; Sport Fairy Tales); *Zur schönen Aussicht* (first performance, 1969; Hotel Grand Vista); *Rund um den Kongreß* (first performance, 1969; Around the Conference); *Ödön von Horváth, Gesammelte Werke* (eds. D. Hildebrandt, T. Krischke, W. Huder, 4 vols., 1970–71; Collected Works); *Von Spießern, Kleinbürgern und Angestellten* (ed. T. Krischke, 1971; Of Stuffed Shirts and White Collars); *Ödön von Horváth: Gesammelte Werke in acht Bänden* (eds. D. Hildebrandt and T. Krischke, 8 vols., 1972; Collected Works in Eight Volumes).

Bibliography: Fritz, A., Hildebrandt, D., and Huder, W., in *Akzente* 19, no. 2 (1972). Jarka, Horst, "Ödön von Horváth und das Kitschige," *Zeitschrift für deutsche Philologie* 91, no. 4 (1972). Kahl, K., Ödön von Horváth, 1966. Krischke, T., ed., *Materialien zu Ödön von Horváth*, 1970 (the bibliography of secondary material is unreliable.) Loram, Ian, "Ödön von Horváth: An Appraisal," *Monatshefte* 59 (spring 1967). Strelka, Joseph, *Brecht, Horváth, Dürrenmatt*, 1962. Weisstein, Ulrich, "Ödön von Horváth: A Child of Our Time," *Monatshefte* 52 (December 1960).

Horst Jarka[▲]

Franz Kafka

Franz Kafka, novelist and short-story writer, was one of the most important prose writers of the first half of the 20th century. He was born on 3 July 1883 in Prague, the son of a prosperous middle-class Jewish merchant, and died on 3 June 1924 at Kierling, near Vienna.

From his early youth on (with the exception of his last few years) Kafka, who was sensitive and introverted, was unhappy in his relationship with his father, who was concerned only with economic and social success. (See the argument and attempt at justification in *Brief an den Vater*; written, November 1919; published, 1953.) After elementary school Kafka attended, from 1893–1901, the German *Gymnasium* in the Old Town of Prague, where he did well despite his own statements to the contrary. He studied Henrik Ibsen and naturalist drama, Spinoza and Friedrich Nietzsche, was influenced by Darwin's theory of evolution, and declared himself a socialist.

During his first year at the university, Kafka vacillated among several courses of study. Under August Sauer he read chiefly Friedrich Hebbel and Adalbert Stifter. Then, in accordance with his father's wishes, he took up the study of law. At the same time he was taking a lively interest in the literary life of Prague. He was influenced by Franz Brentano, became interested in the works of Flaubert and Hugo von Hofmannsthal, and made friends with Max Brod. In the summer of 1903 he took the state examination in the history of law. In July 1905 he was a patient in a sanatorium at Zuckmantel (now Cukmantl), Silesia, where he met a woman who was to become important for him (see *Hochzeitsvorbereitungen auf dem Lande*; written, 1906–1907; published, 1953). Between November 1905 and June 1906 he took his final examinations for the doctorate of law. Kafka returned to the Zuckmantel sanatorium for a few months. From the autumn of 1906 to that of 1907 he worked as a clerk in court, after which he went to work for the Assicurazioni Generali insurance company.

On 30 July 1908 he took the position of a junior executive in the Workers' Accident Insurance Company for the Kingdom of Bohemia, in Prague, and soon built a reputation as an expert on insurance law. Nevertheless, the work did not satisfy him. He withdrew more and more from the literary world and social life and frequented only a limited circle. Dialogue with friends was replaced by the monologue of the diaries, which he kept from 1910 on. They contain unsparing analyses of himself, re-created dreams, projects for literary works, epigrams, and comments on his reading, but nothing of historical or biographical content.

Vacation travel provided breaks in the self-chosen monotony and solitude of Kafka's life. In 1909 he and Max and Otto Brod visited northern Italy (*Aeroplan in Brescia*, 1909); in 1910, he went to Paris; in 1911, with Max Brod to Switzerland, northern Italy, and Paris; in 1912, with Brod to Leipzig, where Kafka met the publishers Rowohlt and Wolff, and to Weimar, the city identified with Goethe.

In 1911 Kafka began to study Judaism and Hebrew. From 1913 (August of that year) to 1917 he was involved in a fluctuating relationship with Felice Bauer, of Berlin, to whom he was twice engaged to be married. In the autumn of 1913 he was a patient at the Riva tuberculosis sanatorium. At the beginning of 1915 he moved into his own apartment in Prague.

Kafka looked on the tuberculosis, which seriously recurred in August 1917, as destiny's judgment on his plans for his life and therefore definitely severed relations with Felice Bauer at the end of the year. He stayed in the country for fairly long periods at a time, first at the home of his youngest sister, Ottla, near Žatec. Intermittently he made attempts to return to his job, but these came to nothing, so that Kafka retired prematurely.

With increased time at his disposal, Kafka's preoccupation with Jewish religious tradition was intensified. During that period he did light farm work, went swimming, and took walks. From 1919 on he stayed in various sanatoriums. In the autumn of 1919 he entered into his third engagement, which, however, did not last long. In 1920 at Merano, he met Milena Jesenska-Pollak (*Briefe an Milena*, 1952). His mental and physical suffering continued. Kafka resumed reading Kierkegaard, and experienced an existential confrontation with Judaism. In 1921 he became acquainted with Robert Klopstock, who as doctor and friend was to watch over Kafka in his final illness.

A turning point in Kafka's life came with his association with Dora Dymant, a twenty-year-old girl from a Polish Hasidic family, whom he met in the summer of 1923 while vacationing on the Baltic. At the end of July 1923 he left Prague and his parents and moved to Berlin. Despite financial difficulties and physical pain, Kafka enjoyed with his companion some relatively happy months of peaceful creative work. But he was already doomed by his disease.

In March 1924, fatally ill, he was brought back to Prague by Brod. Kafka regarded this as a final defeat at the hands of his father and of life in general. The last period of his life was spent at the Kierling sanatorium near Vienna, where, owing to tuberculosis of the larynx, he was barely able to eat and could communicate with Robert Klopstock and Dora Dymant only in writing. On the last day of his life he corrected the proofs of the volume *Ein Hungerkünstler* (written, 1921-24; published, 1924). He died on 3 June 1924 and on 11 June was buried at the Jewish cemetery at Strašnice, Prague.

Kafka himself published, or prepared for publication, only six rather short books and some contributions to periodicals. The major part of his work was prepared for publication by Max Brod from the papers Kafka left, against Kafka's express wish that everything unpublished should be destroyed. From the textual point of view these Brod editions are not without defects. In particular, scholars seriously question the order of chapters in the novels.

Kafka's work is as fascinating as it is difficult to get into. To a large extent it has the qualities of a prototype, which is to say that individual situations, episodes, or actions, seen as in a vision or written in a surrealist or dreamlike manner, represent inner laws of the world, laws so all-inclusive that they seem to permit the most diverse interpretations. In Kafka's work it is no longer the well-rounded individual man who occupies the center of the stage. Rather it is an average type, who functions as one element in a total matrix that is no longer understood, cannot be surveyed, and is, as it were, driven automatically, a matrix in which God, too, no longer reveals himself. With an inventiveness that is paradoxical, grotesque, sometimes humorous but often grisly, types of human life are set face to face with the eschatological questions, and their existential guilt is showed them. Archetypal symbols, exact description, and imagination combine with extremely logical execution and diction to form a compelling whole that represents the hopelessness of modern life with matchless force. No answers are given to the eschatological questions. Kafka's works have had the most profound effect on prose written in German—and not only in German—during the middle years of the 20th century.

Surveying Kafka's work, we distinguish seven stages:

(1) Little plays that were performed on family occasions, poems, and an unfinished novel, *Das Kind und die Stadt*, on which Kafka was working in 1903, have disappeared; they were probably destroyed by Kafka himself. Poems that have been preserved in early letters, and the letters themselves, show that Kafka was influenced by Prague literary circles and by the style of the periodical *Der Kunstwart*, and contain little that is original.

(2) Under the influence of 19th-century literature, of Franz Brentano, and of Hofmannsthal's *Gespräch über Gedichte*, Kafka broke away from the *Kunstwart* style. From 1904 on he wrote little sketches of everyday life in simple language, though seen with an alienated eye. Kafka's first publication was a contribution made up of eight sketches entitled *Betrachtung*, which appeared in 1908 in the review *Hyperion*. These sketches made up the greater part of the little volume of the same title published at the beginning of 1913.

(3) From the early summer of 1912 until 1914, Kafka worked on the novel *Der Verschollene*, which he did not finish. (It was posthumously published by Brod under the title *Amerika* in 1927, and dramatized in 1957.) In May 1913 the first chapter was published separately under the title *Der Heizer*. For this Kafka was awarded the Fontane Prize in 1915. In the novel the young emigrant Karl Rossman arrives in the U. S. A., symbolized by the Statue of Liberty, and in his inexperienced simplicity repeatedly comes into conflict with his social and personal environment. Eventually he finds his very modest place in society at the "nature theater" of Oklahoma, a utopian institution in which every man is granted a place appropriate to his real inner potential. The utopia outlined, itself a fragment, seems to be intended to make the inward coincide with the outward, the here with the beyond, because under these conditions man realizes himself.

In Kafka's own view his real creative achievement began with *Das Urteil* (written, 22–23 September 1912; published, 1916) and *Die Verwandlung* (written, 1912; published, 1916). In these stories and later works his surrealistic invention exclusively served the elaboration of an absolute construct. In *Die Verwandlung*, for instance, Kafka presented a construct of the forces that divide the ego from the family and from the world of work with its duties; they also destroy the ego, for it cannot exist in a condition of absolute isolation.

(4) From the fall of 1914 on, the sphere of law is the formative influence in the structure of Kafka's model world. The high points of this period are the story *In der Strafkolonie* (written, 1914; published, 1919) and the fragmentary novel *Der Prozeß* (written, 1914–15, published, 1925; made into a film, 1962).

In der Strafkolonie, by depicting the jurisdiction and the last execution according to the "old" system, illustrates the transition from the medieval conception of life and God, which was cruel but gave meaning to suffering and death, consequently bringing redemption at the end of life, to the modern attitude, which is humane but ignorant of any higher meaning, which expresses itself in the dull work routine of the masses and the mindless pleasures of the privileged, and which can no longer triumph over death.

Der Prozeß confirms the key sentence spoken in *In der Strafkolonie* by the old commandant: "Guilt is never in doubt." One morning Josef K., a senior bank employee, is arrested, without knowing either the court or the charge. But neither is he put in prison. He is enmeshed in the offenses that he has committed, consciously or unconsciously—offenses against his own existence, his fellow men, and a higher meaning unknown to him. As he does not understand this, he opposes the verdict of guilty and tries by all possible means to defend himself. But this only involves him all the more deeply in his existential guilt, because he approaches everything and everyone only from the point of view of their usefulness in terms of his acquittal. It is precisely because of this that he fails to be truly human, is no longer equal to his profession, misses the (perhaps liberating) opportunity of love, is finally executed, and dies "like a dog." The heart of *Der Prozeß*'s meaning is the parable "Before the Law," which is communicated to Josef K. by the priest in the cathedral—a parable for which even the priest suggests several alternative meanings and which keeps the explicators permanently busy.

(5) After Kafka's world had found its highly significant expression in the rigorous limitation of a juridical-logical structure, his invention became freer, though he did not allow the validity of the model or the consistency of the execution to relax. In 1916 and 1917 he wrote the stories that were published under the title *Ein Landarzt* (1919). In the title story Kafka narrates a doctor's failure which begins at the moment when he seeks to be only a physician, because as such he cannot recognize the man's real "wound." In the story *Ein Bericht für eine Akademie*, the Darwinian theory of evolution is with great irony focused on the transformation of a single monkey into "man," who thereby loses more and more of his freedom and is more and more tied to external things. This provides Kafka an opportunity for some sharp thrusts at the alleged progress of civilization. Though some stories contain touches of humor, the collection offers no relief to the hopelessness of the human situation.

After Kafka's physical collapse in 1917 several more short prose pieces were written between the fall of 1917 and the beginning of 1918. Then his creativity dried up for some while amid self-tormenting attempts at justifying himself.

Only the impact of his meeting with Milena reawakened his creative powers. At the end of 1920, Kafka began to write tiny, static visions and parables, which he did not take seriously and therefore never published, and then some longer prose pieces. In a form of hitherto unequaled concision he worked out his parable model. The attempt at large-scale form led to the most important and most enigmatic of his novels, *Das Schloß* (written, 1921-22; published, 1926; dramatized by Max Brod, 1953), which failed in that it remained unfinished.

Das Schloß is a kind of counterpart to *Der Prozeß*, with, according to the narrow section of the world on which Kafka focuses, a related, but as it were inverted, theme. The main character, K., has left wife and child, his previous environment and profession, in order to traverse the wintry desolation in obedience to a call from Count Westwest for a surveyor. Because he reaches the village late at night, he cannot get to the castle. He never gets to it. Everything is densely symbolic: the lofty situation of the castle; the humble subservience of the villagers toward the most insignificant officials of the castle; the count's hopelessly hermetic official system, with its hierarchy and functions that no one understands, not even the officials themselves; the noises in the telephone; the tectonics of the landscape; the season; the profession of the main character; and other elements.

The surveyor then begins a forlorn struggle—for recognition of his appointment as the count's surveyor; for a conversation with his superior; for admission to the castle; and for enlightenment on its institutions, which would enable him to understand his situation and thus himself. When he gets nowhere in this direct struggle with the absolute, universal, all-controlling powers, but instead appears to be being driven farther and farther away from his goal, he makes an approach from a different direction—he attempts to reach the authorities through members of the village community. But he is not really able to join the community. At one point he comes upon inhabitants who are themselves excluded from the real community for some reason.

And when the surveyor does come closer to someone, as with Frieda, a castle official's mistress whom he makes his own mistress, he fails in essentials. For he does not love Frieda for her own sake, but takes her at first only with the ulterior motive of finding out something about her previous lover, and later to satisfy his physical desire. He is given no official duties as surveyor to the count, but at the same time he is not allowed to fill the most minor posts in the village. Thus he becomes estranged from everyone without achieving anything as a result. Even the occasional meetings with officials have only negative results because the surveyor expects something important in the wrong place and so misses it.

There is nothing in the entire novel, or in Kafka's work as a whole, to suggest that a happy ending was planned for the surveyor, as various interpreters think probable. For the individual, the world is always inscrutable; finite and limited as he is, he can never be happily merged in it. Though the novel remained, in line with its construction, incomplete, it shows human behavior within the context of supra-individual forces—namely, the conflict between the ego and society in the community at large and in love; the interweaving of archetype and individuality from the social to the religious sphere; the tension between instinctive living, which cannot achieve a higher happiness in the world, and conscious existence, which preserves itself only by breaking with the instincts; the antagonism between physical existence and mind; the antithesis, irreconcilable in the world, between liberty and the law. To merge into an all-encompassing whole is not granted to man in this life. These ultimate questions arise in the everyday life of a little village; they would arise in just the same way in any other social setting. Thus this great unfinished novel contains a cosmos that, by parable, symbol, and metaphor, raises, by a slight twist of alienation, the most ordinary everyday affairs and conditions into bearers of the most profound meaning.

(7) In his final creative phase, Kafka wrote the little volume *Ein Hungerkünstler* and other prose pieces (which he did not publish). The effort to create a complete cosmos was abandoned in favor of more concise themes. On the other hand he succeeded in completing what he intended. The artistic message achieved perfect equilibrium between what he was signifying and the signified. Mastery of diction and style was achieved. A new freedom in narration became apparent in the restrained humor that helped to overcome the tension and solipsism of the earlier works. A new objectivity proclaimed itself in the circumstance that several possible views were now open to the facts of the case (as was true earlier in the parable "Before the Law" in *Der Prozeß*). Thus totality is shown here no longer in the multiplicity of the world encompassed by the work but in the comprehensive and integrated interpretation of the relationships in which the individual is enmeshed. The acme of spiritualization of the most insignificant has been achieved.

Works: *Gespräch mit dem Beter* (published in the journal *Hyperion*, 1909; Eng. tr., Conversation with the Supplicant, 1948); *Gespräch mit dem Betrunkenen* (published in the journal *Hyperion*, 1909; Conversation with the Drunkard); *Aeroplan in Brescia* (published in the Prague daily *Bohemia*, 1909; Eng. tr., The Aeroplanes at Brescia, 1946); *Betrachtung* (1913; Eng. tr., Meditation, 1940); *Der Heizer,* (chapter 1 of *Amerika,* 1913; The Coal Stoker); *Die Verwandlung* (1916; Eng. tr., The Metamorphosis, 1937); *Das Urteil* (1916; Eng. tr., The Judgment, 1945); *In der Strafkolonie* (1919; Eng. tr., In the Penal Colony, 1941); *Ein Landarzt* (1919; Eng. tr., The Country Doctor, 1940); *Ein Hungerkünstler* (1924; Eng. tr., Hunger-Artist, 1938); *Der Prozeß* (1925; Eng. tr., The Trial, 1937); *Das Schloß* (1926; Eng. tr., The Castle, 1930); *Amerika* (1927; Eng. tr., America, 1938; Kafka's original title, *Der Verschollene* [The Missing Man]); *Beim Bau der chinesischen Mauer* (1931; Eng. tr., The Great Wall of China, 1933); *Gesammelte Schriften* (ed. M. Brod, 6 vols., 1935–37; Collected Writings); *Beschreibung eines Kampfes* (1936; Eng. tr., Description of a Struggle, 1958); *Tagebücher und Briefe* (1937; Diaries and Letters); *Gesammelte Werke* (9 vols., 1950–58; Collected Work); *Tagebücher 1910–23* (1951; Eng. tr., The Diaries of Franz Kafka, 1948); *Briefe an Milena* (1952; Eng. tr., Letters to Milena, 1953); *Brief an den Vater* (1953; Eng. tr., Letter to My Father, 1954); *Hochzeitsvorbereitungen auf dem Lande, und andere Prosa aus dem Nachlaß* (1953; Eng. tr., Wedding Preparations in the Country, 1954); *Briefe 1902–1924* (ed. M. Brod, 1958; Letters 1902–1924); *Briefe an Felice Bauer* (eds. E. Heller and J. Born, 1967; *Letters* to Felice Bauer).

Bibliography: Benson, A. T., "Franz Kafka: An American Bibliography," *Bulletin of Bibliography* 22 (1958):112–14. Brod, Max, *Franz Kafka: A Biography*, 1947; *Franz Kafka's Glauben und Lehre*, 1948; *Franz Kafka als wegweisende Gestalt*, 1951; and *Verzweiflung und Erlösung im Werk Franz Kafkas*, 1959. Camus, Albert, *Le mythe de Sisyphe*, 1942. Emrich, W., *Franz Kafka: A Critical Study of His Writings*, 1968. Flores, Angel, ed., *The Kafka Problem*, 1946. Heller, Erich, *The Disinherited Mind: Essays in Modern German Literature and Thought*, pp. 157–81, 1952. Janouch, G., *Conversations with Kafka*, 1953. Politzer, H., *Franz Kafka: Parable and Paradox*, 1962. Sokel, Walter H., *Franz Kafka*, 1966. Urzidil, Johannes, *There Goes Kafka*, 1968.

Jacob Steiner

Rudolf Kassner

Rudolf Kassner, essayist, philosopher, and narrative writer, was born on 11 September 1873 in Groß-Pavlovitz; he died on 1 April 1959 in Siders, Switzerland. The son of a factory- and estate-owner, he was afflicted with crippling poliomyelitis at the age of nine months. Everything he created, everything he experienced, was achieved in defiance of appalling physical handicaps—his excellent command of some eight languages, of world literature in general, and of the most diverse branches of knowledge ranging from philosophy and history to mathematics and the natural sciences; his many travels, which took him to the more inaccessible countries of the Far East; his active social life, which kept him in rewarding contact with the intellectual elite of Europe between 1895 and 1955; his literary productivity; and the serenity and firmness of character that he displayed in all these fields. Only at the age of eighty did he agree to give up his crutches for a wheelchair.

After a childhood, which in spite of his physical condition was happy, Kassner studied philology, history, and philosophy in Vienna and Berlin. In his youth he was under the influence of Nietzsche, though he early turned definitively away from him.

Externally Kassner's life was uneventful. His memorable friendship with Rainer Maria Rilke, began in 1907. His ambitious travels ended with World War I, during which he, like Rilke, lived mainly in Munich. From then until 1946 he lived in Vienna, suffering some difficulties through his negative attitude toward the Third Reich. During World War II he did not publish anything. In 1946 the generous maecenas Werner Reinhart became his benefactor, making it possible for Kassner to move to Switzerland. While the numerous books of this last period, in which his concept of physiognomics no longer plays the dominant role, unquestionably tend at times to recapitulate earlier works, there is no question of any failing of his powers. Some of these last works—*Die Geburt Christi* (1951), for instance—rank among his most valuable.

For all his philosophical and poetic talent, Kassner cannot be called either a philosopher or a poet, except in the sense that Plato (whom he so admired) was both. His physiognomical, mystical vision of the world is set down in essays, aphorism cycles, parables, dialogues, symbol-laden character sketches, short stories, personal memoirs, observations on the history of civilization, and extensive treatises on physiognomics. The charge of impenetrable obscurity often brought against Kassner can be upheld, if at all, only in these treatises, of which *Zahl und Gesicht* (1919) is the most important. His syntax is always orderly, his language, for all its solipsism, lively and direct, while humor, wit, and irony pervade all. Kassner is a master of the gnomic statement, comparable in this respect to Novalis or Goethe, and at the same time an excellent storyteller, as is evidenced especially in his three great books of memoirs—*Buch der Erinnerung* (1938; 2nd ed., 1954), *Die zweite Fahrt* (1946), and *Umgang der Jahre* (1949). The difficulty of his writing stems chiefly from his often puzzling terminology—which, however, can never be called jargon—and from his confusing abrupt transitions, or rather leaps, from one thought to another.

Beginning his literary career as a critic under the spell of neo-romantic aestheticism, he wrote, after a long stay in England, *Die Mystik, die Künstler und das Leben* (1900), a volume of essays on English romantics and pre-Raphaelites. Throughout his life Kassner was to retain this cordial affinity with the language, culture, and people of England that henceforth would become intensified. Later it was only with certain reservations that he allowed this first work—and the similarily oriented *Der Tod und die Maske* (1902)—to remain in his *oeuvre*.

A decisive factor in Kassner's discovery of his own nature was his encounter with Sören Kierkegaard and with Indian scriptures. *Der indische Idealismus* (1903) was the first work that was truly characteristic of him.

Not until his old age, however, did he become reconciled to the term mysticism, appropriate as it is to his cast of mind.

Among the works he published before the outbreak of World War I, *Von den Elementen der menschlichen Größe* (1911) and *Die Chimäre* (1914) deserve to be singled out. Here, as in all his later works Kassner is attempting an interpretive synopsis of all manifestations of the spirit—in nations, classes, and individuals; in all stages, transitional phases, and crises of culture; in history; in myths, religions, philosophical ideas, and systems; in poetry and other works of art; in science of all kinds; in dreams; even in numbers; and in the whole physical world as perceived in its symbolic configuration. In all these things Kassner, who hardly differentiates between thought and ocular sensory perception, perceives spiritual and intellectual relationships and processes that need explaining. To explain them, he uses primarily pairs of contrasting concepts, such as space and time, eye and ear, the world of the father and the world of the son, number and vision.

The meaning revealed to Kassner by a world looked at and interpreted in this way differs essentially from, say, the meaning that would emerge from a scientific examination of all things according to a category of causality, which he does not recognize. It also differs essentially from the meaning that is often sought behind appearances, beneath the surface. For Kassner the surface, rightly seen—the "skin" of things—is actually their true essence. To denote this intellectual-sensual relationship to the world peculiar to himself, Kassner in 1919 coined the expression physiognomics. This term dominates his work throughout the interwar period; among other elements it includes a protest against psychoanalysis, which Kassner detested.

Kassner's physiognomical interpretation of the world becomes considerably clearer when one recognizes that everything he wrote is essentially concerned with an analysis of Christianity. The salient factor in his work is his ruthless criticism of the modern spirit and antispirit, not only for its atheistic materialism but precisely for its metaphysical strivings. It would seem self-evident that this defender of the Christian tradition against all the anti-Christian tendencies of the modern world (who has so much in common with Pascal and Kierkegaard) must himself be a devout Christian, especially since his interpretation of the world is concerned with such apparently Christian ideas as "turning" (conversion), "sacrifice," "the holy," and "the god-man" (incarnation). Yet Kassner himself says that his thinking evolved out of a certain "rancor" against Christianity, and in his old age he was still rejecting belief in a personal God and in the Christ of the church. As to Kassner's strained relationship to Christianity, it should in the first place be noted that he regarded his own resistance to the Christian as something entirely different from the anti-Christian attitude of the typical modern man, which he so sharply castigated. He himself called it "the pagan in me," the pagan being for him perhaps even more definitely opposed to the modern spirit than to the Christian spirit. In a sense, the pagan is concerned with the pre-Christian, the modern spirit with the post-Christian.

Kassner often spoke quite openly of a dualism between the Christian and the pagan in his own nature. In 1931, for instance, he wrote to Spoerri that "the pagan and the Christian never completely coincide in my nature. But I tell myself that if they did coincide I could perhaps not live." Kassner recognized in the most diverse phenomena a mixture of the Christian and the pagan that was particularly appealing to him—in the personality of Goethe, in ancient Indian mysticism, and in Catholicism.

The major preoccupation of Kassner's physiognomics is nothing other than a synthesis of the Christian and the pagan (which, however, cannot coincide). The most extreme form this synthesis takes is that of an "esoteric Christianity"—a Christianity lacking an absolute personal God-the-Father, a Christianity concerned not with redeeming man from sin but with redeeming God "from man's incarnate heathenness," a Christianity in which "imagination" replaces "belief." For the sake of this esoteric Christianity, Kassner transposed Jesus from his Old Testament Jewish background to a setting of Greek culture and philosophy as the realization of the presentiments of Plato and the dreams of Socrates. Or he ranked Jesus with the Indian saints who need no god. What Kassner was attempting here is comparable in many respects to the aspirations of some of the great heretical mystics—and he did sometimes feel a spiritual kinship with Meister Eckart (ca. 1260–1327) or Jakob Boehme (1575–1624). But we may well ask whether in fact he was not even closer to the specifically modern spirit that he elsewhere so violently repudiated. Kassner's great argument with Christianity, which in his work remained unresolved to the very end, was, however, resolved in his life. One year before his death he was formally reconciled with the church.

Works: *Sonnengnade* (1895; Sun-Grace); *Der ewige Jude in der Dichtung* (1896; The Wandering Jew in Literature); *Die Mystik, die Künstler und das Leben* (1900; The Mystic, Artists and Life; republished as *Englische Dichter* [1920; English Poets]); *Zum Tode Oskar Wildes* (1901; On the Death of Oscar Wilde); *André Gide* (1901); *Peter Altenberg* (1901); *Der Tod und die Maske* (1902; Death and the Mask); *Der indische Idealismus* (1903; Indian Idealism); *Die Moral der Musik* (1903; The Moral of Music); *Motive* (1906; Motives); *Melancholia* (1908; Melancholy); *Der Dilettantismus* (1910; Dilettantism); *Von den Elementen der menschlichen Größe* (1911; On the Elements of Human Greatness); *Der indische Gedanke* (1913; Indian Thought); *Aus den Sätzen der Joghi* (1913; From the Tenets of Yogi); *Die Chimäre* (1914; Chimera); *Zahl und Gesicht* (1919; Number and Face); *Die Grundlagen der Physiognomik* (1922; Foundations of Physiognomy); *Die Verwandlung* (1925; Metamorphosis); *Das Leben und die Ansichten Tristram Shandys* (1925; Life and Opinions of Tristram Shandys); *Die Mythen der Seele* (1927; The Myths of the Soul); *Narziß, oder Mythos und Einbildungskraft* (1928; Narcissus, or Myth and Power of Imagination); *Das physiognomische Weltbild* (1930; The Physiognomic Conception of the World); *Physiognomik* (1932; Physiognomy); *Das Buch der Gleich-*

nisse (1934; Book of Parables); *Von der Einbildungskraft* (1936; On Imagination); *Buch der Erinnerung* (1938; Book of Recollection); *Der Gottmensch* (1938; God-Man); *Die zweite Fahrt* (1946; The Second Journey); *Transfiguration* (1946); *Das neunzehnte Jahrhundert* (1947; The Nineteenth Century); *Umgang der Jahre* (1949; Procession of the Years); *Sören Kierkegaard* (1949); *Die Agonie Platons* (1950; Plato's Agony); *Die Nacht des ungeborenen Lebens* (1950; The Night of the Unborn Life); *Die Geburt Christi* (1951; The Birth of Christ); *Das inwendige Reich* (1953; The Internal Realm); *Der Zauberer* (1955; The Sorcerer); *Das deutsche Antlitz* (1955; The German Countenance); *Der goldene Drachen* (1957; The Golden Dragon); *Gleichnis und Essay* (1958; Allegory and Essay); *Der Gottmensch und die Weltseele* (1960; God-Man and the Soul of the Universe); *Die Blinde schaut* (1963; The Blind Woman Looks); *Sämtliche Werke* (ed. Ernst Zinn, 1969; Collected Works).

Bibliography: Kensik, A. C., and Bodmer, D., eds., *Gedenkbuch zu Rudolf Kassners 80. Geburtstag*, 1953. Kensik, A. C., *Gespräche mit Kassner*, 1960. Mason, Eudo C., in *German Life and Letters*, 1953–54. Spoerri, T., "Das Vermächtnis Rudolf Kassners," *Schweizer Monatshefte* 41 (1961):55–62. Usinger, F., *Geist und Gestalt*, 1941; and *Tellurium*, 1966. Wieser, T., *Die Einbildungskraft bei Rudolf Kassner*, 1949.

Eudo C. Mason[▲]

Theodor Kramer

Born 1 January 1897, the son of the municipal doctor of Nieder-Hollabrunn in Lower Austria. Went to secondary school in Vienna, graduating in 1914; active service as a soldier 1915–18. After brief studies in Vienna Theodor Kramer entered the book trade. Every year he undertook extensive hiking tours through out-of-the-way parts of Lower Austria and northern Burgenland. In 1931 he fell seriously ill and became unemployed. Emigrated in 1939 to England, where he learned that his mother had been murdered in the concentration camp at Theresienstadt. From 1942 to 1957 he was librarian at the County Technical College at Guilford. In 1957 he returned to Vienna, a sick man, and died there on 3 April 1958.

Kramer, who came back from World War I seriously disabled, felt a brotherly sympathy for the outsiders in modern society. The subject of his poems is the life of simple people and their often vain attempt to cope with the pitiless harshness of their lives. His book *Mit der Ziehharmonika* (1936) is dedicated "To those who have no voice." His entire work is written for the brickmakers, limeburners, and moonshiners, outsiders in a village where the peasants' pride is the care of their land, for the journeymen and loafers, the wine and brandy drinkers, to whom he always felt attracted and whose despair is existentially akin to his own.

Kramer's world is narrowly limited. Austria's Waldviertel and Weinviertel, the river landscapes of the Danube and the outskirts of Vienna, found their voice in him, together with the preoccupations of the people living there. His style is influenced by Georg Trakl and Bertolt Brecht, but something of François Villon's attitude toward life continues in Kramer's writing, too. From his first publication, *Die Gaunerzinke* (1929), Kramer struck his own chord, which only occasionally and superficially has anything in common with the "new objectivity" (*Neue Sachlichkeit*). It is the chord of the folk song and the barrel organ, an "organ of dust" on which he played a subdued and melancholy melody, forever repeating himself and, when all the suffering is done, still praising the world. Every line is full of an undistorted vision and a specific, vernacular vocabulary.

These new discoveries in language and their unpretentious presentation, together with the absence of any kind of reflection, were no doubt factors that helped Kramer's poems to immediate success. It was not until the Nazi period that the universal popularity of his often bitter, always dry, and yet singable verses came to an end. After 1945 his poems failed to make an impression on the general public.

Kramer's poetry is rooted in his own experience. Whenever he leaves that ground and ventures into reflective verse, his poems lose their force and freshness. But as long as he remains in the world to which he belongs, the world of poor, abused humanity, his verse gains color and form and becomes the image of a self-contained universe.

Works: *Die Gaunerzinke* (1929; Rogue's Marking); *Kalendarium* (1930; Almanac); *Wir lagen in Wolhynien im Morast* (1931; We Were Lying in the Mud in Volyhynia); *Mit der Ziehharmonika* (1936; With the Accordion); *Verbannt aus Österreich* (1943; Exiled from Austria); *Die untere Schenke* (1946; The Lower Tavern); *Wien 38. Die grünen Kader* (1946; Vienna 38. The Green Cadres); *Lob der Verzweiflung* (1947; Praise of Desperation); *Vom schwarzen Wein* (1956; On Black Wine); *Einer bezeugt es* (1960; One Bears Witness).

Bibliography: Chvojka, Erwin, "Theodor Kramer," *Akzente* 9 (1962): 143–57. Zuckmayer, Carl, "Der Lyriker Theodor Kramer," *Forum* 4 (1959): 272–73.

Wieland Schmied

Karl Kraus

Karl Kraus, satirist, cultural critic, aphorist, and lyrical poet, was born on 4 April 1874 in Jičín, Bohemia, and died on 6 December 1936 in Vienna. When Kraus was two years old, his father, who was a wealthy manufacturer, moved with his family to Vienna. Kraus's school and university years coincided with the heyday of the Viennese Burgtheater and the lively literary activity so characteristic of the Austro-Hungarian capital. From both Kraus received decisive impressions. Though he matriculated in the law school at the university, he attended only philosophical and literary lectures without ever working toward a degree. He resisted his strong inclinations toward the stage; his dramatic gifts, however, evolved subsequently into his uncommon accomplishments as a reader of his own works and those of others.

Kraus's bent for polemics and satire is manifest in his early pamphlets, *Die demolierte Literatur* (1896) and *Eine Krone für Zion* (1898). An event of decisive importance for his literary career was the founding of *Die Fackel* (1899). The early contributors to this periodical included August Strindberg, Frank Wedekind, Detlev von Liliencron, Richard Dehmel, Peter Altenberg, Georg Trakl, Otto Stoessl, Else Lasker-Schüler, and Berthold Viertel, but from 1911 on to the time of Kraus's death in 1936, *Die Fackel* was written exclusively by Kraus himself. It was, in a sense, a spiritual diary, but it was also a militantly ethical periodical that began before long to play a unique role in the world of German letters. As conceived by Kraus the concern of his fighting mission, though pursued in *Die Fackel* by purely literary means, was less with literary matters than it was with generally spiritual and ethical matters. His writing posed a constant challenge to the prevailing corruption of the spirit in all domains of public life—in politics, law and justice, literature, and art. Kraus came to be the irreconcilable accuser of everything that was rotten in the State of Austria. The target of his most embittered hatred was the press, which he attacked with a persistence that might suggest that he considered such activity the purpose of his life. Indeed, to unmask the press as the embodiment of intellectual prostitution, as the instrument par excellence of the trivialization and mechanization of life, as a menace to the already sorely imperiled state of peace, was to him a fate-imposed obligation.

That Kraus saw the press and the dangers of its enormous power as he did—the Vienna press of his age showed journalism in its ugliest form—followed inevitably from the ethical imperative that was the supreme law of his life and his every endeavor. Because he measured everything by absolute standards, condoning no compromise however trivial, he was bound to regard the journalist who works under the aegis of day-to-day contingencies rather than of ultimate principles as the embodiment of everything evil. The slightest deviation from absolute integrity signified to him man's dehumanization, which, undermining society, must finally lead to its general collapse.

Kraus's polemical essays, in which he fought against the enslavement of man's natural drives by state and church, appeared in book form in the volumes *Sittlichkeit und Kriminalität* (1908) and *Die chinesische Mauer* (1910). Like all his writing, these essays were first published in *Die Fackel*.

Kraus's conception of language was of central importance to him and is of similar importance in any evaluation of his work. The word and the thing, he held, were one. In language he saw the magic passkey to unlock all doors. Indeed, his feared and fearful attacks—the purpose of which was to unmask the hypocrisy and the corruption of his age by making them, through the instrumentality of his mordant wit, a laughing stock for his readers—used language as a means to destroy the adversary. Purity of language was to him the measure of the writer's integrity.

"Since he considered language a direct index of morality, he believed that to purify language would produce a corresponding salutary effect on the ethical plane. Kraus assigned to language the primary role in human existence and elevated it to a vital position as man's only essential concern, to which every other consideration, regardless of its merits, becomes subordinate and tangential. When language loses its meaning by losing its firm basis in life, its definite correspondence to thoughts and deeds—the situation which he felt had occurred in his time—then the entire culture, which is constructed of language and exists only in language, is endangered. His aim was to restore this relationship. . . . His uncompromisingly idealistic program aimed at restoring meaning to language, the basis of the cultural and intellectual life of a nation" (Donald D. Daviau).

Kraus was thus not only the merciless and uncorruptible critic of his age but also the teacher of a new and wakeful awareness of language. There are many whose ears he trained to discern the hollow ring of vacuous phrases, of puff and lie, of shamelessness and perfidy that assaulted them from the columns of the daily press. And there are many whom he strengthened in the integrity of their conduct.

The world-war drama *Die letzten Tage der Menschheit*, which bursts all conventional dimensions, was a climax in Kraus's creative career. In Kraus's words, "by earthly measurements" a performance would require some ten nights on the stage. Actually a reading drama, the imagination of the reader has to provide the stage. The work was written during World War I. It appeared in special issues of *Die Fackel* and in 1922 as a book. Kraus never doubted that Austria's declaration of war in 1914 marked the beginning of the end of that state. This satirical tragedy evolves through the prophetic power of its creator into an apocalyptic warning of an impending world-engulfing disaster. It represents a vast fresco of events at the front as well as behind the lines and back home. A more powerful denunciation of war has never been written. The work has no single hero, though each scene, in this immense concert of scenes, has a hero of its own. There is no unity of time or of place or of action, but the unity of the idea is for that very reason only the more compelling.

Admittedly, today's general reader is not likely to follow all the details of this apocalyptic tragedy without explanatory notes. But this fact will not in any way diminish the impact on the reader; the drama remains uncannily timely, as exemplified by the epilogue *Die letzte Nacht* [The Last Night].

Kraus was one of the very few who never succumbed even for a moment to the chauvinistic poison that filled the air in those years. The only writer of rank to stand firmly against the Austrians who were embracing the war en masse, he challenged with absolute courage the powers that be. In Berlin, where the tide of warlike enthusiasm was running high, he read in public his sketch *Kant und ein Kantianer*, in which he contrasted the author of *Zum ewigen Frieden* with Emperor William II, who liked to fancy himself as fashioned in the mold of Kant and as one who embodied Kant's categorical imperative, but who was here referred to as a "second-class stage hero." The hope that the war would end in a German victory was to Kraus absolute treason, high treason against the spirit. On the basis of *Die letzten Tage der Menschheit*, professors at the Paris Sorbonne repeatedly proposed Kraus for the Nobel Peace Prize.

In his satirical sketches, epigrams, and dramas, Kraus waged a relentless war of cultural criticism, against which the press, his favorite target, had no defense but that of trying to ignore the attacker. His other victims, hopelessly discredited and held up as laughingstocks, also preferred on the whole to limit themselves to reproaching him with the negative character of his criticism, which they claimed "could only destroy but not build up." To be sure, a great satirist must have a clear conception of absolute values. His endeavor to remove the worthless must be inspired by the desire to make room for the worthwhile: and a profound faith in positive values and affirmative truths is actually the basic prerequisite for his creativity.

Kraus was always ready to praise excellence where he saw it. In the area of public life, he supported Liebknecht, Masaryk, and Lamasch; in the area of artistic creation, the great satirists Georg Lichtenberg, Johann Nestroy, and Jacques Offenbach; among his contemporaries, Strindberg, Wedekind, Altenberg, Trakl, Else Lasker-Schüler, and others. He revived interest in the great poets of the German baroque, and through his public readings of Shakespeare's plays he successfully opposed the trend of abandoning Shakespeare's works to the commercialized theater of the big city with its optical illusions and sound effects. In his public-reading series, standing alone at the lectern, he revealed the true power of the works of Goethe and Gerhart Hauptmann, of Ferdinand Raimund, Nestroy, Offenbach, and others.

In matters of form Kraus was no innovator. He said of himself that he was one who continued in the tradition of Shakespeare (in the Schlegel-Tieck translation) and the "lambent flame of language" of the older Goethe, both of whom exerted the strongest influence on him. In matters of content, however, his work is far removed from the poetry of the neoclassicists and neoromanticists. It bears the imprint of his age, having its roots in the past and at the same time pointing the way to the future.

Many of Kraus's poems are cerebral, their content frequently identical with his militant prose. Yet among his poems there are pieces of great lyrical power in which beauty of language and emotional content merge in perfect harmony. They are to be found in Kraus's nine volumes of *Worte in Versen* (1916–30). A collection of penetrating essays on questions of language, which he was preparing for publication during the years 1933 and 1934, appeared only after his death under the title of *Die Sprache* (1937). The collected volumes *Sprüche und Widersprüche* (1909), *Pro Domo et Mundo* (1912), and *Nachts* (1918) prove Kraus to be one of the greatest masters of the aphorism.

Kraus died when Austria was facing the menace of National Socialism at its western borders—this was two years before the forced Anschluß. The outbreak of barbarism in neighboring Germany may have precipitated his death. His last work, written during this time, was not published until 1952. Through an analysis of language and speech, *Die dritte Walpurgisnacht* portrays the horror of the Hitler era, his dictatorship and its literary henchmen. In this work Kraus provides a perceptive analysis of the diabolical nature of the Third Reich.

During his lifetime the impact of Kraus's work was essentially restricted to Vienna. Since the end of World War II wider circles in the realm of German letters have begun to bear witness to his importance and have acknowledged his influence, though not as yet in full proportion to his extraordinary contribution to the artistic and intellectual life of his age. Although Kraus's works condemned his time and although he foresaw prophetically the dangers inherent in modern civilization, leading to an ultimate apocalypse, his work in its totality is nevertheless a profession of faith in man and in the worth of life. It was his deep confidence that his work would endure and that through it he would "live on when I am gone." In this, too, he has proved prophetic.

Works: *Die demolierte Literatur* (1896; Literature Demolished); *Eine Krone für Zion* (1898; A Crown for Zion); *Sittlichkeit und Kriminalität* (1908; Morality and Criminality); *Sprüche und Widersprüche* (1909; Arguments and Counterarguments); *Die chinesische Mauer* (1910; The Great Wall of China); *Heine und die Folgen* (1910; Heine and Consequences); *Promo Domo et Mundo* (1912); *Nestroy und die Nachwelt* (1912; Nestroy and Posterity); *Worte in Versen* (1916–30; Words in Verse); *Nachts* (1918; At Night); *Weltgericht* (1919; World on Trial); *Ausgewählte Gedichte* (1920; Selected Poetry); *Literatur, oder Man wird doch da sehn* (1921; Literature, or What Can You Expect?); *Die letzten Tage der Menschheit* (1922; The Last Days of Mankind); *Untergang der Welt durch schwarze Magie* (1922; Destruction of the World by Black Magic); *Traumstück* (1923; Dream Play); *Wolkenkuckucksheim* (1923; Cloud Cuckoo-Land); *Traumtheater* (1924; Dream Theater); *Epigramme* (1927; Epigrams); *Die Unüberwindlichen* (1928; The Unconquerable Ones); *Literatur und Lüge* (1929; Literature and Lie); *Zeitstrophen* (1931; Timely Stanzas); *Shakespeares Sonette* (translations of the sonnets; 1933); *Die Sprache* (1937; The Language); *Die dritte Walpurgisnacht* (1952; The Third Walpurgis Night); *Werke* (ed. H. Fischer, 1952; Works).

Bibliography: Heller, Erich, *"The Last Days of Mankind," Cambridge Journal*, 1948; and *Disinherited Mind*, 1952. Kohn, C., *Karl Kraus: Le polémiste et l'écrivain defenseur des droits de l'individu*, 1962. Kraft, W., *Karl Kraus: Eine Einführung in sein Werk und eine Auswahl*, 1952. Liegler,

Leopold, *Karl Kraus und die Sprache*, 1918. Mayer, Hans, "Karl Kraus und die Nachwelt," *Sinn und Form* 9, no. 5 (1957). Muschg, Walter, *"Die letzten Tage der Menschheit,"* in *Von Trakl zu Brecht*, 1961. Rollet, E., "Karl Kraus," in *Deutschösterreichische Literaturgeschichte*, 1934. Schick, Paul, *Karl Kraus in Selbstzeugnissen und Bilddokumenten*, 1965. Stoessl, Otto, "Sprüche und Widersprüche," in *Lebensform und Dichtungsform*, 1914.

Frederick Ungar▲

Alfred Kubin

Born 10 April 1877 in Litoměřice, northern Bohemia. Alfred Kubin grew up in Salzburg and Zell-am-See. He was burdened, from an early age, by the death of his mother, difficult relations with his father, failure at school, and a high-strung and melancholic disposition. After an unrewarding three-years' apprenticeship to a photographer at Klagenfurt, he succumbed to a severe depression.

After his recovery, Kubin went to Munich in 1898 to study art and took lessons from Schmidt-Reutte and Gysis. But his artistic talent developed mainly under the influence of the words in the Munich museums of older artists such as Breughel, Holbein, Velasquez, and Goya—artists whom he cherished all his life—and the pictures of contemporary artists and personal acquaintance with some of them, such as Edvard Munch and Paul Klee.

It was the paintings and etchings of Max Klinger that, at a period of crisis in his artistic life, gave Kubin a new inspiration, through which he discovered his real talent as a draftsman. In 1902 Kubin held his first one-man exhibit at Paul Cassirer's gallery in Berlin. His pictures shocked the public but also gained recognition for him. A year later the first Kubin portfolio appeared, which made him more widely known.

In 1904 Kubin married the sister of the writer Oskar A. H. Schmitz, very well known in his day. Kubin traveled to Vienna, Prague and, in 1905, to Paris, where he met Odilon Redon, whom he much admired. In 1906 he acquired the little baroque castle of Zwickledt in Upper Austria close to the German border. In 1907 he went with Fritz von Herzmanovsky-Orlando to northern Italy and Venice. Subsequently he traveled chiefly in the Danube countries and in Yugoslavia with his close friend Karl Wolfskehl. He died at Zwickledt on 20 August 1959.

The period of traveling was marked by a great deal of varied artistic activity, by experiments with different techniques in which work in color alternated with black and white pen drawings. In 1911 Kubin began to illustrate books by contemporary authors as well as ones by earlier writers such as E. T. A. Hoffmann, Edgar Allan Poe, and Fiodor Dostoyevski. These illustrations constitute an important part of his body of drawings. After the formation of the new artists' association in Munich, in which Kandinsky, Jawlensky, and Erbslöh participated, Kubin helped to found the Blaue Reiter, the members of which, in particular Franz Marc, became his close friends. He was also an acquaintance or friend of Max Dauthendey, Gerhart Hauptmann, Thomas Mann, Ernst Jünger, and Max Beckmann.

In many of his drawings Kubin is a "narrator." He became a narrative writer under the impact of an overwhelming afflux of ideas and visions following an illness during which he was preoccupied with Eastern mysticism. After his subsequent journey to Italy with Herzmanovsky-Orlando, he wrote in 1907, in less than three months, the fantastic novel *Die andere Seite* (1909), which he later illustrated. The book describes a "dream state" and its decline and fall. It is the world of a second reality, a world in which Austrian novelists, in particular, tend to be especially interested. The wealth of visions is both fascinating and terrifying. In Kubin's dream world, the laws and logic of reality are constantly and unexpectedly transmuted into the impenetrable dream logic of the second reality of the novel. In this meticulously written and extremely vivid record of an apocalyptic collapse, elements from the life of dreams are incorporated in the action—which is uncanny and baffling to the rational consciousness—and woven into a texture of manifold meanings.

After World War I, *Die andere Seite* aroused great interest, for the collapse of the dream world it depicted was seen as an early prefiguration of the political and cultural collapse of the old Europe. The novel had a direct influence on Franz Kafka, in whose *Das Schloß* a number of scenes and elements of the action recall *Die andere Seite*, as well as on Gustav Meyrink and Hermann Kasack (see Kasack's *Die Stadt hinter dem Strom*).

Works: *Die andere Seite* (1909; Eng. tr., The Other Side, 1967); *Die sieben Todsünden* (1914; The Seven Mortal Sins); *Die Blätter mit dem Tod* (1914; Drawings of Death); *Kritiker* (1920; Critics); *Wilde Tiere* (1920; Wild Animals); *Von verschiedenen Ebenen* (1922; From Different Levels); *Der Guckkasten* (1925; The Peep Show); *Vom Schreibtisch eines Zeichners* (1939; From the Desk of a Graphic Artist); *Abenteuer einer Zeichenfeder* (1941; Adventures of a Drawing Pen); *Schemen* (1943; Phantoms); *Ein neurer Totentanz* (1947; A New Dance of Death); *Nüchterne Balladen* (1949; Sober Ballads); *Abendrot* (1950; Sunset Light); *Phantasien im Böhmerwald* (1951; Phantasies in the Bohemian Forest); *Dämonen und Nachtgesichte* (1959; Demons and Night Specters); *Ringen mit dem Engel: Künstlerbriefe 1933-1955* (1964;

Wrestling with the Angel: Artist's Letters 1933–1955); *Briefe an eine Freundin* (1965; Letters to a Friend).

English translations in collections: *Alfred Kubin: Oils, Watercolors, Drawings* (1957).

Bibliography: Hewig, A., *Phantastische Wirklichkeit*, 1967. Otte, K., and Raabe, Paul, eds., *Alfred Kubin: Leben, Werk, Wirkung*, 1957. Praschek, Helmut, in *Germanistik*, 1963, p. 724.

Wolfgang Schneditz

Christine Lavant

Christine Lavant (pseudonym of Christine Habernig, née Thonhauser) was born on 4 July 1915, the ninth and youngest child of a miner, at Groß-Edling near St. Stefan in the Lavant valley, Carinthia. Began writing when still very young. Has been married since 1939. For many years she earned her living by knitting, although she soon gained recognition for her writing and was encouraged by receiving several prizes, including the Trakl Prize in 1964.

The volume of poems *Die Bettlerschale* (1956) won Christine Lavant recognition as an original poet. The preceding book of poems, *Die unvollendete Liebe* (1949), was still strongly marked by the impact of Rilke; several slender prose volumes with their "erratic vagueness and fairy-tale remoteness" (Wieland Schmied) are of lesser stature than her poetry. From *Die Bettlerschale* through *Spindel im Mond* (1959) to *Der Pfauenschrei* (1962), her poetry gained in depth without deviation from its chosen course.

To this day, Christine Lavant's outward life and her poetic themes are dictated by her modest circumstances and the fact that she has never left St. Stefan. In an unquestioned personal Catholic faith, the poet in her asserts itself in worldly love and in longing for divine love, striving for a new experience of the world and God alike. Her verse sometimes sounds monotonous owing to the consistent use of iambs and trochees in long lines, either unrhymed or else interwoven in intricate rhyme patterns. Yet her poems are animated by a passion for language that occasionally seems almost mannered—note especially the eccentric compound words, the use of endless new variants for favorite images like moon, room, garden, or tree, and the frequent use of diminutives.

Christine Lavant's most recent prose, perhaps, does point to a new departure. In *Lumpensammler* (1961) a graphic and humorously rustic narrative style combines with naive religious feeling. It would be wrong to regard the work of Christine Lavant as a provincial idyll. It is, instead, an unspoiled human being's determined effort to understand and express the things of life and the world in terms of her own everyday surroundings.

Works: *Das Kind* (1948; The Child); *Die unvollendete Liebe* (1949; Unfinished Love); *Das Krüglein* (1949; The Small Jug); *Baruscha* (1952); *Die Bettlerschale* (1956; The Beggar's Bowl); *Die Rosenkugel* (1956; Ball of Roses); *Sonnenvogel* (1960; Sun Bird); *Spindel im Mond* (1961; Spindle in the Moon); *Lumpensammler* (1961; Rag Collector); *Wirf ab den Lehm* (1961; Throw off the Clay); *Der Pfauenschrei* (1962; The Cry of the Peacock); *Nell* (1969); *Gedichte* (ed. G. Lübbe-Grothues, 1972; Poems).

Bibliography: Aichinger, Ingrid, "Alles geht im Schwermutkreise: Christine Lavant zum fünfzigsten Geburtstag," *Österreich in Geschichte und Literatur* 9 (1965):429–47. Blomster, Wesley V., "Christine Lavant," *Symposium* 19 (1965):19–37. Langer, Norbert, "Christine Lavant," *Wort in der Zeit* 2 (September 1956):20–22. Lübbe-Grothues, G., "Zur Gedichtsprache der Christine Lavant," *Zeitschrift für deutsche Philologie* 87 (1968):613–30. Schwarz, Robert, on *Nell*, in *Books Abroad* 44, no. 2 (1970):305–306.

Inge Meidinger-Geise

Josef Leitgeb

Born 17 August 1897 into a South Tyrolese family in Bischofshofen (province of Salzburg). Josef Leitgeb's father was an employee with the railways. The family moved to Innsbruck when Josef was still very young, and, having lost his mother, he lived a few years in an orphanage before his father again set up house. Straight from school he went into active military service in 1915, fought in World War I, and was taken prisoner. After his return he became a schoolteacher, first in several villages of the Tyrol and then at Innsbruck. Along with his teaching duties, he studied law and received his doctorate in 1925, but he did not abandon the teaching profession. As an officer in World War II he served in Russia, France, and Italy. Afterward, in 1945, he became city-school supervisor at Innsbruck. Together with Friedrich Punt and Hermann Lechner he founded the literary almanac *Wort im Gebirge* in 1948. He remained its chief editor until his death on 9 April 1952.

Leitgeb's earliest works were poems, which were published in 1921 in the periodical *Der Brenner*. His poetry of the years of World War I was collected in the slender volume *Gedichte* (1922), which was followed at long intervals by other collections of poems: *Musik der Landschaft* (1935), *Läuterungen* (1938), *Vita somnium breve* (1943), and *Lebenszeichen* (1951). As these books of poems succeeded each other, they marked the poet's slow progress from the initial influence of Georg Trakl and Rainer Maria Rilke to a message and forms of expression all his own. His poems are a single paean to life, which he absorbs with all his senses; yet the sensuous impression is sublimated by thought into pure humanity and floating melody. He is a sovereign master of form, from the simple quatrain to the sonnet and ode. His outstanding achievement is his lyrical portrayal of landscapes from the south and from his native region; in these poems impressions and reflections are combined in masterly polyphonic writing. It should not be forgotten that Leitgeb, under a pseudonym, wrote satirical anti-German poems, which were published in the little magazine *Der Sumpf* in 1933. They are no longer extant.

The first of Leitgeb's narrative works is the novel *Kinderlegende* (1934). Although its subject is an episode taken from the time of the witchcraft trials in Tyrol, it is not an historical novel, inasmuch as the author's main concern is with the demonic nature of evil, whereby an innocent child is convicted and so destroyed. The novel *Christian und Brigitte* (1936) describes the life of a young teacher who struggles through restlessness and aberrations toward balance and finds it in love and in his profession.

Leitgeb's own development is described in the autobiographical volume *Das unversehrte Jahr* (1948). It is a chronicle of his childhood, from the first events fixed in the boy's memory until his father's death. In spirit and form the work is akin to Hans Carossa's books of reminiscences, but Leitgeb has more profound insights into the abyss of the soul and the contradictory nature of life. The volume *Kleine Erzählungen* (1951) is a collection of a few short stories in which occurrences from the author's own experience are retold with a realistic touch.

Of major significance is Leitgeb's reflective and critical prose, published in the volumes *Am Rande des Krieges* (1942), *Trinkt, O Augen* (1943), and *Von Blumen, Bäumen und Musik* (1947). The finest of the pieces not published during his lifetime are now collected in the volume *Abschied und fernes Bild* (1959). *Brief über den Süden*, previously available only in a privately printed edition, is a jewel of German prose. The same balanced flow of language is apparent in Leitgeb's translations of Antoine de Saint-Exupéry, which can be regarded as stylistic exercises for his own stories.

Works: *Gedichte* (1922; Poems); *Kinderlegende* (1934; Children's Legend); *Musik der Landschaft* (1935; Music of the Landscape); *Christian und Brigitte* (1936); *Läuterungen* (1938; Purifications); *Am Rande des Kriegs* (1942; At the Edge of War); *Trinkt, O Augen* (1943; Drink, O Eyes); *Vita somnium breve* (1943); *Von Blumen, Bäumen und Musik* (1947; Of Flowers, Trees, and Music); *Das unversehrte Jahr* (1948; The Intact Year); *Kleine Erzählungen* (1951; Short Tales); *Lebenszeichen* (1951; Signs of Life); *Sämtliche Gedichte* (1953; Complete Poems); *Abschied und fernes Bild* (1959; Farewell and Far-off Picture).

Bibliography: Bithell, Jethro, *Modern German Literature 1880–1950*, pp. 528–29, 1959. Punt, Friedrich, "Josef Leitgeb," *Wort in der Zeit* 3, no. 9 (1957):1–10. Wolf, Josef, *Josef Leitgeb: Leben und Werk*, 1966.

Eugen Thurnher

Nikolaus Lenau

Nikolaus Lenau (pseudonym of Nikolaus Franz Niembsch von Strehlenau) was born 13 August 1802 in Csatád near Temesvár in southern Hungary (now in Rumania), the son of a middle-class German family. The "von" was added to the name in 1821 when Lenau's paternal grandfather was honored with a patent of nobility for his faithful service to the state as a civil servant. Lenau's parents were unhappily married, and the troubled atmosphere of his home, as well as his irregular schooling, and his temporary loss of religious faith as a young man, only served to foster Lenau's basic instability. His father, Franz von Niembsch, a minor government official and former army officer who was given to gambling and dissipation, died in 1807 at the age of twenty-nine. He had been divorced from his wife, Therese, a nervous, emotional woman, who spoiled her son and protected him from all discipline. Lenau was always passionately devoted to his mother as evidenced by his many letters to her. In 1811 she married Karl Vogel, a wealthy Budapest physician, and the young Lenau was sent to live with his grandparents in Stockerau, Austria.

His new home enabled Lenau later to attend the University of Vienna, where he studied philosophy for three years. Subsequently he studied Hungarian law at Preßburg (now Bratislava), agriculture at Altenburg, German law at Vienna, and finally medicine at Heidelberg. He never completed any course of study but came closest to earning a degree in medicine. Just prior to taking his final examination in 1830, however, he was left a modest inheritance by his grandmother, and he withdrew abruptly in order to follow his inclination to become an independent writer.

This basic inability to persevere in any undertaking is symptomatic of Lenau's general character, temperament, and approach to life. He lacked inner stability, and a constant feeling of restlessness and yearning drove him daimonically, making it impossible for him to persist in any enterprise or to find peace of mind anywhere. He seemed to suffer from a split personality, which is reflected outwardly in his constant shuttling between Vienna and Stuttgart and inwardly in his vacillation between the extremes of devout religious belief and the feeling of total nihilism. He suffered intensely from such a tormented existence, and it is not surprising that the mood of melancholy and resignation predominates in his writings.

Lenau had been drawn to poetry by his friendships with young writers in Stockerau and Vienna, and in 1827 he published his first poems in the journal *Aurora*. When he traveled to Stuttgart in 1831, he was already known there and was warmly received by the circle of Swabian poets including Gustav Schwab, Justinius Kerner, Karl Mayer, and Ludwig Uhland. Schwab was particularly drawn to the young Lenau and arranged for the publication of his first volume of lyric verse, *Gedichte* (1832). The pseudonym Lenau was adopted in order to avoid possible consequences of the strict censorship of the Metternich era, although neither the contents of Lenau's works nor his political activities were radical enough to warrant such a precaution. When his real name was discovered, he was summoned by the Austrian authorities for an interview, but no further consequences resulted.

Lenau's first collection of poems, which are predominantly lyric descriptions of nature, portraying the seasons, the limitless Hungarian steppes, and scenes of peasant life, was well received, and it seemed that he had found his true career. He became engaged to Schwab's niece Lotte Gmelin and for a time was truly happy. He was soon gripped once more by restlessness, however, or by what he himself called his inner "daimon of unhappiness." Recognizing that he was not stable enough for marriage, he abruptly broke his engagement, a step that clouded his friendship with Schwab, who felt he could no longer trust the young Lenau. Lenau's state of mind was further aggravated by the loss of half his inheritance in a speculative business deal in Austria.

Characteristic of the romantic dreamer that he was, Lenau conceived the notion that a trip to America would restore both his equilibrium and his fortunes. He anticipated receiving great poetic inspiration from the primeval forests and particularly from Niagara Falls. In a letter to Schwab explaining his decision to go to America, Lenau wrote that he wanted to accomplish great things in art: "My artistic education is the highest goal of my life. I would crucify myself if it would help me to produce a good poem." At the same time he expected great financial gain from land investments and planned to return to Europe after five years a wealthy man.

The trip seems to have been ill-fated from the beginning. Only after great difficulty and the loss of more of his funds did Lenau arrive in Baltimore on 7 October 1832. He bought land in Ohio, but through impatience he resold it before he realized any profit. He suffered from homesickness, was depressed by the winter climate and the absence of songbirds, and was plagued by ill health. The wild forests repelled rather than inspired him (*Der Urwald*), and although his visit to Niagara Falls resulted in a number of memorable poems, most notably *Niagara* and *Die drei Indianer*, in general he experienced none of the joyous uplift that he had expected in the new world of freedom and opportunity.

The most significant and positive result of Lenau's trip to America came from his visits to the religious colony of Father George Rapp in Economy, Pennsylvania, where Lenau's religious belief was revived. Although he had been raised as a Catholic, he had gone through lengthy periods of skepticism and pantheism. Despite this reawakening of religious belief, which became an important influence in his later works, Lenau returned to Europe in 1833 disappointed, disillusioned, and thoroughly contemptuous of America and Americans, who, in his opinion, had no ideals and were interested only in making money. Despite their inaccuracy, his negative views of American life gained wide circulation in Europe and prevailed into the twentieth century.

Back in Vienna again, Lenau fell deeply in love with Sophie von Löwenthal, the wife of an Austrian government official. Although he realized the hopelessness of his position, he was powerless to break away from her despite a number of attempts to do so. Later he became engaged first to Karoline Unger and at another time, in 1844, made plans to marry Marie Behrends. Before he could organize his personal life, however, he suffered a nervous breakdown and eventually lapsed into mental illness from which he never recovered. He died at the asylum in Oberdöbling, near Vienna, in 1850.

Lenau's poetic reputation was established immediately with his first collection of poems and became more widespread with the appearance of *Neuere Gedichte* (1838). His talent was primarily lyric even in his longer epic works, partly because of the basic musicality of his nature (he was an accomplished violinist and guitarist); and partly because all of his writings are intensely personal expressions of his own moods and feelings. He was endowed with unusually acute visual and auditory perceptions, evident in the striking images and metaphors in which he captures scenes from nature. The Austrian Alps and the ocean are among his favorite settings, while autumn, transitoriness, and death represent his principal themes. He is still regarded as one of Austria's greatest lyric poets. A memorial library has been established in his former home in Stockerau, and a scholarly journal called the *Lenau Forum* was founded in 1969 to promote research on Lenau and his period.

Although his epics and dramas are less successful than his lyrical poems, they are important for tracing Lenau's philosophical development and his struggle with ultimate questions of spiritual and moral freedom. His drama *Faust* (1836) was the immediate result of the resurgence of religious feeling that he had experienced in Economy, Pennsylvania. Rejecting Goethe's *Faust*, which Lenau found repugnant, he turned back to the original Faust legend for his work, and presented a Faust who, completely disillusioned at the end, takes his own life. Thus, despite its seemingly orthodox Christian outlook, this work actually symbolizes Lenau's feeling of hopelessness in life, for which he sees no possibility of remedy.

Lenau's search for religion is further evidenced in his epic *Savonarola* (1837), a mystical glorification of religious faith, written under the influence of Hans Martensen, who later became Primate of the Danish Church. This epic was planned as the central work in a trilogy, but the remaining works on Huss and Luther were never completed. Instead, Lenau produced another epic, *Die Albigenser* (1842), which treats the crusade, promoted by Pope Innocent III, against a minority religious group in southern France in the thirteenth century. Influenced by Hegelian dialectics and philosophy of history, Lenau was less interested in the issue of religious freedom than in showing that despite the successful oppression by the majority, there was actually no victor in the struggle. The possibility of reading this work as a parable of government suppression in Austria, however, caused his contemporaries to view Lenau as a champion of political freedom.

In Lenau's final epic, *Don Juan* (1844), in which he dispenses with all religious questions, the dark side of his nature is much in evidence. Although Lenau suffered a breakdown before he could give the work its final form, it is essentially complete in structure and thematic execution. A gifted individual becomes disillusioned with life and finally allows himself to be killed by an inferior opponent simply out of disgust with the emptiness of life. It is Lenau's most personal work, demonstrating two basic aspects of his personality: emotional restlessness and existential despair.

In the years since his death, attempts have been made to categorize Lenau as a representative of Byronian *Weltschmerz*, as a poet of pessimism and melancholy, or as a champion of political and religious freedom. He is too complex an individual, however, to be contained in any shallow formula. Essentially he is a subjective poet who wrote out of his own inner need. Yet, his finest poems transcend all limitations and labels and have touched responsive chords in readers from his time to the present.

Works: *Gedichte* (1832; Poems); *Faust* (1836; revised, 1840); *Savonarola* (1837; revised, 1844); *Neuere Gedichte* (1838; Newer Poems); *Die Albigenser* (1842; The Albigenses); *Don Juan* (1851); *Helena* (1851); *Nikolaus Lenau: Sämtliche Werke und Briefe* (ed. H. Engelhard, 1959; Complete Works and Letters); *Nikolaus Lenau: Briefe an Sophie von Löwenthal* (ed. P. Härtling, 1968; Letters to Sophie von Löwenthal); *Nikolaus Lenau: Briefwechsel* (ed. J. Buchowiecki, 1969; Correspondence).

English translations in collections: Poems and Letters of Nikolaus Lenau (ed. W. H. Root, 1964).

Bibliography: Arndt, Karl J. R., "The Effect of America on Lenau's Life and Work," *Germanic Review* 33 (1958). Auerbach, Berthold, *Nikolaus Lenau: Erinnerungen und Betrachtungen*, 1876. Bischoff, Heinrich, *Nikolaus Lenaus Lyrik: Ihre Geschichte, Chronologie und Textkritik*, 2 vols., 1921. Castle, Eduard, *Lenau und die Familie Löwenthal*, 1906. Greiner, Leo, *Nikolaus Lenau*, 1911. Grün, Anastasius, *Nikolaus Lenau: Lebensgeschichtliche Umrisse*, 1855. Schmidt, Hugo, "Religious Issues and Images in Lenau's Works," *Germanic Review* 39 (1964):163–82. Stamm, Israel S., "Lenau's Faust," *Germanic Review* 26 (1951). Turóczi-Trostler, József, *Lenau*, 1961.

Donald G. Daviau[▲]

Alexander Lernet-Holenia

Born 21 October 1897 in Vienna. Alexander Lernet-Holenia's mother was descended from an old Carinthian family, and his father was a naval officer of French origin. Lernet-Holenia himself was a cavalry officer in World War I and witnessed the collapse of the Hapsburg Empire when serving on the Russian front—an experience that was to leave its mark on him for the rest of his life. As a writer, he traveled frequently after the war, lived for a fairly long time in South America, and returned to Austria before the outbreak of World War II. He fought in the campaign against Poland, was wounded, and was thereupon assigned to the army film service as chief dramatic consultant. He now lives alternately at Saint Wolfgang on the Lake and in Vienna. Since 1969 he has been president of the Austrian P. E. N. Club.

Lernet-Holenia was able to turn his hand with equal facility to comedies, social novels, austere short stories, and the difficult hymnic forms of poetry. Even though he scored his first successes in the theater (*Demetrius*, 1926; *Österreichische Komödie*, 1926; *Ollapotrida*, 1927), Lernet-Holenia regards his poetry as his true message. His most important works, however, are probably his novels and short stories.

As an Austrian, who, like so many others, was haunted by the experience of the empire's fall, nowhere does Lernet-Holenia speak more clearly than in what he almost deprecatingly describes as his "army novels." In these he interpreted in almost mythical terms the events in which the doom of the monarchy was consummated: the cavalry regiments in *Ljubas Zobel* (1932; republished as *Die Frau im Zobel*, 1954) or in *Die Standarte* (1934; republished as *Das Leben für Maria Isabella*, 1966; film, *Mein Leben für Isabell*) go through a sort of experience of the end of the world on horseback. In his most successful novel, *Die Standarte*, he combined a romance with an account of the military end of the monarchy in Belgrade—a constellation of which Lernet-Holenia was rather fond. Astonishingly like Joseph Roth's *Radetzkymarsch*, this novel is essentially an analysis of Austria's internal disintegration.

A new approach, though still in the old tradition, is apparent in *Mars im Widder* (1947; banned after initial magazine publication in

1941) and *Beide Sizilien* (1942). In *Mars im Widder,* in which the story of an enigmatic love affair is interwoven with that of the Polish campaign, Lernet-Holenia tried to combine dream and reality in an "in-between" realm in which "the true event" comes to pass. The style is modeled on Kleist; concise, gripping, and most often dramatic, it contains much dialogue.

Lernet-Holenia holds his own against literary fashion and the drawing-room nobility. In his life and his work he upholds the image of the Austrian *grand seigneur* in a spiritual and spirited sense. Even though since World War II he has come to terms with the new circumstances (see the novels *Die Inseln unter dem Winde,* 1952, and *Der Graf Luna,* 1955), his originality and significance derive from the heritage of his generation and family background.

Works: *Pastorale* (1921); *Kanzonair* (1923); *Demetrius* (1926); *Österreichische Komödie* (1926; Austrian Comedy); *Ollapotrida* (1927); *Das Geheimnis Sankt Michaels* (1927; The Secret of Saint Michael); *Erotik* (1927; Erotic); *Parforce* (1928; Steeple-chase); *Die Frau in der Wolke* (1928; The Woman in the Cloud); *Tumult* (1929); *Die nächtliche Hochzeit* (1929; The Wedding at Night); *Kavaliere* (1930; Cavaliers); *Die Attraktion* (1930; The Attraction); *Kapriolen* (1931; Caprioles); *Die Abenteuer eines jungen Herrn in Polen* (1931; The Adventures of a Young Gentleman in Poland); *Ljubas Zobel* (1932; Ljuba's Sable); *Ich war Jack Mortimer* (1933; I Was Jack Mortimer); *Jo und der Herr zu Pferde* (1933; Jo and the Gentleman on Horseback); *Die goldene Horde* (1933; The Golden Horde); *Die Frau des Potiphar* (1934; Potiphar's Wife); *Die Standarte* (1934; The Flag; republished as *Das Leben für Maria Isabella* [1966; Life for Maria Isabella]); *Die neue Atlantis* (1935; The New Atlantis); *Der Herr von Paris* (1935; The Gentleman from Paris); *Der Baron Bagge* (1936; Baron Bagge); *Die Auferstehung des Maltravers* (1936; The Resurrection of Maltravers); *Der Mann im Hut* (1937; The Man in a Hat); *Mona Lisa* (1937); *Riviera* (1937); *Greta Garbo* (1938); *Strahlenheim* (1938); *Ein Traum in Rot* (1939; A Dream in Red); *Glastüren* (1939; Glass Doors); *Beide Sizilien* (1942; The Two Sicilies); *Die große Liebe* (1942; The Great Love); *Der 27. November* (1946; November 27th); *Spangenberg* (1946); *Die Titanen* (1946; The Titans); *Germanien* (1946; Ancient Germany); *Die Trophäe* (2 vols., 1946; The Trophy); *Mars im Widder* (1947; Mars in Aries); *Der 20. Juli* (1947; July 20th); *Der Graf von Saint Germain* (1948; The Count of Saint Germain); *Spanische Komödie* (1948; Spanish Comedy); *Drei große Liebesgeschichten* (1949; Three Great Love Stories); *An klingenden Ufern* (1950; At Ringing Shores); *Der junge Moncada* (1950; Young Moncada); *Die Wege der Welt* (1952; The Ways of the World); *Die Inseln unter dem Winde* (1952; Islands in Lee); *Monologische Kunst?—Ein Brief-*

wechsel zwischen Alexander Lernet-Holenia und Gottfried Benn (1953; Monologue Art?—A Correspondence between Alexander Lernet-Holenia and Gottfried Benn); *Die Lützowschen Reiter* (1955; Lützow's Riders); *Spionage* (1955; Espionage); *Der Graf Luna* (1955; Count Luna); *Das Finanzamt* (1955; The Internal Revenue Office); *Radetzky* (1956); *Das Goldkabinett* (1957; The Gold Cabinet); *Die vertauschten Briefe* (1958; The Interchanged Letters); *Die Schwäger des Königs* (1958; The King's Brothers-in-Law); *Land, das meine Sprache spricht* (1958; Land That Speaks My Language); *Prinz Eugen* (1960; Prince Eugene); *Mayerling* (1960); *Das Halsband der Königin* (1962; The Queen's Necklace); *Das Bad an der belgischen Küste* (1963; The Spa on the Belgian Coast); *Götter und Menschetn* (1964; Gods and Men); *Die weiße Dame* (1965; The White Lady); *Pilatus* (1967; Pontius Pilate); *Die Geheimnisse des Hauses Österreich* (1971; The Secrets of the House of Austria).

Bibliography: Bednall, J. B., "Alexander Lernet-Holenia," *Modern Languages* 43 (1962):28–31. Rippley, La Vern J., "Horse and Rider: Motif for the Dissolution of the Austrian Empire in Works by Lernet-Holenia," *University of Dayton Review* 6, no. 1:15–23. Schneditz, Wolfgang, "Alexander Lernet-Holenia," *Books Abroad* 22 (1948):229–32. Spiel, Hilde, "Alexander Lernet-Holenia: Zu seinem 60. Geburtstag," *Der Monat* 10 (October 1957):65–72.

Frank Trommler

Jakov Lind

Jakov Lind, born 10 February 1927 in Vienna, emigrated with his parents to the Netherlands in 1938. Survived the deportation of Jews by staying in hiding during the German occupation. Went to Palestine after World War II, where he was employed in a variety of jobs. Now lives in London as a writer.

Lind's prose is cruel, sometimes paralyzing; it deals with horror as though it were something one had to live with as a matter of course. His themes bear the mark of terror of fascism, of persecution, gas chambers, and concentration camps—that is to say, of personal experience. But he does not make heroes of the victims of all this suffering; on the contrary, in a sort of "twilight of the heroes" he goes out of his way to display the weakness and baseness to which people are prone in exceptional situations. Lind is fond of exaggerations, which sometimes go with lack of artistic discipline. What was still deeply moving in the stories in *Eine Seele aus Holz* (1962) became almost macabre attitudinizing in his novel *Landschaft in Beton* (1963).

Works: *Eine Seele aus Holz* (1962; Soul of Wood); *Landschaft in Beton* (1963; Eng. tr., Landscape in Concrete, 1966); *Die Öse* (1963; The Eyelet); Anna Laub (1965; Eng. tr., 1968); *Die Heiden* (1965; The Heathens); *Das Sterben der Silberfüchse* (1965; The Silver Foxes Are Dead); *Die Auferstehung* (1965; The Resurrection); *Eine bessere Welt* (1966; Eng. tr., Ergo, 1967); *Angst und Hunger* (1968; Eng. tr., Fear and Hunger, 1968); *Selbstporträt* (1970; Eng. tr., Counting My Steps . . . Then Yours, 1969); *Numbers* (in English, 1972); *Nahaufnahme* (1973; Close-up); *The Trip to Jerusalem* (in English, 1973).

English translations in collections: Soul of Wood, and Other Stories (1964); *The Silver Foxes Are Dead, and Other Plays* (1968).

Bibliography: Geismar, Maxwell, on *Soul of Wood*, in *New York Times Book Review*, 24 January 1965. Opitz, Kurt, on *Angst und Hunger*, in *Books Abroad*, 1969, p. 263. Pawel, Ernst, on *Numbers*, in *New York Times Book Review*, 11 June 1972, pp. 6, 22. Zohn, Harry, on *Eine bessere Welt*, in *Books Abroad*, 1967, p. 437.

Martin Gregor-Dellin

Georg Lukács

Georg (von) Lukács was born on 13 April 1885, the son of an ennobled Budapest banker. He studied in Heidelberg, Paris, and Berlin. The most lasting influences on him at that time were those of the philosophers Wilhelm Windelband, Wilhelm Dilthey, and Max Weber. He soon espoused the workers' cause and frequented revolutionary circles in Zurich and Paris.

In 1919 Lukács took part in the communist uprising in Budapest and became People's Commissar for Education and Culture in Béla Kun's revolutionary government. After the failure of the revolt, Lukács fled to Berlin in 1920 and lived there as a writer and publicist. Most of his work, published in communist newspapers and periodicals, was intended as a contribution to political, literary, and aesthetic debates within the Communist Party, of which he was a member. In 1933 he emigrated with his friend Johannes R. Becher to the Soviet Union, where he developed, within the framework of socialist realism (the ruling communist literary doctrine), his own concept of realism. But Lukács's concept was quite different from the officially approved doctrine, and although in his studies he repeatedly made references to the principles of socialist realism, these principles underwent a shift in emphasis and meaning.

In 1945 Lukács returned from Moscow to Budapest, which by then had been taken by the Russians. There he was given a university chair in cultural philosophy and aesthetics. But he soon came into conflict—and one that was to grow—with the officially approved doctrine of literature. The Communist Party reproached him with overestimating the "bourgeois heritage" in socialist art, with valuing Balzac, Lev Tolstoi, and Thomas Mann above the best proletarian writers, and with measuring the latter's work by abstract standards of quality having nothing to do with the real class struggle.

After Stalin's death Lukács became one of the leading personalities in the ideological thaw in Hungary. He developed the thesis that the main contradiction in today's world was not that between capitalist and communist countries, but that between "the forces of peace, progress, and rationalism on the one side and the forces of war, reaction, and irrationalism on the other." In the Hungarian intellectual group, the so-called Petőfi circle, he advocated the liberalization of political life. During the 1956 revolt, Lukács was Minister of Education in the Nagy government and after its collapse was deported to Rumania by the Russians. Later he was allowed to return to Budapest, where he lived as a private scholar until his death on 4 June 1971.

Lukács's aesthetic views are enormously influential both in the West and the East. In line with Dilthey's methodology of types, his *Die Theorie des Romans*, written during World War I and published in 1920 (new edition, 1963), presented a metaphysical phenomenology of the novel and warned of its impending crisis. This book had a revolutionizing effect on literary theory. In 1923 he published a book entitled *Geschichte und Klassenbewußtsein*, in which, joining with Hegel (and without being acquainted with the early works of Marx, which were not to be published until 1932), he developed a "theory of man's alienation from his product." Lukács was concerned above all with the aesthetic consequences of this alienation and interpreted great works of literature, in a somewhat involved manner, as "the complicated reflection in ideas of social processes." He thus created the model that all Marxist literary critics have since followed.

In the mid-1920s Lukács became involved in a controversy with Ernst Bloch regarding the position of expressionism and modern literature as a whole (James Joyce, Marcel Proust). Whereas Bloch defended expressionism as an extension of artistic means of expression, Lukács condemned it as "bourgeois decadence." This interpretation led him in the 1930s to the view that the bourgeois novel from Balzac to Thomas Mann represented the binding code of law for great contemporary art, which meant setting up the methods of the bourgeois novel as the model of "new socialist art." With this view he laid himself open to attack from two sides: from the modern bourgeois men of letters, who took their bearings from the methods of Franz Kafka or Proust, and from the champions of the "cult of the proletariat," which set the "writing worker" against the art of the past and was incapable of reflecting the "totality" of all social relationships. This was the war on two fronts in which Lukács was engaged until his death.

In a voluminous work on aesthetics, which was not completed before his death, Lukács built up a system from the scattered remarks on literature to be found in the works of Marx and Engels and formulated the literary doctrine of Marxism: "Art is a specific way of reflecting social reality; it must express the totality of this social reality; its method must be rationalistic and it must contain a dimension of the future—that is, it must have a social perspective."

It cannot be gainsaid that Lukács's aesthetic dogmatism has had a baneful influence on literature in the communist camp. But with Lukács, God dwelled in the detail: the subtlety of his concrete case studies aroused the admiration of all his great contemporaries and assured him of a safe place in literature. Another interesting matter is the discussion that he carried on for years with French existentialists, especially with Jean-Paul Sartre; this turned mainly on epistemological and political questions and increasingly lead to a close rapprochement between him and Sartre.

Noteworthy, too, is his book *Die Zerstörung der Vernunft* (1954 and 1962), which is a sharp criticism of German philosophy "from Schelling to Hitler." Lukács regarded German philosophy as a reflection of "Germany's political calamity" and interpreted it sweepingly as a process leading "from rationalism to irrationalism."

Works: *Die Seele und die Formen: Essays* (1911; The Soul and the Forms); *Die Theorie des Romans: Ein geschichtsphilosophischer Versuch über die Formen der großen Epik* (1920; Eng. tr., The Theory of the Novel, 1971); *Geschichte nud Klassenbewußstein: Studien über marxistische Dialektik* (1923; Eng. tr., History and Class Consciousness: Studies in Marxist Dialectics, 1971); *Lenin: Studie über den Zusammenhang seiner Gedanken* (1924; Eng. tr., Lenin: A Study on the Unity of His Thought, 1970); *Moses Hess und die Probleme der idealistischen Dialektik* (1926; Moses Hess and the Problems of Idealistic Dialectics); *Goethe und seine Zeit* (1947; Eng. tr., Goethe and His Age, 1968); *Der junge Hegel: Über die Beziehungen von Dialektik und Ökonomie* (1948; The Young Hegel: The Relationship between Dialectics and Economy); *Essays über den Realismus* (1948; Essays on Realism); *Schicksalswende: Beiträge zu einer neuen deutschen Ideologie* (1948; Turning Point of Fate: Contributions to a New German Ideology); *Karl Marx und Friedrich Engels als Literaturhistoriker* (1948; Karl Marx and Friedrich Engels as Literary Historians); *Der russische Realismus in der Weltliteratur* (1948; Russian Realism in World Literature); *Thomas Mann* (1949; Eng. tr., Essays on Thomas Mann, 1964); *Deutsche Realisten des 19. Jahrhunderts* (1951; German Realists of the 19th Century); *Balzac und der französische Realismus* (1952; Balzac and French Realism); *Skizze einer Geschichte der neuern deutschen Literatur* (1953; Outline of the History of Modern German Literature); *Die Zerstörung der Vernunft* (1954; The Destruction of Reason); *Beiträge zur Geschichte der Ästhetik* (1954; Contributions to the History of Aesthetics); *Der Historische Roman* (1955; Eng. tr., The Historical Novel, 1962); *Probleme des Realismus* (2nd, enl. ed. of *Essays über den Realismus*, 1955; Problems of Realism); *Wider den mißverstandenen Realismus* (1958; Brit. tr., The Meaning of Contemporary Realism, 1963; Am. tr., Realism in Our Time: Literature and the Class Struggle, 1964); *Schriften zur Literatursoziologie* (ed. Peter Ludz, 1961; Writings on

Literary Sociology); *Werke: Gesamtausgabe* (15 vols., 1962 ff.; Works: Collected Edition); *Von Nietzsche zu Hitler, oder Der Irrationalismus und die deutsche Politik* (1966; From Nietzsche to Hitler, or Irrationalism and German Politics); *Schriften zur Ideologie und Politik* (ed. Peter Ludz, 1967; Writings on Ideology and Politics); *Ausgewählte Schriften* (4 vols., 1967 ff.; Selected Writings); *Über die Besonderheit als Kategorie der Ästhetik* (1967; On the Special as a Category of Aesthetics); *Gespräche mit Georg Lukács: Hans Heinz Holz, Leo Kofler, Wolfgang Abendroth* (ed. by Theo Pinkus, 1967; Conversations with Georg Lukács); *Solschenizyn* (1970; Eng. tr., Solzhenitsyn, 1970); *Zur Ontologie des gesellschaftlichen Seins: Hegels falsche und echte Ontologie* (1972; On the Ontology of Social Existence: Hegel's False and True Ontology).

English translations in collections: *Studies in European Realism* (1950; includes translations of chapters from *Der russische Realismus in der Weltliteratur* and *Balzac und der französische Realismus*); *Writer and Critic, and Other Essays* (1970; includes essays from *Probleme des Realismus*).

Bibliography: Althaus, Horst, *Georg Lukács, oder Bürgerlichkeit als Vorschule einer marxistischen Ästhetik*, 1962. Demetz, Peter, *Marx, Engels and the Poets: Origins of Marxist Literary Criticism*, translated by Jeffrey L. Sammons, revised and enlarged edition, 1967; and "The Uses of Lukács," *The Yale Review* 54 (1964–65):435–40. Heller, Agnes, "Lukács' Aesthetics," *The New Hungarian Quarterly* 7, no. 24 (1966):84–94. Kofler, Leo, *Zur Theorie der modernen literatur*, 1962. Lichtheim, George, *George Lukács*, Modern Masters 6, 1970. Man, Paul de, "George Lukács' Theory of the Novel," *Modern Language Notes* 81 (1966):527–34. Maslow, Vera, "Georg Lukács and the Unconscious," *The Journal of Aesthetics and Art Criticism* 22 (1964):465–70. Mészáros, István, ed., *Aspects of History and Class Consciousness*, 1970. Mitchell, Stanley, "Georg Lukács and the Historical Novel," *Marxism Today*, December 1963, pp. 374–82. Parkinson, G. H. R., ed., *Georg Lukács: The Man, His Work and His Ideas*, 1970. Rieser, M., "Lukács' Critique of German Philosophy," *The Journal of Philosophy* 55 (1958):177–96. Sanders, Ronald, "George Lukács: A Study in European Realism," *Midstream* 18 (January 1972):31–53. Sontag, Susan, "The Literary Criticism of Georg Lukács," in *Against Interpretation*, pp. 90 ff., 1969. Steiner, George, "Georg Lukács and Solzhenitsyn," *East Europe* 20 (1971):31–32. Zitta, Victor, *Georg Lukács' Marxism: Alienation, Dialectics, Revolution. A Study in Utopia and Ideology*, 1964. Bahr, Ehrhard, and Kunzer, Ruth G., *Georg Lukács*, 1973.

Günter Albrecht Zehm

Max Mell

Born 10 November 1882 in Marburg on the Drau (now Maribor, Yugoslavia), the son of an instructor of the blind; died 12 or 13 December 1971 in Upper Austria. Max Mell spent his youth in Vienna, where he studied philology and received his Ph.D. in 1905. He lived in Vienna until his death, for many years spending the summer months at Pernegg in Styria. The crucial experience in his life seems to have been World War I and the collapse of the Hapsburg monarchy, both seen by him as an irruption of chaos. Recipient of many honors and prizes, including the Great Austrian State Prize in 1954 and the Stifter Prize in 1957.

For decades Mell enjoyed an undiminished literary reputation that has never seriously been questioned or, indeed, examined by the critics. It is not clear whether this reputation rests more on the early praise that distinguished patrons such as Hugo von Hofmannsthal gave him, or on the firm ground of Mell's Christian convictions, or on the fashionable ground of his attachment to the country folk and their landscape. All these elements, and others as well, are combined in an amiable absence of discord.

Mell can hardly be said to have started his literary career under the spell of Hofmannsthal or Rainer Maria Rilke. Even the language of his early poems was dry and sober. If anything, one is reminded of the tradition of 19th-century enthusiasm for the renaissance; e.g., in *Lateinische Erzählungen* (1904) and *Die drei Grazien des Traums* (1906). Soon Mell turned his attention to his own age and to the people of Styria, as in *Jägerhaussage* (1910) and *Barbara Naderers Viehstand* (1914). Then he conceived the idea of reviving the old folk play for the purposes of his own theatrical inventions (see the autobiographical sketches on Styria and Styrian life, *Steirischer Lobgesang*, 1939). From 1923 on, Mell wrote a series of popular religious plays that made him famous, thanks to his peculiar skill in combining criminal and inspirational elements.

In *Das Apostelspiel* (1923; television play, 1959; recording, 1960) two thieves are converted by the simple faith of a peasant girl who believes them to be apostles. In *Das Schutzengelspiel* (1923) the belief in miracles is like something in medieval legend. *Das Nachfolge-*

Christi-Spiel (1927) gives the miraculous conversion of a band of robbers a certain touch of credibility by the nobleness of soul of a count. The robbers try to crucify the count, but he is rescued. Then, in a pure spirit of sacrifice, the count enters upon the imitation of Christ as expressed in love for his enemies.

Through the rejuvenated folk play Mell endeavored to bring myth and mysticism to the stage. The simple folk's concern with salvation is transposed into tragedy in the play *Die Sieben gegen Theben* (1932), into a mystical Christian vision in *Der Nibelunge Not* (first performance, 1944; published together with *Kriemhilds Rache*, 1951), and into a Christian-national vision in *Jeanne d'Arc* (1957). The Nibelungen drama shows most clearly how the old subject, the *Nibelungenlied,* has been made less remote and more acceptable by more recent interpretations (Wagner's version of the Valkyrie) and Mell's own interpretation (the figure of Dietrich von Bern). In the process, however, the old, handwoven fabric has taken on the arty-crafty look of a faded peasant brocade.

Critics have paid scant attention so far to the singular problem of Mell's renewal of the modern theater via the folk play. The peasant models make no artistic claim at all; but Mell's imitations do claim to be "religious plays in the theater" or ,even to displace the theater by the play (much to the satisfaction of the pageant play movement). But this is not at all alien to modern literary currents. Mell's intention was no less and no more than to challenge the modern theater with the primitive theater of the Styrian peasant plays. But that fits into the series of attempts to renew the sophisicated theater by drawing on the folk theater, attempts such as those made also by Bertolt Brecht, Carl Zuckmayer, and Friedrich Wolf. Even the Christian optimism regarding the entire possibility of salvation for everyone, which Mell professed in his plays, probably has a touch of modern utopianism.

Works: *Lateinische Erzählungen* (1904; Latin Tales); *Die drei Grazien des Traumes* (1906; The Three Graces of the Dream); *Die Pächterin von Litchfield* (1907; The Farmer's Wife of Litchfield); *Jägerhaussage* (1910; Legend of the Hunter's Lodge); *Das bekränzte Jahr* (1911; The Garlanded Year); *Der Barbier von Berriac* (1913; The Barber of Berriac); *Barbara Naderers Viehstand* (1914; Barbara Naderer's Livestock); *Gedichte* (1919; enlarged editions, 1929, 1953; Poems); *Das Wiener Kripperl von 1919* (1921; The Little Viennese Crêche of 1919); *Die Osterfeier* (1921; Easter Festival); *Alfred Roller* (1922); *Das Apostelspiel* (1923; The Apostle Play); *Das Schutzengelspiel* (1923; Guardian Angel Play); *Ein altes deutsches Weihnachtsspiel* (1924; An Old German

Christmas Play); *Morgenwege* (1924); Morning Walks); *Mein Bruder und ich* (1924; My Brother and I); *Das Nachfolge-Christi-Spiel* (1927; The Play of the Imitation of Christ); *Schauspiele* (1927; Dramas); *Die Sieben gegen Theben* (1932; The Seven against Thebes); *Das Spiel von den deutschen Ahnen* (1935; The Play about the German Forebears); *Das Donauweibchen* (1937; The Danube Water Nymph); *Steirischer Lobgesang* (1939; Styrian Hymn); *Adalbert Stifter* (1939); *Verheißungen* (1943; Promises); *Gabe und Dank* (1949; Gift and Gratitude); *Das Vergelt's Gott* (1950; The "God Bless You"); *Der Nibelunge Not* (1951; The Song of the Nibelungs; also includes *Kriemhilds Rache* [Kriemhild's Revenge]); *Aufblick zum Genius* (1955; Looking up to Genius); *Jeanne D'Arc* (1957); *Prosa, Dramen, Verse* (4 vols., 1962; Prose, Dramas, Verse).

Bibliography: Bithell, Jethro, *Modern German Literature 1880–1950*, pp. 239–41, 1959. Emich, Isolde, *Max Mell: Der Dichter und sein Werk*, 1957. Enderlin, Fritz, in *Licht aus der Stille*, edited by Isolde Emich, 1962. Hill, Joseph Francis, Jr., "Max Mell: Dramatist," *Dissertation Abstracts* 19 (1959):2952–53.

Clemens Heselhaus

Gustav Meyrink

Gustav Meyrink (originally Gustav Meyer) was born 19 January 1868 in Vienna. He was the illegitimate son of a Munich actress and an aristocrat who was minister of state of Württemberg. Secondary schooling in Munich, commercial college in Prague. At the age of twenty, took a job in the banking firm of Morgenstern and settled into the role of a youthful *bon vivant* in Prague society.

Failures in business together with private troubles made something of a misanthropist of Meyrink, who was of convinced antibourgeois and professed antierotic leanings. He fancied he sensed the presence of supernatural forces in the atmosphere of old Prague, and he understood these forces to be opposed to modern civilization and demanding its destruction, but not to be beyond rational apprehension. He discovered in the occult a manifestation of a superior spiritual world, which, in his prose extravaganzas and fantastic novels, he played off against his contemporaries' illusionary materialism with sarcasm and telling effect. Meyrink died on 4 December 1932 at Starnberg on Lake Starnberg, where he had been living since 1911.

Meyrink's first strange tale, *Der heiße Soldat*, was published in 1903 by Ludwig Thoma in *Simplizissimus*. It is the story of a foreign legionnaire who, after drinking an Indian magic draught, runs a high fever while otherwise in perfect health. His temperature rises to boiling point and beyond. Eventually his clothes burn on his body. The natives roast their chickens in his fire. A German professor of medicine pronounces a scientifically foolproof diagnosis and considers that the monstrous phenomenon is thereby fully explained. The subject of this extravaganza—the gulf between magic reality and materialistic "superstition"—contains Meyrink's whole problem in a nutshell.

The first three volumes of his "Sonderbare Geschichten" appeared in 1909, with additions, under the overall title *Des deutschen Spießers Wunderhorn*. Meyrink's soberly bizarre prose style, on the one hand, records the most improbable, cruel, and absurd events in the terse, jerky style of a newspaper reporter. And on the other hand, it accurately mimics the cultural philistine's stilted way of expressing himself. The style is more convincing in the short stories than in the voluminous novels in which Meyrink tried to set forth his mystical rationalism in detail and to popularize it with the help of forced melodramatic effects.

Nevertheless, his first novel, *Der Golem* (1915), became his most successful book. Here, Meyrink recreates the impact Prague made upon him, making a sort of ballad out of dream visions of the legendary figure of the Jewish Golem and the miracle-working rabbi, who, by his spiritual power, brings his artificial likeness to life. In Meyrink's later works, too, the irruption of the experiences of night and dream into the world of the senses remained his central theme. In the novels *Das grüne Gesicht* (1916) and *Walpurgisnacht* (1917), the historical catastrophe of World War I appears as a mystic vision of an apocalypse coming upon mankind to wipe out the nightmare of a despiritualized, mechanized civilization.

Meyrink saw the century's writing on the wall early enough. But as the years passed, the master of the supernatural fantastic became more and more like one of his own characters. He came to feel he was an initiate, a prophet and professor of the occult sciences, standing *An der Schwelle des Jenseits* (at the threshold of the beyond), to quote the title of his confessional work, published in 1923. Thereby he not only lost contact with temporal reality, but even stepped outside the artistic realm of the eccentric fantasies with which he had meant to shock the German philistines and amuse the nonphilistines.

Compared with such writers as Hanns Heinz Ewers, for instance, who took advantage of the literary fashion for the fantastic, Meyrink —who declared E. T. A. Hoffman to be his favorite German author— appears as the legitimate successor of "black" romanticism. Like Franz Kafka's work, Meyrink's fantastic stories are, in part, inspired by the "daimon" of the city of Prague. Without wishing to compare Meyrink's literary eccentricity with the genius of a man like Kafka, one may yet describe Meyrink as a master of fantastic prose. Only a few of his works, it is true, approach the level of writing that creates a symbol.

Works: *Der heiße Soldat* (1903; The Hot Soldier); *Orchideen* (1904; Orchids); *Das Wachsfigurenkabinett* (1907; The Waxworks); *Jörn Uhl und Hilligenlei* (1908); *Des deutschen Spießers Wunderhorn* (1909; The German Philistine's Magic Horn); *Die Uhr* (with A. Roda-Roda, 1914; The Clock); *Der Golem* (1915; Eng. tr., The Golem, 1928); *Der Kardinal Napellus* (1915); *Das grüne Gesicht* (1916; The Green Face); *Fledermäuse* (1916; Bats); *Der Löwe Alois und andere Geschichten* (1917; Alois the Lion, and Other Stories); *Gesammelte Werke* (6 vols., 1917; Collected Works); *Walpurgisnacht* (1917; Walpurgis Night); *Der Engel vom westlichen Fenster* (1920; The Angel of the Western Window); *Der weiße Dominikaner* (1921; The White Dominican); *Der violette*

Tod und andere Novellen (1922; The Violet Death, and Other Novellas); *And der Schwelle des Jenseits* (1923; At the Threshold of the Beyond); *Die heimtückischen Champignons und andere Geschichten* (1925; The Malicious Mushrooms, and Other Stories); *Meister Leonhard* (1925).

Bibliography: Bithell, Jethro, *Modern German Literature 1880–1950*, pp. 72–74, 1959. Buskirk, W. R. van, "The Bases of Satire in Gustav Meyrink's Work," *Dissertation Abstracts* 19 (1958):141–42. Frank, Eduard, *Gustav Meyrink: Werk und Wirkung*, 1957. Schwarz, Theodor, in *Weimarer Beiträge*, 1966. Sperber, H., *Motiv und Wort bei Meyrink*, 1918.

K. H. Kramberg

Erika Mitterer

Born 30 March 1906 in Vienna. After secondary school Erika Mitterer did social work for a while. She married in 1937. During the Third Reich she wrote for the periodical *Das innere Reich*, edited by Paul Alverdes and Benno von Mechow. She now lives in Vienna.

Erika Mitterer started writing early and at the age of eighteen sent Rainer Maria Rilke some of her poems. These poems so struck the aging poet as evidence of a mysterious affinity with himself that he arranged a personal meeting with her in November 1925. Their correspondence, which was published in 1950 under the title *Briefwechsel in Gedichten: 1924–1926*, bears witness to their intellectual and spiritual relationship.

Although at first spellbound by Rilke, Erika Mitterer emancipated herself with her first volume of poems, *Dank des Lebens* (1930), which writers such as Stefan Zweig and Ernst Lissauer hailed as showing "an unusually pure and limpid talent." Ernst Lissauer praised her spontaneity and freshness and "the naturalness of her nature." Both parts of this volume (part one, *Buch des Dankes*; part two, *Wandlungen*), however, also reveal her inner conflicts. In the *Wandlungen* it is the conflict between faith and doubt in confronting life. In such turns of phrase as "the suffering of the circumscribed form" one can sense the influence of Gottfried Benn. Many poems in this volume still make their impact today; *e.g., Sturm,* a powerful hymn, and *Der heilige Tag*, a pastoral vision filled with humble affection for the "simple" forms of life.

The 1935 collection of new poems, *Gesang der Wandernden*, is made up of three sequences: *Gnade der Heimat, Landschaft der Seele,* and *Tempelgesang*. The last sequence, especially, shows an inner bond between Erika Mitterer and Hugo von Hofmannsthal. Her *Zwölf Gedichte: 1933–1945* (1946) are composed in strict, hymnic form. The theme of these poems is the common suffering of the persecuted and the appalling problems facing the individual; they culminate in a profession of faith: "To purify the world needs love's bright fire,/Not belching yellow smoke of vengeful ire."

Erika Mitterer made her mark as a prose writer in 1940 with a voluminous novel, *Der Fürst der Welt* (new edition, 1964), which she herself regards as her main work. Its subject is the "evil spirit's accession to power." Painting on a broad canvas, she deals with the upheavals of the time around 1500, the waning of the Middle Ages. The short story *Begegnung im Süden* (1941) is set against the colorful background of the Italian landscape; it describes the brief, fateful encounters of two people. The tragic destiny of orphaned twins is the subject of the novel *Wir sind allein*, which was written in 1932 but published only in 1945. *Die nackte Wahrheit* (1951) is the story of a woman whose confused existence in the years after World War I leads to fulfillment in her encounter with a poet. In the fairy-tale novel *Wasser des Lebens* (1953), Erika Mitterer tried to give substance to the medieval legend of a Spanish alchemist. All these novels and stories, while often broad in conception, lack the unmistakable originality of her poetry.

Works: *Dank des Lebens* (1930; Life's Gratitude); *Charlotte Corday* (1932); *Höhensonne* (1933; Mountain Sun); *Gesang der Wandernden* (1935; Song of the Wanderers); *Der Fürst der Welt* (1940; new edition, 1964; The Prince of the World); *Begegnung im Süden* (1941; Encounter in the South); *Die Seherin* (1942; The Seeress); *Wir sind allein* (1945; We Are Alone); *Zwölf Gedichte: 1933–1945* (1946; Twelve Poems: 1933–1945); *Briefwechsel in Gedichten: 1924–1926* (1950; Correspondence in Poems); *Die nackte Wahrheit* (1951; The Naked Truth); *Wasser des Lebens* (1953; Water of Life); *Kleine Damengröße* (1953; Small Size for Ladies); *Gesammelte Gedichte* (1956; Collected Poems); *Verdunkelung* (1958; Blackout); *Tauschzentrale* (1958; Swap Shop); *Die Welt ist reich und voll Gefahr* (1964; The World Is Rich and Full of Danger); *Weihnacht der Einsamen* (1968; Christmas of the Lonely Ones); *Klopfsignale* (1970; Wall-Tapping Code).

Annemarie Groß-Denker

Robert Musil

Born 6 November 1880, Klagenfurt; died 15 April 1942, Geneva. Robert Musil's father, Alfred von Musil, of an old Austrian family of officials, scholars, engineers, and officers, was for a long while professor at the Brünn Technical University. Musil intended to pursue a career in the military, but discovered his talent for the technical while studying artillery. Making a sudden decision, he left military school and studied mechanical engineering. In 1901 he passed the state engineering examination at the Brünn Technical University. From 1902 to 1903 he was an instructor at the Stuttgart Technical University. He then took up the study of philosophy, concentrating on logic and experimental psychology (1903–1908), for which a new research center in the Helmholtz tradition had been established in Berlin. He built the Musil color gyroscope, and wrote an epistemological thesis on Ernst Mach. But he refused the offer of an academic appointment. As he had meanwhile gained some international fame with his first book, *Die Verwirrungen des Zöglings Törleß*, he decided on the profession of writer.

From 1911 to 1914 he was library assistant and later librarian at the Vienna Technical University. In 1914 he became an editor of the Berlin periodical *Die Neue Rundschau*. During World War I he was an officer on the Italian front. From the end of 1918 to 1920 he was employed as a writer at the Foreign Ministry; from 1920 to 1922 he worked as consultant to the war department. In addition to full-time work, he became dramatic critic (*Prager Presse*), wrote essays, etc. He returned to Berlin because there the tensions and conflicts of German intellectual life could be more keenly experienced than in Vienna. In 1933, after Hitler came to power, he turned his back on Germany, though he was not being subject to harassment. For five years he lived in Vienna, sacrificing everything to the completion of his main work, *Der Mann ohne Eigenschaften*. In 1938, Musil emigrated to Zurich and then to Geneva.

In his work Musil integrated the many strands of the narrative tradition that had evolved since Goethe's *Wilhelm Meisters Wanderjahre*. In so doing he exploited, refined, and intensified these strands with such logical consistency that the result is something entirely original. To a degree that was not previously imagined possible, the interrelations of the ego and the world, of time and space, the individual and the community, reflex and feeling, are made transparent and imbued with autonomy. Reality is largely shaped by opinions. The imagination is stimulated as much by what does not happen as by events themselves; indeed, more strongly by possibilities than by reality.

In the presence of the absent, Musil's "constructive irony" demonstrates just how absent are those present. What has not yet happened and what has ceased to happen are given equal weight, so that only the circumstances that happen to create any current reality prevent the reality from changing at once into other possibilities. In every definition and relation the variables are more important than the constants, for that creative "spirit" that simultaneously calls forth the complementary emotion reveals itself:

> He mixes up, dissolves, and recombines things. Good and evil, above and below, are not concepts of skeptical relativity for him. They are labels of a function, values depending upon the context in which they are set. (This view is consistently expressed by means of the language.) He has learned from the history of the centuries that vices can become virtues and virtues vices. He accepts nothing as permitted and nothing as forbidden, for everything may have a quality by which some day it will find its place in some great new context. Secretly he hates like death everything that behaves as though it were certain once and for all, great ideals and laws and their petty, fossilized imprint, the character who has made his peace with everything. He takes nothing as certain, no ego, no order . . . believes in no ties . . . everything maintains its value only until the next act of creation.

These interrelations, revaluations, and intellectual experiments make visible connections that hitherto have been unexposed or underexposed. They reconcile contradictions, alienate the familiar, raise the meaningless to significance, and reduce the meaningful to unimportance.

Inasmuch as everything is an electric field for Musil, he needs a style that enables him to keep track, simultaneously and equally, of all the ceaselessly moving and reciprocally causal effects and antieffects. The unreal develops against a background of reality; possibilities evoke realities. Cool representation is charged with the energy of irony or satire. Musil's intimacy with the reader answers his great detachment from the subject matter. Similes are extremely condensed; they cram together the heterogeneous and the complementary and suggest unknown relationships, create unheard-of effects.

Musil has a range of expression that harbors the unambiguous and at the same time displays the ambiguous. There are tension contrasts between syntax and statement, just as there are between noun and verb; each is the counterpoise to the other so that the expressive energies are forever being rebalanced. Possibilities are given free scope in an unrestricted field of multiple tensions between essence and existence, the special and the typical, the imaginary and the tangible, the temporal and the timeless. With unflagging power Musil keeps control of multiplicity and simultaneity. What has not yet been done appears as done already, and what has been done appears as potentially yet to be done: "Before and after are not binding. The content spreads out in a timeless way." The revealing subjunctive, which governs the time of narration as well as the set of characters in the aggregate and in their interrelations, is the appropriate mood for such timelessness.

Musil is inaccessible to that simplifying ordering that enables one to say, "When that had happened, this occurred." He looked at everything from the angle of the various time dimensions. Every moment intensifies the states of synchronism, the overlapping and effect of sequence and simultaneity; this applies to the ego as much as to the world.

States of consciousness, wishes, premonitions, confer on everything a changeable "sense color," permeate things with feelings (and are permeated by them in reverse), and form a superstructure over the familiar relations of space and time. Man energizes this field and is in turn determined by it. One recognizes "potential" man who experiences identity in diversity, and in that diversity the identifying modes of consciousness. Like time-field and time-space, the ego is an electric field. There is no such thing as an immutable character but only "more strongly linked groups of elements," while at the same time the ego is "the imaginary meeting place of the impersonal."

This preservation of variability, the ultimate refusal to define, causes the difficulty of Musil's dramatic works. The tentative nature of the characters inevitably gives rise to something intangible, something that eludes theatrical realization. As "intellectual comedies," they may be compared to the works of Paul Valéry. The plurality in every situation continually produces new constellations, equations, and symbols. Coagulated reality regains its original fluidity; possibilities achieve the density and impact force of objects. Causal concatenations cannot always satisfy the demands of the reasoning mind. Thus Musil brings to mind the interconnections of events and motives, always intent upon "incorporating the infinitely refracted polygon of a chain of feelings and thoughts into the absolute and indefinably rounded whims of diction, into the aura of the characters, into silence, and into all that is unrenderable." He was intent upon coming to grips with that "central activity of the personality," which "only begins behind all the surfaces of pain, confusion, weakness, and passion." Everything erratic and abrupt, the discontinuities, the pre-image and the pre-echo occupy the space that has hitherto denied them.

All of this is illustrated in the volume of stories *Vereinigungen* (1911). Here, crowded together, we find the preexperience and the experience, the event and the nonevent, the doing and the feeling that nothing should be done, the fantasized and the conscious, the unending interaction of attracting and repelling forces, the integration of the irreconcilable, "a quivering dissolution of all apparent opposites." What is happening in a character's consciousness is offered. The activity is shown in phases, and moments become states in a splitting and pinpointing that had never before been carried so far by a writer.

Acute observation and exactitude of imagination are expressed in numerous parallel analyses and obsessive experimentation. Musil saw his task as being that of "discovering new solutions, connections, constellations, variables; of creating prototypes of the course of events; of devising tempting prefigurations of how one can be a man; of inventing the inner man." In doing so he preferred to imagine disturbing, deviant relationships because of the wealth of possibilities. These borderline cases of limited and special validity are reminiscent of the freedom with which the mathematician sometimes makes use of the absurd in order to get to the truth.

In seeking to define the undefinable, to understand exactly supralogical procedures, Musil is to be ranked with Pascal, Lichtenberg, Novalis, and Valéry. There is an extraordinary analogy to the theory of relativity and quantum physics in Musil's structures, in his knowledge about the uncertainty of relations, the supersession of Aristotelian logic by truth values (which instead of *tertium non datur*, admit intermediate values and situations that may be true or may be false, the "coexisting possibilities" [Werner Heisenberg]), the breach in unconditional determinism and the causal principle. Similarly we find pulsating conceptions instead of rigid concepts, analogies instead of identities, probability instead of truth.

Recognition of these objectives sheds light on Musil's approach to language. Writing is "a simultaneous effect of mutually illuminating words." That is, the statement is not to be made with any one word but with each sentence, for the "structure of good prose is not something rigid but is like a swaying bridge that changes as step follows step."

The unusual clarity about things and about himself that Musil achieved, the dual detachment of easy accessibility and incorruptible distance, qualified him equally as a creative writer and as a critic, not least is he to be heeded as a critical interpreter of himself. Proof of this lies in his *Skizze zur Erkenntnis des Dichters*. That clarity confers on his beginnings in *Die Verwirrungen des Zöglings Törleß* (1906) the same unerring assurance that was brought to its perfection in *Der Mann ohne Eigenschaften* (written, 1898–1942). The depiction of reality became a means of ascertaining "knowledge of feelings" and "upheavals of thought," that "system of sentiments" by which each individual shapes "the confusion of orbiting centers" into a universe that lasts until the next moment of creation. This writing that overcomes the prejudgment of Either/Or, gives form to innumerable self-contradictions, and unifies the real and the unreal, "precision and soul," mysticism and mathematics. It is the "most daring intellectual adventure" in 20th-century German literature.

Works: *Die Verwirrungen des Zöglings Törleß* (1906; Eng. tr., Young Törless, 1921); *Vereinigungen* (1911; Unions); *Die Schwärmer* (1921; The Dreamers); *Grigia* (1923); *Die Portugiesin* (1923; The Portuguese Woman); *Vinzenz und die Freundin bedeutender Männer* (1924; Vinzenz and the Girl Friend of Important Men); *Drei Frauen* (1924; Three Women; includes *Grigia, Die Portugiesin*, and *Tonka*); *Rede zur Rilke Feier* (1927; Speech at the Rilke Celebration); *Der Mann ohne Eigenschaften* (3 vols., 1930–43; Eng. tr., The Man without Qualities, 1953–54, 1965); *Nachlaß zu Lebzeiten* (1936; My Posthumous Works); *Über die Dummheit* (1937; On Stupidity); *Gesammelte Werke* (3 vols., ed. A. Frisé, 1952–57; Collected Works).

English translations in collections: *Five Women* (1966; includes translations of *Vereinigungen* and *Drei Frauen*).

Bibliography: Arntzen, H., *Satirischer Stil in Robert Musil's "Der Mann ohne Eigenschaften,"* 1960. Baumann, Gerhart, *Robert Musil: Zur Erkenntnis der Dichtung*, 1965. Fleischmann, Wolfgang Bernard, in *Wisconsin Studies in Contemporary Literature*, 1967, pp. 480–81. Kaiser, E., and Wilkins, E., *Robert Musil: Eine Einführung in das Werk*, 1962. Karthaus U., *Der andere Zustand, Zeitstrukturen im Werke Robert Musils*, 1965. Kermode, Frank, introduction to *Five Women*, 1966. Peter, F., *Robert Musil*, 1973. Pike, Burton, *Robert Musil: An Introduction to His Work*, 1961.

Gerhart Baumann

Franz Nabl

Born 16 July 1883 in Lautschin (now Loučeň, Czechoslovakia), the son of an estate manager. From 1886 to 1913, lived in Vienna where he studied law, philosophy, and German language and literature. Moved to Baden near Vienna in 1913. From 1924 to 1927 worked as editor on a newspaper in Graz, where he has been living and writing since 1934. Received an honorary degree from the University of Graz in 1943.

Franz Nabl is a typical representative of those nostalgic Austrians who, even after the collapse of the Hapsburg empire, remained faithful to the idea of a greater Austrian mission. All Nabl's works (novels, short narratives that are occasionally treated as stories within a story, and his contributions to contemporary drama), while not explicitly handling the theme of the decline of Austria's power, are nevertheless latently overshadowed by it. Rather like Robert Musil, whom he surpasses in narrative power but whose speculative and analytical perspicacity he does not match, he takes a view of life that is as bitter as it is penetratingly realistic and that, at first sight, has little in common with what is usually regarded as specifically Austrian. Against the generally gray background characteristic of Nabl's writing, his characters stand out graphically in sharp outline.

Nabl's importance lies primarily in the narrative genres, where his strict objectivity built bridges from naturalism, in its moderate, late form, to the new realism; he has no room either for lyrical softness or for sympathy with any sort of political ideology. Underlying his cool social criticism of both the individual and society is always the absolute question of ethical behavior. In a certain sense this may be regarded as carrying the work of Ferdinand von Saar one step further, but also as a contrast to Adalbert Stifter's *Nachsommer* mood. The very title of Nabl's main work, the two-volume novel *Ödhof* (1911; "bleak farm"), suggests his conception of people and their styles of life.

Nabl's work has sometimes been neglected, perhaps in part because of his conservative style and his aloofness from the popular prejudices of the new Austria. Very occasional touches of surrealism provide a glimpse of the dark foundations on which Nabl erected the solid architecture of his work.

Works: *Noch einmal* (1905; Once Again); *Weihe* (1950; Consecration); *Geschwister Hagelbauer* (1906; The Hagelbauer Siblings); *Hans Jäckels erstes Liebesjahr* (1908; Hans Jäckel's First Year of Love); *Narrentanz* (1911; Fool's Dance); *Ödhof* (1911; Bleak Farm); *Das Grab des Lebendigen* (1917; Grave of the Living; republished as *Die Ortliebschen Frauen* [1936; The Ortlieb Women]); *Der Tag der Erkenntnis* (1919; Day of Recognition); *Requiescat . . .* (1920); *Der Schwur des Martin Krist* (1920; Martin Krist's Oath); *Die Galgenfrist* (1921; The Reprieve); *Die Augen* (1923; The Eyes); *Trieschübel* (1925); *Schichtwechel* (1929; Change of Shifts); *Kindernovelle* (1932; Children's Novella); *Ein Mann von gestern* (1935; A Man of Yesterday); *Das Meteor* (1935); *Der Griff ins Dunkel* (1936; Grab into the Dark); *Der Fund* (1937; The Find); *Steirische Lebenswanderung* (1938; Life's Journey of a Styrian); *Die Weihnachten des Dominik Brakel. Pilatus im Credo* (1938; Dominik Brakel's Christmas. Pilate in the Credo); *Kleine Freilichtbühne* (1943; Small Open-Air Stage); *Spätlese* (1943; Late Vintage); *Mein Onkel Barnabas* (1946; My Uncle Barnabas); *Johannes Krantz* (1948); *Das Rasenstück* (1953; The Grass Plot); *Der Teufel an der Wand* (1958; The Devil on the Wall); *Der erloschene Stern* (1962; The Burned-Out Star); *Die zweite Heimat* (1963; Second Home Country); *Ausgewählte Werke* (4 vols., 1966; Selected Works).

Bibliography: Alker, Ernst, *Die deutsche Literatur von Goethes Tod bis zur Gegenwart*, pp. 759 ff., 1949; and "Franz Nabl," *Wort in der Zeit* 2 (January 1956):1–7. Langfeldt, Johannes, "Franz Nabl," *Sudetenland* 3 (1961):99–105. Metelmann, Ernst, in *Die schöne Literatur* 29 (1928): 237–39.

Ernst Alker

Johann Nestroy

Johann Nepomuk Nestroy, Austria's most popular writer of comedies, was born 7 December 1801 in Vienna and died 25 May 1862 in Graz. His literary roots are in the primitive farces, romantic comedies, and *Zauberstücke* (magic fairy plays) popular in Vienna's outskirts in the early 19th century. He raised those genres to great heights by his wit, satire, insight into human foibles, and a superb use of words. Every major stage in Austria has produced several of his eighty three plays, and many theaters have a special Nestroy actor who plays those quick-witted, nimble-tongued charmers and scoundrels that Nestroy wrote as roles for himself. When the two-hundred-year-old Vienna Burgtheater went on its first world tour in 1967–68, the directors selected Nestroy, together with Friedrich Schiller, Franz Grillparzer, and Arthur Schnitzler, to represent German-language playwrights. Modern critics have compared Nestroy with Molière, Swift, Goldoni, and even Shakespeare—and yet he is hardly known outside Austria. The reason for this obscurity is that he wrote in the Viennese idiom, and that his wit is expressed largely in linguistic somersaults and plays on words that resist translation. Thornton Wilder recognized the potential of Nestroy's work by taking one of Nestroy's comedies, *Einen Jux will er sich machen,* as the basis for the play *The Matchmaker,* from which the musical "Hello, Dolly!" emerged, proving that Nestroy, with proper adaptation, can become popular with American audiences.

Nestroy's plays are deceptively simple, even crude. He took plots from earlier sources—French vaudeville plays, English comedies, German farces. If the story was primitive or implausible, so was Nestroy's adaptation. He had two main ambitions: to come up with comical situations and to create good roles for himself and the actors of the two Viennese theaters in which he played (the Carltheater and the Theater an der Wien). It took his public two generations to realize that Austria's greatest comedy writer had also been one of Austria's greatest philosophers.

Nestroy's philosophy, concealed in the slapstick, is one of bitter satire—against the pretense and fraud of the degenerating aristocracy; the selfishness of the newly emerging rich middle class; the oppressions of the absolute monarchy as represented by Austria's foreign-affairs minister, Prince Metternich, and his censors; the stupidity of the bureaucracy; and the laziness, superstition, and fickleness of the common man. Nestroy spotted weakness in man on all levels and was ruthless in ridiculing it. He probably was not aware that he was instrumental in helping to bring down the crumbling values of his own time. Although etchings exist showing him on the barricades during the essentially unsuccessful revolution of 1848, his plays indicate that his enthusiasm for that revolution was limited to his desire to get rid of censorship. He wrote a few plays about the new freedom, but he soon seemed to despair about the people, too. "The people are a giant," he wrote, "a giant in a cradle: he wakes up, staggers about, tramples everything down, and in the end collapses somewhere, where he lies even more uncomfortably than in the cradle."

In exposing human weakness, some of Nestroy's sharpest darts were directed against an institution common to all classes: marriage. "Love is a string that ties hearts," he has one of his characters say, "and marriage is a rope that ties hands; the string can be broken, but the rope—never." His dim view of marriage was no doubt the result of his own experience: he married young, divorced his wife when he found her with a lover, and for the rest of his life had one affair after another while living with a common-law wife whom he, as a Catholic, could not marry. Marriage, to Nestroy, was a "mutual life-annoyance company," which, however, did not keep him from including one and, more often, several marriages in the conventional happy endings of his plays. "I've never found anything distasteful," he wrote, "in seeing someone else getting married."

Nestroy was the son of a lawyer whose ancestry can be traced to Polish Silesia, which accounts for his Slavic-sounding name. Johann, too, studied law but did not finish. Instead he became an opera singer and actor of serious plays in the Austrian provinces. His talent for comedy is said to have been discovered when he disliked one of the parts and tried to "throw" it by exaggerating it into a grotesque parody. The story, probably apocryphal, is in line with documented evidence of his gift of achieving comical effects by gestures, glances, and intonations. His favorite trick was to outwit the censor by submitting a harmless-looking play and then to imply subversive meanings by a raised eyebrow, a twitching lip, or a special stress.

At the age of thirty, Nestroy returned to Vienna, where theater life was divided between the literary drama presented in the heart of Vienna and the popular shows performed in the outskirts. He was able to transfer the stereotyped figures of folk comedy and *commedia dell'arte* into flesh-and-blood characters so genuinely Viennese that even visitors who knew the plays that Nestroy was adapting did not recognize them and believed they were typical Austrian folk originals. He also enriched his characters by bestowing on them a language so full of mental twists, and puns that he is considered the father of a special type of satirical writing, one that later became popular in German and Austrian cabarets and produced such writers as Frank Wedekind and Bertolt Brecht. Brecht also is indebted to Nestroy for the use of songs in plays. Nestroy took the stereotyped musical banalities of the popular farces of his era and used them as a vehicle for witty comments on human weaknesses or social conditions. He had the actor step out of his role and address the audience directly. Nestroy initiated the tradition of adding stanzas commenting on events of the day, an idea that Brecht adapted for his own purposes. Nestroy also invented the art of ridiculing the reverence and pomposity with which historical and mythological figures often are treated (for example, in his *Judith and Holofernes*, 1849), an art that Bernard Shaw lifted to even more sophisticated levels.

Nestroy was such an outstanding theatrical personality that after his death his plays were not considered playable by other actors. Only twelve of his farces had been published during his lifetime, and his work was in danger of oblivion. This was prevented and Nestroy's true nature discovered by the Viennese satirist and critic Karl Kraus, who in 1912, on the occasion of the fiftieth anniversary of Nestroy's death, drew public attention to this towering playwright-actor-philosopher. More recently, the Viennese playwright and critic Hans Weigel has published an extensive evaluation of Nestroy and has adapted, as also did Kraus, many of his plays.

Among Nestroy's works, *Der böse Geist Lumpazivagabundus, oder Das liederliche Kleeblatt* (1835) was the greatest success during his lifetime. It is still rooted in the world of magic, a style that Nestroy later abandoned. Today's most popular plays include *Einen Jux will er sich machen* (1844), *Der Zerrissene* (1845), *Der Talisman,* (1843), *Liebesgeschichten und Heiratssachen* (1843), *Das Mädel aus der Vorstadt* (1845), *Eine Wohnung zu vermieten . . . , Der Unbedeutende* (1849), *Die schlimmen Buben in der Schule* (1847), *Kampl* (1852), *Der alte Mann und die junge Frau* (1849), *Die verhängnisvolle Faschingsnacht* (1841), and the political farce about the 1848 revolution, *Freiheit in Krähwinkel,* (1849).

Works: *Der konfuse Zauberer* (1832; The Mixed-up Magician); *Robert der Teuxel* (1833; Robert the Devil); *Der böse Geist Lumpazi-*

vagabundus, oder Das liederliche Kleeblatt (1833; The Evil Spirit Lumpazivagabundus, or The Slovenly Cloverleaf); *Die Familien Zwirn, Knieriem und Leim, oder Der Weltuntergang* (1834; The Families Thread, Stirrup, and Glue, or the End of the World); *Weder Lorbeerbaum noch Bettelstab* (1835; Neither Laurel Tree nor Beggar's Staff); *Eulenspiegel* (1835); *Die beiden Nachtwandler* (1836; The Two Sleepwalkers); *Das Haus der Temperamente* (1837; The House of Tempers); *Zu ebener Erde und erster Stock* (1838; In the Basement and on the First Floor); *Die verhängnisvolle Faschingnacht* (1841; The Fateful Carnival Night); *Der Talisman* (1843; Eng. tr., in *Three Comedies*, 1967); *Liebesgeschichten and Heiratssachen* (1843; Eng. tr., Love Affairs and Wedding Bells, in *Three Comedies*, 1967); *Einen Jux will er sich machen* (1844; He Would Like to Pull a Practical Joke); *Der Zerissene* (1845; Eng. tr., A Man Full of Nothing, in *Three Comedies*, 1967); *Das Mädel aus der Vorstadt* (1845; The Gal from the Factory District); *Die schlimmen Buben in der Schule* (1847; The Naughty Boys in School); *Der Unbedeutende* (1849; The Insignificant Man); *Der alte Mann mit der jungen Frau* (1849; The Old Man with His Young Wife); *Judith und Holofernes* (1849); *Freiheit in Krähwinkel* (1849; Freedom in Krähwinkel); *Tannhäuser* (1852); *Johann Nepomuk Nestroy: Ausgewählte Werke* (ed. F. Mautner, 1938); *Johann Nepomuk Nestroy: Gesammelte Werke* (6 vols., ed. O. Rommel, 1948); *Johann Nepomuk Nestroy: Werke* (2 vols., ed. P. Reimann, 1962).

Bibliography: Battaglia, Otto Forst de, *Johann Nestroy*, 1962. Kraus, Karl, "Nestroy und die Nachwelt," in *Die Fackel*, May 1912. Mautner, Franz H., *Johann Nestroy und seine Kunst*, 1937. Weigel, Hans, "Johann Nestroy," *Der Monat*, December 1951; and *Flucht vor der Größe*, 1960.

Max Knight and Joseph Fabry▲

Robert Neumann

Born 22 May 1897 in Vienna, the son of a professor of mathematics and bank director who was a founding member of the Austrian Social Democratic Party. In Vienna Robert Neumann studied chemistry, medicine, and German language and literature, and in 1919 published his first volume of poems, *Gedichte*, which he later repudiated. During the inflation period he rose from apprentice bookkeeper to director of a chocolate factory and senior partner in a corporation. He lost all his money and became a seaman on a tanker. In 1927 he suddenly achieved literary fame and success with his collection of parodies *Mit fremden Federn*.

In his novels of social criticism Neumann exposed to ridicule, among others, the National Socialists, then pressing for power, and in 1933 his books were publicly burned. In 1934 he emigrated to Great Britain, became an English citizen, and lived at Cranbrook, Kent. Since then he has also written in English. He is now living at Locarno. In 1966 he became vice-president of the International P.E.N.

Neumann's body of works falls into four groups:

(1) The parodies of style—*Mit fremden Federn* (1927; 2nd edition, 1955) and *Unter falscher Flagge* (1932).

(2) "Factual" topical novels, satiric reportage, and critical biographies—e.g., *Sintflut* (1929), *Die Macht* (1932; republished as *Macht*, 1964), *Sir Basil Zaharoff: Der König der Waffen* (1934), the novel *Struensee* (1935; republished as *Der Favorit der Königin*, 1953; filmed under the title *Herrscher ohne Krone*), *By the Waters of Babylon* (1939), *Die Puppen von Poshansk* (1952; television play, 1955), *Die dunkle Seite des Mondes* (1959), and *Festival* (1962).

(3) Stories of a satirical, parodistic content in which the author writes a "disguised" language that is to be in the manner and jargon of the characters—e.g., *Hochstapler Novelle* (1930; new edition as *Die Insel der Circe*, 1952), *Karriere* (1931; the confessions of a Hungarian call girl), *Olympia* (1961; the controversial autobiography of the sister of Thomas Mann's confidence man Felix Krull, a lady whom Mann himself refers to only incidentally).

(4) Narrative prose, excluding parodies, which Neumann writes in the style of famous writers (from Boccaccio to James Joyce), such

as the inserted tales in *Die Pest von Lianora* (1927) or the stories collected in the volume *Jagd auf Menschen und Gespenster* (1928).

Neumann's unusual gift for adapting the cadence and diction of other writers enables him to use literary parody, which he never allows to sink to the level of mere banter, as a method of critical literary phenomenology. In this kind of mimicry he is not surpassed by any German-language writer at the present time. But Neumann's natural gift for parody has proved an almost unsurmountable obstacle to the development of a personal style unique to Neumann himself. Though he has made great efforts toward such a style, he has only achieved it, if at all, in the markedly objective style of his topical novels in the 1920s. Among his narrative works he reached his highest artistic level in the novels written, as it were, in disguise, such as *Karriere* and *Olympia*. Neumann's outstanding capacity for an intuitive understanding of alien language and form is matched by his sympathy, secret or overt, for all the characters he has created.

Works: *Gedichte* (1919; Poems); *Zwanzig Gedichte* (1923; Twenty Poems); *Mit fremden Federn* (1927; Borrowed Feathers); *Die Pest von Lianora* (1927; The Pest of Lianora); *Jagd auf Menschen und Gespenstern* (1928; Hunt of Men and Ghosts); *Stintflut* (1929; Flood, 1930); *Hochstapler-Novelle* (1930; Novel of a Confidence Man; republished as *Die Insel der Circe* [1952; The Isle of Circe]); *Passion* (1930); *Panoptikum* (1930); *Das Schiff "Espérance"* (1931; The Ship *Espérance*); *Karriere* (1931; Career); *Unter falscher Flagge* (1932; Under False Colors); *Hochstaplerkomödie* (1932; Comedy of a Confidence Man); *Die Macht* (1932; republished as *Macht* [1964; Power]; Mammon, 1933); *Sir Basil Zaharoff: Der König der Waffen* (1934; Sir Basil Zaharoff: The Munition's King); *Struensee* (1935; The Queen's Doctor, 1936; republished as *Der Favorit der Königin* [1953; The Favorite of the Queen]); *Die blinden Passagiere* (1935; The Stowaways); *Eine Frau hat geschrieen* (1938; A Woman Screamed; republished as *Die Freiheit und der General* [1958; Freedom and the General]); *By the Waters of Babylon* (1939; German, An den Wassern von Bablon, 1945); *Twenty-Three Women: The Story of an International Traffic* (1940); *Scene in Passing* (1942; German, Tibbs, 1948); *The Inquest* (1944; German, Bibiana Santis: Der Weg einer Frau, 1950); *Children of Vienna* (1946; German, Kinder von Wien, 1948); *Blind Man's Buff* (1948); *Sur les Pas de Morell* (1952; English, In the Steps of Morell, 1952); *Die Puppen von Poshansk* (1952; The Dolls of Poshansk); *Meine schöne Mama* (1956; My Beautiful Mama); *Mein altes Haus in Kent* (1957; My Old House in Kent); *Die dunkle Seite des Mondes* (1959; The Dark Side of the Moon); *Gesammelte Werke in Einzelausgaben* (1959ff; Collected Works in Single Editions); *Voruntersuchung* (1960; Preliminary Inquiry); *Madame Sephardi* (1960); *Silver-*

man (1960); *Treibgut* (1960; Flotsam; also includes *An den Wassern von Babylon*); *Ausflüchte unseres Gewissens* (1960; Evasions of Our Conscience); *Das Leben von Adolf Hitler* (1961; The Life of Adolf Hitler); *Hitler—Aufstieg und Untergang des Dritten Reiches* (with H. Koppel, 1961; Hitler—Rise and Fall of the Third Reich); *Geschichte einer Geschichte* (1961; Story of a Story); *Olympia* (1961); *Die Parodien* (1961; Parodies); *Festival* (1962); *Ein leichtes Leben: Bericht über mich selbst und Zeitgenossen* (1963; An Easy Life: Report on Me and Contemporaries); *Die Staatsaffäre* (1964; State Affair); *Der Tatbestand, oder Der gute Glaube der Deutschen* (1965; Factual Findings, or The Good Faith of the Germans); *Vielleicht das Heitere* (1968; Serenity Perhaps); *Palace de la Plage und der finstere Hintergrund* (1968; Palace de la Plage and the Sinister Background); *Komma Sutra: Die Hochvollkommene Ehe* (1969; Kamasutra: The Highly Perfect Marriage); *Dämon Weib* (1969; Demon Woman); *Nie wieder Politik* (1969; Never Again Politics); *"Vorsicht Bücher"* (1969; "Careful, Books"); *Deutschland diene Österreicher. Österreich deine Deutschen* (1970; Germany, Your Austrians. Austria, Your Germans); *Oktoberreise mit einer Geliebten* (1973; October Journey with a Beloved).

Bibliography: Beerman, Hans, in *Books Abroad*, 1967, p. 316. Desch, Kurt, ed., *Robert Neumann: Stimmen der Freunde. Der Romancier und sein Werk*, 1957. Kricheldorf, Hans, on *Festival*, in *Neue deutsche Hefte*, May-June 1963. On *Vielleicht das Heitere*, in *New York Times Book Review*, 13 October 1968.

K. H. Kramberg

Alfred Polgar

Born 17 October 1873 in Vienna. The son of a composer, Alfred Polgar studied music and piano construction. He became a journalist, author of theatrical sketches, theater critic, and poet. In 1925 he went to Berlin, where he joined the *Weltbühne*. Returned to Vienna in 1933, went to Paris in 1938 and to the United States in 1940. Lived in New York and Hollywood and became an American citizen. In 1947 he went to Zurich, the haven of returning emigrants. He died there on 24 April 1955.

Polgar was already over fifty when he began to collect his essays and reviews in book form, notably *Stücke und Spieler* and *Noch allerlei Theater*, both published in 1926. From then on, however, they appeared in a steady stream, which ended with the Nazi burning of books on the Opera Square in Berlin in 1933. As a theater critic he was the contemporary of the theater critics Siegfried Jacobsohn, Alfred Kerr, and Herbert Ihering, but in historical terms, which are rather more significant in taking the measure of his work, he takes his place between Fontane and Ernst Penzoldt. To borrow a phrase from Nietzsche, he chiseled away at each page of prose as though it were a statue.

The two volumes *Ich bin Zeuge* (1928) and *Schwarz auf Weiß* (1929) contain reflections, comments, short stories, and anecdotes. These are unique, incomparable prose gems that have to be given a new name, his name: Polgarisms.

All his life Polgar wrote almost nothing but such "small prose." It belongs to the great prose of German literature. He never took ten pages to say what could be said in one; on the contrary, he might condense ten pages until only one was left. Instead of diluting his impressions and feelings, he distilled their essence. He wrote "novels" only a few pages long (*Der Mantel* and *Einsamkeit*); a telephone booth was all the setting he needed to make plain a human destiny. In a manner of speaking, entire corn fields grew on his palm.

Shy and skeptical, Polgar presented in a veiled fashion what was to emerge as poetry. For his poems, verse had too much pathos, rhyme was too vulgar, song too loud. And so he wrote what the French would call *poèmes en prose*: for example, *Aber der Frühling*, *Es geht uns gut, Flieder, Klage um einen geliebten Menschen.* As he wrote, he had "a vision of the touching halo of the ridiculous, which hovers over things and people, and hence also over one's own head." He had a sense of humor and, a rarer gift, the ability to be ironic about himself. The weapon with which he attacked and defended himself was the punch line—a sharp point hitting the bull's eye with a single sentence. As an artist needs only a line to draw a portrait, so Polgar needed only one sentence to do so, amicably or maliciously, or, even better, amicably and maliciously. The subject might be the actor Kainz, the singer Fritzi Massary, the poet Ringelnatz, the polemicist Karl Kraus, or, for that matter, the tailor Sedlak. Polgar knew the celebrities of his time well enough, but—and perhaps for that very reason—it was not they who engaged his interest most deeply, but the "unknown man." He could have collected for publication his aphorisms like Lichtenberg and Kraus, but he was too modest, as was Nestroy, to pick the raisins out of the cake.

Polgar took his work seriously but made no claim of importance for it, "at least not so far as others are concerned." He was not one of those who pretend they are "showing us a way across the dreadful abyss yawning beneath us." But he was conscious of it, "black and boundless like eternity's night." Above this dark background sparkled the lightning flashes of his wit. And some stars, too: delicate, cool, and somewhat flickering—with the courage of uncertainty.

Works: *Der Quell des Übels* (1908; The Source of Evil); *Goethe im Examen* (1908; Goethe During Examination); *Der Petroleumkönig, oder Donauzauber* (with E. Friedell, 1908; The Petroleum King, or the Charm of the Danube); *Bewegung ist alles* (1909; Motion Is Everything); *Brahms Ibsen* (1910; Brahm's Ibsen); *Soldatenleben im Frieden* (with E. Friedell, 1910; Soldier's Life in Peacetime); *Der Freimann* (with E. Friedell, 1910; The Freeman); *Talmas Tod* (with A. Friedmann, 1910; Talma's Death); *Hiob* (1912; Job); *Kleine Zeit* (1919; Small Time); *Pallenberg* (1921); *Gestern und Heute* (1922; Yesterday and Today); *An den Rand geschrieben* (1926; Written on the Margin); *Orchester von oben* (1926; Orchestra from Above); *Noch allerlei Theater* (1926; Some More Theater); *Ja und Nein* (4 vols., 1926; Yes and No); *Stücke und Spieler* (1926; Plays and Actors); *Ich bin Zeuge* (1928; I Am a Witness); *Schwarz auf Weiß* (1929; Black on White); *Hinterland* (1929); *Bei dieser Gelegenheit* (1930; At This Occasion); *Die Defraudanten* (1931; The Defrauders); *Ansichten* (1933; Opinions); *In der Zwischenzeit* (1934; In the Meantime); *Der Sekundenzeiger* (1937; The Second Hand on the Clock); *Handbuch des Kritikers* (1938; Manual of the Critic); *Geschichten ohne Moral* (1942; Stories without a Moral); *Im Vorübergehen* (1947;

In Passing By); *Anderseits* (1948; On the Other Hand); *Begegnungen im Zwielicht* (1951; Encounters in the Twilight); *Standpunkte* (1953; Points of View); *Im Lauf der Zeit* (1954; In the Course of Time); *Fensterplatz* (1959; Window Seat); *Auswahl, Prosa aus vier Jahrzehnten* (1968; Selection, Prose of Four Decades).

Bibliography: Lestiboudois, H., "Alfred Polgar: Meister der kleinen Form," in *Literarische Miniaturen*, 1948. Luft, F., "Alfred Polgar," *Der Monat*, no. 81 (1955). Reich-Ranicki, Marcel, "Alfred Polgars sanfte Gewalt," *Die Zeit*, no. 24 (1968). Torberg, Friedrich, "Alfred Polgar," *Der Monat*, no. 66 (1954). Viertel, Berthold, "Über Alfred Polgar," in *Deutsche Literaturkritik im 20. Jahrhundert*, edited by H. Mayer, 1965.

Nino Erné

Ferdinand Raimund

Born 1 June 1790, Vienna; died 5 September 1836, Pottenstein, Lower Austria. Ferdinand Raimund, Franz Grillparzer, and Johann Nestroy are the most significant Austrian playwrights of the 19th century.

Raimund, a craftsman's son, grew up on the outskirts of Vienna. He lost his father when he was eight, his mother six years later. His formal schooling ended early. As apprentice to a pastry cook, he sold refreshments in the Burgtheater and watched the performances. At eighteen, he ran away to join a theater troupe. For years he led the life of an itinerant actor. First success as actor in Vienna in 1815. In 1819 he fell in love with Toni Wagner, daughter of a coffeehouse owner; her parents objected to a marriage with an actor. In 1820 Raimund married Luise Gleich, daughter of a playwright. They separated after one year, and Raimund returned to Toni. The two lived together until his death without the sanction of the church but with that of society and finally with that of her parents when Raimund became artistic director of the Leopoldstädter Theater in Vienna (1828–30). Raimund was the greatest comic actor in the Vienna of his time. The last six years of his life he also appeared on stages in Germany. When he was bitten by a dog one day, his old fear of rabies returned, and he committed suicide. He is buried in Gutenstein, Lower Austria.

Raimund's life with its melodramatic episodes, its neurotic instability, and its tragicomic dilemmas defies every notion of a Biedermeier existence. Similarly, his work is marked by tensions and contradictions. Grillparzer pointed to a significant polarity in Raimund's plays when he said: "People have often regretted that Raimund lacks education; [they] fail to realize that it is precisely the juxtaposition of the intuitively poetic and his ordinariness and lack of sophistication that constitutes the special charm of his works." What Grillparzer saw as a virtue, Raimund himself considered his handicap, and his talents often conflicted with his aspirations as an artist. A born comic talent, he wanted to become a tragic actor. He was a comedian and playwright of genius in the tradition of Viennese popular theater, but it was his ambition to advance to "Burgtheater status" (the famous theater of the German-speaking world) by raising his plays to the level of sublimity. His misunderstanding of his own genius and of his situation made him also misunderstand Nestroy, whom he considered his rival but who, in effect, only continued a development that, ironically, Raimund had prepared for with his realistic scenes.

Like Molière and Nestroy, Raimund combined in himself the talents of actor and playwright. It was only after fifteen years of acting—and out of disgust with the plays available—that he started to write plays himself; all his life he remained an actor, appearing in one hundred and seventy-three roles. His plays are, first of all, theater plays, not literary plays. They are deeply rooted in the baroque tradition, particularly the tradition of the Viennese popular theater in which, contrary to the development in Germany, *homo ludens* had survived the chill of the Enlightenment. All the elements of the traditional popular comedy of his day are present in his work, but never before had they been realized so purely. The message in his plays is as simple as that of a conventional *Besserungsstück* (an unsophisticated play of moral conversion); it can be summed up in an adage and yet is presented as convincingly as a newly discovered truth. As in the popular comedies of his times, the effect of his plays greatly depends on the comic figure and the personality of the actor, but Raimund raised the comic type to the level of character.

Music had always played an important role in Viennese popular theater, but instead of using conventional vocal numbers written for a certain play and soon forgotten, Raimund himself composed songs for his plays that have become folk songs still sung today. And like other popular comedies, his plays are rich in visual effects (from emblematic tableaus and inscriptions to scene changes that allow full play to stage machinery). Yet, in his most powerful "visual" scenes, Raimund employs simple allegorical figures in which the miracle of the human theater triumphs over the spectacle of mechanics. His emphasis on the visual was the outcome of his fundamentally pictorial imagination, so evident in his metaphoric language; every idea became an image to him, every inner change of a character a visible transformation.

Raimund's work is slender in volume, consisting of only eight plays written within ten years. They are all *Zauberstücke*, plays set within the baroque tripartite order of spirits, humans, and demons, in which the life of man is governed by supernatural powers. The interrelationship of the realms is sometimes intricate (as in *Der Barometermacher auf der Zauberinsel* and *Das Mädchen aus der Feenwelt, oder Der Bauer als Millionär*), sometimes merely functional (as in

Der Alpenkönig und der Menschenfeind). The difference in tone reflects Raimund's ambivalent feelings toward the baroque heritage. In the earlier plays, it is the tone of localized parodies (fairies speak dialect) in which the intermingling of the realms creates comic contrast (again, as in *Der Barometermacher auf der Zauberinsel* and *Das Mädchen aus der Feenwelt, oder Der Bauer als Millionär*). In the later plays he tended to restore the original seriousness to the realm of fairies and spirits, while he relegated humor to the realistic scenes set in the world of mortals.

In his first play, *Der Barometermacher auf der Zauberinsel* (1823), based on the Fortunatus legend, Raimund aimed only at entertainment in the general manner of the local farce. Raimund's individuality is apparent in the absence of obscenities and in his fascination with verbal play (he was then reading Abraham a Santa Clara). *Der Diamant des Geisterkönigs* (1824) was his first effort to juxtapose serious elements (in this case rather shadowy ideal lovers) and humorous, realistic characters. Florian Waschblau, no longer a mere clown, is a lovable, though not an idealized person. In 1948 Hans Christian Andersen adapted this play for the Danish stage, *More than Pearls and Gold*.

Raimund's first great success was *Das Mädchen aus der Feenwelt, oder Der Bauer als Millionär* (1826). He no longer depended on literary sources. The central figure, Fortunatus Wurzel, was created from the life around Raimund. Fortunatus is a farmer who has become rich overnight and, just as quickly, is reduced to poverty. Topical social criticism deepens into a moving parable on the worth of contentment and the transitoriness of human existence (as in the famous lyric *Aschenlied*). *Die gefesselte Phantasie* (1826; first performance, 1828), *Moisasurs Zauberfluch* (1827), and *Die unheilbringende Zauberkrone* (1829) illustrate Raimund's determination to rise above the "theater of amusement" of his time ("I don't want to write local plays! I don't want to hear of the popular theater!"). The intricate mythological apparatus, the often stilted, literary language in the serious scenes, did not appeal to his audience. Perhaps a more basic reason for the lukewarm reception of these plays was that his contemporaries simply did not share Raimund's allegorical way of thinking and could not enter into the elaborate baroque dream world of these plays. They preferred his realism as long as it was humorous, as in for example, the figure Nachtigall; they resented it when it was bitter, as in the treatment of the character Gluthahn, the greedy, heartless farmer in *Moisasurs Zauberfluch*, who is a demon in everyday clothes. These three plays have not been performed very frequently. With stage sets by Oskar Kokoschka, however, they were revived with some measure of success in the early 1960s.

Der Alpenkönig und der Menschenfeind (1828; first English performance, London, 1831) is Raimund's most powerful play. "Even Molière could not have thought out a more ingenious design. A misanthrope is healed by having his own behavior brought before his very eyes. No other writer of comedies has ever thought of an idea that is at the same time psychologically more convincing and richer in dramatic possibilities" said Grillparzer. Raimund intensifies the old theme of the misanthrope. Rappelkopf's hatred is not motivated by the evil around him (as in Molière's play). Instead his destructive suspicion is but a projection of his self-hatred. The play becomes a cure in which Raimund tries to overcome his own paranoid tendencies. Around the central image of a mirror, he created a unique tragicomedy of subjectivism.

The unity Raimund achieved in *Der Alpenkönig und der Menschenfeind*, in which he was writing about his innermost self, was not sustained in his last play, *Der Verschwender* (1833, first performance, 1834). The strength of the play lies not in the supernatural or mysterious elements (the self-confrontation in the figure of the beggar is more haunting in an eerie way than truly moving) but in the human qualities of the servant Valentin, the carpenter, who does not hesitate to provide for the impoverished count and thus rewards his master's often unthinking magnanimity with the generosity of his heart. Valentin counteracts his wife's unforgiving hardness, disguised as common sense, with the words: "When I am very old one day I want to have something else to remember than that I glued on some chair legs and put a cabinet together."

On the stage, Raimund's best plays radiate a magic hardly explainable through a critical analysis of their text or of their structure. Their effectiveness does not depend on dramatic coherence (perfect unity is evident only in *Der Alpenkönig und der Menschenfeind*) but on the power of individual elements: on the human warmth of the comic characters (Florian, Wurzel, Nachtigall, Valentin), which overcomes the shadowy coolness of the figures that often surround them; on the songs ("Brüderlein fein"; "So leb denn wohl"; "Hobellied"), which are organic parts of the plays and cannot be separated from the stage without losing their simplicity and becoming sentimental; on scenes of stark realism usually redeemed by humor; and on moments when in a unique fusion of stage-sense and imagination Raimund creates truly poetic images of human existence. Martin Esslin, commenting on the allegorical figures of Youth and Old Age in

Das Mädchen aus der Feenwelt, oder Der Bauer als Millionär, sees in such dramatic images an elemental kinship between Raimund's plays and the nonliterary theater of our time: "Here, as in the best works of the theater of the absurd, the human condition is concretized in visual metaphor."

In spite of their immense, inherent effectiveness on the stage, it is not easy to recreate the transparent magic of Raimund's plays in the theater. As Kurt Kahl wrote: "One must never reduce them to charming trivialities, never treat Raimund as a Biedermeier clown. We must follow this melancholy dreamer into his dreams at the risk of suddenly coming face to face with most disturbing realities."

Works: *Der Barometermacher auf der Zauberinsel* (1823; The Maker of Barometers on the Magic Isle); *Der Diamant des Geisterkönigs* (1824; The Diamond of the King of the Spirits); *Das Mädchen aus der Feenwelt, oder Der Bauer als Millionär* (1826; The Girl from the Fairy World, or The Peasant as Millionaire); *Die gefesselte Phantasie* (1826; The Shackled Fantasy); *Moisasurs Zauberfluch* (1827; Moisasur's Magic Curse); *Der Alpenkönig und der Menschenfeind* (1828; Eng. tr., The King of the Alps, 1850); *Die unheilbringende Zauberkrone* (1829; The Magic Crown that Bears Disaster); *Der Verschwender* (1833; Eng. tr., The Spendthrift, 1949); *Sämtliche Werke* (4 vols., 1837); *Sämtliche Werke* (6 vols., ed. F. Schreyvogel, 1960).

Bibliography: Bender, Wolfgang, "Verkennung und Erkennung in Ferdinand Raimunds Alpenkönig," *Germanisch-romanische Monatsschrift*, Neue Folge, no. 18, 1968. Claude, David, "Ferdinand Raimund—*Moisasurs Zauberfluch*," in *Das deutsche Lustpiel*, vol. 1, ed. H. Steffen, 1968. Erken, Günter, "Ferdinand Raimund," in *Deutsche Dichter des 19. Jahrhunderts*, edited by B. von Wiese, 1969. Krügel, Fred A., "Ferdinand Raimund's Gutenstein Poems," in *Essays on German Literature in Honor of G. J. Hallamore*, edited by Batts and Marketa, 1969. Michalski, John, *Ferdinand Raimund*, 1968. Prohaska, Dorothy James, "Raimund's Contribution to Viennese Popular Comedy," *German Quarterly* 42, no. 3 (May 1969); also, *Raimund and Vienna*, 1970.

Horst Jarka[▲]

Rainer Maria Rilke

Born 4 December 1875 in Prague. Rilke's father, after the failure of his military career, had become a railroad-company employee, and Rilke's mother for the rest of her life never got over their exclusion from high society. Rilke's own speculations about his aristocratic origin were undoubtedly an outgrowth of his mother's attitude. Throughout his school years in Prague, both before and after his unsuccessful attempt to pursue an army officer's career (1886–90, cadets' school at St. Pölten; 1890–91, military college in Mährisch-Weißkirchen), his cultural environment was that of a linguistic diaspora. His first literary experiences were influenced by the German-speaking milieu of Prague. At that time it was Detlev von Liliencron who not only served as the model for Rilke's budding talent, but who also supported and actively encouraged its development.

In 1896 Rilke went to Munich and entered into a more lively literary world. It was there that he first met Lou Andreas-Salomé, whom he followed to Berlin in 1897. From then on he traveled a great deal and continued to do so until his last years in Switzerland. He visited Italy frequently; in 1899 and 1900 he traveled with Lou Andreas-Salomé to Russia, where he visited with Lev Tolstoi; he also made visits to France, Sweden, Egypt, Spain, and Switzerland. Between trips he made vain attempts to establish a permanent residence, often with the financial support of friends.

The most stable periods of Rilke's life were: 1901–1902, when he lived with his wife, the sculptor Clara Westhoff, in the vicinity (that is, in Westerwede) of the Worpswede artists' colony; 1902, when he lived at intervals in Paris (where he met Auguste Rodin and Paul Cézanne, both of whom had an important influence on the development of his more mature art); and 1910 and 1911–12 at Duino Castle on the Adriatic, where he enjoyed the hospitality of Princess Marie von Thurn und Taxis.

During the last phase of his career, after World War I, Switzerland provided Rilke with the spacious environment and the security he needed in his efforts to find a balance between art and life. He spent the year 1920 at Berg on the Irschel, and from 1921 on he lived at the castle of Muzot (in the canton Valais), which was put at his disposal by his patron Werner Reinhart of Winterthur. Except for short stays in Paris he never left the castle until he went to the Val-Mont sanatorium, where after a painful illness he died on 29 December 1926. He was buried in the cemetery at Raron, amid the Valais countryside, which he had loved and praised.

Rilke, through the effect of his nature upon his companions, through his friendships, and through his extensive correspondence, made his personality and life a center of unusual attention. One consequence of this propensity to exert his personality, not only as a creative artist but also as an individual, was the stream of reminiscences that began to be published soon after his death. Such works vary greatly in value and have encouraged interpretations that confuse purely personal matters with the literary work. It cannot be denied that Rilke took an active interest in the creation of his own legend. As a result the books of reminiscences, in which private and chance occurrences are stressed more than his lyrical works, seem like an echo of the personal image that he himself cultivated. On the other hand Rilke's stylization of himself as a poet was particularly affected by the influence of his associates.

Three women in succession not only decisively contributed to Rilke's growing awareness of his poetic vocation but also quite probably determined specific features and manifestations of his sense of mission. They contributed to his utilization of his natural poetic gift, but they did so in a way that produced a strained, exaggerated, and esoteric effect. His mother, who was herself the author of a collection of aphorisms, *Ephemeriden* (1900), and who was disappointed by her inescapable middle-class life, instilled in the boy the notion that he had a special destiny by virtue of his talent and that he should therefore set himself apart from his surroundings. Lou Andreas-Salomé was his close friend during his beginning years as a poet and later remained as confidante who was understanding but kept her distance. Rilke, who repeatedly succumbed to the inclination to let himself drift, was led by her back to his true self. She was of service to his work by her interpretations, suggestions, and repeated references to the quality of his talent and the necessity for him to preserve it. Princess Marie von Thurn und Taxis also played a special role. To Rilke's basic experiences concerning the manner in which his poems "emerged," she gave the special character of a "dictation" that was independent of himself. Thus, when the "unforeseeable" that was communicated to him as "grace" was viewed by him as something beyond his own control, this interpretation of his creative process owed a great deal to the princess.

The major figures who inspired and shaped Rilke's creative life included Jens Peter Jacobsen in the early period, Friedrich Klopstock and Friedrich Hölderlin in the later years, and the French sculptor Auguste Rodin (1840–1917), whose influence was decisive. It was due to Rodin that Rilke, after the vague lyricism of his beginnings, changed to precise apprehension of the object and to the development of a craft that would always be at his disposal, irrespective of inspiration. It was a great stroke of luck for Rilke that, in addition to the influence of the three women who set him on his own path and helped him to become aware of his own nature, he was exposed to the discipline of Rodin, who directed him away from himself and taught him to understand the work of art as a mission and an achievement.

The main source of information about Rilke's life and conception of art is his voluminous correspondence and his diaries. Of the diaries, *Das Florenzer Tagebuch* (1898) is particularly important in providing an early example of his poetic originality. Following the first seven-volume collection of letters, written between 1899 and 1926 (*Briefe*, 1929–37, later revised; also published in a two-volume abridged edition, 1950), the most important correspondences appeared in separate editions that contain the letters of both parties. The most important as biographical references are the volumes of correspondence with Marie von Thurn und Taxis (1951), Lou Andreas-Salomé (1952), Katharina Kippenberg (the wife of Rilke's publisher, Anton Kippenberg; 1954), Benvenuta (Magda von Hattingberg; 1954), Merline (Baladine Klossowska; 1954), André Gide (1952, 1957), Émile Verhaeren (1955), and Inga Junghanns (1959). In addition there are Rilke's letters to his publisher (1934; 2nd edition in two volumes, 1949), to Countess Sizzo (1950), and the shorter series of letters to a young poet and to a young woman (1929, 1930). Among the memoirs the outstanding ones are those of Lou Andreas-Salomé (*Rainer Maria Rilke*, 1928; and the Rilke chapter in her autobiography, *Lebensrückblick*, 1951), and of J. R. von Salis (*Rainer Maria Rilkes Schweizer Jahre*, 3rd edition, 1952).

To an extent unusual among poets, Rilke's transposition of the poetic vision into language is shaped by impressions of landscapes. For him the contours of certain landscapes had the effect of celestial constellations. His verbal images and their sequence grew out of his ideas of space. One of the most striking characteristics of Rilke's poetry is that it expresses intellectual and spiritual concepts in spatial terms. He wrote with grandeur whenever vast spaces were at hand to correspond to his inner experiences, as in the early period at Worpswede (where he lived from 1900 until his marriage to Clara

Westhoff) and in Russia. This was also true later at Duino, and in Egypt, Spain, and the Swiss canton of Valais. These landscapes provided an inner vision. In his letters Rilke often discussed these interconnections.

To characterize Rilke is still a difficult task even today. Our view of the man and poet as he really was is obstructed by too many subjective opinions, both positive views of friends and the negative criticisms of his enemies. His deliberate stylization of himself, which has already been mentioned, also contributes to the confusion. In approaching Rilke, as with any great personality, it is necessary to draw boundaries and make distinctions. In intellectual matters there is no other choice. The main goal is to do justice to the true quality of his work, which was not the achievement of a delicate, tranquil soul but of a challenging, violent, intransigent personality.

The interpretation of Rilke's poetry, especially that of the later period, is still in its beginnings, particularly with respect to language and form. Considerably more effort will be required to achieve understanding. Rilke himself, by his manner of expression, made an exact elucidation of his message difficult. In the poetry of his early period, critical comprehension is hampered mainly by the sound, the flowing melody, the magical persuasiveness. In the later poetry, as in the letters, the main obstacle is his strenuous effort to present the uncertain as certain and the questionable as unequivocal. He does so with an intransigence that precludes contradiction, and the reader is put in the position of one who, if he does not agree, contradicts truth itself. Yet, in strange contrast to this assertive approach, there is a humility toward the secret of existence. Rilke felt that his greatness was a matter of being defeated "by the ever greater."

The demanding attitude that Rilke adopts is the expression of a sense of vocation, which communicates itself in religious paraphrases and sentiments. There has been nothing comparable in German poetry since Hölderlin. (The utilization by the Young German movement of such religious types as the seer, the apostle, the evangelist, derived from the sociopolitical insistence that the writer dedicate himself to the portrayal of essentially nonpoetic, didactic tendencies.) Rilke's sense of vocation emerges from a fear of life that turns into an affirmation of life. He assents to life in order to endure it. His struggle to accept life in spite of its "hells" determined Rilke's view of his poetic "mandate," which he interpreted as a religious one.

This inner experience found noteworthy expression in Rilke's frequent accounts concerning the genesis of his poetry, particularly of his late poetry. It is certain that in developing these concepts he was subject to outside influences, above all that of the Princess Marie von Thurn und Taxis. As already stated, however, these ideas corresponded to his own interpretation of the poetic process, which he experienced as "dictation, being brought to one's knees, grace, storm, a hurricane in the spirit" *Diktat, Geworfenwerden, Gnade, Sturm, Orkan im Geiste.*" Rilke explained his poems as something that transcended him, "as though they were not mine; in their nature something more than by me." In short, the meaning that was striving for communication "made use" of him, "in order to find expression in human terms."

The *Duineser Elegien* and *Sonette an Orpheus* are not the result of thought but an experience of being charged with a duty. Therefore he required—and there is hardly anything comparable in the personal statements of other poets—"surrender" to his word. He demanded for his poetry what is usually only insisted upon in regard to a religious revelation: namely, believing acceptance. Just as the creative process is felt as an ascendance into the religious sphere—Rilke himself compared this experience to that of Moses on Mount Tabor—from which it is a long way back to men, so, too, is the content of the message inescapable and capable of transforming men, "wie das Aufheben einer Monstranz über einer Menge, die ins Knie bricht" (as when a monstrance is elevated above a crowd that falls to its knees). This attitude explains the hardness that Rilke exercised toward himself in his artistic work. The great transformation after he met Rodin was an unparalleled achievement wrung from what had hitherto been a casual involvement with art. This also makes understandable Rilke's pitiless rejection of amateurish efforts among his associates.

The content of Rilke's sense of vocation, which began to assume increasingly definite form after *Das Stundenbuch* (written, 1899–1903), can be described by the poet's own phrase as "earth's mandate." In his poetry he set out not only to interpret the world, to illuminate existence, as is usual in other poetry, but to save the world. He wanted to give not just to man but to the whole of life the possibility of being present, of "belonging to this world" and therefore "capable of being expressed." In keeping with this definition the poetry of the 1920s was expanded far beyond the great claim of expressionism, which was to render the "essence" of man. The stability and permanency of the world, which "has fallen into the hands of men," had to be safeguarded. The world in a comprehensive sense, the substance and meaning of existence, became the task of poetry.

The great aspect of Rilke's poetry is the slow but consistent reshaping of his understanding of this mandate. It was a laborious road from the interpreting of his mandate as the artistic mastery of things to the last phase, when he recognized his task as a human one. This perhaps explains much that is strained and misleading in his late poetry and also the greatness of his sense of mission.

The phrase from the seventh elegy in *Duineser Elegien,* "The nearest is remote for men," strikingly formulates the problem of maturing. What is most inward and original can be attained only perilously and by circuitous means. Part of the originality of Rilke's work is that it moves in a single line from the less important to the more important. No one could have foreseen that the vague, early work would develop into the density of the middle period and the sublimity of the late poems. Rilke's work does not add dimension to dimension but, at each stage, supersedes what has preceded it. This does not mean that the individual poems after *Das Stundenbuch* cannot lay independent claim to validity. But each new group of poems is an attempt at a deeper and more precise mastery of the same task—"earth's mandate."

In the early poems—*Leben und Lieder* (1894), *Larenopfer* (1896), *Traumgekrönt* (1897), *Advent* (1898; in *Erste Gedichte,* 1913), and *Die frühen Gedichte* (1909; originally *Mir zur Feier,* 1899; includes the poems *Engellieder, Mädchengestalten, Lieder der Mädchen, Gebete der Mädchen zu Maria,* and the dramatic poem *Die weiße Fürstin*)— the solution is a noncommittal one based on a sentimental, verbose celebration of things that are not apprehended with the intent of presenting their true, "definitive" shape in a work of art. The decisive factor is not the things themselves, but the animation of the soul that they evoke: "celebration of *myself* (*mir zur Feier*); "it moves *me* so much" (*mich rührt so sehr*); "spread *thyself* like a festive robe over the pensive things" (*breite dich wie ein Feierkleid über die sinnenden Dinge*). *Das Stundenbuch* (in "three books"; written, 1899, 1901, 1903; published, 1905) remains essentially on the same level, although it contains one new feature in the fraternal relation to things and to God. For the first time a religious sense enters Rilke's experience of the world, a Franciscan compassion for the world. At this time it was still understood in a social sense, but later it recurred on an essentially different level.

In a few poems—*Du dunkelnder Grund* (Thou Darkling Ground), in the first part, and *Die Könige der Welt* (The Kings of the World), in the second part—the beginnings of a movement, the meaning of which is not yet grasped by Rilke, toward things that need man can be seen. Before this attitude was fully developed, a radical reversal took place in Rilke's relationship to the world and the task it imposed upon him. This change was necessary to enable him to accept things lovingly as they really are and for their own sake. First their essence had to be *grasped*. This happened in the later poems of the *Buch der Bilder* (written, 1898–1906; published, 1902; 2nd edition, 1906) and especially in the two parts of the *Neue Gedichte* (written, 1903–1908; published, 1907–1908) and *Der neuen Gedichte anderer Teil* (1908).

The second stage was closely connected with Auguste Rodin's personal and artistic influence on Rilke. In 1902 Rilke, whose wife Clara had been a pupil of the sculptor's, went to Rodin in Paris and at Meudon. In 1905 he returned to Paris, where he lived in close association with Rodin, working as his secretary for part of the time. Then, because of certain conflicts between them, there was finally a complete break in 1906. The crucial point of the association was that Rodin, with his ruthless severity, lifted Rilke's work out of the *à peu près*, out of an imprecise lyricism, and into exact and graphic presentation. Rilke learned how to apprehend the object feature by feature as something totally apart from himself. This was the origin of the *Dinggedichte* (thing poems), concerning which references to phenomenology have been made with some justice. By means of precise observation and artistic transformation, these poems go back to the essential nature of the thing, be it animal, plant, art object, or human figures and relationships.

Die Aufzeichnungen des Malte Laurids Brigge (written, 1904–1910; published, 1910) represent a kind of autobiographical and factual commentary on the *Neue Gedichte*, which were written at the same time. Yet, in form the *Aufzeichnungen* anticipate the new features of the late period: the event is disobjectivized, and logical, psychological, and factual connections are dissolved in inner movement. "Work and be patient" was what Rilke learned from Rodin. This middle, or classical, period of Rilke's life was fundamentally contrary to his inmost nature. But it was necessary in order to exorcise the danger of dissolution visible in the wordiness and shapelessness of *Das Studenbuch*. Rilke broke off his work on *Das Stundenbuch*, and the fourth part he had begun was never completed.

The third and last period in Rilke's writing led him back again in the direction of the early period. Whereas during the period of the *Neue Gedichte* he attempted to see the thing purely in itself, independent of his own wishes and intentions, Rilke now once more directed his love and interest toward things. During the middle period, movement was from things to the poet. Now it proceeds from the poet to things, as in the early period, with the difference that now the intensity and the purpose have become greater and deeper. It is no longer a question of transfiguring things, but of preserving them, of ensuring their survival, and thus of saving existence altogether.

In the poem *Wendung* of 1914, he tells how "looking" is replaced by "heartwork,". which draws things into itself: "For, lo, there is a limit to looking/and the more looked-at world longs to prosper in love./ Work of seeing is done,/now do heartwork" (*Denn des Anschauens, siehle, ist eine Grenze/und die geschautere Welt will in der Liebe gedeihn./Werk des Gesichts ist getan,/tue nun Herzwerk*). No longer, as was the case in the *Neue Gedichte*, is "earth's mandate" understood in a purely artistic sense as saving the form, as transposing accidental existence into something necessary and definitive, as mastering the world by the aesthetic process. Now it is understood in the human sense as saving the world from a seemingly unavoidable decline brought on by man, a decline that can be resisted and conquered only by man himself in the person of the singer, of Orpheus.

In a process that is as grandiose as it is weird, the aesthetic task coincides more and more with the human. Man is nothing but the singer, and only as such is he in a position to preserve the world and thereby himself. It is one of the most intense and yet one of the most exultant attempts at self-redemption through art. At the center of this phase stand the following works: the *Duineser Elegien* (1923), begun in 1912 at Duino Castle and, after a long interruption, finished at Muzot in February 1922; the two series of *Sonette an Orpheus* (1923), which were produced at the same time "in an after-storm" to the *Elegien*; the groups of poems in French of Rilke's last years (*Vergers suivi des quatrains Valaisans*, 1926; *Les Roses*, 1927; *Les Fenêtres*, 1927; all collected in 1935 under the title *Poèmes français*); and the *Späte Gedichte* (1934).

The poems of the *Späte Gedichte* were first collected in the third volume of the *Gesammelte Werke* (1927), under the heading "Letzte Gedichte und Fragmentarisches." They later appeared, complete, in the volume *Gedichte 1906 bis 1926* (1953), and in a more meaningful arrangement in the second volume of the *Sämtliche Werke* (1956). Some of these poems were written before and some after the *Elegien* and the *Sonette* and contain many of Rilke's lasting works. Some of those poems created after the peak of achievement reached in the two Muzot cycles attain a tranquil simplicity, perhaps adumbrating a new stage of development, which was never to be completed.

The background to the new stage was the experience of the decline of things, an experience that from World War I on became increasingly distressing. Rilke connected this with historical observations, particularly of the late Middle Ages, when (so it is expressed in *Malte Laurids Brigge*) external things were "equivalents" for inner states. Since then, with the advance of reason and the scientific and technological world dependent on it, the outer has become separated from the inner. The thing and its meaning no longer coincide. The machine, "the tense drive" (*der spannende Drang*), destroys the things that were "prayed to, served, knelt to" (*gebeteten, gedienten, geknieten*)—the "temples" that were the "heart's extravagance" (*Herzens Verschwendung*). The "temples" are now replaced by a "contrived form" (*erdachtes Gebild*), by "an acting without an image, by an acting under crusts" (*ein Tun ohne Bild, Tun unter Krusten*).

The seventh and ninth elegies as well as the "machinery" sonnets (Part I, numbers eighteen and nineteen; Part II, number 10) give an elegiac description of this process. In the two elegies—neither of which is a "product of weariness" as has, incomprehensibly, been said—this lament turns into rejoicing that it should be possible for man, "the most fleeting of fleeting things," to arrest this decline and to make existence healthy and enduring. The *Elegien*, with their precisely developed transition from "lament" to "praise" (in the course of which each elegy has its prescribed place, so that before the whole had been completed, the position of each had been unalterably determined, resulting in an indescribably harmonious unity), celebrate this promise given to man. And the *Sonette* show him at work transforming things into "constellations" (*Sternbild*) and transposing them into the beyond, into "pure relationship" (*reinen Bezug*).

By *transforming* things, decline can be arrested. Rilke meant by this something quite real as he explained in some of his letters—namely, the possibility of increasing the frequency of oscillations of things and thus transforming them into a new state that will confer permanence upon them. In Rilke's poetry this is celebrated as the vision of a new state of the world. The transformation takes place through songs of praise, through language, through the transposition of things by the spoken word into a new form of existence: "And these things that live on departure, understand when you praise them; transient, they trust in rescue through us, the most transient of all" (*Und diese von Hingang/lebenden Dinge verstehn,/daß du sie rühmst; vergänglich,/traun sie ein Rettendes uns, den Vergänglichsten zu*). This transforming praise is "accomplished" by grasping things in our feelings, "in the overfull gaze and the speechless heart" (*im überfüllbaren Blick und im sprachlosen Herzen*).

The "heartwork" that thus absorbs things means to transform them inwardly, to make them invisible, and thereby to transpose them into the new quality of being that Rilke described by the spatial concept of *Weltinnenraum* (earth's inner space). Earth's "dream" is to "arise invisibly within us" (*unsichtbar in uns erstehn*): "What is your urgent command, if not transformation?" (*Was, wenn Verwandlung nicht, ist dein drängender Auftrag?*—ninth elegy). And in the seventh elegy: "Nowhere, beloved, can world exist but within. Our life passes with transformation" (*Nirgends, Geliebte wird Welt sein, als innen. Unser/Leben geht hin mit Verwandlung*). The strength of the *Elegien* lies both in this radiant conviction of being able to arrest a universal doom and in the fact that Rilke attributes this capability to man, regardless of whoever we may be (*wer wir auch seien*).

Earth's inner space" is both a state of the world, the existential form of the new world (behind which ultimately lie secularized wishes for a "new heaven and new earth"), and the spiritual space of things and of men. In it there is no distinction between here and beyond, between death and life, and between outward and inward. In earth's inner space" there is no sense of hierarchy, everything is simultaneously present and interrelated. It is an extreme antithesis to the Christian view of the universe. Rilke's religious feeling was fundamentally opposed to the Christian viewpoint. Hence he protested more violently than Nietzsche against Christ, who for him was an alien figure (see, among many sources of evidence, the *Brief des jungen Arbeiters*, in *Über Gott*, 1933). He was devotedly attached to the religious spirit of the Old Testament and thereby to the Jewish people.

Among earth's creatures it is the lovers, those who die young, heroes, children, and animals who, insofar as we do not prevent them, have the possibility of seeing "the open, the pure, and entire relationship" (*das Offene, den reinen, den ganzen Bezug*), "the circle of the whole change" (*den Umkreis des ganzen Wandels*). They have no "opposite" as we do, and therefore no "fate." They know their place and their seasons and have not dropped out of their place in the total unity. Anyone who makes distinctions, disintegrates the pure, experiences "fate"—he misses the "open," because his feeling, instead of being allowed to remain mere direction, is directed at an opposite, which he wants to seize and by which he wants to be seized, which he wants to still and by which he wants to be stilled.

In the eighth elegy, in connection with certain concepts of Rudolf Kassner, Rilke celebrated this "openness" as the fateful space of true existence, the "nowhere without no, the pure, unsupervised" (*Nirgends ohne Nicht, das Reine, Unüberwachte*), "the eternal current" (*die ewige Strömung*) into which animals and children enter, while we have "world" before us.

No special proof is required to show that this experience of a new state of world in the form of "earth's inner space" is the result of an inner disposition of Rilke's decreed by fate. For him, love of man and, as in the parable of the prodigal son in *Die Aufzeichnungen des Malte Laurids Brigge*, love of God dissolves into a "tendency of the heart." For this reason he praised the ones whose love is unrequited, of whom in the *Elegien* and again in *Malte Laurids Brigge* he gives individual examples. In the first, second, and fourth elegies, in language that continually changes and becomes ever-more moving, he describes the nature of unpossessing love. He feels that the "forsaken" are richer than the "satisfied," and that we must therefore "lovingly free ourselves from the beloved and endure it in living" (*liebend uns vom Geliebten befrein und es lebend bestehn*), just as "the arrow endures the bowstring." Then a new clarity invades him: it is false to want to feel permanence in "caresses," or to promise oneself "eternity" from embraces, to want to think that lovers will enrich one another, with each gaining in "plenitude" from the other. This feeling that lovers believe they experience is no guarantee that each is not "waning," being diminished by the abundance he is receiving.

For Rilke, the way to overcome a false, hollow, selfish togetherness is *not* to set the other free on his own terms, is *not* to come into one's own self through devotion to the fully affirmed and accepted beloved, but to surrender completely to the emotion itself. The force of love is important, not the person evoking that force. The beloved and God are the turbulence of the emotion of love itself and no longer its goal, repository, and destiny. No one will contest the intensity that Rilke was capable of feeling, but by the same token, it cannot be overlooked that his love always violently recoiled upon himself. This is made unmistakably clear by the evidence concerning Rilke's relations with women and friends that is to be found in their reminiscences and in his letters. Poetry, however, has the power to communicate the contrary of the literal statement. Hence, it may be that the passionate tone of the statements about love in the *Elegien*, even when this tone is contradicted by his words, is the expression of an affirmation contrary to his own conviction. It is a scarcely believable process to be able to create so magically the nature of a real meeting in love (as in the second elegy), and then to have to expend so much real, not imaginary, effort in order to deny it. Above the poem *Wendung* Rilke inscribed a quotation from Rudolf Kassner: "The path from ardor to greatness lies through sacrifice."

The poetic realization of "earth's mandate" on various levels and with continually growing power and decisiveness is one of the greatest intellectual adventures of modern time. Rilke is a poet of mysterious, terrifying vision. The greatest moments of his poetry are the outcome of an extreme "exposure upon the mountains of the heart" (*Ausgesetzseins auf den Bergen des Herzens*), which is at the same time an extreme abandonment within himself. It is evident that there is a limit to the greatness of this poetic achievement, even though it elevates the poet to the rank of world savior and guardian of mankind. No real transcendence is produced, despite the angel. The *Weltinnenraum* remains enclosed within itself and is not susceptible to any meaning beyond itself. What has been willed is in itself divine. God has disappeared from the *Elegien*. Man is the ultimate and extreme possibility of being; his singing is world salvation and self-redemption.

Works: *Leben und Lieder: Bilder und Tagebuchblätter* (1894; Life and Songs: Pictures and Notes from a Diary); *Larenopfer* (1896; Sacrifice to the Lares); *Jetzt und in der Stunde unseres Absterbens* (1896; Now and at the Hour of Our Death); *Christus, Visionen* (1896–98; Eng. tr., Visions of a Christ, 1967); *Traumgekrönt* (1897; Dream-crowned); *Im Frühfrost* (1897; In the Early Frost); *Ohne Gegenwart* (1898; Without a Present); *Am Leben hin* (1898; By the Side of Life); *Das Florenzer Tagebuch* (1898; The Florence Diary); *Advent* (1898; republished in *Erste Gedichte*, 1913); *Zwei Prager Geschichten* (1899; Two Prague Stories); *Mir zur Feier* (1899; Celebration of Myself; republished under the title *Die frühen Gedichte* [1909; The Early Poems]); *Vom lieben Gott und Anderes* (1900; About God and Others; republished under the title *Geschichten vom lieben Gott* [1904; Eng. tr., Stories of God, 1963]); *Die Letzten* (1902; The Last); *Das tägliche Leben* (1902; Daily Life); *Das Buch der Bilder* (1902; The Book of Pictures); *Worpswede* (1903); *Auguste Rodin* (1903); *Das Stundenbuch* (1905; in three parts, *Das Buch vom mönchischen Leben, Das Buch von der Pilgerschaft,* and *Von der Armut und vom Tode*; Eng. tr., The Book of Hours: Of the Monastic Life, Of Pilgrimage, and Of Poverty and Death, 1961); *Die Weise von Liebe und Tod des Cornets Christoph Rilke* (1906; Eng. tr., The Lay of the Love and Death of Cornet Christopher Rilke, 1959); *Auguste Rodin* (1907; includes the 1903 essay and a second essay); *Neue Gedichte* and *Der neuen Gedichte anderer Teil* (1907 and 1908; Eng. tr., New Poems, 1964); *Requiem* (1909); *Die Aufzeichnungen des Malte Laurids Brigge* (1910; Eng. tr., The Notebooks of Malte Laurids Brigge, 1949); *Erste Gedichte* (1913; First Poems); *Rückkehr des verlorenen Sohnes* (1913; translation of André Gide's *Le Retour de l'enfant prodigue*); *Das Marienleben* (1913; Eng. tr., The Life of the Virgin Mary, 1947); *Die weiße Fürstin* (1920; The White Princess); *Duineser Elegien* (1923; Eng. tr., Duinese Elegies, 1930); *Sonette an Orpheus* (1923; Eng. tr., Sonnets to Orpheus, 1936); *Vergers suivi des quatrains Valaisans* (1926); *Les Fenêtres* (1927); *Les Roses* (1927); *Gesammelte Werke* (6 vols., 1927; Collected Works); *Erzählungen und*

Skizzen aus der Frühzeit (1928; Stories and Sketches from the Early Years); *Briefe an A. Rodin* (1928; Letters to A. Rodin); *Verse und Prosa aus dem Nachlaß* (1929; Verses and Prose from the Posthumous Writings); *Briefe an einen jungen Dichter* (1929; Eng. tr., Letters to a Young Poet, 1954); *Briefe* (7 vols., 1929–37; republished in an abridged edition in 2 vols., 1950); *Briefe an eine junge Frau* (1930; Letters to a Young Woman); *Über Gott: Zwei Briefe* (1933; On God: Two Letters; includes "Der Brief des jungen Arbeiters" [The Letter from a Young Workingman]); *Späte Gedichte* (1934; Eng. tr., Later Poems, 1938); *Briefe an seinen Verleger* (1934; Letters to His Publisher); *Poèmes français* (1935; includes the three earlier collections of poems in French); *Gesammelte Briefe* (6 vols., 1936–39; Collected Letters); *Tagebücher aus der Frühzeit* (1942; Diaries from the Early Years); *Ewald Tragy* (1944; Eng. tr., 1959); *Nachlaß vier Teile* (1950; Posthumous Writings, Four Parts); *Die Briefe an Gräfin Sizzo 1921–26* (1950; The Letters to Countess Sizzo 1921–26); *Aus dem Nachlaß des Grafen C. W.: Ein Gedichtkreis* (1950; Eng. tr., From the Reminiscences of Count C. W., 1952); *Briefwechsel mit Marie von Thurn und Taxis* (1951; Eng. tr., The Letters of Rainer Maria Rilke and Princess Marie von Thurn und Taxis, 1958); *Rainer Maria Rilke und Lou Andreas-Salomé* (1952); *André Gide: Correspondance 1909–26* (1952); *Briefe an Frau Gudi Nölke* (1953; Eng. tr., Letters to Frau Gudi Nölke, 1955); *Gedichte, 1909–26* (1953); *Briefwechsel in Gedichten mit Erika Mitterer* (1954; Eng. tr., Correspondence in Verse with Erika Mitterer, 1953); *Rainer Maria Rilke an Benvenuta* (1954; Eng. tr., Letters to Benvenuta, 1954); *Rainer Maria Rilke et Merline: Correspondance 1920–26* (1954); *Rainer Maria Rilke und K. Kippenberg* (1954); *Rainer Maria Rilke et André Gide/Émile Verhaeren: Correspondance inédite* (1955); *Sämtliche Werke* (1956; Complete Works); *Lettres Milanaises, 1921–26* (1956); *Rainer Maria Rilke und Inga Junghanss: Briefwechsel* (1959); *Briefe an Sidonie Náherny von Borutin* (1969).

English translations in collections: *Poems by Rainer Maria Rilke* (1918; enlarged ed., 1943); *The Journal of My Other Self* (1930); *Requiem, and Other Poems* (1935); *Translations from the Poetry of Rainer Maria Rilke* (1938); *Wartime Letters of Rainer Maria Rilke, 1914–21* (1940); *Fifty Selected Poems* (bilingual ed., 1940); *Primal Sound, and Other Prose Pieces* (1943); *Letters* (2 vols., 1945–48); *Thirty-one Poems by Rainer Maria Rilke* (1946); *Selected Letters of Rainer Maria Rilke, 1902–26* (1946); *Five Prose Pieces* (1947); *Rainer Maria Rilke: His Last Friendship* (1952); *Selected Works* (1954 ff.); *Poems 1906–26* (1957); *Selected Works: Prose and Poetry* (2 vols., 1960).

Bibliography: Andreas-Salomé, Lou, *Memoirs*, edited by Ernst Pfeifer, 1952. Batterby, K. A., *Rilke and France: A Study in Poetic Development*, 1966. Hamburger, Käte, *Rainer Maria Rilke*, 1950. Hartman, Geoffrey H., *Unmediated Vision*, 1966. Holthusen, Hans Egon, *Der späte Rilke*,

1949; and *Rainer Maria Rilke*, 1957. Kunisch, Hermann, *Rainer Maria Rilke*, 1944. Mandel, Siegfried, *Rainer Maria Rilke: The Poetic Instinct*, 1966. Mason, Eudo C., *Rilke, Europe and the English-speaking World*, 1961. Puknat, E. M., and S. B., "American Literary Encounters with Rilke," *Monatshefte* 60 (1968):245–56. Shaw, Priscilla, *Rilke, Valéry and Yeats: The Domain of Self*, 1964. Wood, F., *Rainer Maria Rilke: The Ring of Forms*, 1958.

Hermann Kunisch

Joseph Roth

Born 2 September 1894 in Schwabendorf in Galicia; died 27 May 1939 in Paris. The son of Jewish parents, Joseph Roth later converted to Catholicism. Studied German literature and philosophy in Vienna. Served in the Austro-Hungarian army and was prisoner of war in Russia. After demobilization, he was a journalist in Vienna and Berlin and then a writer in Frankfurt on the Main, contributing features to the *Frankfurter Zeitung*. He lived mostly in hotels and traveled a great deal. He was a refugee in Paris at the time of his death.

Roth was an important novelist, essayist, and critic. His search for the past and a lost native land made him a notable chronicler of the vanished Danube monarchy. According to him, only the past is luminous and genuine, while the present appears strangely pallid and derivative; everything exists only insofar as it is past. It is thus that Roth looks through his childhood eyes at an Austria long since gone. People never embrace the present moment, but instead they inhabit an ever-present past; what is close at hand holds something arbitrary, something disturbing, and only what is far away acquires conclusive validity, indeed becomes symbolical.

Restless and on a "flight without end"—see his novel *Flucht ohne Ende* (1927)—Roth delighted in the roles of "high comedy." His stories are not autobiographical, certainly, but he displays sympathy for many of his characters that sometimes develops into actual identification with them. Characteristically, they linger hopelessly in what is over and done with. A superpersonal force dominates their recurrent fate, sometimes disrupting their identity and forcing them into a false existence. The narrator's attitude alternates between passionate sympathy and ironic detachment, a circumstance that gave Roth an extraordinary gift for portraiture. Simultaneously virtuoso and moralist, adventurer and believer, admirer and critic, he casts a varied light on characters and events, likes to let the complementary colors stand out, so that reality appears as a refraction through the prism of the characters. These characters remain solitary figures even when they appear in company. They live in a reality as this reality appears to them; unsuspected changes in this appearance remain incomprehensible to them, for the perspective vanishing points of the "world bioscope theater" are continually changing.

The action in Roth's work develops out of individual situations, episodes, anecdotes, traits of character—a typical melange of theatrical and descriptive representation. The conversations are laconic, descriptions are done with a broad brush. The passage of time and the individual's sense of time do not coincide; Roth creates powerful effects from this difference, for the characters remain completely enmeshed in their own particular time, as the novel *Radetzkymarsch* (1932) admirably demonstrates.

As in time, so too in space Roth prefers the isolated setting. The landscape of the old Austrian-Russian frontier is the basic setting of his writing; it sends forth the characters who make their way all through his work and insures unity in variety. The themes may be predictable, but they are presented in a multitude of forms. With the kaleidoscopic structure of his tales, the detail is often more striking than the whole, the brief passage more penetrating than the extended one.

Works: *Hotel Savoy* (1924); *Die Rebellion* (1924); *April* (1925); *Der blinde Spiegel* (1925; The Blind Mirror); *Juden auf Wanderschaft* (1927; The Wandering Jews); *Die Flucht ohne Ende* (1927; Eng. tr., Flight without End, 1930); *Das Spinnennetz* (1928; The Spider Web); *Zipper und sein Vater* (1928; Zipper and His Father); *Rechts und Links* (1929; Right and Left); *Hiob* (1930; Eng. tr., Job: The Story of a Simple Man, 1931); *Panoptikum* (1930; Panopticon); *Radetzkymarsch* (1932; Eng. tr., Radetzky March, 1933); *Der Antichrist* (1934); *Studien* (1934; Essays); *Tarabas, ein Gast auf dieser Erde* (1934; Eng. tr., Tarabas: A Guest on Earth, 1934); *Die hundert Tage* (1936; Eng. tr., The Ballad of the Hundred Days, 1936); *Beichte eines Mörders* (1936; Eng. tr., Confessions of a Murderer Told in One Night, 1937); *Das falsche Gewicht* (1937; Short Weight); *Die Kapuzinergruft* (1938; The Capuchin Crypt); *Die Geschichte von der 1002. Nacht* (1939; The Story of the 1002nd Night); *Die Legende vom heiligen Trinker* (1939; Eng. tr., The Legend of the Holy Drinker, 1943); *Der Leviathan* (1940); *Werke* (ed. H. Kesten, 3 vols., 1956; Works); *Romane, Erzählungen, Aufsätze* (1964; Novels, Stories, Essays); *Der stumme Prophet* (1966; The Silent Prophet).

Bibliography: Bronsen, David, "Das literarische Bild der Auflösung im *Radetzkymarsch*," *Jahrbuch der Grillparzer Gesellschaft*, vol. 4, pp. 130–43, 1966. Cusatelli, G., "Realismo di Roth," *Palatina* 9, no. 3 (1965): 55–70. Kesten, Hermann, *Meine Freunde*, 1953. Linden, H., *Joseph Roth: Leben und Werk*, 1949. Rosenfeld, Sidney, "Die Magie des Namens in

Joseph Roths Beichte eines Mörders," *German Quarterly* 40 (1967):351–62. Trommler, Frank, *Roman und Wirklichkeit*, 1966. Ziolkowski, Theodore, *Dimensions of the Modern Novel*, p. 273, 1969.

Gerhart Baumann

Ferdinand von Saar

Born 30, September 1833 in Vienna. Ferdinand von Saar's parents, Ludwig and Karoline von Saar, both came from the recently ennobled families of government officials. His father, who had left government service for a career in business, died five months after Ferdinand's birth, and the boy spent an unhappy childhood in the home of his disciplinarian grandfather, privy councilor Ferdinand von Nespern. He attended the Benedictine Schottengymnasium, and in 1849, at the age of sixteen, he was persuaded to join the Austrian army, although he had no inclination for a military career. During the next years he served in many of the widely scattered military garrisons of the Austrian monarchy, gaining valuable experience that later formed the basis for his novellas and poems. He once noted: "From my writings one can deduce much—perhaps everything that I have lived and experienced."

Although his early poems and dramas were unsuccessful, Saar resigned his lieutenant's commission in 1860 after his return from the Italian campaign, determined upon a literary career. His writings brought little recognition and even less income, and he was arrested several times for debt. Until late in life he remained dependent in some measure on the generosity and hospitality of wealthy patronesses, particularly Josefine von Wertheimstein and Princess Salm-Lichtenstein, to whom he owed "the best of my production, a home, and the freedom to pursue my muse." He led a nomadic existence, wandering from the country estate of one patroness to another, interrupted only by occasional stays in Vienna. After his return from Italy in 1860—except for a trip there in 1877—he never traveled beyond the borders of the Austro-Hungarian Empire, not even in his stories or poems. His disconsolate life is reflected in his letters, written over a twenty-five-year period, to Princess Maria zu Hohenlohe, who, because she believed in Saar's talent, did all that she could to advance his career. She not only gave him constant encouragement, but she also offered critical judgment of his works and used her influence to build his reputation.

Saar's marriage to Melanie Lederer in 1881 provided his life with a happy interlude, which was ended by her suicide three years later to escape the suffering of a severe illness. Throughout the following difficult years Saar never lost faith in himself despite the lack of public response, and on his sixtieth birthday he finally received widespread acclaim. This acclaim came particularly from the young generation of Viennese writers led by Hermann Bahr, the so-called Young Vienna, who hailed him as a model and forerunner. He was further distinguished by being named an honorary member of the upper house of the Austrian parliament, the only writer besides Franz Grillparzer ever honored in this way. Despite his belated success, Saar never overcame a basic disposition toward pessimism and melancholy. Afflicted with incurable cancer, he committed suicide with his army revolver on 24 July 1906.

In Austria the theater is generally regarded as the preeminent literary art, and Saar regarded it as his most bitter blow of fate that his dramas never found success on the stage. *Eine Wohltat* (1861), his peasant tragedy, and *Die beiden de Witt* (1875), a historical drama, were performed for a short time in the Vienna Burgtheater. His two-part historical tragedy, *Hildebrand* (1863) and *Heinrichs Tod* (1867), which treats the conflict between the German emperor and Pope Gregory VII, has, however, never been staged. He had no better luck with the later tragedies *Tempesta* (1881) and *Thassilo* (1886). Saar's frustration at his failure as a dramatist—he considered tragedy the highest form of art—resulted in seven years of unproductivity, lasting from 1865 to 1872. Only gradually did he come to the realization that his talent was primarily descriptive and lyric and hence best suited to prose and poetry.

As a fiction writer Saar did not possess the inventiveness of a born storyteller, but he excelled in recreating characters, situations, and places that he knew from personal experience. His finest stories were published under the title *Novellen aus Österreich* (1877), and all of his thirty-two stories could be included under this heading. The political and social life of the Austro-Hungarian monarchy after 1848, that is, the reign of Franz Joseph, provided the themes, settings, characters, and atmosphere for all of his works. Although other prominent Austrian writers, such as Karl Emil Franzos, Leopold von Sacher-Masoch, and Marie von Ebner-Eschenbach, have described the same period, none surpasses Saar in the ability to evoke this age, its people, its social values, and its historical significance. Saar's use of the first-person narrative and the leisurely, elegiac tone of his stories, which is rarely lightened by humor, make them appear somewhat ponderous and old-fashioned today, but his richly detailed descriptions and backgrounds endow his works with lasting power and beauty.

Saar, who was strongly influenced by Ivan Turgenev and Arthur Schopenhauer, generally depicts characters who are defeated in life, often for reasons beyond their control, such as hereditary factors (as in *Tambi, Doktor Trojan*). The themes of renunciation of love and the transitoriness of life recur as leitmotifs throughout his works beginning with his first story, *Innocens* (1865). His usually passive characters succumb to misfortune because they fail to act or to reveal their true feelings. Saar is a master at depicting the inner feelings of women, and many of his stories such as *Marianne, Ginevra, Ninon, Die Parzen,* and *Requiem der Liebe*, are psychological portraits of feminine characters. Unrequited love is a frequent theme, as is the erotic triangle in its many variations (*Die Geigerin, Die Geschichte eines Wienerkindes, Der Exzellenzherr*). He was attracted to characters who were the victims of daimonic impulses (in *Die Troglodytin, Sappho*) and felt sympathy for those of his characters who were so rooted in times past that they were unable to adapt to change. Many of his tales concern the kind of people encountered during his military years, e.g., *Der Exzellenzherr, Das Haus Reichegg, Vae Victis, Leutnant Burda,* and *Schloß Kostenitz*. Although Saar made no attempt to connect his stories into an organized portrait of his time, he nevertheless emphasized that "only by recognizing their interconnection, can one understand and evaluate them completely."

Saar, who early worked to communicate his belief that milieu is the shaper of human destiny considered himself "a bridge" to the modern writers. *Die Steinklopfer* (1829) is often referred to as the first story in German of the working man and his milieu. Many of his novellas are case histories in the naturalistic writer's sense of the term. Once having established setting and character, Saar allows events to move inexorably to their conclusion, however gloomy. It is this inner integrity combined with Saar's meticulous craftsmanship that endows these stories with lasting literary value, over and above their significance as cultural documents of a bygone historical era.

The same elegiac tone predominates in Saar's lyric poetry, in which he combines dream and observation, reflection and melancholy, longing for the past and love of one's country. His most successful poetic works are *Wiener Elegien* (1892), revealing his love for Vienna, and *Die Pincelliade* (1897), a burlesque epic of barracks life.

Works: *Hildebrand* (1863); *Innocens* (1865; Innocence); *Heinrichs Tod* (1867; Heinrich's death); *Kaiser Heinrich IV* (1872); *Marianne* (1873); *Die Steinklopfer* (1874; Eng. tr., The Stonebreakers, 1907); *Die Geigerin* (1875; The Woman Violinist); *Die Beiden de Witt* (1875; The Two de

Witts); *Novellen aus Österreich* (1877; Novellas from Austria); *Das Haus Reichegg* (1877; The House of Reichegg); *Tempesta* (1881); *Gedichte* (1882; Poems); *Der Exzellenzherr* (1883; His Excellency); *Benvenuto Cellini* (1883); *Tambi* (1883); *Vae Victis* (1883); *Thassilo* (1886); *Eine Wohltat* (1887; A Benevolence); *Leutnant Burda* (1889; Lieutenant Burda); *Schicksale* (1889; Destinies); *Seligmann Hirsch* (1889); *Die Troglodytin* (1889; The Troglodyte); *Geschichte eines Wienerkindes* (1892; Story of a Viennese Child); *Ginevra* (1892); *Schloß Kostenitz* (1892; Kostenitz Castle); *Wiener Elegien* (1893; Viennese Elegies); *Herbstreigen* (1896; Autumn Dance); *Die Pincelliade* (1897); *Herr Fridolin und sein Glück* (1897; Mr. Fridolin and His Happiness); *Ninon* (1897); *Requiem der Liebe* (1897; Requiem of Love); *Nachklänge* (1899; Reminiscences); *Conte Gasparo* (1899); *Doktor Trojan* (1899); *Sündenfall* (1899; Fall of Man); *Ludwig XVI* (1899); *Camera Obscura* (1900); *Der Bauer von Hadrovan* (1901; The Peasant from Hadrovan); *Die Brüder* (1901; The Brothers); *Der Burggraf* (1901; The Count of the Castle); *Dissonanzen* (1901; Dissonances); *Die Parzen* (1901; The Furies); *Hermann und Dorothea* (1902); *Außer Dienst* (1904; Retired); *Die Heirat des Herrn Stäude* (1904; The Marriage of Mr. Stäude); *Der Hellene* (1904); *Die Familie Wrel* (1906; The Wrel Family); *Hymen* (1906); *Die Pfründner* (1906; The Beneficiaries); *Sappho* (1906); *Tragik des Lebens* (1906; Tragedy of Life); *Sämtliche Werke* (ed. J. Minor, 12 vols., 1908; The Complete Works); *Briefwechsel* (ed. A. von Sonnenthal, 2 vols., 1912; Correspondence).

English translations in collections: Selected works can be found in *The German Classics of the 19th and 20th Centuries* (vol. 8, 1913–15).

Bibliography: Bettelheim, Anton, *Ferdinand von Saars Leben und Schaffen*, 1908. Hodge, James L., "The Novellen of Ferdinand von Saar: Anticipations of 20th-Century Literary Themes and Techniques," dissertation (Penn State), 1961. Kretzschmar, Hadwig, *Ferdinand von Saar*, 1965. Lukas, M., *Leben und Werk von Ferdinand von Saar*, 1947. Mailly, A. von, "Ferdinand von Saars eigene Welt," *Österreichische Rundschau* 1 (1946). Pick, Robert, "Ferdinand von Saar. Poet of a Declining Age," *German Life and Letters* (New Series) 4, no. 2 (1951). Shears, L. A., "Theme and Technique in the Novellen of Ferdinand von Saar," *The Journal of English and Germanic Philology* 24 (1925). Vogelsang, H., *Ferdinand von Saars Dichtung und Weltbild*, 1957.

Donald G. Daviau[▲]

George Emmanuel Saiko

Born 5 February 1892 in Seestadtl (now Ervěnice, in Czechoslovakia). At the University of Vienna George Saiko studied philosophy, psychology, archaeology, and history of art, earning a Ph.D. In 1939 he joined the staff of the Albertina, the famous museum of graphic arts in Vienna. During World War II and the postwar period, he successfully safeguarded this priceless collection, becoming the acting director in 1945. In 1950 he left the service of the museum and embarked on a writing career. He died on 23 December 1962 in Vienna.

Though his works are few in number, Saiko has a definite place in literary history within the development of the modern Austrian novel that leads from Adalbert Stifter's *Nachsommer* via Hugo von Hofmannsthal, Arthur Schnitzler, Robert Musil, and Hermann Broch to Heimito von Doderer. He displays the characteristics typical of the whole range of themes and forms. By disposition and education he was equipped with the intellectual acumen of the critical writer as well as with an understanding of the nature and problems of depth psychology (especially the theories of Sigmund Freud). It was on this basis that he constructed his narrative themes.

Like almost all representative writers of the analytical novel, Saiko, in his novels and short stories, presents the problems of human relationships largely in terms of depth psychology and social criticism. The novels *Auf dem Floß* (1948) and *Der Mann im Schilf* (1955) are, on the surface, novels of topical interest that depict the Austria of the interwar period—*Auf dem Floß*, the Austria of 1934–38, and *Der Mann im Schilf*, the attempted National Socialist putsch in 1934. But in both works Saiko contributed to the solution of problems that the crisis of the novel as a form of art had made precipitate. He sees the writer's task as one of mastering a "magical realism," which is capable of raising the irrational instincts and other driving forces concealed beneath convention to the rational level, to the level of what can be seen and told.

Saiko's progression into myth and totemism is perceptible in his short stories, such as *Der feindliche Gott* (1964). For Saiko, as for other Austrian novelists, the seemingly real world—real in a popular sense— is in fact interpenetrated by the vestiges of archetypal, magical, and mythical images and sensations. Saiko believed that these can ultimately be rendered harmless only by the writer and not by social convention. He, like the physician, has the power of transforming what is dangerous in the unconscious into something conscious and constructive.

Works: *Auf dem Floß* (1948; On the Raft); *Der Mann im Schilf* (1955; The Man in the Reed); *Die dunkelste Nacht* (1961; The Darkest Night); *Giraffe unter Palmen* (1962; Giraffe under Palm Trees); *Der Opferblock* (1962; The Sacrificial Block); *Der feindliche Gott* (with H. Polster, 1964; The Hostile God); *Die erste und die letzte Erzählung* (1968; The First and the Last Story).

Bibliography: Benesch, Kurt, "In Memoriam George Saiko," *Wort in der Zeit* 9, no. 2 (1963):1–5. Csokor, Franz Theodor, on *Auf dem Floß*, in *German Life and Letters*, 1954–55, p. 85; and "Später Beginn in Vollendung," *Wort in der Zeit* 9, no. 2 (1963):1–5. Reider, Heinz, "Ein magischer Realist: Zum 70. Geburtstag Georg Saiko am 5. Februar 1892," *Wort in der Zeit* 8, no. 1 (1962):15–19.

Robert Mühlher

Richard von Schaukal

Essayist, novelist, poet, and translator, born 27 May 1874 in Brünn (now Brno, in central Czechoslovakia), the son of a businessman. Studied law in Vienna (1892–96) and received his doctorate of law degree. Schaukal then entered the civil service and worked in Moravia. In 1903 he received an appointment to a post in the ministerial presidium in Vienna. In 1908 he traveled in Europe, and in the same year he became an important official of the Ministry of Labor. In 1918 he was raised to the nobility. From 1918 on, he lived in Vienna as a writer and died there on 10 October 1942.

With the collapse of the Hapsburg monarchy in 1918, Schaukal applied for retirement from the Austrian civil service. "Long sick of the sterile drudgery," he retired into private life at the age of forty-four. The criticism of the period that was implied in this step had years before found literary expression in his ironic and satirical novel *Leben und Meinungen des Herrn Andreas von Balthesser, eines Dandy und Dillettanten* (1907). The chapters of this novel, which are rather like separate essays written in the polished, epigrammatic style characteristic of Schaukal, take issue with the most varied manifestations of "the swamp of modern civilization" and demonstrate how much the age is threatened by mediocrity, stupidity, decline in taste and sense of form, by materialism and opportunism. Following his early, aestheticizing poems, many of which were close to Viennese impressionism and French symbolism, this novel was the first of Schaukal's works to show him as the incisive critic of civilization and society that he was later to prove to be in his collections of aphorisms and essays.

With his emphatically aristocratic and traditionalist attitude, Schaukal had no use for modern utilitarianism, for the cult of progress, for culture turned into business, for the manifestations of the mass era. He denounced bad taste in every field, from fashion and interior decoration to language and social life. And against all this he upheld the culture, dignity, and civilized way of life of the aristocracy and of the steadily receding prerepublican period upon which the aristocracy had left its mark. Beneath his trenchant, sarcastic, and often haughty observations, he was as little able to conceal his distress over the times and his ever-increasing isolation as he was his melancholy and resignation.

In turning his back on the present, Schaukal began to be increasingly absorbed in his own personal past. The affectionate depiction of his childhood in Brünn and of the people of that time, the evocation of little incidents, of vanished streets, houses, rooms, and bygone implements, displays his sensitive, poetic nature in its most attractive form and the subtlety of his observation and feelings. These qualities appear much more genuine and spontaneous in his poetry than in his stories, the immediate effect of which is often prejudiced by an all too obvious stylistic polish and by the resulting stiltedness. His poems of nature and meditation written in these years are conservative in style and contain a great deal of weary sadness and self-indulgent lament, at times considerable emotionalism and a great deal that is only barely tolerable to modern ears. But the poet also strikes a tender folk-song note, sincere and naive.

As a commentator, editor, and essayist he was primarily concerned with E. T. A. Hoffman, Adalbert Stifter, Richard Dehmel, and Karl Kraus.

Works: *Gedichte* (1893; Poems); *Rückkehr* (1894; Return); *Verse* (1896; Verses); *Meine Gärten* (1897; My Gardens); *Tristia* (1898); *Tage und Träume* (1899; Days and Dreams); *Sehnsucht* (1900; Longing); *Intérieurs aus dem Leben der Zwanzigjährigen* (1901; Interiors of the Lives of Twenty-Year-Olds); *Von Tod zu Tod* (1902; From Death to Death); *Pierrot und Columbine, oder Das Lied von der Ehe* (1902; Pierrot and Columbine, or The Song of Marriage); *Einer, der seine Frau besucht und andere Scenen* (1902; One Who Visits His Wife, and Other Scenes); *Vorabend* (1902; Eve); *Mimi Lynx* (1904); *Ausgewählte Gedichte* (1904; Selected Poems); *E. T. A. Hoffmann* (1904); *Wilhelm Busch* (1905); *Kapellmeister Kreisler* (1906; Conductor Kreisler); *Großmutter: ein Buch von Tod und Leben* (1906; Grandmother: A Book on Death and Life); *Eros Thanatos* (1906); *Giorgone, oder Gespräche über die Kunst* (1907; Giorgone, or Discourses on Art); *Literatur* (1907; Literature); *Leben und Meinungen des Herrn Andreas von Balthesser, eines Dandy und Dilettanten* (1907; Life and Opinions of Mr. Andreas von Balthesser, a Dandy and Dilettante); *Die Mietwohnung: Eine Kulturfrage* (1907; The Apartment: A Cultural Problem); *Schlemihle* (1907); *Richard Dehmels Lyrik* (1908; The Poetry of Richard Dehmel); *Buch der Seele* (1908; Book of the Soul); *Verse: Der ausgewählten Gedichte erster Teil* (1909; Verses: The Selected Poems' First Part); *Bilder: Der ausgewählten Gedichte zweiter Teil* (1909; Pictures: The Selected Poems' Second Part); *Vom Geschmack* (1910; On Taste); *Vom unsichtbaren Königreich* (1910; On the Invisible Kingdom); *Beiläufig* (1912; By the Way); *Neue Verse* (1912; New Verses); *Kinder-*

gedichte (1913; Children's Poems); *Zettelkasten eines Zeitgenossen: Aus Hans Bürgers Papieren* (1913; Filing Box of a Contemporary: From Hans Bürger's Papers); *Die Märchen aus Hans Bürgers Kindheit* (1913; The Fairy Tales of Hans Bürger's Childhood); *Herbst* (1914; Autumn); *Kriegslieder aus Österreich* (1914–16; War Songs from Austria); *Eherne Sonette* (1914, 1915; Sonnets of Brass); *Das Buch Immergrün* (1916; The Book Evergreen); *Widmungen* (1916; Dedications); *Zeitgemäße deutsche Betrachtungen* (1916; Timely German Reflections); *Dem Gedächtnis weiland Kaiser Franz Joseph I.* (1916; In Memoriam of the Late Emperor Franz Joseph I.); *Heimat der Seele* (1916; Homeland of the Soul); *Heimat* (1917; Homeland); *Gedichte 1891–1918* (1918; Poems 1891–1918); *Erlebte Gedanken* (1918; Experienced Thoughts); *Österreichische Züge* (1918; Austrian Trends); *Dionys-bácsi* (1922; Dionysos-bácsi); *Jahresringe* (1922; Annual Rings); *Ausgewählte Gedichte* (1924; Selected Poems); *Gezeiten der Seele* (1926; Tides of the Soul); *Adalbert Stifter* (1926); *Gedanken* (1931; Thoughts); *Herbsthöhe* (1933; Autumn Summit); *Karl Kraus* (1933); *Beiträge zu einer Selbstdarstellung* (1934; Contributions to a Self-Representation); *Erkenntnisse und Betrachtungen* (1934; Perceptions and Meditations); *Von Kindern, Tieren und erwachsenen Leuten* (1935; On Children, Animals, and Grown-up People); *Neue Gedanken* (1943; New Thoughts); *Spätlese* (1943; Late Harvest); *Einsame Gedankengänge: 1934–39* (1947; Lonely Trains of Thoughts: 1934–39); *Frühling eines Lebens* (1949; Springtime of a Life); *Gedichte aus dem Nachlaß* (1954; Poems from the Posthumous Works); *Wie ganz bin ich dein eigen* (1960; How Completely I Am Thine); *Musik der ruhenden Welt* (1960; Music of a World in Repose); *Über Dichter* (1966; On Poets).

Bibliography: Bithell, Jethro, *Modern German Literature 1880–1950*, pp. 208–209, 1959. Nadler, J., *Schaukals lyrisches Werk*, 1932. Pitrou, R., "Richard von Schaukal, poète autrichien," *Revue Germanique* 29 (1938). Thomas, R. Hinton, "Richard von Schaukal: A Poet of Austria in Decline," *German Life and Letters* 3 (1939). Tschulik, Werner, *Die österreichische Dichtung im Rahmen der Weltliteratur*, 1949.

Charlotte Nennecke

Arthur Schnitzler

Born 15 May 1862 in Vienna; died there on 21 October 1931. The son of a well-known laryngologist, Arthur Schnitzler studied medicine in Vienna and became a specialist for nervous disorders. Later became a professional writer in Vienna.

Schnitzler is the representative writer of pre-World War I Vienna and had far-reaching influence as an exponent of Austrian letters. His themes, though narrow in range, were treated with a rare wealth of nuances: dream and death, play and compulsion, appearance and reality, mask and inner self. This was a set of themes common to his contemporaries among Viennese writers, so they occasionally dealt with the same subject from different points of view. In *Die Schwestern, oder Casanova in Spa* (1919), Schnitzler takes up the theme of Hugo von Hofmannsthal's *Gestern*. Shunning the obtrusively emotional and the stridently tragic, Schnitzler preferred an indirect approach, ironic refractions, "to trace the minor impulses and the minor passions, the play and sideplay of the sentiments, to spread out everything that is divided, all that is an offshoot of the main stem" (Georg Brandes). He is concerned not with dialectical debate, but with diagnosis as unobtrusive as it is unerring and yet not devoid of didactic intent.

The flexible and detached diction is in contrast to the profundity of the themes. Schnitzler is a master at writing conversational exchanges, in which the speakers unintentionally reveal themselves, even by what they do not say. However casual the dialogue technique may seem, every exchange has been carefully thought out. Reflections of objects become more revealing than the objects themselves, gestures often more than words, the intonation is more expressive than the content, and everything that is said has overtones of the inexpressible. These preconditions result in conversations that have a true-to-life nature.

A rich web of relations and suggestions is woven around insoluble paradox; the *Buch der Sprüche und Bedenken* (1927) displays the diction appropriate to this form of thought, and the illuminating diagrams of *Der Geist im Wort und der Geist in der Tat* (1927) reveal the nearness of the diverse and the divisivenesses in affinities. Schnitzler allots ample space to the contradictions within his characters; in the "vast domain" (title of play, *Das weite Land*) of the soul there is room for faithfulness and unfaithfulness, for the conscious dream, for the repetition of the unrepeatable, for timelessness in the bondage of time, for loneliness in the nexus of relationships. The living dead confront those who live like puppets. For the figures lack the courage to be themselves, lack the imperious ability to prevail; sometimes they lose themselves altogether, as shown in the ironic refractions in the comedy *Fink und Fliederbusch* (1917). Reality refutes its appearance, the unassailable are lost by their own doing. They all cling desperately to the illusion of uniqueness while in fact there is endless repetition.

Misled by worldliness and occasional frivolity, the uncritical eye perceived only what offered pleasure and was suggestive; wit was equated with levity, the macabre game of love with immorality. The theatergoer looked only at the *süßen mädeln* and the adventurers, without noticing their melancholy and despair. Neither did he notice the conflict between the mere moment's noncommittal encounter and the bondage of sorrowful memories and thoughts. For Schnitzler's characters never live in an unbroken present—their present is already past, and only the past is at hand; memories are projected into the future as wishful dreams. And so they succumb again and again to the cruel "comedy of seduction" (title of play, *Komödie der Verführung*), possible realities that never lead to real possibilities. They see fate not as what happens, but as what might happen; a comedy that does not liberate, a tragedy that does not ennoble, but lays bare the tension of contradiction, the strangeness in trust, the delusion of appearance, the inexorable distance in every approach. For every beginning harbors the seed of the end—a cruel merry-go-round most appropriately represented by Schnitzler's play *Reigen* (written, 1896/97; private printing, 1900; published in public edition, 1903; first performance, 1920).

Schnitzler's characters seek a whirlwind of social life, and yet they know that they must walk lonely to the end of their roads. With affected ease they touch the heaviness of fate. Like Hofmannsthal, Schnitzler knew how to hide profundity under the surface. Tact and unobtrusiveness do not preclude the obstinate pursuit of insight, as can be shown by comparative analysis. Schnitzler's writings are those of a moralist and of a merciless critic of society. Passions are the expression of veiled skepticism; ambiguities hide the dreaded unambiguous; wisdom has a background of disillusionment, and knowledge is granted only to those who are lost at the threshold of death. Behind different masks the same figures keep reappearing; each figure experiences no life other than his own although under different names. Each longs to fulfill his destiny and yet studiously evades it; their tragic situations are often "comedies of words" (title of play, *Komödie der Worte*). When the hour to remove the mask comes, Schnitzler is at his most impressive: in *Casanovas Heimfahrt* (1918), for example, we find that it is at a miserable inn that sleep, "dreamless and dull," takes pity on Casanova, "who has long been driven through the world not by youth's spirit of adventure, but by the restlessness of old age."

The insoluble conflicts between apparent freedom and merciless compulsion, between the face and the mask, the feigned joke and hopeless gravity, pretense and reality, led Schnitzler into tragicomedy. Early hints of this direction he was to take can be found in the grotesque, confusing web of reality and appearance of *Der grüne Kakadu* (1899). This technique of double exposure was later perfected in *Die letzten Masken* (in *Lebendige Stunden*, 1902), *Das weite Land* (1911), and *Große Szene* (in *Komödie der Worte*, 1915). It is in the plays that we find the most powerful examples of the summarizing moment, of the episode encompassing all the multiplicity of its apparent content and testifying to an instinctive grasp of stage effect. This can be observed even in the early *Anatol* (1893; republished in 1964, complete and with background material for interpretation). Schnitzler did not always successfully avoid the pitfall of historicizing trappings.

Schnitzler's stories achieve compelling artistic unity. The moment's fullness is perfectly expressed by means of the interior monologue, showing man (and Schnitzler, too) as a creature of the instant's grace. *Leutnant Gustl* (1901) and *Fräulein Else* (1924) are outstanding examples of this style. Everything takes place in a limited setting, the internal is revealed in the external, the suprapersonal in personal impulses; semiconscious strata of feeling and the sinister consequences of fleeting contact are made patent, acts of consciousness become comprehensible. Light is thrown on the "floating elements" in man, which never center on one point and therefore never coalesce into unity. Schnitzler knows the man of mere qualities as well as he does qualities without man. The writer is the "fluid mirror of the world ... even though the mirror may at times be so clouded as to be opaque." Space and landscape receive and give out illuminating reflections. Schnitzler has shown how discontinuities and erratic associations assume reality, how dissonances become valid modes of expression, how the dividing line between waking and dreaming is blurred, and thereby he has opened up important avenues to modern writing.

Concurrently with Sigmund Freud and Josef Breuer, Schnitzler discovered the significance of the unconscious and of the subconscious, the significance of instinctive life. In addition he followed up on the thinking of Ernst Mach and the Vienna school of philosophy. Most clearly of all, he showed the influence of French writers such as Alfred de Musset and Anatole France, of the society play and critical comedy of morals (Dumas fils, Augier, Sardou).

Works: *Anatol* (1893; Eng. tr., Anatol: A Sequence of Dialogues, 1911); *Das Märchen* (1894; The Fairy Tale); *Sterben* (1895; To Die); *Liebelei* (1896; Eng. tr., Light-O'-Love, 1912); *Freiwild* (1898; Eng. tr., Free Game, 1913); *Die Frau des Weisen* (1898; The Sage's Wife); *Das Vermächtnis* (1899; The Legacy); *Der grüne Kakadu* (1899; Eng. tr., The Green Cockatoo, and Other Plays, 1913); *Der blinde Geronimo und sein Bruder* (1900; Blind Geronimo and His Brother); *Leutnant Gustl* (1901; Eng. tr., None but the Brave, 1926); *Der Schleier der Beatrice* (1901; The Veil of Beatrice); *Frau Bertha Garlan* (1901; Eng. tr., Bertha Garlan, 1913); *Lebendige Stunden* (1902; Living Hours); *Reigen* (1903; Eng. tr., Hands Around, 1920; film, La Ronde, 1950); *Der einsame Weg* (1904; Eng. tr., The Lonely Way, 1904); *Die griechische Tänzerin* (1905; The Greek Dancer); *Zwischenspiel* (1906; Intermezzo); *Marionetten: Drei Einakter* (1906; Marionettes: Three One-Act Plays); *Der Ruf des Lebens* (1906; The Call of Life); *Dämmerseelen* (1907; Twilight Souls); *Der Weg ins Freie* (1908; Eng. tr., The Road to the Open, 1923); *Der tapfere Kassian: Singspiel in einem Aufzug* (1909; Gallant Kassian: Singspiel in One Act); *Komtesse Mizzi, oder Der Familientag* (1909; Eng. tr., Countess Mizzie, 1907); *Der junge Medardus* (1910; The Young Medardus); *Der tapfere Cassian: Puppenspiel in einem Akt* (1910; Eng. tr., Gallant Cassian, 1914); *Der Schleier der Pierrette* (1910; The Veil of Pierrette); *Die Hirtenflöte* (1911; The Shepherd's Pipe); *Der Mörder* (1911; The Murderer); *Das weite Land* (1911; The Vast Domain); *Professor Bernhardi* (1912; Eng. tr., Professor Bernhardi, 1927); *Masken und Wunder* (1912; Masks and Miracles); *Die Theaterstücke* (5 vols., 1912–22; Plays); *Erzählende Schriften* (6 vols., 1912–28; Narrative Writings); *Frau Beate und ihr Sohn* (1913; Eng. tr., Beatrice, 1926); *Die griechische Tänzerin, und andere Novellen* (1914; The Greek Dancer, and Other Novellas); *Komödie der Worte* (1915; Comedies of Words); *Fink und Fliederbusch* (1917); *Doktor Gräsler, Badearzt* (1917; Eng. tr., Dr. Graesler, 1923); *Casanovas Heimfahrt* (1918; Eng. tr., Casanova's Homecoming, 1921); *Die Schwestern, oder Casanova in Spa* (1919; The Sisters, or Casanova at Spa); *Die dreifache Warnung* (1924; The Triple Warning); *Fräulein Else* (1924; Eng. tr., 1925); *Komödie der Verführung* (1924; Comedy of Seduction); *Die Frau des Richters* (1925; The Judge's Wife); *Traumnovelle* (1926; Eng. tr., Rhapsody: A Dream Novel, 1927); *Der Gang zum Weiher* (1926; The Walk to the Pond); *Buch der Sprüche und Bedenken* (1927; Eng. tr., Reflections and Aphorisms, in prep.); *Der Geist im Wort und der Geist in der Tat* (1927; Eng. tr., The Mind in Words and Actions: Preliminary Remarks

Concerning Two Diagrams, 1972); *Spiel im Morgengrauen* (1927; Eng. tr., Daybreak, 1927); *Therese: Chronik eines Frauenlebens* (1928; Eng. tr., Theresa: The Chronicle of a Woman's Life, 1928); *Im Spiel der Sommerlüfte* (1930; In the Play of the Summer Breezes); *Flucht in die Finsternis* (1931; Eng. tr., Flight into Darkness, 1931); *Traum und Schicksal: Sieben Novellen* (1931; Dream and Destiny: Seven Novellas); *Die kleine Komödie: Frühe Novellen* (1932; The Little Comedy: Early Novellas); *Abenteurernovelle* (1937; Novella of an Adventurer); *Flucht in die Finsternis, und andere Erzählungen* (1939; Flight into Darkness, and Other Stories); *Über Krieg und Frieden* (1939; Eng. tr., Some Day Peace Will Return: Notes on War and Peace, 1972); *Ausgewählte Erzählungen* (1950; Selected Stories); *Der Briefwechsel Arthur Schnitzler—Otto Brahm* (1955; Correspondence of Arthur Schnitzler—Otto Brahm); *Meisterdramen* (1955; Master Dramas); *Georg Brandes und Arthur Schnitzler: Ein Briefwechsel* (1956; Georg Brandes and Arthur Schnitzler: An Exchange of Letters); *Egon Friedell: Briefe* (1959; Egon Friedell: Letters); *Große Szene* (1959; The Big Secne); *Die erzählende Schriften* (2 vols., 1961; The Narrative Writings); *Die dramatischen Werke* (2 vols., 1962; The Dramatic Works); *Hugo von Hofmannsthal—Arthur Schnitzler Briefwechsel* (1964; Hugo von Hofmannsthal—Arthur Schnitzler Correspondence); *Erzählungen* (1965; Stories); *Spiel im Morgengrauen, und acht andere Erzählungen* (1965; Play at Daybreak, and Eight Other Stories); *Jugend in Wien: Eine Autobiographie* (1968; Youth in Vienna: An Autobiography).

English translations in collections: The Green Cockatoo, and Other Plays (1913; includes "The Green Cockatoo," "The Mate," and "Paracelsus"); *Living Hours* (1913; includes "Living Hours," "The Lady with the Dagger," "Last Masks," and 'Literature"); *Viennese Idylls* (1913; includes "Flowers," "The Sage's Wife," "Blind Geronimo and His Brother," "Andreas Thameyer's Last Letter," "The Farewell," and "The Dead Are Silent"); *The Lonely Way* (1915; includes "The Lonely Way," "Intermezzo," and "Countess Mizzie, or the Family Reunion"); *Anatol. Living Hours. The Green Cockatoo* (1917; includes "Anatol," "Living Hours," "The Lady with the Dagger," "Last Masks," "Literature," and "The Green Cockatoo"); *Comedies of Words, and Other Plays* (1917; includes "The Hour of Recognition," "The Big Scene," "The Festival of Bacchus," "Literature," and "His Helpmate"); *The Shepherd's Pipe, and Other Stories* (1922; includes "The Shepherd's Pipe," "The Murderer," and "The Blind Geronimo and His Brother"); *"Beatrice," and Other Stories* (1926; includes "Beatrice," "Flowers," "A Farewell," "The Wife of the Wise Man," "The Hour of Fame," and "The Dead Are Silent"); *Little Novels* (1929); *Viennese Novelettes* (1931); *Reigen, The Affairs of Anatol, and Other Plays* (1933).

Bibliography: Allen, Richard H., *An Annotated Arthur Schnitzler Bibliography*, 1966; additions to the above by Urbach, Reinhard, in *Literatur und Kritik* 15 (June 1967):324–28. Bailey, Joseph W., "Arthur Schnitzler's

Dramatic Work," *Texas Review* 5, no. 4 (July 1920):294–307. Beharriell, Frederick J., "Arthur Schnitzler's Range of Theme," *Monatshefte für deutschen Unterricht* 43, no. 7 (November 1951):301–311. Bentley, Eric, *The Playwright as Thinker: A Study of Drama in Modern Times*, pp. 263–64, 1951. Bithell, Jethro, *Modern German Literature 1880–1950*, pp. 229–37, 1959. Kann, Robert A., "Schnitzler as an Austrian Writer in the World Today," *Journal of the International Arthur Schnitzler Research Association* 1, nos. 4–5 (Autumn–Winter 1962):3–4. Politzer, Heinz, "Arthur Schnitzler: Poetry of Psychology," *Modern Language Notes* 78, no. 4 (October 1963: 353–72. Reichert, Herbert W., "Arthur Schnitzler and Modern Ethics," *Journal of the International Arthur Schnitzler Research Association* 2, no. 1 (Spring 1963):21–24. Reik, Theodor, *Arthur Schnitzler als Psycholog*, 1913. Seidlin, Oskar, "In Memoriam Arthur Schnitzler: May 15, 1862–Oct. 21, 1931," *American-German Review* 28, no. 4 (April–May 1962):4–6. Specht, Richard, *Arthur Schnitzler: Der Dichter und sein Werk. Eine Studie*, 1922. Urbach, Reinhard, *Arthur Schnitzler*, 1973.

Gerhart Baumann

Karl Schönherr

Born 24 February 1867, the son of a village schoolmaster, at Axams near Innsbruck. When Karl Schönherr was still very young, his father, who had been transferred to Schlanders in South Tyrol in 1872, died. His mother supported her family of six and made it possible for her son to attend secondary school. In 1886 he enrolled at Innsbruck University and after a year changed from the study of philosophy to medicine. In 1891 he went to Vienna, where he received his M. D. degree and started to practice medicine in 1896. But he was not happy as a doctor. Amid the bustle of the big city he was haunted by the mountain ranges, and the poet awoke in him. In 1905, after having some successes in the theater, he gave up his medical practice. He spent the winter in Vienna and the summer at his country home, Telfs, in the Tyrol. In his later years he withdrew more and more. He died after a long illness on 15 March 1943 in Vienna.

Schönherr began by writing dialect poems (*Inntaler Schnalzer* 1895; *Tiroler Marterln für abg'stürzte Bergkraxler*, 1895), short stories (*Allerhand Kreuzköpf*, 1895), and plays (*Der Judas von Tirol*, first version 1897, second version 1927; *Die Bildschnitzer*, 1900; *Karrnerleut'*, 1904). His plays, in which he treated social themes and combined a naturalistic style with regional flavor, gave him a successful entry into Vienna theater, including the Burgtheater.

Intellectually Schönherr was influenced by the Young Tyrol movement, with its German nationalist, liberal-anticlerical attitude— the drama *Sonnwendtag* (1902) and the tragedy *Glaube und Heimat* (1910) are examples of this influence. Ludwig Anzengruber, Ludwig Thoma, and Peter Rosegger were his forebears as writers on peasant themes. According to his own statement, he "went through Ibsen's school." His connection with the Austrian-Tyrolese theatrical tradition was also of crucial importance. He was an expert on and a practiced hand in the theater. Thus his work with the Exl Theater from 1910 until his death in 1943 was an ideal collaboration.

In his mature plays (from about 1906 to 1918) Schönherr combined naturalism and symbolism, and he sharply defined characters and types. Everything centers on life, vigorous and harsh, or otherwise. His peasant homeland becomes the scene of the struggle for existence, becomes Earth pure and simple (see his comedy *Erde*, 1908, one of his major works). In 1809 the Tyrolese were primarily defending their ancestral way of life (*Volk in Not*, 1916). The strongest representatives of the will to live acquire daimonic and mythical traits: examples are old Grutz in *Erde*; the Sandwirt, who is the embodiment of the collective aspirations of the Tyrolese in *Volk in Not*; and the woman in *Der Weibsteufel* (1915). But there is no unconditional adoration of the strong and the victorious. There is room for sympathy with children who are broken by the cruelties of life, as is evident in *Kindertragödie* (1919), and with the maternal women who accept the law of the earth and yet overcome it by their sacrifice, as the Rotadlwirtin in *Frau Suitner* (1917).

The characteristics of Schönherr's style are concentration on a few basic instincts and characters, single-minded characters, sharp contrasts, terse phrases, and impressive gestures. The limitations of Schönherr's world are shown by his rather unconvincing plays about doctors and life in the big city, Vienna. Nor was he able to manage dramatic attempts on higher levels, as can be seen by his portrayal of Christ in *Passionsspiel* (1933) and by *Das Königreich* (1909). Rather than reaching the humor that liberates, his sense of humor scarcely goes beyond the grimly pessimistic kind; it is especially gloomy in the collection of short stories in *Schuldbuch* (1913). Schönherr did not so much create naturalistic images as archetypes of the Tyrolese world.

Works: *Inntaler Schnalzer* (1895; Inntaler Clickers); *Tiroler Marterln für abg'stürzte Bergkraxler* (1895; Tyrolese Memorial Tablets for Mountain Climbers Who Plunged to Their Death); *Allerhand Kreuzköpf* (1895; Sundry Blockheads); *Der Judas von Tirol* (1897; Judas of Tyrol); *Die Bildschnitzer* (1900; The Wood Carvers); *Sonnwendtag* (1902; Solstice); *Karrnerleut'* (1904; The Carters); *Caritas* (1905); *Familie* (1905; Family); *Erde* (1908; Earth); *Über die Brücke* (1908; Across the Bridge); *Das Königreich* (1909; The Kingdom); *Glaube und Heimat* (1910; Creed and Homeland); *Aus meinem Merkbuch* (1911; From My Notebook); *Tiroler Bauernschwänke* (1913; Tyrolese Peasant Farces); *Schuldbuch* (1913; Ledger); *Tiroler Bauern von 1809* (1913; Tyrolese Peasants from 1809); *Der Weibsteufel* (1915; The She-Devil); *Volk in Not* (1916; A People in Distress); *Frau Suitner* (1917); *Narrenspiel des Lebens* (1919; Fool's Play of Life); *Kindertragödie* (1919; Child Tragedy); *Der Kampf* (1920; The Struggle; republished as *Vivat Academia!* [1922]; republished as *Der Spurius* [1927]; republished as *Herr Doktor, haben Sie zu essen?* [1930; Doctor, Do You Have Anything to Eat?]); *Es* (1922; It); *Maitanz* (1923; May Dance); *Der Komödiant* (1924; The Comedian); *Die Hunger-*

blockade (1925; Starvation Blockade; republished as *Der Armendoktor* [1926; Poor Man's Doctor]; republished as *Der Nothelfer* [1926; The Deliverer]); *Gesammelte Werke* (4 vols., 1927; Collected Works); *Passionsspiel* (1933; Passion Play); *Die Fahne weht* (1937; The Flag Is Flying); *Gesammelte Werke* (2 vols., 1948); *Gesamtausgabe: Band 1, Bühnenwerke* (1967; Complete Works; Volume 1, Dramas).

Bibliography: Cysarz, Herbert, "Karl Schönherr," in *Neue österreichische Biographie ab 1815: Große Österreichischer*, vol. 14, pp. 137–51, 1960. Hölzl, Norbert, "Karl Schönherr zum 25. Todestag," *Österreich in Geschichte und Literatur* 12 (1968):159–65. Lederer, Max, "Karl Schönherr, 1867–1943," *Books Abroad* 18 (1944):23–25. Paulin, Karl, *Karl Schönherr und seine Dichtungen*, 1950. Waldinger, Ernst, in *German Life and Letters*, 1956–57, pp. 108–109.

Walter Weiss

Adalbert Stifter

Born 23 October 1805 into a family that worked a small farm in Oberplan, southern Bohemia. He got his basic education in the Benedictine monastery of Kremsmünster in Upper Austria and studied at the University of Vienna, earning his living as a private tutor. Though not without some initial sympathies with the revolutionary cause, he hurriedly left Vienna for Linz after the events of March 1848. He then took up the post of a government school inspector (at first unpaid), from which he retired on a pension in 1865. Throughout his life he treasured memories of an unhappy early love affair; his marriage (1837) to an uneducated working-class girl remained childless and was the source of much friction. As a student he could not decide whether to become a landscape painter or writer. In spite of some literary success, he never achieved financial independence and resented the demands of his job. After a long illness, diagnosed as cirrhosis of the liver, he ended his life on 25 January 1868. Apart from a brief journey to Trieste (1857), Stifter's entire life was spent in the region between the Bohemian Forest, Vienna, and the Danube. The humble and straitened circumstances of his life suggest an important source of the increasingly stylized quality of his fiction.

Besides minor poetry and a number of articles on political, moral, and pedagogic topics, Stifter wrote two major novels and more than thirty novellas, many of which are now available in the versions in which they were originally published in magazines as well as in their heavily revised final form. His writings up to the middle 1840s show traces of romantic fantasy and of the influence of Jean Paul Richter. But later his narrative structures became increasingly simple, drawn from modest anecdote, folk tale, ancient chronicle, or village annual. The relatively complex psychological insights of mid-19th-century German prose writers are bypassed, and the sophisticated social realism of contemporary French and English fiction remains completely alien to these stories. (Significantly, the only foreign influence is that of James Fenimore Cooper.) Instead, Stifter uses a simple psychology of humors, his concern is with the fate of his characters within natural, rural, and patriarchal settings, and he confines his social milieu to the family, the village, or the utopian country estate.

The air of anachronism of such settings is accentuated by complex, occasionally pedantic stylistic devices, which derive from the enlightened prose of the previous century and from contemporary Austrian official diction. Accurate descriptions of natural phenomena, of man-made things, objects of antiquarian interest move into the foreground of the action, partly by way of the pathetic fallacy, partly because Stifter's characters seek to protect themselves by means of these *Dinge und Geräthe* (things and tools) against the blows of untoward fate. These descriptions and the incomplete causality alike suggest again and again that men, through their impatience or the exercise of their will, are alienated from the true grounds of their being and at the mercy of a power (*Strafgericht*) they can neither understand nor appease. Yet Stifter does not indulge in the ready irrationalism of the German romantics. On the contrary: his originality, and the most characteristic achievement of his stories, lies in the strenuous elaboration of highly rational, almost "scientific" descriptive means toward rationally inaccessible ends (*letzte Unvernunft des Seins*; ultimate senselessness of life). Being an indifferent critic of his own work and apt to stress merely its high-minded moral intention, Stifter gives no hint of the extent of his literary self-consciousness.

Of Stifter's two great novels, one, *Der Nachsommer* (1857), has become a classic in the language, while the other, *Witiko* (1865-67), the first and only part of a projected trilogy about medieval Bohemia, carries the expatiatory mode to lengths that few readers are willing to follow. *Der Nachsommer* is a long novel of development and initiation into the good life, in which an old man's gentle wisdom is purposefully and gradually conveyed to a young man of great receptivity and eagerness to learn. The only dramatic element it contains is a novella of passion, recalled from the past, which explains (not wholly convincingly) how the old man, Freiherr von Risach, came by his maturity and wisdom. For the rest there is no conflict, no tension, and no breath of adversity. The many years von Risach spent in distinguished public service are said to have counted for little in the attainment of his serenity. The model country estate that von Risach has planned and built in the Indian summer of his life, its mansion (with its many rooms), its park, landscape, the highly ordered harmonious life of its inhabitants (which are described in detail)— all these are sealed off against the world of passion and strife, against the common social world, and only briefly contrasted with the disaffecting life of the city. But all these descriptions are now set out to provide patterns of harmony, practical and aesthetic, for young Heinrich Drendorf's instruction and spiritual refinement. The story ends with Heinrich's marriage to Natalie, daughter of von Risach's beloved Mathilde, and with his taking up the management of the estate.

In biographical terms the novel represents the consummation of Stifter's relentless pursuit of a golden Eden that would veil the gray wretchedness of his life. In literary terms it is an experiment in the irenic mode that is likely to be unique. The gradualness of development, absence of dramatic effects, and single-minded creation of idyll give *Der Nachsommer* a quality and distinction all its own. In that sense it is the most remarkable prose fiction of 19th-century Austrian and indeed German literature.

Works: *Wien und die Wiener in Bildern aus dem Leben* (1844; Vienna and the Viennese in Pictures of Life); *Studien* (6 vols., 1844–50; includes *Der Kondor, Feldblumen, Das Haidedorf, Der Hochwald, Die Narrenburg, Die Mappe meines Urgroßvaters, Abdias, Das alte Siegel, Brigitta, Der Hagestolz, Der Waldsteig, Zwei Schwestern, Der beschriebene Tännling;* Studies: The Condor, Field Flowers, The Village on the Heath, Forest of Tall Trees, Pictures of Life [Eng. tr., 1847], Rural Life in Austria and Hungary [Eng. tr., 1850], Abdias, The Old Seal, Brigitta [Eng. tr., 1957], The Recluse [Eng. tr., 1968], The Forest Path, Two Sisters, The Small Fir Tree with Carved Inscriptions); *Bunte Steine* (2 vols., 1853; includes *Granit, Kalkstein, Turmalin, Bergkrystall, Katzensilber, Bergmilch*; Colored Stones: Granite, Limestone Tourmaline, Rock Crystal [Eng. tr., 1945], Mica, Rock Milk); *Der Nachsommer* (3 vols., 1857; Indian Summer); *Witiko* (3 vols., 1865–67); *Erzählungen* (2 vols., 1869; includes *Prokopus, Die drei Schmiede ihres Schicksals, Der Waldbrunnen, Nachkommenschaften, Waldgänger, Der fromme Spruch, Der Kuß von Sentze, Zuversicht, Zwei Witwen, Die Barmherzigkreit, Der späte Pfennig, Der Tod einer Jungfrau;* Stories: Procopus, The Three Smiths of Their Fates, The Well in the Forest, Descendants, The Wanderer in the Forest, The Pious Adage, The Kiss of Sentze, Confidence, Two Widows, Mercifulness, The Late Pfennig, The Death of a Virgin); *Briefe* (3 vols., 1869; Letters); *Vermischte Schriften* (2 vols., 1870; Selected Writings); *Sämtliche Werke* (24 vols., 1901–1960; Complete Works); *Auswahl von Briefen* (ed. F. Seebaß, 1936; ed. M. Enzinger, 1947; ed. H. Schumacher, 1947; ed. G. Fricke, 1949; Selected Letters); *Gesammelte Werke* (7 vols., 1939ff.; Collected Works); *Werge* (9 vols., 1952–60; Works); *Erzählungen in der Urfassung* (1952; Stories in Their Original Version); *Jugendbriefe* (1954; Letters from His Youth); *Die Schulakten Adalbert Stifters* (1955; Adalbert Stifter's School Documents); *Pädagogische Schriften* (1960; Pedogogical Writings); *Leben und Werk in Briefen und Dokumenten* (1962; Life and Work in Letters and Documents).

English translations in collections: *Limestone, and Other Stories* (1968).

Bibliography: Blackall, E. A., *Adalbert Stifter: A Critical Study*, 1948. Hein, A. R., *Adalbert Stifter*, 2nd edition, 1952. Hohoff, C., *Adalbert Stifter: Seine dichterischen Mittel und die Prosa des 19. Jahrhunderts*, 1949. Muschg, W., *Tragische Literaturgeschichte*, 1948. Pascal, R., *The German Novel*, 1957. Silz, W., *Realism and Reality*, 1954. Staiger, E., *Stifter als Dichter der Ehrfurcht*, 1943. Stern, J. P., *Reinterpretations*, 1964. Stopp, F. J., "The Symbolism of Stifter's *Kalkstein*," *German Life and Letters*, January 1954.

J. P. Stern[▲]

Otto Stoessl

Novelist, poet, essayist, and dramatist, born 2 May 1875, Vienna; died there, 15 September 1936. Otto Stoessl was the son of a physician who made a name for himself by several publications in his special field (pediatrics). His father's early death not only clouded his youth —Stoessl was deeply devoted to his father—but also explains the sadness that pervades his writings. Early in his life his eyes were opened to the futility of human destiny, to the tragedy of wasted, ruined, lost life and happiness. The unburdening of oppressive childhood remembrances—the grievous memory of a beloved father, so early lost, and of an unmotherly mother—is a recurring motif in his writings.

Stoessl's early literary endeavors and successes—he published his first longer novella *Leile* in 1898—brought him into contact with Peter Altenberg, Karl Kraus, and Adolf Loos, the architect. He contributed to Kraus's periodical *Die Fackel* until 1911, when Kraus proceeded to do all the writing for this publication by himself. In spite of his aspirations to establish himself as a writer, Stoessl continued his studies at the University of Vienna and took his degree as a doctor of law in 1900. However, the insecurity of a writer's existence, more difficult then than today, together with his obligations to his family (he married in 1900) prompted him to enter the service of the Kaiser Ferdinand Nordbahn railroad. This bread-winning employment was to bring him the security enabling him to establish himself as a writer, but the double exertion of energy also made for the doubled consumption of his strength. The problem of such division of an artist's life, in the midst of an uncomprehending, indifferent, even hostile environment, occurs in always new refractions in Stoessl's writings. After 1919 he was the Burgtheater critic of the *Wiener Zeitung*. He left his position at the Nordbahn (as *Hofrat*) in 1923. In the same year he received the Prize of the City of Vienna awarded then for the first time.

The decade before World War I was the happiest and most productive of Stoessl's life. In rapid succession a number of works appeared that made him favorably known and brought him the friendships of noteworthy personalities. At first he was drawn to the drama and toward naturalistic social criticism, but he soon turned his attention to the art of narration. His models were the past masters of poetic realism, Gottfried Keller, C. F. Meyer, and Adalbert Stifter, about whom he wrote superb critical essays, thereby describing that kind of poetic writing most congenial to his own.

"Criticism and self-criticism," wrote Ernst Krenek in the *Wiener Zeitung* (5 May 1935) "guarantee the purity of Otto Stoessl's language, a value whose preservation has become one of Austria's special tasks. Perhaps this is the most important Austrian responsibility in the realm of German culture due to the wretched debasement of the language in Germany in the Third Reich. It is certainly no accident that the most passionate and unyielding defender of the German language, Karl Kraus, is an Austrian. German culture owes him an eternal debt for stimulating Austria's best minds to maintain unflagging vigil over the dignity and purity of the German language."

The Austrian school of the novella is the heir of a great tradition beginning with Franz Grillparzer and Ferdinand von Saar. Stoessl carried on this tradition in a truly noble way. What gives his novellas their vigor and conviction is, beyond all aesthetic merits, their profound humanity.

Stoessl did not want to be anything but a quiet observer, who, from his window, watched people's lives. His keen but kindly eye pierced the most secret and most ramified passageways of the anthill called human society. But what compelled his greatest compassion were the strangely blurred border areas of this seemingly so solidly built society and the people who lived in an oddly hazy, indescribable twilight. These outsiders of society, who despised bourgeois life yet were caricatures of its members, are his favorites. Unforgettable for everyone who has met them are: Heinrich Frantzel in *Das Haus Erath* (the Frantzels are to Austria what the Buddenbrooks and Forsytes are to Germany and England); or that master of the art of living, Lieutenant Roszkowski in *Sonjas letzter Name* (1908); or that funniest specimen of an ingenious heel, Egon de Alamor, in the magnificent story *Egon und Danitza* (1911). But in addition to buffoons, hypocrites, and adventurers, we meet such wondrously fine women as the patiently suffering Antonia and the angelic Agnes in *Das Haus Erath*.

The end of World War I, the collapse and destruction of the Austro-Hungarian monarchy, seemed to deprive Stoessl of the main elements of his life and art, but his unbroken creative energy turned this downfall too from a painful experience into a subject of artistic creation. The novel *Das Haus Erath* (1920) shows this collapse by means of presenting the fate of three generations of a widely branched-out, originally solid and wealthy family; its moral and financial decline represents the degeneration of the middle class generally and so warrants the empire's ruin. *Das Haus Erath*, justly considered Stoessl's main achievement, was his most successful work. About it Karl Nötzel in the *Kunstwart* (February 1926) wrote: "It would be hard to find in the current crop of novels one that compares with Stoessl's *Erath* in its richness—no word is more apt—of psychological penetration, warmth, brilliance and breadth of ideas, inventive power, beauty and rightness of language. . . . With this writer-we live an undreamed-of multidimensional and strangely enchanting existence. We forget ourselves in the process, yet know that we have a right to do so because we return to ourselves richer, more knowing, and inwardly gayer."

In the novel *Sonnenmelodie* (1923), Ludwig Mainone, through whom Stoessl speaks, describes his relation to the collapsed monarchy: "For he loved it, although he suffered from it. One cannot have been born in a country and have wandered through all its regions, have delighted in the sight of them—the plains and the Alps, the powerful river streaming through it, the southern landscape, people with many customs and idioms—and not partake with one's heart of this century-old structure." In the same novel Mainone calls himself a mourner of the Austrian empire, because by its destruction his favorite toy had been smashed.

When, in 1933, the first volume of his collected works (4 vols., 1933–37) appeared, Stoessl titled it *Arcadia*, gathering in it a series of poetic creations almost all of which deal with classical antiquity or are rooted in antiquity. The typical Austrian, a synthesis of German and Mediterranean elements, of antiquity and Christianity, pervades Stoessl's work. This is particularly apparent in his *Griechisches Tagebuch* (in the above-mentioned volume; also published separately, 1930), which combines Goethe's wide vision with the realism of Grillparzer's notes on a similar journey through Greece. The problems of artistic creation of the novellas had been preoccupying Stoessl. They are treated in *Das Erlebnis des Dichters* (which can be freely translated as "The Creative Process of the Literary Artist"), which is one of the most significant articles in the third volume of the collected works.

For the volumes comprising his novellas Stoessl planned a division into *Schöpfer* (Creators) and *Geschöpfe* (Creatures). He did not live to see their publication. Only the volume *Schöpfer* appeared after his death in 1937. With the emigration of his publisher in 1938 this edition of his collected works came to an end.

Behind every poetic creation of Stoessl a spiritual, moral force is operative. To look at it from a merely aesthetic point of view does not do justice to Stoessl's work. In his own words: "The homeland of all morality is art. It gives direction and uniqueness, it enlivens man's wretched life through its manifold interpretations, it provides variety for the moments of perpetual tension and so lightens the burden on his shoulders."

Works: *Ware* (1897; Merchandise); *Leile* (1898); *Tote Götter* (1898; Dead Gods); *Kinderfrühling* (1904; Children's Spring); *Gottfried Keller* (1904); *Conrad Ferdinand Meyer* (1906); *In den Mauern* (1907; Within the Walls; republished as *Das Schicksal pocht an die Pforte* [1956; Fate Knocks at the Gate]); *Sonjas letzter Name* (1908; Sonja's Last Name); *Negerkönigs Tochter* (1910; The Black King's Daughter); *Allerleirauh* (1911); *Egon und Danitza* (1911); *Morgenrot* (1912; Dawn); *Was nützen mir die schönen Schuhe?* (1913; What Good Are the Pretty Shoes to Me?); *Unterwelt* (1914; Underworld); *Lebensform und Dichtungsform* (1914; Form in Life and Literature); *Basem, der Grobschmied* (1916; Basem, the Blacksmith); *Das Haus Erath* (1920; The House of Erath); *Der Hirt als Gott* (1920; The Shepherd as God); *Irrwege* (1922; Blind Paths); *Opfer* (1923; Victim); *Sonnenmelodie* (1923; Melody of the Sun); *Adalbert Stifter* (1925); *Johannes Freudensprung* (1926); *Nachtgeschichten* (1926; Tales of the Night; republished as *Menschendämmerung* [1929; The Twilight of Man]); *Die Schmiere* (1927; The Seedy Little Stage); *Antike Motive* (1928; Motifs of Antiquity); *Griechisches Tagebuch* (1930; Greek Diary); *Die wahre Helena* (1931; The True Helena); *Gesammelte Werke* (4 vols., 1933–38; Collected Works); *Nora, die Füchsin* (1934; Nora, the Vixen); *Schöpfer* (1937; Creators).

Bibliography: Alker, E., "Zu Otto Stoessls 50. Geburtstag," *Die Literatur* 27 (1924–25):61. Bing, S., "Otto Stoessl, Ein Dichter Österreichs," *Frankfurter Zeitung*, 9 July 1925, p. 1. Krenek, E., "Otto Stoessl," *Wiener Zeitung*, 5 May 1935. Leszer, J., "Otto Stoessl," *Neue Schweizer Rundschau*, 1928, pp. 753–58. Lissauer, E., "Ein Gedichtband Otto Stoessls," *Die Literatur* 31 (1928–29):17. Nötzel, K., "Otto Stoessl," *Kunstwart*, February 1929. Wied, M., "Otto Stoessl zum 60. Geburtstag," *Wiener Zeitung*, 1 May 1935.

Frederick Ungar[▲]

Friedrich Torberg

Friedrich Torberg (pseudonym of Friedrich Kantor-Berg) was born on 16 September 1908 in Vienna, where he spent his childhood and youth. Studied philosophy in Prague. When he was twenty-two, his novel *Der Schüler Gerber hat absolviert* (1930; new version, *Der Schüler Gerber*, 1954) gained not only a wide public for him (it has been translated into ten languages and new editions are still appearing), but also the friendship of older writers such as Franz Werfel, Hermann Broch, Max Brod, and Karl Kraus. Three more novels appeared in quick succession. Outstanding among these is the sports novel *Die Mannschaft* (1935), which is of lasting value both from a literary and a factual point of view (Torberg was an outstanding water-polo player).

The events of 1938 drove Torberg first to Switzerland and then to France, where he served as a volunteer in the army from 1939 to 1940. Then going to Spain and Portugal, he finally reached the United States, where he lived from 1941 to 1951. Whereas there had hitherto been no mention of politics in Torberg's books, this was now reversed. The short story *Mein ist die Rache* (1943) and the novel *Hier bin ich, mein Vater* (written, 1943–46; published, 1948) take individual destinies as examples of the fate of the Jews under the Nazi regime. For the setting of the novel *Die zweite Begegnung* (1950) Torberg returned to a Bohemia now enslaved by communism. These books of his emigré years have two things in common: the emphasis in subject matter on the extreme case, and the transposition of political problems into universal human terms. But at bottom they are books of homesickness, books of pain at the horrors committed in the places where the writer is forever at home.

Since 1951 Torberg has again been living in Vienna, and his literary career has taken yet another turn. In many essays, reviews, comments, and parodies he has become the irrepressible, kindly critic of his native land. The major work of this third period in his life and career is the monthly review *Forum*, which he not only edited but truly made his own. It is one of the liveliest periodicals in the German-speaking world.

Through all the stages of his work, Torberg's creed has been a threefold one based on the German language, his Austrian homeland, and the Jewish faith. The literary outcome is a forward-looking conservatism, such as generally distinguishes Austrian from German literature. Accordingly, as a critic Torberg campaigns on two fronts—against what is old and necrotic on the one hand and what is new but stillborn on the other, against both mustiness and modernity. Similarly, in his narrative prose and his poetry he preserves this Austrian sense of balance by keeping a tight stylistic rein on even what is extreme in his subject matter. He is daring in his ideas but not in his style: for instance, the experiment of revealing a truth not in victory but in defeat—from the suicide of the pupil Gerber in *Der Schüler Gerber hat absolviert*, via the defeats of the team in *Die Mannschaft*, to the prodigal son (if he really is one) in *Hier bin ich, mein Vater*. Even in disrupted lives a red thread may be traced: a love for his fellowman.

Works: *Der ewige Refrain* (1929; The Eternal Refrain); *Der Schüler Gerber hat absolviert* (1930; The Student Gerber Graduated from School; republished under the title *Der Schüler Gerber* [1954]); *. . . und glauben, es wäre die Liebe* (1932; . . . And Think This Were Love); *Die Mannschaft* (1935; The Team); *Anna sagt Nein* (with A. Hoffmeister, 1935; Anna Says No); *Der Pfarrer von Kirchfeld* (1937; The Priest of Kirchfeld); *Abschied* (1937; Farewell); *Mein ist die Rache* (1943; Vengeance Is Mine); *Hier bin ich, mein Vater* (1948; Here I Am, My Father); *Die zweite Begegnung* (1950; The Second Meeting); *Komödianten des Lebens* (1952; Comedians of Life); *Nichts ist leichter als das* (1956; Nothing Is Easier than That); *Adenauer und die Intellektuellen* (1957; Adenauer and the Intellectuals); *Lebenslied* (1958; Song of Life); *Gesammelte Werke* (1962 ff.; Collected Works); *P. P. P. Pamphlete, Parodien, Post-Scripta* (1964; P. P. P. Pamphlets, Parodies, Postscripts); *Das fünfte Rad am Thespiskarren* (2 vols., 1966–67; The Fifth Wheel of the Thespian Cart); *Golems Wiederkehr* (1968; Golem's Return); *Süßkind von Trimberg* (1973).

Bibliography: Ahl, Herbert, *Literarische Portraits*, p. 583, 1962. Beer, Otto F., on *Die zweite Begegnung*, in *Neues Österreich*, 14 December 1963. Hellmann, Winfried, on *P.P.P. Pamphlete, Parodien, Post-Scripta*, in *Germanistik*, 1966, p. 327. Nedomansky, Herbert, in *Die Presse*, 10 October 1968. Urbach, Reinhard, on "Golems Wiederkehr," in *Literatur und Kritik*, 1968, pp. 185–86. Vormweg, Heinrich, on *Golems Wiederkehr und andere Erzählungen*, in *Süddeutsche Zeitung*, 5 December 1968.

Herbert Eisenreich

Georg Trakl

Georg Trakl was born on 3 February 1887 in Salzburg. His father's family came from Hungary, his mother's from Bohemia. His father was a merchant dealing in iron, which afforded the family a prosperous middle-class style. Among the five brothers and sisters, relations were particularly close between Trakl and his highly gifted sister Margarethe, a pianist. Trakl attended the humanistic *Staatsgymnasium* in Salzburg from 1897 to 1905. When he failed to be promoted from the seventh class (he had already had to repeat the fourth), he left school. Without express permission from his father, who knew of his early addiction to drugs, Trakl decided to become a pharmacist. He received his degree in pharmacy after completing the required three years of apprenticeship (1905–1908 in Salzburg) and two years' study (1908–1910 in Vienna).

After a year's military service from 1910 to 1911, Trakl made several attempts to obtain a job in Salzburg, Vienna, and Innsbruck. Ludwig von Ficker, whom he met in Innsbruck in 1912, played a crucial role in his life at this point. In his periodical *Der Brenner*, von Ficker published most of the poems that Trakl wrote during the last two years of his life, and on many occasions he altruistically provided a refuge to the poet, who was drifting from place to place. Trakl's relations, of varying intensity, with Karl Kraus, Oskar Kokoschka, and the architect Adolf Loos in Vienna, with Karl Boromäus Heinrich, Theodor Haecker, and Karl Röck in Innsbruck, and with Else Lasker-Schüler in Berlin in 1914 were less important, but they are not without interest as evidence of the impact of his personality and of contemporary judgment of his work. In 1917 Röck edited a cyclic arrangement of Trakl's late poetry, which was published in 1919 as *Die Dichtungen*.

At the outbreak of World War I, Trakl was drafted and served as a dispenser in the medical corps. After the battle of Grodek, he was transferred to Cracow for medical observation of his mental state as a result of a nervous breakdown and attempted suicide. There, on 3 or 4 November 1914, an overdose of cocaine led to his death, a possible suicide.

In Trakl's work two periods may be clearly distinguished. His writings of the years 1906 to 1910 hint at his later achievement—in the choice of theme, for instance, or sometimes in the cadence—but hardly provide evidence of what was to come. In his early attempts at drama (*Totentag, Fata Morgana*, both produced in Salzburg in 1906, but now lost) Trakl seems to have worked in the tradition of Ibsen and Maeterlinck. The heroes of these two one-act plays both go to their death when they step out of the world of their illusions and see reality as it is. Apart from fragments, the little puppet play *Blaubart* is the only one of Trakl's later dramatic works to have survived. In the lyrical poems of this early period the influence of the French symbolists, especially Baudelaire, is evident. A few prose sketches and pieces of literary criticism complete the picture of an exploratory period, the works of which only show that Trakl had, on the whole, not yet found his own voice.

Seldom has such important poetic work been preceded by such insignificant efforts as Trakl's early *Aus goldenem Kelch*, which was edited in 1939 by his boyhood friend Erhard Buschbeck (2nd enlarged edition, 1951). But in the following years, especially after 1912, Trakl wrote the poems that won him his place in modern German poetry—*Gedichte* (1913) and *Sebastian im Traum* (1915). In these the work of Rimbaud played a part that has often been overestimated; the influence was, all in all, catalytic rather than determining. It must not be overlooked that Trakl really knew the French poet's work only in a not always faithful translation by K. L. Ammers.

Trakl's fundamental experience was that of melancholia. He, if anyone, was a native in Rilke's mountains of "primeval pain." Thanks to statements orally transmitted and to letters (*Erinnerung an Georg Trakl*, edited by Ludwig von Ficker, 1926; 3rd enlarged edition, 1966), it is possible to follow this experience in the poet's life, stage by stage, down to the misery of the war when as a pharmacist, alone without medicine, he was assigned to ninety serious casualties, or at the Cracow garrison hospital, when he was confined in a cell with a delirious officer. More important—from the point of view of his poetry—was Trakl's feeling of being at the mercy of "an infernal chaos of rhythms and images" (1910), which crowded upon him with overwhelming force. The apocalyptic character of these visions became steadily stronger, while the splendor of "bread and wine," which once had made life tolerable in a world that was confused but not vile, became steadily weaker. "It is such an indescribable disaster when the world falls apart for one . . . ," he wrote in 1913.

For Trakl, even the Christian message of salvation was caught in the whirlpool of a disintegrating world. The result was a personally as well as metaphysically experienced sense of guilt, the painfully endured conflict between the Christian belief in divine "mercy" (*Gesang einer gefangenen Amsel*) and "God's silence" (*De profundis*). It will never be possible to judge definitively what the outcome of this conflict was in Trakl's soul because of the obscurity shrouding his death. And finally there remained "nocturnal images of tears" *der Tränen nächtige Bilder*, in *Jahr*). These are primeval images and dream images that sometimes seem understandable considering the biographical information that Trakl repeatedly had recourse to drugs, or from insight into the poet's psychological make-up—though even to know how the images came about does not contribute much to their interpretation.

It should be more illuminating, in regard to the aesthetic character of Trakl's imagery, to examine his creative process. So far, little use has been made of the poet's papers (the Margarethe Langen estate, property of E. Buschbeck, K. B. Heinrich, et al.), which, despite great losses, are still considerable as regards the body of his work. Apart from biographical documents and some one hundred and twenty-five letters, the papers comprise about four hundred pages (partly manuscript drafts and clean copies, partly typescripts of earlier and definitive versions). Editorial attention has been given only to completed poems or to drafts that visibly constitute a whole (*Aus goldenem Kelch*, and *Georg Trakl: Nachlaß und Biographie*, edited by W. Schneditz, 1949). But this attention has often been far from adequate —for example, the poem "Nächtliche Klage" (nocturnal lament) that appears as *Nächtliche Gelage* (nocturnal carouse). The critical edition will therefore have to undertake not only the task of presenting an accurate text of Trakl's known poetry, but also the no less important one of making the remaining papers suitably accessible to research. Since 1958, Walther Killy has published drafts and versions of poems as a consequence of the work on the critical edition. It has become clear from these that the complete publication of the papers promises to offer significant insights into the manner of composition of modern poetry.

The stock of subjects and images, which is astonishingly small for such an important poet as Trakl, is used in "kaleidoscopic play" (Killy), according to the rules of a hidden economy, to produce image structures that are always new even though related in their genesis and theme. The images appear in ever new figurations; they are modified, interchanged, and even replaced by their opposites. The fragments of the world that is falling apart no longer have the qualities that once were peculiar to things that receive their specific value from the context of the whole. The sophistical argument that even a disintegrating world constitutes an entity that leaves the parts their place obstructs the approach to a just assessment of the intensity of the suffering Trakl experienced, endured, and captured in words. The further one plunges into the thicket of his drafts, the more obstinately do his images elude interpretation, that is, conceptual definition. For this reason Rainer Maria Rilke's question "Who may he [Trakl] have been?" is as relevant now as in 1915.

The difficulties that oppose any interpretation, or even an understanding, of Trakl's poems, largely reside in the fact that Trakl's language is a faithful mirror image of a disintegrating world, it is the appropriate expression of an incoherent plenitude of images. The dissolution of conventional sentence formation (ellipsis, etc.) does as much to reduce the predicate to a condition of elusive ambiguity, as does, for example, the emancipation of the adjectives, especially those of color, which are used in such a way that they sometimes suggest an impressionist and sometimes a symbolic interpretation. In fact, the question arises as to whether in Trakl's work words have not altogether lost their communicative character and become signs of relationships experienced only by the poet, so that an exceptional degree of caution is required in any attempt to interpret this poetry.

In regard to form, Trakl increasingly freed himself from the use of the rhyming four-line stanza and the sonnet, which had been a favorite of his until his more mature writing. In their place he turned to forms for the stanza and for the entire poem that were invented only as the poem was being written and were neither separable from it nor transferable. He often discarded the line unit, which is usually used in poetic language, and wrote poems in prose. Hölderlin's late hymns may not have been without influence on the poems Trakl wrote in the summer of 1914—*Das Gewitter, Die Schwermut, Der Abend, Die Nacht.*

A failure from the point of view of middle-class respectability, Trakl, in his brief lifetime, produced a body of work that, though modest in extent, was of almost unfathomable depth and had no equal in its time.

Works: *Totentag* (1906; Day of the Dead); *Fata Morgana* (1906); *Gedichte* (1913; Poems); *Sebastian im Traum* (1915; Sebastian Dreaming); *Die Dichtungen* (1919; The Poetry); *Der Herbst des Einsamen* (1920; Autumn of the Lonely One); *Gesang der Abgeschiedenen* (1933; Song of the Dead); *Aus goldenem Kelch* (1939; From a Golden Chalice); *Die Dichtungen* (3 vols., 1939; The Poetry); *Offenbarung und Untergang*

(1947; Revelation and Downfall); *Gesammelte Werke* (3 vols., 1948 ff: Collected Works); *Nachgelassene Gedichte* (1958; Posthumous Poems).

English translations in collections: Decline (1952); *Twenty Poems* (1961); *Selected Poems* (1968).

Bibliography: Basil, O., *Georg Trakl in Selbstzeugnissen und Bilddokumenten*, 1965. Bleisch, E. G., *Georg Trakl*, 1964. Brown, Russell E., "Attribute Pairs in the Poetry of Georg Trakl," *Modern Language Notes* 82 (1967):439–45. Casey, T. J., *Manshape That Shone: An Interpretation of Georg Trakl*, 1964. Ficker, L., and Zangerle, I., *Erinnerungen an Georg Trakl*, 2nd edition, 1959. Magnuson, K., "Consonant Problems in the Lyrics of Georg Trakl," *Germanic Review* 37 (1962):263–81. Ritzer, W., *Trakl Bibliographie*, 1956. Werner, B., *Erlösungsmotive in der Dichtung Georg Trakls*, 1961.

Hans Szklenar

Franz Tumler

Born 16 December 1912 in Gries, near Bozen (now Bolzano). After the early death of his father, who had taught Latin and Greek at the Bozen *Gymnasium*, his mother and the boy went back to her home in Upper Austria, where Tumler grew up. He attended the local teachers' college and for a number of years taught at the elementary school at Altmünster on Lake Traun. After World War II, in which he served as an officer, Tumler did not return to teaching but instead took up a writing career and moved to Linz. He now lives in Berlin.

Tumler's father had left a mass of material for a comparative dictionary of the Ladin dialects, which are spoken in the Engadine, Switzerland, and adjacent parts of Italy. These notes and a visit to his South Tyrol birthplace inspired the twenty-three-year-old writer's first story, *Das Tal von Lausa und Duron* (1935). The story describes the decline of a remote Ladin village amid the upheavals of World War I. The involved story line is made clear through the sharply outlined characters, but behind the seemingly realistic characterization, powerful individual symbols emerge in which what has remained unsaid about a character's inner life is revealed. In this very first effort, Tumler found his own style, which has become continually more pronounced with the development of his narrative work.

Tumler's stories appeared at intervals—*Die Wanderung zum Strom* (1937), *Der Soldateneid* (1939), *Auf der Flucht* (1943), *Das Hochzeitsbild* (1953), and *An der Waage: Aufzeichnungen aus dem Lagerhaus* (1959). In all of them the action takes place in the present, and all are based either on observations or on experiences lived at first hand. But Tumler does not simply report the event. He probes, ponders, and interprets the experience in terms of the universal, which reveals itself in symbols. He also applied this procedure to his novels, but he has succeeded only gradually in integrating many-layered events in expressive symbols. In the earlier novels, episodic abundance obstructed the main drive of the action. This was the case with *Der Ausführende* (1937), which raises the question of responsibility for one's acts, and above all with the two extensive portraits of the age, *Heimfahrt* (1950) and *Ein Schloß in Österreich* (1953). While these have the dimensions of novels, they lack the compelling power of the form-giving fable.

Tumler avoided the danger of disintegration into formlessness by evermore incisive elaboration of psychological processes through which the episodic is situated in time and subordinated to the course of destiny. This kind of construction first appeared in the novel *Der alte Herr Lorenz* (1949), which makes the experience of aging apparent even in the old man's return to life. The novel *Der Schritt hinüber* (1956) takes as its theme the inexpressible element in human relationships, in that each of the characters fails in his attempt to justify his inner self. *Der Mantel* (1959) again takes up the same problem, but in this novel the protagonist, "a man without qualities," is unable to see what is real for the many things that are possible. All these novels come to an end without any significant conclusion. Tumler carries the action up to the point at which all the threads are visible and all the motifs clearly displayed before us, and then he leaves the further development of the idea to the reader.

Tumler's poems follow no model. The collections *Anruf* (1941) and *Liebeslobpreisungen* (1947) are completely unconventional in form. He deliberately renounces established prosody, for in his view the content must determine the form. It is no accident, therefore, that free verse predominates. Even the boundary between verse and reflective prose is not always evident. The prose pieces *Landschaften des Heimgekehrten* (1948; also published as *Neuer Blick auf die Erde*, 1949) could well be taken as lyrical works, while in the books *Berlin: Geist und Gesicht* (1953) and *Der Gardasee* (1958) the factual interest predominates. But all Tumler's work bears the stamp of an original personality.

Works: *Das Tal von Lausa und Duron* (1935; The Valley of Lausa and Duron); *Die Wanderung zum Strom* (1937; Excursion to the River); *Der Ausführende* (1937; The One Who Carries Out); *Im Jahre 38* (1939; In the Year '38); *Der Soldateneid* (1939; Oath of Enlistment); *Österreich ist ein Land des deutschen Reiches* (1940; Austria Is a Country of the German Reich); *Der erste Tag* (1940; The First Day); *Anruf* (1941; Appeal); *Auf der Flucht* (1943; Fleeing); *Liebeslobpreisungen* (1947; Praises of Love); *Einmal war etwas Gutes geschehen* (1947; Once Something Good Happened); *Landschaften des Heimgekehrten* (1948; Countrysides of the Homecomer); *Der alte Herr Lorenz* (1949; Old Mr. Lorenz); *Ein Schloß in Österreich* (1953; A Castle in Austria); *Heimfahrt* (1953; Homeward Journey); *Das Hochzeitsbild* (1953; The Wedding Picture); *Berlin: Geist und Gesicht* (1953; Berlin: Spirit and Image); *Der Schritt hinüber* (1956; The Step Beyond); *Der Gardasee* (1958; Lake Garda); *An der Waage: Aufzeichnungen aus dem Lagerhaus* (1959; At the Scales: Notes from a Warehouse); *Der Mantel* (1959; The Coat); *Menschen in Berlin*

(1960; Men in Berlin); *Volterra: Wie ensteht Prosa* (1962; Volterra: How Prose Comes into Being); *Nachprüfung eines Abschieds* (1964; Examination of a Farewell); *Aufschreibungen aus Trient* (1965; Notes from Trient); *Welche Sprache ich lernte* (1970; The Language I Learned); *Sätze von der Donau* (1972; Sentences from the Danube); *Pia Faller* (1973).

Bibliography: *Jahr und Jahrgang 1912* (reminiscences), 1966. Tumler, Franz, "Der Schritt hinüber: Ein Selbstporträt," *Welt und Wort* 12 (1957):79–80.

Eugen Thurnher

Johannes Urzidil

Born 3 February 1896 in Prague, the son of a railroad employee and inventor. As a writer, Johannes Urzidil adhered to no literary trend, program, or school. His work bears the stamp of his native Bohemia. It is expressionist to the extent that there was a Prague form of expressionism. In its reverence for all creation and human creativeness, it is close to Adalbert Stifter's work; in its humanism it is classic but also receptive to the supernatural. All these varied and divergent trends radiated from Urzidil's experience of Prague, yet they were unified by a strong language consciousness resting on moral responsibility.

Urzidil studied philology at the German university in Prague. His first volume of poems was published in 1920. From 1921 to 1932 he was press attaché at the German embassy in Prague. In 1939 he emigrated to England and in 1941 to the United States, where he made a living in New York by writing and doing manual jobs. He also worked in broadcasting for the "Voice of America." He died in Rome, where he was on a lecture tour, on 3 November 1970.

Urzidil's diction has a core of unimpeachable stability, so that it always falls into some orderly pattern of its own even when the grammar is loose or the language disintegrates into units of expression. In *Die verlorene Geliebte* (1956), Urzidil reconstructs Prague, the city of his memories, in eleven short stories that are as true to life as Sherwood Anderson's youthful memories in *Winesburg, Ohio*. In *Prager Tryptichon* (1960) Urzidil's narrative style has the more deliberate objectivity of "memoirs." "To be one of the least brings a man closer to the vastness of life than if he were from the safeguard center," he writes in his short story *Der Trauermantel* (1945, 1955), which is based on Stifter's youth in the Böhmerwald.

In the novel *Das große Halleluja* (1959), a symphonic evocation of American life, Urzidil wove the voice of his own vocation into the polyphony. "Humility and patience, these were the two attitudes required to serve the craftsman's raw material." This is what the protagonist Weseritz, a man who applied as much painstaking labor to writing a page as to making a leather box, came to understand. In an age of total mobilization, which has robbed such static phenomena, as state, nation, religion, property, and personality of their validity, the artist is no longer the guardian of "the most sacred values" but a craftsman taking a creative part in the universal process of transformation. To the extent that he produced something unique, however, he stands up to mass civilization in the same spirit of primitive reverence that is at the root of the epic.

This is the explanation for the classical character of the fifteen short stories in the volume *Das Elefantenblatt* (1962). It also explains the perseverance with which Urzidil worked for many years on his tribute of piety, *Goethe in Böhmen,* and brought it to its conclusion in 1962.

Works: *Sturz der Verdammten* (1920; Downfall of the Damned); *Die Stimme* (1930; The Voice); *Goethe in Böhmen* (1932; enlarged edition, 1962; Goethe in Bohemia); *Zeitgenössische Maler der Tschechen* (1936; Contemporary Czech Painters); *Wenceslaus Hollar* (1936); *Der Trauermantel* (1945; Camberwell Beauty); *Über das Handwerk* (1954; On Handicraft); *Die verlorene Geliebte* (1956; The Lost Beloved); *Die Memnonsäule* (1956; The Pillar of Memnon); *Das Glück der Gegenwart: Goethes Amerikabild* (1958; Happiness of the Present: Goethe's Image of America); *Denkwürdigkeiten von Gibacht* (1958; Memorabilia of Gibacht); *Neujahrsrummel* (1959; New Year's Revels); *Das große Halleluja* (1959; The Great Hallelujah); *Prager Triptychon* (1960; Triptych of Prague); *Geschenke des Lebens* (1962; Gifts of Life); *Das Elefantenblatt* (1962; Engraving of an Elephant); *Amerika und die Antike* (1964; America and Antiquity); *Entführungen und sieben andere Ereignisse* (1964; Abductions and Seven Other Events); *Literatur als schöpferische Verantwortung* (1965; Literature as Creative Responsibility); *Prag—Glanz und Mystik einer Stadt* (with A. Jaenicke, 1966; Eng. tr., Prague—Spirit and Grandeur of a European Capital, 1966); *Da geht Kafka* (1966; Eng. tr., There Goes Kafka, 1969); *Die erbeuteten Frauen* (1966; The Women Captives); *Bist du es, Ronald?* (1968; Is It You, Ronald?); *The Living Contributors of Jewish Prague to Modern German Literature* (1969); *Väterliches aus Prag und Handwerkliches aus New York* (1969; Paternal Things in Prague and Craftsmanship in New York).

Bibliography: Brandt, Thomas O., on *Die erbeuteten Frauen,* in *Books Abroad,* 1967, p. 319. Mendels, J., on *Väterliches aus Prag und Handwerkliches aus New York,* in *Books Abroad* 44, no. 3 (1970):481. Trapp, Gerhard, "Des literarische Frühwerk Johannes Urzidils," *Literatur und Kritik* 11 (1967):12–26; and *Die Prosa Johannes Urzidils: Zum Verständnis eines literarischen Werdegangs vom Expressionismus zur Gegenwart,* 1967. Von Gronicka, André, "Johannes Urzidil," *Wort in der Zeit* 2 (February 1956):1–5.

Karl August Horst

Ernst Waldinger

Born 16 October 1895 in Vienna; died 1 February 1970 in New York. Upon graduation from the *Gymnasium*, Ernst Waldinger volunteered for military service and was seriously wounded in August 1917. He studied German literature and art history at the University of Vienna. Having attained his Ph.D., he worked for a commercial firm. But writing poetry was the core of his life.

For his first-published volume, *Die Kuppel* (1934), Waldinger received the Julius Reich Prize of the University of Vienna. In 1938 he had to leave Austria and emigrated to the United States, where a new life and, for a number of years, economic hardships were his lot. In 1947 he became a professor of German literature and language at Skidmore College in Saratoga Springs, New York, where he taught until his retirement in 1965.

Much of what the blows of fate mercilessly did to his life found expression in his lyrical writing: his youth broken because of his war wounds, which left him a semiinvalid throughout his life (his right hand and the right half of his face were paralyzed); his narrow escape to the United States in 1938; his nostalgic longing for his lost homeland, Austrian word and song, the mellow landscape around the Danube and the Wienerwald, and the streets and alleys of Vienna, which remained his sentimental and intellectual home. *Nur der hat Heimat, der die Sehnsucht hat* is one of his most beautiful poems. In it he professed that only he who is tormented by longing has a real homeland, not he who happens to own property.

In a time of complete dissolution of form Waldinger postulated and strove for its stern observance. This artistic deed is professed in many of his poems, particularly in the volume *Der Gemmenschneider* (1936). "His poems are as stern as Dante's Cantos and yet so rich in vocal musicality as sonnets by Rosetti; still the harsh wind of our time blows through them" wrote Ludwig Lewisohn in *The Nation* when *Die Kuppel* was published.

A virtuoso with words, Waldinger masters an extraordinary variety of themes by a multiplicity of metrical forms in poems of a usually contemplative nature. He wrote tercets, ghazels, strophic cantos and, most of all, sonnets. This prosody lends itself best to his dialectical way of thinking, in that it confronts thesis with antithesis to end up in a liberating synthesis of reconciled contrasts.

Not to be forgotten are his magnificent ballads, which would add luster to any anthology of German poetry. Waldinger saw himself, as evidenced by several of his poems, as a preserver of the purity of the German language. He believed in the purifying power of poetry, which could healingly confront our disjointed time and our mechanized life with the concept of a better world.

"It is necessary," he said, "to write poetry in order to hold against that which is most inhuman in us that which is most humane, the longing for what man should be. Poetry is not entertainment, its aim is not to create tension or to relieve it but to lead to concentration and to deepen our humanity, a direction that, in this time of alienation, we so badly need." His life's center, his poetry, was not aloof to the problems and the dark shadows of our time. It was fused with his will to speak to his time, to stand up and be counted.

In spite of all the affliction of his life Waldinger's solidarity with all living remained unshaken. He held high the banner of a common humanity. His clear and pure voice was the noblest lyrical voice of the Austrian, the German emigration. His art and his humanity grew only through the shocks and jolts of our time. It is our own fate poetically heightened, that confronts us in his work.

Ernst Waldinger did not in his lifetime receive the recognition he so richly deserved. His friend, Josef Weinheber, a poet in his own right, may be quoted here as witness to a more judicious assessment: "Just because Waldinger's work is genuine, it can afford to wait. It will endure long after the demise of lyric poetry so noisily predicted by those who killed it."

Works: *Die Kuppel* (1934; The Cupola); *Der Gemmenschneider* (1936; The Gem Cutter); *Die kühlen Bauernstuben* (1946; The Cool Farmhouse Rooms); *Musik für diese Zeit* (1946; Music for these Times); *Glück und Geduld* (1952; Luck and Patience); *Zwischen Hudson und Donau* (1958, Between the Hudson and the Danube); *Gesang vor dem Abgrund* (1961; Song before the Abyss); *Ich kann mit meinem Menschenbruder sprechen* (1965; I Can Talk with My Fellowman).

Bibliography: Brunngraber, Rudolf, "Ernst Waldinger zum 60. Geburtstag," *Wort in der Zeit* 2 (November 1956):1–5. Kauf, Robert, "Stiller Dichter in lärmender Zeit: Zum 70. Geburtstag Ernst Waldingers," *Wiener Bücherbriefe* 6 (1966):181–85; and "Ernst Waldinger: An Austro-American Poet," *American-German Review* 27, no. 6 (1961):11–13. Picard, Jacob, "Ernst Waldinger at Sixty," *Books Abroad* 31 (1957):28–29.

Frederick Ungar▲

Hans Weigel

Born 29 May 1908 in Vienna, Hans Weigel attended a *Gymnasium* that taught the classical languages. He remained in Vienna until 1938, writing cabaret pieces and making adaptations (for example, of Johann Nestroy's plays) and working as coauthor of musical comedies. He survived the Hitler era in Switzerland. Since 1945 he has again settled and been active in Vienna—as poet, novelist, playwright, adapter, essayist, critic, editor, correspondent; as a "pike in a carps' pond" (as the Germans say of an agent that stirs up the members of a sluggish situation) of Austrian literature and culture; as their *enfant terrible* and whatever else he may have been called. He is in his element when he is being provocative, and the motto of his literary career is "One against almost all."

Weigel has tried his hand at everything and has made himself heard through numerous publications, newspapers, theaters, and radio stations. In the sharpest possible contrast to Albert Gütersloh, for instance, or to Heimito von Doderer, he is, more than anyone else in Austria, an *au courant*. As an emigré, he wrote a satirical novel about Nazism, *Der grüne Stern* (1946). About 1950 he gathered the young poets and painters around him at the Café Raimund.

Weigel speaks whenever he thinks that silence cannot be justified, even at the risk of evoking hostility. He is on hand everywhere. By now it would be impossible to catalogue all the stimuli he has provided—to an author here, a publisher there, to a theater, or to a radio station.

As an essayist, however, Weigel has had an influence far beyond just the immediate. His 1958 book on Austria, *O du mein Österreich*, was a good deal more than an expanded newspaper feature. But the real Weigel, behind his manifold topical masks, appeared in the volume *Flucht vor der Größe* (1960), a collection of essays on Franz Schubert, Ferdinand Raimund, Johann Nestroy, Franz Grillparzer, Adalbert Stifter, and Johann Strauss.

Weigel's deepest love is for the theater. He has written plays (*Barabbas*, 1945; *Der eingebildete Doktor*, among others), adapted, translated (from Molière to Terence Rattigan), and reviewed almost everything that for nearly two decades was to be seen on the Vienna stage. He is as much a part of the Viennese theater of this period as Werner Krauss and Inge Konradi.

It is impossible to say of Weigel that as a writer such and such is his theme and such and such is his style. We can only say that he is important. He represents a type of man whose nonexistence we have to imagine in order to become fully aware of his importance and of the necessity of his being with us.

Works: *Axel an der Himmelstür* (1926; Axel at the Heavenly Portals); *Barrabas und der 50. Geburtstag* (1945; Barrabas and the 50th Birthday); *Das himmlische Leben* (1945; Heavenly Life); *Der grüne Stern* (1946; The Green Star); *Das wissen die Götter* (1947; Only the Gods Would Know); *Hölle oder Fegefeuer* (1948; Hell or Purgatory); *Angelika* (1948); *Die Erde* (1948; The Earth); *Unvollendete Symphonie* (1951; Unfinished Symphony); *Masken, Mimen und Mimosen* (1958; Masks, Mimes, and Mimosas); *O du mein Österreich* (1958; O You My Austria); *Flucht vor der Größe* (1960; Flight from Greatness); *Tausend und eine Première* (1961; A Thousand and One First-Nights); *Lern dieses Volk der Hirten kennen* (1962; Come to Know this Nation of Shepherds); *Versuch über Josef Meinrad* (1962; Essay on Josef Meinrad); *Blödeln für Anfänger* (1963; Talking Nonsense for Beginners); *Attila Hörbiger* (1963); *Tirol für Anfänger* (1964; Tyrol for Beginners); *Pünktlichkeit für Anfänger* (1965; Punctuality for Beginners); *Apropos Musik* (1965); *Das kleine Walzerbuch* (1965; The Little Waltz Book); *Das tausendjährige Kind* (1965; The Millennial Child); *Johann Nestroy* (1967); *Das Buch der Wiener Philharmoniker* (1967; The Book about the Vienna Philharmonic Society); *Karl Kraus, oder Die Macht der Ohnmacht* (1968; Karl Kraus, or The Power of Powerlessness).

Herbert Eisenreich

Josef Weinheber

Born 9 March 1892 in Vienna, the son of a butcher, cattle dealer, and innkeeper. After the early death of his parents and sisters, Josef Weinheber was brought up in an orphanage in Mödling, where he also attended the *Gymnasium*. The first of his three autobiographical novels, *Das Waisenhaus* (1925), deals with his unhappy years at the orphanage. He worked in a butcher's shop, and then from 1911 to 1932 in a post office in Vienna. During this time he also traveled in Italy, France, and Dalmatia. From 1932 until his death, he made his living as a writer. He was also a gifted painter.

Weinheber was almost always poor, in spite of the fact that he was awarded important literary prizes, and, from the early 1930s on, he was known throughout the German-speaking world. In 1927 he converted from Catholicism to Protestantism. For a time he was committed to the National Socialists, who promoted his poetry, but whom he inwardly rejected after 1943. He had a tendency toward pathological depression, which he fought, even as a young man, by drinking. He considered his art as therapy. In 1940 he wrote to a friend, the north-German writer Moritz Jahn: "Of course, being a drinker, I am not at all well. All I try to do with art is to keep a balance, to find some compensation for my unstable, pusillanimous, wretched life." He died from an overdose of medication on 8 April 1945 at his country place Kirchstetten in Lower Austria, where he had lived since 1936.

By 1913 Weinheber had proved himself an original poet. But the influence of Richard Dehmel, Rainer Maria Rilke, Arno Holz, and Christian Morgenstern is still perceptible in his early volumes of poems—*Der einsame Mensch* (1920), *Von beiden Ufern* (1923), *Boot in der Bucht* (1926)—as well as in the early poems first printed in the collected edition of his works (edited by J. Nadler; 5 vols., 1953–56). As he said himself, he "learned German" from Karl Kraus. A trip through Italy and to Paris confirmed his predilection for classical forms, though there always remained the countercurrent of his creative delight in the music of Austrian popular speech. As a poet he wavered between Olympus and Ottakring (a lower-class district of Vienna), between Michelangelo and Nestroy.

It was with the volume of poems *Adel und Untergang* (1934)

that Weinheber first succeeded in the classical style modeled on Hölderlin and Horace. In these poems he combined his artistic creed, "Take sorrow and make a song of it," with his vision of the new man. The collection *Späte Krone* (1936) and especially the volume of chiseled, strict odes *Zwischen Göttern und Dämonen* (1938), followed in 1939 by the intimately and delicately stylized *Kammermusik*, display a perfection of form saturated with lyricism that may well be called unique in modern poetry in German. At the same time, *Wien wörtlich* (1935) and the almanac *O Mensch gib acht* (1937) contains verses of a folk-song nature, written partly in Viennese dialect, deeply naive, yet with a light touch of caprice.

Weinheber's almost superabundant body of works includes hymns and odes, sonnets, refrains and songs that recall Friedrich Rückert in their formal mastery. His poetry possesses a dark, orphic verbal music that, in a mood somewhere between intoxication and melancholy, suggests the struggle with a demon to which the poet finally succumbed.

Works: *Der einsame Mensch* (1920; Lonely Man); *Von beiden Ufern* (1923; From Both Shores); *Das Waisenhaus* (1925; The Orphanage); *Boot in der Bucht* (1926; Boat in the Bay); *Der Nachwuchs* (1927; The Rising Generation); *Adel und Untergang* (1934; Nobility and Decline); *Wien wörtlich* (1935; Vienna Verbatim); *Vereinsamtes Herz* (1935; Lonely Heart); *Im Namen der Kunst* (1936; In the Name of Art); *Späte Krone* (1936; Belated Crown); *O Mensch gib acht* (1937; O Man, Watch Out); *Zwischen Göttern und Dämonen* (1938; Between Gods and Demons); *Kammermusik* (1939; Chamber Music); *Blut und Stahl* (1941; Blood and Steel); *Hier ist das Wort* (1947; Here Is the Word); *Über die Dichtkunst* (1949; About Poetry); *Über alle Maßen aber liebte ich die Kunst* (1952; I Loved Art above All Else); *Briefe an Maria Mahler* (1952; Letters to Maria Mahler); *Sämtliche Werke* (5 vols., 1953–56; Collected Works); *Briefe an Sturm* (1956; Letters to Sturm); *Gedichte, Auswahl* (1968; Selected Poems).

Bibliography: Bergholz, Harry, "The Weinheber Controversy," *German Life and Letters* 3 (1949–50):50–59. Finke, E., *Josef Weinheber: Der Mensch und das Werk*, 1950. Ibel, R., *Mensch der Mitte: George—Carossa—Weinheber*, 1962. Nadler, J., and Weinheber, H., *Josef Weinheber und die Sprache*, 1955. Waldinger, Ernst, "A Propos Josef Weinheber," *Books Abroad* 26 (1952):248–50. Wassermann, Felix M., "Between Gods and Demons: Josef Weinheber, the Man and the Poet," *German Life and Letters* 6 (1953):81–87.

K. H. *Kramberg*

Ernst Weiß

Born 28 August 1882, in Brünn (now Brno, in central Czechoslovakia), the second son of a Jewish cloth merchant. Ernst Weiß's life was that of an extremely gifted person who never reached the height of his powers. Since his father died when Weiß was four, the father-son conflict, a constantly recurring theme in his work, would seem to stem from his frustrated desire to have a father to love and admire, one for whom, however, he would have ambivalent, often hostile feelings. In any event, with Weiß this conflict theme stemmed from different grounds than it did with his friend Franz Kafka, who was almost the same age as he and with whom he had more in common than merely regional origin.

Having completed his medical studies in Prague and in Vienna, where the psychoanalysis of Freud claimed his passionate interest, Weiß practiced for a time as a surgeon. His first full-length literary work, *Die Galeere,* a novel that recounts the life story of a Viennese physicist and radiologist, first appeared in 1913 and was republished in a revised version in 1919. From the medical point of view it is astonishing to note that at that time Weiß had already clearly recognized the harmful effects of repeated exposure to Röntgen rays. He describes these effects exhaustively, right up to the death by cancer of the central character.

Before World War I Weiß contracted tuberculosis and was obliged to give up surgery. He took the position of ship's doctor for a cruise to Asia. His knowledge of the tropics was later to prove decisive for one of his most important novels, *Georg Letham, Arzt und Mörder* (1931). Actually, his own professional experience as a doctor, particularly his experiences as an army doctor in World War I, is the determining factor throughout his work.

The 1920s, in the course of which Weiß moved from Prague to Berlin and later to Munich, were his most productive years; he wrote novels and plays in rapid succession. He was on the threshold of still greater success when, with the advent of Hitler, he was forced to leave Germany. Paris became his refuge, as it did for many others. But when the German troops marched into Paris in 1940, his strength failed him. Finding himself unable to flee further, he took his own life on 14 or 15 June 1940.

All the tensions and contrasts of character portrayed in his ample body of work must have been present in Weiß himself: a cutting analytical acumen and a capacity for warm feelings; anxiety toward life, and at the same time a dominant sensibility toward all living things; on the one hand, an uncanny attraction for misfortune, and on the other, an uncommon capacity for camouflaging the vulnerable ego and identifying with the destinies, as if with roles, of others. Weiß's major works follow in the tradition of the psychological, realistic novel, with expressionistic pathos here and there. The delineation of character and the construction of a convincing plot obviously interested him more than language and unity of form.

Georg Letham, Arzt und Mörder is the story of the transformation of a man's character. A physician and bacteriologist, a man whose calling is meant to be the preservation of life, becomes a destroyer of life and the murderer of his wife owing to a scientific, subtly reasoned orientation toward evil. An icy intellect, avarice, self-revulsion, and disgust for his fellowmen have made him an extreme outsider. This Letham, with his egomanic arrogance and cynical lack of faith, is sentenced for life to a penal colony in the tropics. There, among the outcasts, Letham's character undergoes a purification in the tradition of the classical fables: he stakes his life on seeking a cure for yellow fever and has a decisive part in the discovery that will benefit the human race for all time.

Der arme Verschwender (1936) depicts a doctor's development and career from the end of the 19th century until the end of the 1930s. Behind the individual life story a historical break becomes clearly visible—the collapse of the Austro-Hungarian Empire.

But in regard to the plot, the most unusual and original of all Weiß's novels is the posthumously published *Der Augenzeuge*, which first appeared in 1963 under the title *Ich—der Augenzeuge*. Before his suicide Weiß had sent the manuscript to New York as an intended entry to a proposed competition. For a long time it was believed lost and was only published twenty-three years after submission. The narrator, again a doctor, treats a private first class, one A. H., in a field hospital. He diagnoses A. H.'s case as blindness induced by hysteria rather than that of temporary blindness caused by gas poisoning from which Hitler himself claimed to have suffered. The doctor cures the hysterical man and by so doing frees the subsequent political dynamism of the dictator.

In this last work Weiß finds a term for the overwhelming omnipotence of an impersonal destiny—his main theme—a term he takes up and uses again with the finality of total conviction: "that which crushes." It is exemplified in the feelings of guilt and the desires to escape in all of Weiß's characters. They are condemned to existence and stand accused by the Unknown. In the picture he conveys of the unalterable nature of the decrees of fate, in his highly vulnerable, overwrought sensibility lies Weiß's intellectual kinship with Kafka.

Works: *Die Galeere* (1913; rev., 1919; The Galley); *Der Kampf* (1916; The Struggle; republished under the title *Franziska: Mensch gegen Mensch* [1919; Franzisca: Man against Man]); *Die Herznaht* (1918; The Seam in the Heart); *Tiere in Ketten* (1918; rev., 1922; Animals in Chains); *Das Versöhnungsfest* (1920; The Celebration of Reconciliation); *Stern der Dämonen* (1920; Star of the Demons); *Tanja* (1920); *Nahar* (1922; continuation of *Tiere in Ketten*); *Die Feuerprobe* (1923; rev., 1929; Trial by Fire); *Atua* (1923); *Olympia* (1923); *Die kleine Heilige* (1923; The Little Saint); *Hodin* (1923); *Daniel* (1924); *Der Fall Vukobrankovics* (1924; The Vukobrankovic Case); *Männer in der Nacht* (1925; Men at Night); *Boëtius von Orlamünde* (1928; republished under the title *Der Aristokrat Boëtius von Orlamünde* [1966; The Aristocrat Boëtius of Orlamünde]); *Das Unverlierbare* (1928; What Cannot Be Lost); *Dämonenzug* (1928; The Train of Demons); *Georg Letham, Arzt und Mörder* (1931; George Letham, Physician and Murderer); *Der Gefängnisarzt, oder Die Vaterlosen* (1934; The Prison Doctor, or The Fatherless); *Der Geisterseher* (1934; One Who Sees Ghosts); *Der arme Verschwender* (1936; The Poor Spendthrift); *Der Verführer* (1938; The Seducer); *Ich-Der Augenzeuge* (1963; I—the Eyewitness).

Bibliography: Taylor, Harley U., "Ernst Weiß: Fortune's Stepchild," *West Virginia University Philological Papers* 15 (1966):43–48. Wendler, Wolfgang, "Ernst Weiß," in *Expressionismus als Literatur: Gesammelte Studien*, edited by Wolfgang Rothe, pp. 656–68, 1969. Wondrák, Eduard, *Einiges über den Arzt und Schriftsteller Ernst Weiß mit einer autobiographischen Skizze von 1927 . . . und einer Bibliographie*, 1968.

Dieter Lattmann

Franz Werfel

Franz Werfel, born 10 September 1890, was the son of a prosperous merchant in Prague. While still a student in Prague he became a friend of Max Brod and Franz Kafka. After further studies at Leipzig and Hamburg, he worked for a while in a shipping firm in Hamburg. From 1911 to 1914 he was a reader for the publisher Kurt Wolff of Leipzig and Munich and in 1913 helped to found the literary series *Der jüngste Tag*. During World War I he served in the Austrian army at the eastern front. After the war he settled in Vienna, where he later married Alma Mahler, the widow of composer Gustav Mahler. During the 1920s he traveled in Italy, Egypt, and Palestine. In 1938, after the Anschluß, he was forced to leave Vienna, coming to the United States in 1940. He died on 26 August 1945 in Beverly Hills, California.

Werfel's voluminous literary works comprise short stories, novellas, sketches, poems, essays, lectures, plays, and ten novels plus the unfinished *Die schwarze Messe* and *Cella, oder Die Überwinder*. His writing is closely bound up with the places in which he lived. The majority of his short stories and some of his novels take place in Vienna and Prague. Many of his poems are on themes from the cities and landscapes of his native region. His stay in Turkey led to the novel *Die vierzig Tage des Musa Dagh* (1933). As a result of his travels in Italy, he wrote the poem *Venezianische Melancholien* and the novels *Verdi* (1924), *Die Geschwister von Neapel* (1931), and *Der veruntreute Himmel* (1939), first published under the title *Der gestohlene Himmel*, as well as some short stories.

Werfel's European journeys as a refugee after 1938 may be traced by the settings of the works he conceived during that period. In France he wrote sketches of life in Paris and decided to write the novel *Das Lied von Bernadette* (1941), the action of which takes place in France. Spain is the scene of *Die arge Legende vom gerissenen Galgenstrick* (1948), while America is the recognizable setting for the posthumously published utopian novel *Stern der Ungeborenen* (1946).

Werfel's late work, however, is noticeably marked by a certain loss of a geographical base of reference. In the narrative *Eine blaß-*

blaue Frauenschrift (1941), Vera, a Jewish woman on the point of emigration, has a conversation in which someone says to her that Montevideo is terribly far. To this she asks, "Far from where?" Werfel then added: "This was a reference to a melancholy joke current among the exiles who had lost their geographical center of gravity." The reporter F. W. in *Stern der Ungeborenen* is such a character.

The "astro-mental" world of *Stern der Ungeborenen* is likewise curiously faceless: it has no vegetation to characterize it, no mountains, there is no active means of traversing its space. It is true that the latter peculiarity is supposed to be a mark of astro-mental civilization, the purpose of which is "to abolish the contradiction between man's boundless inner capacity for experience and his earthly and physical limitations." Therefore, "astro-mentalism may be defined as the art of giving body to the infinitely mobile mental images of our psyche and setting them in space and time." But no doubt it was only Werfel's situation as an exile that prompted him to conceive such a "reality." The annexation of what is spatially remote by means of "sharply focused wishes" corresponds exactly to the process by which the exile brings to mind his homeland and in memory walks about the place from which he is barred.

Werfel's work is quite unmistakably characterized by his ties with Austria—not only in the settings of his plots, but also with regard to its characteristic intellectuality—and with his Jewishness. His Jewish conflicts may be reduced to two main strands: namely, Judaism as an historical phenomenon and as a metaphysical problem. The two were inextricably linked in Werfel's mind, as indeed he never isolated human destinies from a metaphysical frame of reference in the shape either of private or of historical and political events. Werfel was particularly concerned with the relationship between Judaism and Christianity. Although he repeatedly declared himself a Jew, Christian thought is traceable throughout his work. Along with the Old Testament prophets we find the 19th-century Saint Bernadette among the characters of his books, while piety is seen as an essential element of the human soul that has nothing to do with organized religion.

Nevertheless, Werfel saw in the special position of Israel its specific religious role. In his novel *Die wahre Geschichte vom wiederhergestellten Kreuz* (1942; revision of the ninth chapter of the unfinished *Cella, oder Die Überwinder*), he refers expressly to Romans 11:25 when he writes: "Obduracy has gripped part of Israel until the full number of heathens has come in." The rabbi interprets this passage as follows:

"And then, what would happen if all the Jews in the world were baptized? Israel would disappear. And with it the only real witness to God's revelation would vanish from the world. The holy scriptures, which, through our existence, are a documented truth, would become a vapid, impotent legend like any of the Greek myths. Does the Church not see this danger? We belong together, Reverend, but we are not one. In the Epistle to the Romans it is written that the communion of Christ is based on Judaism. I am convinced that, as long as the Church exists, Israel will exist, but also that the Church must fall if Israel falls."

Also in *Stern der Ungeborenen* the "Jew of the Age" believes, in line with divine ordainment, that he is linked in an indissoluble union with Christianity. Werfel's attitude seems to have been like that of his characters. It may be for that reason that he never converted to the Christian faith.

Werfel was deeply interested in the forces of contemporary change—in technology, psychology, and social problems—as well as in the relation of the individual to the state, but he remained all his life an individualist. All the collectivist manifestations of the 20th century were suspect to him. In his writings he dwelled on human communities, for example, on family life.

Werfel's particular affection went out to those who serve, who sacrifice themselves. In sacrifice and self-abandonment man's value as a person remains inviolate. Traditional, humanistic ideas of self-sacrifice are linked by Werfel with religious orientation. Since one's metaphysical destiny is fixed, one's integrity is inalienable.

Werfel saw the development of the cosmos as a whole from the same point of view. He was, above all, suspicious of progress. In his last novel, *Stern der Ungeborenen*, he shows that astro-mental civilization cannot solve man's existential problems. Even infinitely refined civilization contains the seeds of revolution, decline, destruction, internal and external. In *Stern der Ungeborenen* the archbishop makes this crucial observation: "The other half of truth is very simple, my son: we not only depart from God through time, but we also approach God through time, inasmuch as we move away from the beginning of all things and toward the end of all things."

Werfel first gained recognition as a lyric poet. His early volumes, particularly those of poems up to 1920, were among the most important products of expressionism. Even the titles of his best-known books of poetry, *Der Weltfreund* (1911), *Wir sind* (1913), and *Einander* (1915), express his fraternal affection for others, his sympathy with men and all living things, his universal love that, despite its awareness of transience, again and again soars up to the Creator in intoxicated rejoicing.

While many of Werfel's poems are in conventional form (he sometimes used the simple quatrains of folk song), there are others that tear apart syntax with their ecstatic, hymnlike outbursts, placing all the emphasis on a few words and sacrificing the clarity of the image to associations loaded with emotion. An example is the poem *Lächeln Atmen Schreiten,* which is one of the most effective that young Werfel wrote.

The aim of the early poems is not to provide a meditative summary or to make a statement, but to call out a proclamation. Even though no actual "character" poems are to be found in Werfel's poetry, it is clear that there is an intention of dialogue. In addressing himself, the poet appeals at the same time to the reader or listener and thus, with persuasive and dynamic purpose, continually addresses an imaginary interlocutor.

It is not surprising therefore that Werfel wrote such effective stage works as *Euripides: Die Troerinnen* (1915); an adaptation of Euripides's *Trojan Women*), *Spiegelmensch* (1920), *Juarez und Maximilian* (1924), *Paulus unter den Juden* (1926), and *Jacobowsky und der Oberst* (1944). *Das Reich Gottes in Böhmen* (1930) ranks with Franz Grillparzer's *Ein Bruderzwist in Habsburg* and Hugo von Hofmannsthal's *Der Turm* as one of the great Austrian historical dramas on the problem of power and the vanity of action.

In his early years Werfel wrote prose pieces and sketches, but it was not until about 1926 that he began to publish technically developed stories and novels. In these he usually followed traditional narrative methods—a continuous line of action, told chronologically in the first or third person, often enclosed within a framework. In his middle and later periods, a metaphysical interpretation of the characters replaced the psychological approach that had been frequent in his early work. Characteristic of his style are a wealth of imagery and a predilection for symbolic allusions in which the setting is brought into close connection with the action.

Werfel's criticism of himself was often incorporated in the fictitious character of a literary man to whom he attributed shortcomings for which he himself had been reproached—intellectual trifling, an undisciplined tendency to write too much, carelessness in expression, a liking for baroque exaggeration and operatic finales.

Works: *Der Weltfreund* (1911; The Philanthropist); *Die Versuchung* (1913; Temptation); *Wir sind* (1913; We Are); *Einander* (1915; Together); *Euripides: Die Troerinnen* (1915; Euripides: The Trojan Women, adaptation); *Gesänge aus den drei Reichen* (1917; Songs from the Three Realms); *Der Gerichtstag* (1919; The Day of Judgment); *Die Mittagsgöttin* (1919; The Noon Goddess); *Der Besuch aus dem Elysium* (1920; The Visit from Elysium); *Nicht der Mörder, der Ermordete ist schuldig* (1920; Eng. tr., Not the Murderer, 1937); *Spielhof* (1920; Play Ground); *Spiegelmensch* (1920; Eng. tr., Mirror Man, n.d.); *Bocksgesang* (1921; Eng. tr., Goat Song, 1926); *Schweiger* (1922; Eng. tr., 1926); *Arien* (1922; Arias); *Beschwörungen* (1923; Incantations); *Verdi* (1924; Eng. tr., Verdi, a Novel of the Opera, 1947); *Juarez und Maximilian* (1924; Eng. tr., 1926); *Paulus unter den Juden* (1926; Eng. tr., Paul Among the Jews, 1928); *Gesammelte Gedichte* (1927; Collected Poems); *Der Snobismus als geistige Weltmacht* (1927; Snobism as a Spiritual World Power); *Der Tod des Kleinbürgers* (1927; Eng. tr., The Man Who Conquered Death, 1927); *Geheimnis eines Menschen* (1927; Eng. tr., Saverio's Secret, 1937); *Gesammelte Werke* (8 vols., 1927 ff; Collected Works); *Der Abituriententag* (1928; Eng. tr., Class Reunion, 1929); *Barbara, oder die Frömmigkeit* (1929; Eng. tr., The Pure in Heart, 1931); *Dramatische Dichtungen* (1929; Dramatic Writings); *Das Reich Gottes in Böhmen* (1930; God's Kingdom of Bohemia); *Kleine Verhältnisse* (1931; Eng. tr., Poor People, 1937); *Die Geschwister von Neapel* (1931); Eng. tr., The Pascarella Family, 1932); *Die Kämpfe der Schwachen* (1933; The Struggles of the Weak); *Die vierzig Tage des Musa Dagh* (1933; Eng. tr., The Forty Days of Musa Dagh, 1934); *Schlaf und Erwachen* (1935; Sleep and Awakening); *Der Weg der Verheißung* (1935; Eng. tr., Eternal Road, 1936); *Höret die Stimme* (1937; republished as *Jeremias*, 1956; Eng. tr., Hearken unto the Voice, 1938); *Von der reinsten Glückseligkeit des Menschen* (1938; On the Purest Happiness of Man); *Gedichte aus dreißig Jahren* (1939; Poems of Thirty Years); *Der veruntreute Himmel* (1939; Eng. tr., Embezzled Heaven, 1940); *Das Lied von Bernadette* (1941; Eng. tr., Song of Bernadette, 1942); *Eine blaßblaue Frauenschrift* (1941; Pale-Blue Handwriting of a Woman); *Zwischen Gestern und Morgen* (1942; Between Yesterday and Tomorrow); *Die wahre Geschichte vom wiederhergestellten Kreuz* (1942; The True Story of the Restored Cross); *Jacobowsky und der Oberst* (1944; Jacobowsky and the Colonel); *Gedichte aus den Jahren 1908–1945* (1945; Eng. tr., Poems from the Years 1908–1945, 1945); *Zwischen Oben und Unten* (1946; Eng. tr., Between Heaven and Earth, 1944); *Stern der Ungeborenen* (1946; Eng. tr., Star of the Unborn, 1946); *Die arge Legende vom gerissenen Galgenstrick* (1948; The Evil Legend of a Cunning Good-for-Nothing); *Erzählungen aus zwei Welten* (3 vols., 1948, 1952, 1954; Tales from Two Worlds); *Gesammelte Werke* (13 vols., 1948 ff.; Collected Works); *Die Dramen* (2 vols., 1959; The Dramas); *Das lyrische Werk Franz Werfels* (1967; The Lyrical Work of Franz Werfel).

English translations in collections: Twilight of the World. Poor People. Class Reunion. Saverio's Secret. The Staircase. The Man Who Con-

quered Death. The House of Mourning. Not the Murderer (1937); *Poems by Franz Werfel* (1947).

Bibliography: Blumenthal, W., "Sin and Salvation in the Works of Franz Werfel," *Dissertation Abstracts* 18 (1968):2674A. Foltin, Lore B., *Franz Werfel*, 1960; and "The Franz Werfel Archives in Los Angeles," *German Quarterly* 39 (1966):55–61. Fox, W. H., "Franz Werfel," in *German Men of Letters*, edited by A. Natan, vol. 3, pp. 107–25, 1964. Grenzmann, Wilhelm, *Dichtung und Glaube*, 1950. Klarmann, Adolf D., "Das Weltbild Franz Werfels," in *Wissenschaft und Weltbild*, 1954. Lea, H. A., "Prodigal Sons in Werfel's Fiction," *Germanic Review* 40 (1965): 41–54. Puttkamer, A. von., *Franz Werfel*, 1952. Zahn, L., *Franz Werfel*, 1966.

Anneliese Kuchinke-Bach

Martina Wied

Martina Wied (Alexandrine Martina Augusta Weisl, née Schnabel) was born on 10 December 1882 in Vienna, the daughter of a lawyer. In her parents' home she came into contact with literature at an early age. She studied German philology, philosophy, history, and the history of art, and widened her knowledge in the course of visits to Poland, France, England, and Italy. In 1910 she married the manufacturer Sigmund Weisl. After his death in 1930, she was to devote herself entirely to her work. In 1924, together with Robert Musil, Richard Billinger, and Otto Stoessl, she was awarded the Writers' Prize of the City of Vienna. She contributed to many periodicals, including *Der Brenner* (beginning in 1913). In 1938 she emigrated to Great Britain and subsequently taught for some years in Scotland, where she wrote her best-known works. In 1947 she returned to Austria. She died in Vienna on 25 January 1957.

Martina Wied first came to public attention with the neoromantic, impressionist poems of *Bewegung* (1919). In 1952 she collected her life's work as a poet (1912–52) in the volume *Brücken ins Sichtbare*. Her plays *Spuk* (written, 1922), *Der Gast* (written, 1923), and *Der Spielberg* (written, 1924) have not yet been published. At an early stage in her career she was already writing essays and critical articles on literature.

Martina Wied's strongest gifts lay in the narrative genres, on which she concentrated almost exclusively after 1924. Her basic concern—namely, how to give meaning to a life that in the world's confusion cannot find its way to divine mercy—was first apparent in her novel *Das Asyl zum obdachlosen Geist* (written, 1925–26; published in *Wiener Zeitung*, 1934; first published independently under the title *Kellingrath*, 1950). The novel *Rauch über Sankt Florian, oder Die Welt der Mißverständnisse* (1949) is a monument to Paul Ernst. She saw Ernst as a representative of pure but powerless intellect.

After World War II, Martina Wied published a number of short stories—*Das Einhorn* (1948), *Das Krähennest* (1951), *Der Ehering* (1954), and *Das unvollendete Abenteuer* (1955)—and the novel *Die Geschichte des reichen Jünglings* (1952), which was begun in Zakopane in 1928 and finished in Glasgow in 1943. The novel depicts the life of a young Polish manufacturer's son, Adam Leontjew, amid the upper-middle class, with its self-satisfaction, satiety, and lack of instinctive feelings. Martina Wied's prose work is an attempt to show the threat to the individual in the chaos of modern times. But her extremely alert mind and acute critical understanding are more evident than human sympathy and religious feeling. Her work has an easy, lively style that slips into reportage from time to time.

Works: *Bewegung* (1919; Movement); *Rauch über Sankt Florian, oder Die Welt der Mißverständnisse* (1936; Smoke over Saint Florian, or the World of Misunderstandings); *Das Einhorn* (1948; The Unicorn); *Kellingrath* (1950); *Das Krähennest* (1951; The Rookery); *Jakobäa von Bayern, ihr Leben und ihre Welt 1401–1436* (1951; Jakobäa of Bavaria, Her Life and Her World 1401–1436); *Die Geschichte des reichen Jünglings* (1952; The Story of the Rich Youth); *Brücken ins Sichtbare* (1952; Bridges into the Visible World); *Nikodemus* (1952); *Das fremde Haus* (1953; The Strange House); *Der Ehering* (1954; The Wedding Ring); *Das unvollendete Abenteuer* (1955; The Unfinished Adventure).

Bibliography: Berry, Jesse L., "Martina Wied: Austrian Novelist 1882–1957," *Dissertation Abstracts* 27 (1967):3446A (Vanderbilt). Bithell, Jethro, *Modern German Literature 1880–1950*, pp. 513–15, 1959. Winter, Hanns, "Martina Wied," *Wort in der Zeit* 3, no. 5 (1957):1–5.

Wolfram Mauser

Anton Wildgans

Born 14 April 1881 in Vienna. At the urging of his family with its legal tradition, Anton Wildgans studied law and for two years worked as a trial judge. The responsibility this involved and the torments of a pretrial hearing provided the subject matter of his first attempt at drama, *In Ewigkeit, Amen* (1913). In 1912 Wildgans resigned from a post that was uncongenial to him and made his living as a writer. He was director of the Vienna Burgtheater from 1921 to 1923 and again from 1930 to 1931. He died in Vienna on 3 May 1932. After his death a number of hitherto unknown manuscripts of complete novels and plays were brought to light.

During his lifetime Wildgans's significance as a writer was scarcely disputed. He stood between two eras, and his work displayed the most diverse stylistic trends of the 19th and 20th centuries. After his early poems, which were influenced by Hugo von Hofmannsthal and Rainer Maria Rilke, his *Die Sonette an Ead* (1913) contained lyrics of graphic sensuousness and emotionally inspired imagery. He was most gifted as a poet, but he skillfully acquired the craftsmanlike traditions of the Austrian theater, finding inspiration in the most varied subject matter. His treatment of the question of sexual morality in the play *Liebe* (1916) owes something to Frank Wedekind, while the stylistic means by which Wildgans implies that a young married couple has already used up its portion of sensual happiness recalls Arthur Schnitzler.

The tragedy *Armut* (1914), which uses the surroundings of the poor as its setting, continues to show the influence of naturalism, though the expressionist style becomes apparent in, for instance, the transitions from prose to verse or in the poetic outburst at the father's death. The final act of *Dies irae* (1918), the introduction and conclusion of which are in verse, makes clear the social indictment. The suicide of the son, who fails in life and love, is interpreted as the tragedy of the "unwanted" child. Contrary to other expressionist dramas that are concerned with the conflict between the generations, *Dies irae* condemns the father not as educator but as progenitor.

Wildgans combined his feeling for tradition with his open-mindedness toward modernity in a most convincing manner in the epic *Kirbisch, oder Der Gendarm, die Schande und das Glück* (1927), which is composed in hexameters. This satirical, humorous poem deals with the weaknesses of the age, with the changes brought about in Austria by World War I, and with the belief in a better future. The village idyll expands and becomes a symbol of the way of the world, in which the naturalistic depiction of everyday life is enveloped in Wildgans's religious faith.

Works: *Vom Wege* (1903; Off the Way); *Herbstfrühling* (1909; Autumnal Spring); *Und hättet der Liebe nicht* (1911; bilingual edition published in Vienna, And Have Not Charity, 1965); *Die Sonette an Ead* (1913; Sonnets for Ead); *In Ewigkeit, Amen* (1913; Forever and Ever, Amen); *Armut* (1914; Poverty); *Österreichische Gedichte* (1915; Austrian Poems); *Liebe* (1916; Love); *Dreißig Gedichte* (1916; Thirty Poems); *Mittag* (1917; High Noon); *Dies irae* (1918); *Kain* (1920); *Die bürgerlichen Dramen* (3 vols., 1920; The Middle-Class Dramas); *Die sämtlichen Gedichte* (3 vols., 1923; The Complete Poems); *Sonette aus dem Italienischen* (1924; Sonnets from the Italian); *Wiener Gedichte* (1926; Vienna Poems); *Kirbisch, oder Der Gendarm, die Schande und das Glück* (1927; Kirbisch, or The Gendarme, Disgrace, and Good Luck); *Musik der Kindheit* (1928; Music of Childhood); *Gedichte um Pan* (1928; Poems about Pan); *Buch der Gedichte* (1929; Book of Poems); *Rede über Österreich* (1930; Speech on Austria); *Gesammelte Werke* (5 vols., 1930; Collected Works); *Die Berufung* (1932; The Calling); *An einen Freund* (letters to F. Winterholler, 1932; To a Friend); *Ich beichte und bekenne* (1933; I Confess and Admit); *Späte Ernte* (1933; Late Harvest); *Briefwechsel mit Hofmannsthal* (1935; Correspondence with Hofmannsthal); *Briefe* (ed. L. Wildgans, 1937; Letters); *Ein Leben in Briefen* (1937; A Life in Letters); *Sämtliche Werke* (7 vols., 1948; Complete Works).

Bibliography: Breuer, Robert, "An Austrian Poet's Literary Heritage," *Books Abroad* 24 (1950):16–18. Kallos, Alexander, "The Social Problem in the Work of Anton Wildgans," *Dissertation Abstracts* 16 (1956):1688 (Penn.). Pablé, Elisabeth, "Anton Wildgans und das Wiener Theater," in *Jahrbuch der Gesellschaft für Wiener Theaterforschung*, pp. 3–68, 1954–55 (published, 1958). Wildgans, Lilly, "Anton Wildgans als Goetheverehrer," *Chronik Wiener Goetheverein* 62 (1958):1–10. Wurm, Ernst, "Anton Wildgans," *Wort in der Zeit* 4, no. 10 (1958):1–4.

Lutz Weltmann

Ludwig Wittgenstein

Born 26 April 1889 in Vienna. Between the years 1907 and 1911 Wittgenstein's interests shifted from applied mathematics to pure mathematics, and finally to the philosophical foundation of mathematics. After initial studies at the Berlin-Charlottenburg School of Engineering and after aeronautical experiments carried out chiefly at Manchester University, Wittgenstein began studies at Cambridge in the fall of 1911. His relations with Bertrand Russell, the well-known philosopher of mathematical logic, were those of a friendship between equals. The philosophers Alfred North Whitehead and George Edward Moore, as well as the economist John Maynard Keynes, likewise accepted the student as their intellectual peer.

World War I, in which Wittgenstein fought as an officer in the Austrian army, interrupted this philosophical communion, but not Wittgenstein's work on logic. By 1918 he had completed the manuscript of the *Tractatus logico-philosophicus* (published in German, 1921, in Wilhelm Ostwald's *Annalen der Naturphilosophie*; published in a bilingual German-English edition, with an introduction by Bertrand Russell, 1922, in London). While the *Tractatus logico-philosophicus* began to exercise its influence on the public, Wittgenstein withdrew from it, perhaps under the impact of the war and imprisonment, but certainly under the influence of Lev Tolstoi's writing. He gave away the fortune he inherited, became an elementary-school teacher, helped monks to tend their gardens. In these years he did, however, make the acquaintance of the philosopher Moritz Schlick, who gained recognition for Wittgenstein among the Vienna circle of neopositivists.

Ten years after World War I, in 1929, Wittgensten finally returned to Cambridge, first as a research student. In 1930 he became a fellow of Trinity College and in 1939 succeeded Moore as the professor of philosophy. His academic activity was interrupted by World War II, during which he worked as a hospital orderly, siding with England. In 1947 he gave up teaching altogether in order to devote himself entirely to his *Philosophische Untersuchungen* (published posthumously in a bilingual edition, 1953, in Oxford; also in separate German and English editions), on which he had been working since the

1930s despite Russell's growing disapproval and ultimate aversion. Wittgenstein died of cancer on 29 April 1951.

A discussion of Wittgenstein's philosophy centers mainly on the alleged conflict between *Philosophische Untersuchungen* and *Tractatus logico-philosophicus*. The seven principal propositions of *Tractatus logico-philosophicus*, together with the minor propositions associated with them by decimal classification, outline a theory of how the world is depicted by language, how facts are expressed in statements. Accordingly, the first four principal propositions read: (1) "The world is all that is the case"; (2) "What is the case—a fact—is the existence of states of affairs"; (3) "A logical picture of facts is a thought"; (4) "A thought is a proposition with a sense." This actually adds up to work of epistemology in the grand style, but Wittgenstein presents it in large part as contribution to the solution of special questions of logic such as had arisen since Russell's *Principia Mathematica*.

In the *Tractatus logico-philosophicus*, words such as "proposition" or "meaningful" are used as terms in mathematical logic, which Wittgenstein himself did much to advance (*e.g.*, by his truth functions). "Language" always means solely and exclusively the language of logic, which can, at will, be formulated in symbols and is the only language that counts. This position seems reversed in the *Philosophische Untersuchungen*, in which Wittgenstein speaks of many languages, that is, of the so-called language games: "Giving orders, forming and testing a hypothesis, making up a story, guessing riddles, asking, thanking, cursing, greeting, praying"; the logic appears to be no longer mathematical but hermeneutical like that of Hans Lipp, or it sometimes seems to come close to Karl Kraus's critique of language. Wittgenstein's literary and philosophical style also seems to have undergone some change between the two books. He no longer claims to have solved the problems "in essentials" and "definitively." The apodictic assertion has given way to perpetually renewed questions.

The diaries related to the *Tractatus logico-philosophicus* (for the years 1914–16; published in *Wittgenstein's Schriften*, 1960), show, however, that Wittgenstein did not alter his line of thought. The *Tractatus logico-philosophicus* ventures some temporary answers to questions that preoccupied its author both before and after writing it. Bertrand Russell's division of Wittgenstein's work into Wittgenstein I and Wittgenstein II—with mathematical logic associated with the early Wittgenstein, and the (largely Anglo-Saxon) critique of language with the late Wittgenstein—may well turn out to be a philosophical error. Certain key sentences in both works prove that the *Philo-*

sophische Untersuchungen has certainly not given up the theory of representation of the *Tractatus logico-philosophicus*. The language of logic still depicts the world, but with *Philosophische Untersuchungen* it now depicts the language games in addition.

Works: *Tractatus logico-philosophicus* (1921; German-English bilingual edition, 1922); *Philosophische Untersuchungen* (1953; Eng. tr., Philosophical Investigations, 1953; also in a bilingual edition, 1953); *The Blue and Brown Books* (British, 1958; German, Blau-Buch/Braun-Buch/Zettel, 1969; Am. tr., Preliminary Studies for the Philosophical Investigations, 1970); *Bemerkungen über die Grundlagen der Mathematik* (1958; Eng. tr., Remarks on the Foundations of Mathematics, 1964); *Tagebücher 1914–1916* (1960; Eng. tr., Notebooks 1914–1916, 1961); *Schriften* (3 vols., 1960; Writings); *Philosophische Bemerkungen* (1964; Philosophical Remarks); *Schriften zu philosophischen Bemerkungen* (1964; Writings on Philosophical Remarks); *Wittgenstein und der Wiener Kreis* (as recorded by R. Waismann, 1967; Wittgenstein and the Vienna Circle); *Philosophische Grammatik* (1970; Philosophical Grammar).

Bibliography: Black, M., *A Companion to Wittgenstein's "Tractatus,"* 1964. Morrison, J. C., *Meaning and Truth in Wittgenstein's "Tractatus,"* 1968. Mundle, C. W. K., *A Critique of Linguistic Philosophy*, 1970. Patzig, G., *Sprache und Logik*, 1970. Rochelt, H., "Das Creditiv der Sprache: Von der Philologie J. G. Hamanns und Ludwig Wittgensteins," *Literatur und Kritik* 4 (1969); 169–76. Janik, Allan, and Toulmin, Stephen, *Wittgenstein's Vienna*, 1973.

Joachim Schickel

Herbert Zand

Born 14 November 1923 in Knoppen near Bad Aussee (in the province Styria); died 14 July 1970 in Vienna. Herbert Zand spent his childhood on his father's small farm. During World War II he was severely wounded while serving on the eastern front. He lived alternately in Vienna and Knoppen, making a living as a writer and translator. He was also active in the Austrian Society of Literature. Zand's first novel, *Die Sonnenstadt*, appeared in 1947. In creatively expressing the reflection and language of nature—the nature that he also makes an effort to explore in his poems—it is a precursor of his later novels.

It was not until 1953, in *Letzte Ausfahrt*, the novel of "the encircled," that Zand achieved a narrative style of his own. The novel is the record of a personal war experience at the front and shows how, in the machinery of total war, fighting degenerates into senseless destruction. The story line recounts the events of the big battle that threatens to trap the inhabitants and defending troops of an eastern German town. The circumstances symbolize the ego encased in fear, in greed for power, and in the desperate will to live, struggling hopelessly until it must capitulate to the encircling superior power of death. Zand took a number of sharply outlined scenes from reality, and these not only illustrate but also interpret the war by their mood. In this way he arrived at a spiritualized, multilevel realism. Nature, people, things, conversations, and thoughts very consciously point to the theme of encirclement, and the image of the circle in the first chapter unfolds into an apocalyptic dance of death in the last chapter.

The feeling that there is no way out, whether this is really so or only seemingly so, dominates Zand's later novels as well. In *Der Weg nach Hassi el emel* (1956) a pilot who has crashed escapes the destructive power of the desert by a superhuman strength of will. The record of the stream of consciousness disrupts the time and space of an otherwise monotonous plot. The characters of the novel *Erben des Feuers* (1961), which is set in Vienna, are bound by tradition and bourgeois convention. People who are unable to give up the lifestyle of the Austro-Hungarian monarchy are at variance with a society that, for the sake of money and ambition, has sacrificed all sense of the deeper significance of life. The young generation, which can find support neither in honorable tradition nor in an honorless society, is melted down in a daimonic fire (as is the character Manfred Galland) or else recast in it (as is Sascha Mallovan), and thus prepared for a new beginning.

Works: *Die Sonnenstadt* (1947; Sun-City); *Letzte Ausfahrt* (1953; Eng. tr., The Last Sortie, 1955); *Die Glaskugel* (1953; The Glass Sphere); *Weg nach Hassi el emel* (1956; Eng. tr., The Well of Hope, 1957); *Erben des Feuers* (1961; Heirs to the Fire); *Kerne des paradiesischen Apfels* (1971; Pits from the Apple of Eden).

Bibliography: Bithell, Jethro, *Modern German Literature 1880–1950*, pp. 533–35, 1959. Holzinger, Alfred, Introduction to *Der Weg nach Hassi el emel*, 1965.

Alfred Doppler

Stefan Zweig

Stefan Zweig was born on 28 November 1881 in Vienna, into an Austrian Jewish, affluent upper-middle-class family. He studied philosophy, German, and Romance languages and literatures in Berlin and Vienna, receiving his Ph.D. Traveled all around the world. Early successes as a poet and essayist. Was a bibliophile, owner of an internationally famous collection of autographs and manuscripts, which was confiscated and sold for much less than its worth by the Nazis. As a confirmed European, spent the end of World War I in Switzerland, working for world peace. Friendship with Romain Rolland. After 1919 lived in Salzburg. From 1934 on, Zweig maintained a second residence in England. He emigrated to England in 1939, then to New York in 1940, and eventually to Brazil in 1941. During the last years of his life, Zweig suffered from melancholia, which he attributed partly to the collapse of his humanitarian ideals in Europe and partly to personal emotional crisis. On 23 February 1942, he and his second wife committed suicide in Petropolis near Rio de Janeiro.

When still a schoolboy, Zweig's delight in toying with language led him to discern what sort of life would suit him. His first lyric poems, *Silberne Saiten* (1901) and *Die frühen Kränze* (1906), testify to the influence of Hugo von Hofmannsthal and of the new romantic school, of French symbolism, and of the Viennese variant of impressionist poetry—a high-strung, accomplished art. Zweig translated works of Paul Verlaine, Charles Baudelaire, and all the works of his friend Émile Verhaeren. Under the impact of Freudian psychology, he frequently explored, in his short stories, the labyrinths and points of crisis of the soul. This applies especially to the short-story collections *Erstes Erlebnis* (1911), *Amok* (1922), and *Verwirrung der Gefühle* (1927), but just as much to his last complete prose work, the accomplished *Schachnovelle* (1942; film, 1960). Decisions of dramatic world import are recalled in the "historical miniatures" of *Sternstunden der Menschheit* (1927; enlarged editions, 1936, 1943).

Zweig's famous biographies of writers were brought together and republished in 1935 under the title *Baumeister der Welt*. This book contains three earlier, separate volumes: *Drei Meister* (1920), treating the lives of Balzac, Charles Dickens, and Fiodor Dostoyevski;

Der Kampf mit dem Dämon (1925), about Friedrich Hölderlin, Heinrich von Kleist, and Friedrich Nietzsche; and *Drei Dichter ihres Lebens* (1928), about Casanova, Stendhal, and Lev Tolstoi. His humanist and pacifist convictions found indirect expression in *Triumph und Tragik des Erasmus von Rotterdam* (1934).

Of Zweig's works for the stage, only two won theatrical success: his libretto for Richard Strauss's opera *Die schweigsame Frau* (1935) and his free adaptation of Ben Jonson's *Volpone* (1925). His autobiography *Die Welt von gestern* (1944; first published in English, *The World of Yesterday*, 1943) reflects the dying glory of a Europe of the past. Zweig's sensitive analyses of the creative process, his gripping style, and, above all, his intelligent efforts as a mediator among nations have won him a place in European literature that promises to be something more than the in part fashionable success in smart society that he enjoyed in his lifetime.

Works: *Silberne Saiten* (1901; Silver Strings); *Die Liebe der Erika Ewald* (1904; The Love of Erika Ewald); *Verlaine* (1905); *Die frühen Kränze* (1906; Early Wreaths); *Tersites* (1907); *Verhaeren* (1910); *Erstes Erlebnis* (1911; First Experience); *Das Haus am Meer* (1912; The House at the Sea); *Der verandelte Komödiant* (1913; The Transformed Comedian); *Jeremias* (1917); *Fahrten* (1919; Travels); *Legende eines Lebens* (1919; Legend of a Life); *Drei Meister: Balzac, Dickens, Dostojevskij* (1920; Three Masters); *Der Zwang* (1920; Coercion); *Angst* (1920; Fear); *Marceline Desbordes-Valmore* (1920); *Romain Rolland* (1921); *Amok* (1922; Eng. tr., 1931); *Die Augen des ewigen Bruders* (1922; The Eyes of the Eternal Brother); *Frans Masereel* (1923); *Die gesammelten Gedichte* (1924; Collected Poems); *Der Kampf mit dem Dämon: Hölderlin, Kleist, Nietzsche* (1925; Battle with the Demon); *Volpone* (1925; Eng. tr., 1957; based on Ben Jonson's comedy); *Der Flüchtling* (1927; The Fugitive); *Die Flucht zu Gott* (1927; Flight to God); *Verwirrung der Gefühle* (1927; Eng. tr., Conflicts, 1928); *Abschied von Rilke* (1927; Farewell to Rilke); *Sternstunden der Menschheit* (1927; enlarged, 1936, 1943; Eng. tr., Tide of Fortune, 1955); *Drei Dichter ihres Lebens: Casanova, Stendhal, Tolstoi* (1928; Eng. tr., Adepts in Self-Portraiture, 1952); *Quiproquo* (1928); *Kleine Chronik* (1929; Little Chronicle); *Das Lamm der Armen* (1929; The Lamb of the Poor); *Joseph Fouché* (1929; Eng. tr., 1948); *Die Heilung durch den Geist* (1931; Eng. tr., Mental Healers, 1932); *Marie Antoinette* (1932; Eng. tr., 1952); *Triumph und Tragik des Erasmus von Rotterdam* (1934; Eng. tr., Right to Heresy, 1951); *Die schweigsame Frau* (libretto, 1935; Silent Woman); *Maria Stuart* (1935; Eng. tr., Queen of Scots, 1950); *Baumeister der Welt* (1936; Builders of the World; includes *Drei Meister*, *Der Kampf mit dem Dämon*, and *Drei Dichter ihres Lebens*); *Castellio gegen Calvin* (1936); *Arturo Toscanini* (1936); *Gesammelte Erzählungen*

(2 vols., 1936; Collected Tales); *Begegnungen mit Menschen, Büchern, Städten* (1937; Meetings with People, Books, Cities); *Der begrabene Leuchter* (1937; Eng. tr., Buried Candelabra, 1944); *Kaleidoskop* (1938; Eng. tr., Kaleidoscope, Vol. I, 1949; Vol. II, 1951); *Magellan* (1938); *Ungeduld des Herzens* (1938; Eng. tr., Beware of Pity, 1953); *Brasilien, ein Land der Zukunft* (1941; Brazil, Land of Future); *Schachnovelle* (1942; Eng. tr., Royal Game, 1945); *Amerigo: Die Geschichte eines historischen Irrtums* (1944; Eng. tr., Amerigo, 1942); *Die Welt von Gestern* (1944; Eng. tr., The World of Yesterday, 1943); *Zeit und Welt: Aufsätze und Vorträge, 1904–1940* (1943; Time and World: Essays and Lectures); *Legenden* (1945; Eng. tr., Stories and Legends, 1955); *Balzac* (1946; Eng. tr., 1946); *Briefwechsel 1912–1942: Stefan Zweig–Friederike Zweig* (1957; Eng. tr., Stefan Zweig and Friederike Zweig: Their Correspondence 1912–1942, 1954); *Briefwechsel Richard Strauss–Stefan Zweig* (1957; Correspondence between Richard Strauss and Stefan Zweig); *Europäisches Erbe* (1960; European Heritage); *Gesammelte Werke* (12 vols., 1960; Collected Works); *Die Dramen* (1964; The Dramas); *Unbekannte Briefe aus der Emigration an eine Freundin* (1964; Unknown Letters to a Friend from the Emigration).

English translations in collections: Letter from an Unknown Woman (includes *Royal Game, Amok, Letter from an Unknown Woman*, 1945).

Bibliography: Arens, Hans, *Stefan Zweig*, 1949. Dumont, R., *Stefan Zweig et la France*, 1967. Klawiter, R. J., *Stefan Zweig: A Bibliography*, 1965. Lucas, W. I., "Stefan Zweig," in *German Men of Letters*, edited by A. Natan, vol. 2, pp. 227–48, 1963. Zohn, Harry, ed., *Stefan Zweigs Freundeskreis*, 1953. Zohn, Harry, "Jewish Themes in Stefan Zweig," *Journal of the International Arthur Schnitzler Research Association* 6, no. 2 (1967): 32–38. Zweig, F., *Stefan Zweig*, 1948.

K. H. Kramberg

Index

Achleitner, Friedrich, 7
Aichinger, Ilse, **3–4**
Aktion, Die (periodical), 80
Albertina Museum (Vienna), 230
Alker, Ernst (contributor), 192–93
Altenberg, Peter, **5–6**
Andreas-Salomé, Lou, 209, 210, 211
Antschel, Paul. *See* Celan, Paul
Artmann, Hans Carl, **7–9**
Auernheimer, Raoul, **10–13**
Austrian literature, xiii–xvi
   baroque elements in, 8, 20, 23, 72–73, 109, 121, 128, 205–206
   "black" romanticism and, 183
   censorship of, 167, 194–95
   dialect poetry in, 7–8
   expressionism and, 59, 105, 176, 213, 275, 281
   fantastic prose and, 183
   narrative tradition and, 187–88
   naturalism and, 72
   novel and, 230
   novella and, 78–79, 249
   parody and, 199
   poetic realism and, 249
   "Real-Idealismus" and, 76
   themes in, 37, 103, 108, 161, 179, 227, 230–31, 235, 244
Austrian parliament, members of, 97, 227

Bachmann, Ingeborg, **14–17**
Bahr, Hermann, 10, **18–22**
baroque elements, in literature, 8, 20, 23, 72–73, 109, 121, 128, 205–206
Basil, Otto (quoted), xiii
Baudelaire, Charles, translator of, 288
Baumann, Gerhart (contributor), 23–25, 187–91, 223–25, 235–40
Bayer, Konrad, 7
Beer-Hofmann, Richard, 10, **23–25**
Beethoven, Ludwig van, 98
Bernhard, Thomas, **26–27**
Besserungsstück, 205
Bialik Prize, recipient of, 41
Bible, translation of, 51
Bildungsjargon, 134
Billinger, Richard, **28–30**
"black" romanticism, 183
Blätter für die Kunst (periodical), 119
Blaue Reiter, 160
Blei, Franz, **31–33**, 105
Blick in die Welt (review), 91
Bloch, Ernst, 176
Bodmershof, Imma von, **34–35**
Brandes, Georg (quoted), 235
Brecht, Bertolt, 45, 111, 180, 196
Brenner, Der (periodical), 254
Breuer, Josef, 237–38
Broch, Hermann, **36–40**, 57
Brod, Max, **41–44**, 138–43 passim
Bruckner, Ferdinand, **45–47**
Buber, Martin, **48–54**
Büchner, Georg, 63
Büchner Prize. *See* Georg Büchner Prize
Burgtheater (Vienna), 153, 194
   critics of, 10, 248
   directors of, 20, 281

The bold-face numbers indicate the author entry itself.

Burgtheater (*Cont'd*)
  playwrights and, 135, 204–205, 227, 241
Busta, Christine, **55–56**
Byron, Lord (quoted), 98

Café Raimund, 266
Canetti, Elias, **57–58**
Carltheater (Vienna), 194
Celan, Paul, **59–61**
censorship, under Metternich, 167, 194–95
Cézanne, Paul, 209
Chotjewitz, Peter O., 9
Coudenhove-Calergi, Count R. N., xiv
Court's Theater (Vienna), 97
Csokor, Franz Theodor, **62–64**
Czechoslovak State Prize, recipient of, 41

Däubler, Theodor, **65–69**
Daviau, Donald G. (contributor), 10–13, 18–22, 166–70, 226–29
  quoted, 154
deutsche Rundschau, Die (magazine), 75
dialect poetry, 7–8
Dietz, Gertrud. *See* Fussenegger, Gertrud
Dilthey, Wilhelm, 48, 175, 176
Dimt, Christine. *See* Busta, Christine
Dimt, Maximilian, 55
Doderer, Heimito von, 7, **70–74**, 107
Doppler, Alfred (contributor), 286–287
Dorn, Aloys, 95
Drama Prize of the Oldenburg State Theater, recipient of, 95
Duse, Eleonora, 20

Ebner-Eschenbach, Marie von, **75–79**
Ehrenfels, Christian Freiherr von, 34
Ehrenstein, Albert, **80–82**
Eich, Günter, 3

Eisenreich, Herbert, **83–84**
  as contributor, 70–74, 105–107, 115–16, 252–53, 266–67
Eliot, T. S., translator of, 91
Engländer, Richard. *See* Altenberg, Peter
Erken, Günther (contributor), 80–82
Erné, Nino (contributor), 201–203
Ernst, Max, 88
Esslin, Martin (quoted), 207–208
Ewers, Hanns Heinz, 183
Exl Theater, 241
expressionism, 59, 105, 176, 213, 275, 281

Fabry, Joseph (contributor), 194–197
Fackel, Die (periodical), 80, 153–155 passim, 248
fantastic prose, 183
Ficker, Ludwig von, 254, 255
Fledermaus, Die (cabaret), 93, 94
Fontane Prize, recipients of, 105, 106, 141
Forster, E. M., 77
Forum (review), 252
Freie Bühne, Die (journal), 18
Freud, Sigmund, **85–90**, 237–38, 270, 288
Fried, Erich, **91–92**
Friedell, Egon, **93–94**
Fröhlich, Katharina, 97, 101
Fussenegger, Gertrud, **95–96**

Georg Büchner Prize, recipients of, 14, 59, 60
George, Stefan, 119
Gerhart Hauptmann Prize, recipient of, 111
German neoromanticism, 49
German romantics, 245
Gide, André, 31, 211
Giesinger, G., 9
Gilbert, Prentice, 10
Goethe Prize, recipient of, 51
Grand Prix (Paris), recipient of, 105

Index

Great Austrian State Prize, recipients of, 26, 71, 179
Greene, Graham, translator of, 91
Gregor-Dellin, Martin (contributor), 174
Grenzmann, Wilhelm (contributor), 108–110
Grillparzer, Franz, xiv, 12, 23, 24, **97–104**, 120, 194
  quoted, 41, 207
Groß-Denker, Annemarie (contributor), 185–86
Gruppe 47, 111
Gütersloh, Albert Paris, 7, 70, **105–107**

Habernig, Christine. *See* Lavant, Christine
Handel-Mazzetti, Enrica von, **108–110**
Handke, Peter, **111–14**
Hasidism, 48–49, 52
Henze, Hans Werner, 16
Hern, Nicholas (contributor), 111–114
Herzl, Theodor, 10, 48
Herzmanovsky-Orlando, Fritz von, **115–16**
Heselhaus, Clemens (contributor), 45–47, 179–81
Heuschele, Otto (contributor), 34–35
Hochland (periodical), 108
Hochwälder, Fritz, **117–18**
Hofmannsthal, Hugo von, 10, 28, **119–31**, 179, 236
  paraphrased, xiv–xv
Hohenlohe, Princess Maria zu, 226
Horst, Karl August (contributor), 83–84, 262–63
Horváth, Ödön von, **132–37**
Huder, Walther (contributor), 3–4

ideological thaw, Hungarian, 175–76
Institute of Creative Writing (Ulm), 3

Ivask, Ivar (contributor), 7–9

Jarka, Horst (contributor), 75–79, 132–37, 204–208
Jesenska-Pollak, Milena, 139, 142
Johst, Hanns, 62
Jonson, Ben, adaptation of, 289
journalism, 10–11, 154
Joyce, James, 37
Jugendstil, 48
Julius Reich Prize, recipient of, 264

Kafka, Franz, 41, 42, 88, 115, **138–145**, 183, 270, 272
  influence of, 3, 161
Kahl, Kurt (quoted), 208
Kantor-Berg, Friedrich. *See* Torberg, Friedrich
Kasperle, the, 8
Kassner, Rudolf, **146–50**, 218
  quoted, 219
Keynes, John Maynard, 283
Kiehtreiber, Albert Conrad. *See* Gütersloh, Albert Paris
Killy, Walther, 256
Kleist, Heinrich von, 172
Kleist Prize, recipients of, 29, 132
Klimt, Gustav, 19, 105
Knight, Max (contributor), 194–97
Kohn, Hans (contributor), 48–54
Kokoschka, Oscar, 80, 207
Kramberg, K. H. (contributor), 182–184, 198–200, 268–69, 288–90
Kramer, Theodor, **151–52**
Kraus, Karl, 80, **153–58**, 196, 202, 248, 249, 284
  influence of, 57, 268
Krenek, Ernst (quoted), 249
Kubin, Alfred, 115, **159–61**
Kuchinke-Bach, Anneliese (contributor), 273–78
Kunisch, Hermann (contributor), 119–31, 209–222
Kunstwart, Der (periodical), 140–141

Landauer, Gustav, 50
Lange, Victor (contributor), 59–61
Lattmann, Dieter (contributor), 270–72
Lavant, Christine, **162–63**
Lear, Edward, translator of, 7
Lee, Laurie, translator of, 91
Lehrstücke, 111
Leitgeb, Josef, **164–65**
Lenau, Nikolaus, **166–70**
Lenau Forum (journal), 168
Leopoldstädter Theater (Vienna), 204
Lernet-Holenia, Alexander, **171–73**
Lewisohn, Ludwig (quoted), 264
libretto writing, 16–17, 98, 120, 122, 126, 127–28, 289
Liliencron, Detlev von, 209
Lind, Jakov, **174**
Linné, Carl von, translator of, 7, 8
Lipp, Hans, 284
Lissauer, Ernst (quoted), 185
Literary Prize of the Free City of Bremen, recipient of, 59
Loris. *See* Hofmannsthal, Hugo von
Lukács, Georg (von), **175–78**

Marxist literary doctrine, 176
Mason, Eudo C. (contributor), 146–150
Mauser, Wolfram (contributor), 55–56, 79–80
Mautner, Franz H. (contributor), 5–6
Meidinger-Geise, Inge (contributor), 162–63
Mell, Max, 28, **179–81**
Meyer, Gustav. *See* Meyrink, Gustav
Meyrink, Gustav, **182–84**
Mitterer, Erika, **185–86**
Molière, 125, 205, 207, 266
Moore, George Edward, 283
Mühlher, Robert (contributor), 230–31
Munk, Georg. *See* Winkler, Paula

Musil, Robert, **187–91**
Muth, Carl, 108

Nabl, Franz, **192–93**
National Socialists, xv, 63, 66, 105, 198, 201, 249, 268, 270, 288
naturalism, 72
Nazis. *See* National Socialists
Nennecke, Charlotte (contributor), 14–17, 232–34
neopositivists, 283
Nestroy, Johann, xiv, **194–97**, 266
Neue Freie Presse (newspaper), 10
Neue Rundschau, Die (periodical), 187
Neumann, Robert, **198–200**
Nietzsche, Friedrich, 49, 88
    paraphrased, 201
Nobel Prize, nominee for, 36
Nötzel, Karl (quoted), 250
novel, development of, 230
novella, 78–79, 249

O'Neill, Eugene, 99

parody, 199
Peace Prize of the German Book Trade, recipient of, 51
P. E. N. Club, 62, 63, 171, 198
Peterich, Eckart (contributor), 65–69
Petöfi circle, 176
phenomonology, 87–88
physiognomics, 148–49
poetic realism, 249
Polgar, Alfred, 94, **201–203**
Polgarisms, 201
Politzer, Heinz (contributor), 97–104
Pound, Ezra, 7
Prize of the City of Vienna, recipient of, 248
projection, theory of, 85–86
psychoanalysis, theory of, 86–88

Quevedo, Francisco de, translator of, 7

Index

Raimund, Ferdinand, xiv, **204–208**
Rapp, Father George, 168
Renaissance Theater (Berlin), 45
Rettung, Die (periodical), 105
Rilke, Rainer Maria, 24, 146, 185, **209–222**, 255
  quoted, 24, 257
Röck, Karl, 254
Rodin, Auguste, 209–215 passim
Rosenzweig, Franz, 51
Roth, Joseph, **223–25**
Rühm, Gerhard, 7
Russell, Bertrand, 283, 284
Ruttmann, Irene (contributor), 117–118

Saar, Ferdinand von, 76, **226–29**
Saiko, George Emmanuel, **230–31**
Saint-Exupéry, Antoine de, translator of, 165
Salten, Felix, 10, 23
Salzburg Festivals, 120
Sartre, Jean-Paul, 3, 88, 177
satire, 196
Schaukal, Richard von, **232–34**
Schickel, Joachim (contributor), 57–58, 283–85
Schiller, Friedrich, 194
Schlick, Moritz, 283
Schmied, Wieland (contributor), 91–92, 151–52
  quoted, 162
Schneditz, Wolfgang (contributor), 159–61
Schnitzler, Arthur, 10, 11, 194, **235–40**
Scholl, Inge, 3
Schönherr, Karl, **241–43**
Schubert, Franz, 98
Schwab, Gustav, 167
Schwebell, Gertrude C. (contributor), 95–96
Schwedler, Wilfried (contributor), 26–27
secessionist movement, 20
Shakespeare, William, 91, 156

Simmel, Georg, 48
socialist realism, 175
Sonnemann, Ulrich (contributor), 85–90
Spengler, Oswald (quoted), 93
Sprechstücke, 111
Steiner, Jacob (contributor), 138–145
Stern, J. P. (contributor), 244–47
Stifter, Adalbert, 19, **244–47**, 262
Stifter Prize, recipients of, 95, 179
Stoessl, Otto, **248–51**
Strauss, Richard, 119, 120, 122, 289
Strehlenau, Nikolaus Franz Niembsch von. *See* Lenau, Nikolaus
Strindberg, August, 99, 153
Strobl, Karl (contributor), 31–33
Sturm, Der (review), 80
Swabian poets, 167
Synge, J. M., translator of, 91
Szklenar, Hans (contributor), 254–258

Tagger, Theodor. *See* Bruckner, Ferdinand
theater, Austrian, 9, 20, 227, 267
  Besserungsstück and, 205
  comedy and, 205
  criticism of, 11, 201
  the Kasperle and, 8
  popular stage of Vienna and, 100, 117, 195–96, 205–206, 207
  satire and, 196
  Volksstück and, 133–34, 135, 180
  Zauberstück and, 62, 194, 205–206
Theater an der Wien, 194
themes, in literature, 37, 103, 108, 161, 179, 227, 230–31, 235, 244
Thomas, Dylan, translator of, 91
Thurnher, Eugen (contributor), 164–65, 259–61
Thurn und Taxis, Princess Marie von, 209–213 passim

Tolstoi, Lev, 283
Torberg, Friedrich, **252–53**
  quoted, xv, 115
Trakl, Georg, **254–58**
Trakl Prize, recipient of, 162
Trommler, Frank (contributor), 93–94, 171–73
Tumler, Franz, **259–61**

Ungar, Frederick (contributor), 153–58, 248–51, 264–65
Urzidil, Johannes, **262–63**

Valéry, Paul, 189
Verhaeren, Émile, translator of, 288
Verlag der Autoren, 111
Verlaine, Paul, translator of, 288
Vienna Group, 7
Vienna School of Phantastic Realism, 7
Viennese culture
  fin-de-siècle, 12, 19, 78, 88, 98, 120–21, 132, 153, 192
  of the 1930s, 155
Villon, François, translator of, 7
Volksstück, 133–34, 135, 180

Walden, Herwarth, 80
Waldinger, Ernst, **264–65**
Weigel, Hans, 196, **266–67**
  quoted, xiv
Weinheber, Josef, **268–69**
  quoted, 265
Weiß, Ernst, **270–72**

Weiss, Walter (contributor), 36–40, 241–43
weißen Blätter, Die (periodical), 80
Weltmann, Lutz (contributor), 28–30, 41–44, 62–64, 281–82
Werfel, Franz, 41, **273–78**
Westhoff, Clara, 209–215 passim
Whitehead, Alfred North, 283
Wied, Martina, **279–80**
Wiener, Oswald, 7
Wiener Gruppe, Die, 7
Wiesenthal, Grete, 28
Wiesl, Alexandrine Martina Augusta. *See* Wied, Martina
Wilder, Thornton, 194
Wildgans, Anton, **281–82**
Winkler, Paula, 48
Wittgenstein, Ludwig, **283–85**
Wolff, Kurt, 273
Worpswede, 209, 211
Wort im Gebirge (literary almanac), 164
Writers' Prize of the City of Vienna, recipients of, 279

Young German movement, 212
Young Tyrol movement, 241
Young Vienna movement, 10, 227

Zand, Herbert, **286–87**
Zauberstück, 62, 194, 205–206
Zehm, Günter Albrecht (contributor), 175–78
Zeit, Die (newspaper), 18
Zionism, and Buber, 48–51 passim
Zuckmayer, Carl, 45, 132, 180
Zweig, Stefan, **288–90**